Banking and Monetary Policies in a Changing Financial Environment

The twenty-first century witnessed major changes in the financial environment surrounding bank regulators and banks. *Banking and Monetary Policies in a Changing Financial Environment* delves into three of these developments and challenges.

The first change in the financial environment relates to the rise in the number and sophistication of financial and economic crimes which shaped the international regulatory architecture. New rules and regulations led to the creation of new strategies to combat these crimes, especially those concerning the spread of more advanced money laundering methods and techniques, terrorist financing after the 9/11 attacks, and the proliferation of weapons of mass destruction. The second development concerns the global financial crisis of 2008, which drastically affected the regulatory environment of various international and domestic financial authorities, causing major changes in bank lending and corporate governance policies, and in the development of the Basel III accord on capital adequacy for bank supervision. The third development manifests itself in the creation of a major European monetary union without a fiscal union and a giant European central bank impacting the conduct of monetary policy along with the new monetary policies of quantitative easing to combat the financial crisis. This book combines theory, policy, regulation, and institutional approaches with empirical testing, analyzing applications and case studies of various international regulatory authorities and administrations, countries and jurisdictions, central banks, and commercial banks.

This volume is suitable for those who study international finance, banking economics, and financial crime.

Wassim Shahin is Professor of Business Economics and Assistant Provost for special external projects at the Lebanese American University in Lebanon and served as the founding dean of the school of business in the same institution on its Byblos campus from 1996 to 2011.

Elias El-Achkar is Director of Research and Statistics at the Association of Banks in Lebanon and a university lecturer.

Routledge International Studies in Money and Banking

Banking and Monetary Policies in a Changing Financial Environment

A regulatory approach

**Wassim Shahin and
Elias El-Achkar**

LONDON AND NEW YORK

First published 2017 by Routledge

2 Park Square, Milton Park, Abingdon, Oxfordshire OX14 4RN
711 Third Avenue, New York, NY 10017

Routledge is an imprint of the Taylor & Francis Group, an informa business

First issued in paperback 2018

British Library Cataloguing-in-Publication Data
A catalogue record for this book is available from the British Library

Library of Congress Cataloging in Publication Data
Names: Shahin, Wassim N., 1957- author. | El-Achkar, Elias, author.
Title: Banking and monetary policies in a changing financial environment: a
regulatory approach / Wassim Shahin and Elias El-Achkar.
Description: Abingdon, Oxon; New York, NY: Routledge, 2017.
Identifiers: LCCN 2016011102| ISBN 9781138913530 (hardback) | ISBN
9781315691381 (ebook)
Subjects: LCSH: Banks and banking–State supervision. | Banking law. |
Financial institutions–Government policy. | Monetary policy.
Classification: LCC HG1725 .S45 2017 | DDC 332.1–dc23
LC record available at https://lccn.loc.gov/2016011102

ISBN: 978-1-138-91353-0 (hbk)
ISBN: 978-1-138-32509-8 (pbk)

Typeset in Times New Roman
by Sunrise Setting Ltd, Brixham, UK

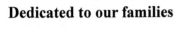
Dedicated to our families

Contents

Illustrations

Figures

Tables

Acknowledgments

We thank the Lebanese American University for funding the presentations of part of this research in international peer-reviewed conferences: namely, the Allied Social Sciences Association annual meetings in the US, the Middle East Economics Association Conferences and the International Symposium on Economic Crime at the University of Cambridge. We are also indebted to many of our colleagues with whom some of our ideas were discussed, the graduate research assistants who helped at various stages of the development of the book, and the score of students whom we taught excerpts from this material. We owe special thanks to our graduate research assistant Mia Cherfane, who assumed the role of a dedicated associate by providing research and technical assistance necessary to finish the book in a timely fashion. Finally, we owe an enormous debt to our families, to whom we dedicate our work.

1 Introduction

The rationale for the book

The twenty-first century witnessed major changes in the financial environment surrounding banks and bank regulators, including central banks. This book is motivated by three of these developments and challenges. The first relates to the rise in the number and sophistication of financial and economic crimes, which shaped the international regulatory architecture. New rules and regulations led to the creation of new strategies to combat these crimes, especially ones concerning the spread of more advanced money-laundering methods and techniques, terrorist financing after 9/11 and the proliferation of weapons of mass destruction experienced lately. The second development concerns the global financial crisis of 2008, which drastically affected the regulatory environment of various international and domestic financial authorities, causing both major changes in bank lending and corporate governance policies and the development of the Basel III accord on capital adequacy for bank supervision. The third development saw the creation of a major European monetary union without a fiscal union and a giant European central bank that impacts on the conduct of monetary policy. The financial crisis also caused monetary authorities to resort to unconventional monetary policies of quantitative easing rarely witnessed previously in terms of their length and operational amount in a recessionary and deflationary environment. Additionally, some central banks resorted to holding more foreign reserves to hedge against future crises.

This changing financial environment necessitated a change in the strategies, measures and regulatory policies governing it, which drastically affected bank and central bank policies. These policies were impacted at the level of compliance with new international and domestic rules and regulations, corporate governance, capital adequacy in quantity, quality and composition, risk management, and various micro-prudential and macro-prudential policies. At the same time, monetary authorities and banks have to survive in a monetary policy environment of monetary unions, quantitative easing, historically low interest rates, and possible deflation. These developments in the financial environment acted as motivators for us to develop this book to address the new policies and monetary policy changes of banks and central banks. The framework and analysis we will use combine theory, policy, and regulatory and institutional approaches, along with some empirical testing, applications, and case studies of a range of international regulatory authorities and administrations, countries, jurisdictions, central banks, and commercial banks.

The organization of the book

The book is divided into three parts, reflecting the three developments and changes in the financial environment addressed above. The first part (including Chapters 2 and 3) deals with banking regulation aimed at combating financial and economic crime. Chapter 2 builds on the fact that the regulatory environment has changed drastically in the twenty-first century, with an increase in the sophistication and number of methods and techniques of money laundering and financial and economic crimes after the 9/11 attacks in the US at the beginning of the century and the proliferation of weapons of mass destruction at the present time. The rise of terrorism necessitated adding eight recommendations in 2001and a ninth in 2004 to the forty recommendations of the Financial Action Task Force on the laundering of money; these nine recommendations were incorporated within the forty new recommendations drawn up in 2012. The purpose of the chapter is thus to highlight the new regulatory environment governing financial and economic crimes by developing a complete list of these crimes and of the various policies, measures and strategies undertaken by all international bodies and organizations in order to combat criminal activities. Such crimes include money laundering, terrorist financing, organized crime, bribery, corruption, fraud, cybercrime, financing proliferation, human trafficking, the smuggling of migrants, identity theft, tax evasion, whistleblowing, stolen assets, and politically exposed persons, among a wider set of criminal activities.

Chapter 2 is a necessary analytical introduction to the following chapter, on bank compliance with measures taken by worldwide financial intermediaries. These compliance policies and measures have changed the nature and structure of bank practices and policies from those of the previous century. Therefore, Chapter 3 is based on the premise that compliance has become, in recent years, a major regulatory and supervisory issue and an essential part of the bank's business activities and corporate culture. Compliance, as addressed in this chapter, refers to the compliance of banking institutions with established domestic and international laws, rules, and standards related to the banking profession. Compliance risk is defined by the Basel Committee on Banking Supervision of the Bank for International Settlements as: "the risk of legal or regulatory sanctions, material financial loss, or loss to reputation a bank may suffer as a result of its failure to comply with laws, regulations, rules, related self-regulatory organization standards, and codes of conduct applicable to its banking activities." Issues addressed by compliance cover anti-money laundering (AML), countering the financing of terrorism (CFT), economic and financial sanctions, and tax evasion regulations. Failure to comply in these areas tends to expose the bank to significant fines and reputational damage. Dealing effectively with compliance risk requires a dynamic, transparent, and centralized approach to compliance and a board of directors and senior management responsible for ensuring full compliance with regulations and enforcing the culture of compliance throughout the banking firm. In addition, a compliance function originating from a compliance policy must be in place; that function could be organized within other functions, when commonalities exist, or located as a separate function with clear lines of cooperation with other functions on the organizational chart. Large differences exist among banks not only regarding the organization of the compliance function but also when it comes to the responsibilities and activities of its staff. What matters, however, is whether banks' compliance functions and adopted policies and procedures adhere to international rules and regulations in the area of compliance and compliance-related issues, and are consistent with existing best industry practices. Though banks in theory and practice support measures aiming at reducing the compliance risk and avoiding reputational damage, they are also concerned with the uncertainty and burden presented by regulatory complexity, and the substantial direct and indirect costs of compliance with new or modified regulations.

This book's second part addresses the causes and origins of the crisis, bank lending policies in a number of countries after the crisis ensued, the changes in governance policies regulating financial institutions and the new Basel III accord on capital adequacy. The discussion in Chapter 4 is based on the premise that the global financial crisis of 2008, and those that subsequently hit many peripheral European countries, reignited interest in the topic of financial instability and financial crises among academics, researchers, and policy-makers. Awareness was similarly awakened following the East Asia financial crisis almost ten years earlier in 1997–8 and other episodes of financial turbulence throughout the current and previous centuries. Financial crises are recurring phenomena and have a long history dating from well before the great depression of 1929. Most crises are similar in many respects, often resulting in serious economic and social costs often associated with a sharp drop in employment and output. Adverse implications may extend as well to the fiscal situation, the effectiveness of monetary policy, and the external sector. In addition, in an interlinked world the damage may not be limited to the economy in which the crisis originated, and the fear of adverse contagion or spill-over effects, involving the rapid spread of the crisis across other economies, is a major policy issue. Therefore, understanding the origins of the crisis and the contributing roles of monetary and fiscal policies and identifying the real causes and linkages are of the utmost importance both to monetary and fiscal authorities and to financial system regulators and supervisors in terms of learning the right lessons, addressing existing weaknesses, strengthening the financial system, and limiting contagion effects.

Chapter 5 empirically examines the effects of the global financial crisis of 2008 on total bank lending in selected countries, as declining bank credit is both one of the major causes of economic slowdown or recession and, in many cases, one of its results. The goal of the chapter is therefore first to investigate whether the global credit crisis and ensuing world economic recession resulted in a decline in bank private sector credit in these countries. Second, given that a decline was found, the chapter addresses whether this decline was supply- or demand-driven by bank borrowers. The supply side effect could result if bank credit to the private sector was constrained by a decline in deposits or an increase in non-performing loans, and if issues of risk aversion by banks reflected in adverse selection and moral hazard mechanisms, whereas the demand side could result from an increase in unemployment, a decline in business opportunities, and risk aversion by borrowers regarding investment profitability. To test whether there has been a contraction of bank credit following the global credit crisis, and if so whether it came from a shift in the demand or a shift in the supply or both, we built on the methodologies commonly used in the literature, addressing both the determinants of bank lending and the means to disentangle shifts in loan supply from shifts in loan demand. Initially we developed a credit theoretical model in line with the existing models in the literature. Then, employing empirical methodology, we estimated with panel data the overall impact on banks' loan extension. The determination of the cause of credit slowdown or retreat has important policy implications: if the credit decline is related to weak demand for bank loans, whether due to pessimistic economic perspectives, deteriorations in borrowers' balance sheets, excessive leverage or other factors, then policies aiming at stimulating aggregate demand could be effective; if, on the other hand, the decline is due to banks' inability and reluctance to lend because of a decline in deposits, capital losses related to loan losses, or asset price collapse and increased riskiness, then other sets of measures, including easy monetary policy, are needed to revive bank lending and foster investment.

Chapter 6 centres on the fact that, since the early 1990s, corporate governance has been receiving increasing attention from international standard-setters, domestic law-makers and regulators, and all domestic and external stakeholders in general, with a rising awareness of its importance for and impact on the soundness and performance of financial and non-financial companies and on certain economic outcomes. The ongoing pressure to adhere to constantly updated international standards in this area as well as to related applicable domestic laws and regulations and a mounting conviction on the part of shareholders and investors of the positive efficiency, profitability and sustainability signals that adequate corporate governance can send to the markets have been the main drivers in influencing the board and senior management of banks and non-banks to incorporate the best corporate governance practices into their daily operations and decision making. There is no single definition of corporate governance, yet it is commonly known to be a set of structures, systems, policies and procedures by means of which corporations are managed and controlled. One of the best definitions is that of the Organization for Economic Co-operation and Development (OECD), which mentions that corporate governance "specifies the distribution of rights and responsibilities among the main participants in the corporation—including shareholders, directors and managers—and spells out the rules and procedures for making decisions on corporate affairs. By doing this, corporate governance provides the structure through which company objectives are set, implemented and monitored." The commitment to and adoption of good corporate governance practices in reference to well-known international standards differ from one company or industry or country to another, because such practices are decided only in part by companies and are dictated to a large extent by laws and regulations. In addition to the regulatory and legal considerations, there are other factors that play a role in the divergence in practices, including the size, complexity, and risk-taking culture of the firm, and the political, institutional, social, and cultural environment. Nevertheless, a company devoted to sound corporate governance has clearly described shareholders' roles and equal rights, an empowered board of directors with well-determined responsibilities to exercise management and oversight, strong internal controls and accountability, and high levels of transparency and disclosure. A corporate governance framework of guiding principles and practices is exceptionally momentous in the banking industry given the role played by banks in the economy and the functions performed, which are central to financial market development and economic growth. The importance of corporate governance in the banking sector is also related to the fact that weak corporate governance and poor management and oversight can lead to bank failures and heighten systemic risk, potentially destroying savings and necessitating costly bailouts by governments. Thus, well-established laws and regulations for proper corporate governance framework at banks and the strong commitment of bank shareholders and management to the implementation of the best practices are essential. This chapter also addresses the Basel III accord, a set of reform measures developed by the Basel Committee on Banking Supervision in the wake of the financial crisis to strengthen the regulation, supervision and risk management of the banking sector, and its ensuing challenges. The aim of the accord is to improve the banking sector's ability to absorb shocks. The reforms are partly bank-level—or micro-prudential—and partly system-level—or macro-prudential. These two approaches to supervision are complementary, as greater regulation and supervision at the bank level tend to reduce systemic risk. The discussion of the Basel III accord thus analyzes the many challenges that the new accord will present to banks. These relate largely to raising more capital, improving the quality of capital, and meeting the liquidity capital requirements of coverage ratio and liquidity requirement tools. At a time when many banks worldwide are still trying to meet the Basel II capital adequacy requirements, banks are asked to address the composition and quality of capital, as well as creating buffer capital zones to address pro-cyclicality. Specifically, it is very challenging for banks that are not operating as public ones to raise the share of common stock in their tier one capital and apply the stricter definition of this equity. In addition, it is difficult to create a capital conservation buffer of common equity to withstand future periods of stress. Such requirements are believed to influence the way banks do business in most countries, especially if Basel III has effects on financial markets and on monetary policy implementation.

The third part of this book addresses issues of monetary policy arrangements, looking at changes that are occurring in the practice of this policy in the current century. The environment and conduct of monetary policy have drastically changed in the last fifteen years, with the establishment of monetary unions without fiscal unions and the adoption of unconventional policies of quantitative easing aimed at combating the financial crisis. This book analyzes these two new developments in the financial environment and conduct of monetary policy and their impact on its administration and its strategy in two chapters. Chapter 7 addresses quantitative easing by the US and the UK in the immediate aftermath of the financial crisis with the aim of addressing the recessionary and deflationary impacts of the crisis in order to restore economic growth and price stability. This involves an analysis of the new unconventional monetary policy, including its background and description; its strategy of instruments–targets–goals; its channels of transmission mechanisms; the experiences of the US and the UK (the first two countries to adopt it after the crisis); the assessment of its success based on empirical support and evidence; and, finally, various exit strategies from quantitative easing on the road to policy normalization. The analysis also addresses the nature of monetary policy when short-term interest rates are zero-bound, using a money demand and velocity framework.

Chapter 8 deals first with the rise of European Monetary Union (EMU) and a European Central Bank (ECB), which shape the conduct of monetary policy for the nineteen countries currently forming the euro area with a common euro currency. This monetary union was not coupled with a fiscal union, making the ECB operate in an environment in which it faces many fiscal authorities rather than one, which was the traditional form of monetary policy until 2000. This monetary union operates in a euro area in which countries are sometimes divided between two tiers on the basis of widely divergent unemployment and growth rates. Inflation rates are calculated based on a harmonized index of consumer prices (HICP), aiming at an average for the nineteen countries below but close to 2 percent to achieve the price stability objective as per the Maastricht treaty. The differences in the macroeconomic indicators cause the common monetary arrangements to be loose for some countries and tight for others, making policy interest rates relatively too low for one group and too high for the other. Differences in economic fundamentals cause the euro sometimes to be overvalued for some countries and undervalued for others, impacting trade activities within the euro area and with the rest of the world. Additionally, the lack of a fiscal union or some type of disciplined fiscal integration has been perceived by many to leave member countries with fiscal imbalances prone to inflows of shocks and crisis, causing declines in aggregate demand with contagious systemic dangers across the eurozone. These salient features require different monetary policy arrangements than the ones practiced by central banks facing one fiscal authority, given that the aim is to achieve the price stability objective and a macroeconomic environment characterized by high output and employment growth across various members. The twenty-first century also witnessed a major financial crisis that has shaped the international financial architecture. This crisis caused many central banks across the world to hold additional reserves for both precautionary reasons, reflected in their responses to various market shocks and attempts to prevent of disorderly market conditions, and non-precautionary reasons, to protect fixed pegged exchange rate arrangements and provide international liquid assets. However, when inappropriate amounts of reserves are accumulated there is believed to be a social cost, and a literature dealing with reserve adequacy, or the determination of the optimal amount of reserves to be held by central banks, is developing. This chapter thus aims at covering two main topics: first, it deals with monetary policy arrangements in monetary unions without fiscal unions by using the EMU as a case study; second, it examines the social cost of reserve accumulation using a set of countries from the Middle East and North Africa region (MENA).

Readership and competition

The readership we expect to reach includes academic scholars, central bankers and other regulators, bankers and other practitioners and professionals, upper-level undergraduates and graduate students. We strongly feel that no book to date has addressed these three facets of change in the regulatory financial environment of banks and central bank policies in the way that we have approached the subject matter. There exists a wide literature, of course, on the financial crisis and its impact on economic activity. There is another, as well, on combating economic and financial crimes using various regulatory measures. Monetary unions in the absence of fiscal unions as well as central bank policies of quantitative easing have also been covered extensively. However, using a regulatory approach to address and examine banks and central banks in a changing financial environment incorporating the three changes discussed earlier has not been attempted, and the choice of topics and the way we approach and analyze them using theory, policy, regulation, country-specific cases, empirical evidence from selected countries and central bank developments after the financial crisis have not been so far addressed in an integrated document.

Part 1

Banking regulation to combat the rise in financial and economic crimes

2   The changing regulatory environment governing financial and economic crimes

Introduction

Hegel's dialectic, consisting of a thesis, an antithesis, and a synthesis, best describes the dynamics among financial and economic criminals, on the one hand, and domestic and international regulators, organizations, and conventions on the other. While regulators are satisfied with enforcing and improving existing laws and regulations constituting the "thesis," financial and economic criminals develop new modes of crime for the purpose of—simply stated—profits and gains. These new criminal modes and techniques become the "antithesis." The new laws and regulations developed to face this antithesis form the "synthesis," which becomes the "new thesis." This new thesis satisfies regulators that crimes are abated, as the cycle of criminal activities decreases from its previous antithesis peak to a trough. However, the low point of the cycle reaches another peak as the substitution of new modes of crime develops, beginning the process again. Technological developments help both sides, but favour the criminals, as they exploit them to strengthen their antithesis—as has happened with cyberspace crimes and terrorism. The moral of the dialectic is that there will always be financial and economic crime, with regulations lagging behind, simply because profits lead ethics and laws. At best, regulators can increase the slope of the cycle, reducing criminal activities faster and extending the periodicity of the cycle, thus keeping economic and financial crimes at a low level for a longer period. Determining whether this glass is half-empty or half-full depends on whether one is drinking or pouring.

The literature on the theory and practice of economic and financial crimes has addressed and is still covering topics that are central to the policy responses aimed at combating criminal, corrupt, fraudulent, terrorist-financing and money-laundering activities. There exists a body of common topics reflecting the most important criminal issues and the internationally accepted and recommended methods of preventing and controlling economically motivated crimes. These topics are presented and debated by academicians and practitioners on an annual basis in the International Symposium on Economic Crime at the University of Cambridge.[1] This chapter will address the regulatory responses to an exhaustive list of financial and economic crimes divided here into fifteen groups of similar criminal issues. Below follows alphabetical coverage of topics, the research for which drew on the most reliable sources specializing in the combating of economic and financial crimes; examples are discussed where relevant.

Responses and measures to counter financial and economic crimes

AML/CFT/compliance/risk-based approach

The Financial Action Task Force on the laundering of money (FATF) has redefined its mission to include, in addition to combating money laundering and countering the financing of terrorism (AML/CFT), the combating of the financing of the proliferation of weapons of mass destruction. Thus, in February 2012 it developed forty new recommendations to replace the 40+9 recommendations (see Chapter 1) and de-emphasized its twenty-five criteria. The requirements have been strengthened in higher-risk areas and in areas where implementation could be enhanced, and made more flexible in low-risk areas, based on the new risk-based approach (RBA). They have also become tougher on corruption and more transparent. Recommendation 7 of the revised recommendations is new and deals specifically with the proliferation of weapons of mass destruction. The financing of terrorism is now incorporated in the body of the forty recommendations (recommendations 5 and 6) instead of being covered in the additional nine special recommendations. Equally important is the introduction of the RBA as recommendation 1. This approach ties and maps the strength of the adopted measures to the risk of the areas involved by ensuring that measures to prevent money laundering and terrorist financing are commensurate with the risks identified in each area for more efficient allocation of countries' resources across the AML/CFT parlance.[2] Thus, countries should ensure that their AML/CFT regime adequately addresses the higher risks identified. Simplified measures may under certain conditions be used for lower risks in terms of some of the FATF recommendations.

The proliferation of weapons of mass destruction or financing proliferation will be addressed below. This section will address recommendations 5 and 6 on CFT, which summarize the additional nine recommendations in the old framework, which were related largely to terrorism. Recommendation 5 states that countries should criminalize terrorist financing, the financing of terrorist organizations and individual terrorists, and ensure that such offences belong to the money-laundering scheme. Recommendation 6 deals with the implementation of financial sanctions in compliance with United Nations Security Council resolutions relating to the prevention and suppression of terrorism and terrorist financing. The resolutions require that funds or other assets are frozen and that no funds or other assets are made available to the parties accused under recommendation 5.

As a result of these forty new recommendations, FATF has developed and regularly updated a list of high-risk jurisdictions that are either subject to countermeasures by the international regulatory bodies, or that have not made sufficient progress in addressing the deficiencies in AML/CFT, or that have only recently provided a high level of political commitment to addressing deficiencies. Initially a large number of jurisdictions were placed on this list, but these have become fewer over the years, as many have shown sufficient progress. So, in October 2013, the list contained thirty-three jurisdictions, but as of October 23, 2015 it included fifteen jurisdictions.[3] A report by the US Treasury Financial Crime Enforcement Network (FinCEN) on January 19, 2016 confirmed the FATF listings of October 2015.[4]

Countries and jurisdictions not complying with some or more of the forty recommendations were found deficient in the following strategic AML/CFT areas:[5] (1) adequately criminalizing money laundering and terrorist financing; (2) establishing and implementing an adequate legal framework for identifying, tracing, and freezing terrorist assets; (3) implementing an adequate AML/CFT supervisory and oversight program for all financial sectors; (4) establishing and implementing adequate procedures for confiscation of assets related to money laundering and other terrorist activities; (5) establishing a fully operational, autonomous, and effectively functioning Financial Intelligence Unit (FIU); (6) establishing and implementing effective controls for cross-border cash transactions; (7) enhancing the framework for international co-operation related to terrorist financing; (8) ensuring that appropriate laws and procedures are in place to provide mutual legal assistance; (9) addressing secrecy provisions; (10) ensuring an effective supervisory program for AML/CFT compliance; (11) improving suspicious transaction reporting requirements; (12) and ensuring comprehensive and effective customer due diligence measures and record-keeping requirements.

Thus, compliance in the following areas and others related to the specific stipulations of each recommendation is necessary for the removal from the list of countries and jurisdictions with AML/CFT deficiencies. While the situations differ among jurisdictions, each has provided a written high-level political commitment and action plan to address the identified deficiencies.

Asset recovery/politically exposed persons (PEPs)

Asset recovery refers to attempts made by individual countries and jurisdictions and international organizations such as the World Bank and the UN to recover stolen assets, largely from developing countries, once these assets have left their home. It is estimated that $20–$40 billion is lost every year in developing countries through corruption alone and the proceeds of all types of crime in the global economy are estimated to represent between $1 trillion and $1.6 trillion annually, with half coming from developing countries.[6] Given the large amounts of funds stolen through acts of bribery, corruption, embezzlement, theft and other criminal activities by high-ranking officials and leaders and their close associates, the United Nations Office on Drugs and Crime (UNODC) and the World Bank initiated the Stolen Asset Recovery (StAR) Initiative in 2007 to assist countries to locate and return their stolen funds, which are generally hidden in outside countries and jurisdictions that mostly enjoy financial secrecy and lax regulatory environments. StAR estimates that only $5 billion in stolen funds has been repatriated to the country of origin over the last fifteen years. Thus, StAR's work covers not just locating and returning assets to home countries; it would also like to seek international cooperation from all regulatory bodies in developing measures to identify and trace stolen assets and in preventing assets from leaving victim jurisdictions and from entering financial centers abroad. Thus, the process of asset recovery starts at home, preventing assets from leaving, and continues through a sequence of identifying, tracing, restraining, confiscating, and repatriating stolen wealth.

An important measure aimed at preventing assets from leaving the country of origin is FATF recommendation 4 on confiscation and provisional measures. It states that countries should develop measures to enable their competent authorities to freeze or seize and confiscate ill-gotten properties and proceeds. Countries should consider adopting measures that allow such proceeds to be confiscated without requiring a criminal conviction, or which require an offender to demonstrate the lawful origin of the property alleged to be liable to confiscation, to the extent that such a requirement is consistent with the principles of their domestic law.

Another measure to prevent stolen funds from leaving the country of origin or from being hidden abroad is the development of guidance relating to politically exposed persons (PEPs), reflected in FATF recommendations 12 and 22. Thus, in June 2013 FATF produced a paper entitled "Guidance on Politically Exposed Persons" to assist countries and the private sector in the development and application of measures to implement recommendations 12 and 22.[7] The crux of these measures is that, in addition to performing normal customer due diligence, financial institutions should be required, in relation to possible foreign PEPs, to have appropriate risk management systems to determine whether the customer or the beneficial owner is a PEP; to obtain senior management approval for establishing or continuing such business relationships; to take reasonable measures to establish the sources of wealth and funds; and conduct enhanced ongoing monitoring of the business relationship. Additionally, financial institutions should be required to take reasonable measures to determine whether a customer or beneficial owner is a domestic PEP or a person who is or has been entrusted with a prominent function by an international organization. The requirements for all types of PEP should also apply to their family members or close associates. The recovery of stolen assets has been enhanced by the development of various international bodies and agreements, such as the United Nations Convention against Corruption (UNCAC). This convention requires signatories to assist countries and jurisdictions that have been victims of corruption by freezing, confiscating, and repatriating any proceeds of corruption deposited in their jurisdictions.

Despite all these international attempts to recover assets, several barriers remain significant. The StAR initiative lists and analyzes these barriers as follows.[8] First are general barriers in the form of a lack of trust among parties involved in asset recovery; the lack of a comprehensive asset recovery policy; deficient resources as a result of originating and requested jurisdictions frequently committing insufficient resources to assist in asset recovery cases; a lack of adherence to and enforcement of AML/CFT measures; and a lack of effective coordination among involved parties. Next are legal barriers and requirements that delay assistance, such as differences in legal traditions; an inability to provide formal mutual legal assistance in criminal and asset recovery cases; a failure to observe and criminalize all offences listed in the United Nations Convention against Corruption (UNCAC) and the United Nations Convention against Transnational Organized Crime (UNTOC); unbalanced notice requirements that allow the dissipation of assets; financial secrecy laws; the lack of a non-conviction-based confiscation mechanism as specified in FATF recommendation 12; the inability to enter into plea agreements by many jurisdictions out of concern that the truth-finding process will be distorted; immunity laws that prevent prosecution and mutual legal assistance; the inability to recognize and enforce foreign confiscation and restraint orders; and, finally, the inability to return assets to originating jurisdictions. Lastly, there are some operational barriers and communication issues, such as the absence or ambiguity of focal points of contact between originating and requesting jurisdictions; a lack of information on mutual legal assistance requirements; unreasonable delays in responses; difficulties identifying foreign bank accounts; and a lack of publicly available registries for properties.

Corruption/bribery/fraud

The issues of corruption, bribery, and fraud in cases where illegal practices are allowed to take hold within firms have been termed "the enemy within." These practices constitute a risk for financial institutions and an encouragement to conduct money laundering to clean the proceeds of these illegal activities. Thus, the topics discussed under this heading can—in addition to matters of risk and money laundering—take the form of the perimeters of corruption in the business world; its presence in the literature on criminology; the strategic importance of corruption as a cause of revolutions; the boundaries of corruption; the possibility of legitimate influence becoming corruption; corruption and fraud using internet intelligence; securities and insurance fraud; and elderly and socially vulnerable victims of financial fraud, among many other topics.[9] Fighting corruption, bribery, and fraud can take place within firms through proper governance and audit, known as "policing from inside," or through government and international initiatives, such as the Inter-American Convention against Corruption, adopted in March 1996 by the Organization of American States as one of the first multilateral anticorruption agreements, the US Foreign Corrupt Practices Act, the UK Bribery Act, the UK Serious Fraud Office, the United Nations Convention against Corruption (UNCAC), the United Nations Office on Drugs and Crime (UNODC), and the G20 Anti-Corruption Working Group (ACWG), as well as various FATF initiatives aimed at preventing the laundering of the proceeds of crime.

Since 2011 the FATF has developed several documents to address the issue of corruption and its impact on the AML/CFT recommendations. Specifically, in July 2011, a report entitled "Laundering the Proceeds of Corruption" was produced to address typologies used for this purpose. Cases were analyzed from a practitioner's perspective to assist in the understanding of money-laundering techniques. In June 2012 a report on "Specific Risk Factors in Laundering the Proceeds of

Corruption: Assistance to Reporting Entities" provided assistance to financial institutions and designated non-financial businesses and professions (DNFBPs) to better analyze and understand the specific risk factors associated with laundering the proceeds of corruption. In October 2012 a document entitled "A Reference Guide and Information Note on the use of the FATF Recommendations to Support the Fight against Corruption (the Corruption Information Note)" was published. This note was aimed at explaining to the general public how to leverage AML/CFT measures in the fight against corruption.

According to the FATF, in various reports on corruption, especially the Best Practices paper of October 18, 2013, "The Use of the FATF Recommendations to Combat Corruption," it was stated that the G20 called upon the FATF to address the problem of corruption as part of its work on combating money laundering and terrorist financing.[10] Corruption and money laundering are linked in the sense that the proceeds of fraud, corruption, and bribery need to be concealed and cleaned. It is true that the FATF recommendations were designed to combat money laundering and terrorist financing, but they can also serve to combat corruption by protecting private sector institutions from criminal abuse, increasing the transparency of the financial system and facilitating the detection, investigation, and prosecution of corruption and money laundering.

In the Best Practices paper it was reiterated that in February 2011, October 2012 and 2013 the FATF held three meetings, jointly with the G20 Anti-Corruption Working Group (ACWG), to provide an international platform for the exchange of views between AML/CFT and anti-corruption experts.[11] It was agreed that there was a need for further tools to enhance understanding of the FATF recommendations so that they might be used more effectively in the fight against corruption.

Cybercrime/information technology

Cyber-terrorism has become the fifth domain of warfare after land, sea, air, and space. Cyber-attacks and threats start with simple individual hacking, wire fraud, credit card fraud, network penetration, cyber-espionage, organized crime, nation state cyber-attacks or cyber-terrorism. Governments, financial organizations, and other groups in society have been penetrated in recent years by cyber-criminals, prompting comparisons to be drawn between threats of cyber-terrorism and historic conventional battles. US secretary of defense Leon Panetta has been quoted as saying that the next Pearl Harbor will be a cyber-attack. Cyber-attacks have been called an electronic Chernobyl, a digital Armageddon, Trojans out of the Trojan horse. We would like to add to the literature a term we have coined: reverse D-Day, where the letter D stands for digital rather than decision, and where 'reverse' reflects that the bad guys are digitally attacking the good ones. There is clearly a need to come up with methods to combat this new type of terrorism.

This new type of terrorism involves rational agents maximizing expected utility based on the occurrence of certain states. We would like, therefore, to rely on the definition of conventional terrorism in defining cyber-space terrorism as the threat or actual use of cyber-attacks to attain a financial or political goal. However, cyber-terrorism differs from the conventional sort in terms of the cost of the terrorist event; the risk that cyber-events may be untraceable and harder to track than activities requiring the attacker's physical presence, such as skyjacking; the location of the attackers, which could be hidden; the impact of the same attack on individuals in different countries (terrorism sans frontiere); and the ungoverned space, or lack of a regulator for cyber-space.

Two political examples can be used to highlight the severity of cyber-attacks. The *Wall Street Journal* of Friday, September 27, 2013 stated that US officials claimed that Iran had hacked unclassified Navy computers in the foregoing weeks in an escalation of Iranian cyber intrusions targeting the US military.[12] The attacks were carried out by hackers working for Iran's government or by a group acting with the approval of Iranian leaders. The most recent incident came in the week starting September 15, before a security upgrade, the officials said. The allegations would mark one of the most serious infiltrations of US government computer systems by Iran. Previously, current and former US officials have said, Iranian-backed infiltration and surveillance efforts have targeted US banks and computer networks running energy companies.

The second case relates to claims arising on October 23, 2013 that the US National Security Agency (NSA) conducted widespread spying on its European allies, including the monitoring of German chancellor Angela Merkel's cell phone. According to a CNN report on Saturday October 26, 2013, Merkel said the assertions that the NSA spied on her and other world leaders had "severely shaken" relationships between Europe and the US, and that trust would have to be rebuilt.[13] Brazilian and German diplomats met to discuss a possible UN resolution regarding the protection of privacy in electronic communication, government officials in Brazil said. The German spying allegation came in the same week that the French daily newspaper *Le Monde* reported claims that the NSA intercepted more than 70 million phone calls in France over a 30-day period, as per the same CNN report.

In a financial case reflecting cyber-attacks from within the organization, a bank in a country in the Arabian Gulf witnessed a fraud in its credit cards issuance in May and June 2013.[14] Around 200 credit cards were issued and sent all over the world to different groups. These cards were issued without withdrawal limits, which the system interpreted to mean no limit, or infinity. Over $40 million was withdrawn from ATM machines worldwide using these cards. Payments software was changed to repair this issue; meanwhile, the perpetrators fled to a country with no extradition agreements with the Gulf country. On another financial note, HSBC has started changing security codes for employees and customers every thirty seconds.

A cartoon in the *New York Times* summarizes it all by stating: "Believe me, it is so much easier to do it on line." With the internet becoming more and more prevalent, commercial websites and internet payment systems are potentially subject to a wide range of risks and vulnerabilities that can be exploited by criminal organizations and terrorist groups. In response, in 2008 FATF published a report entitled "Money Laundering and Terrorist Financing Vulnerabilities of Commercial

Websites and Internet Payments Systems." The study analyzed money-laundering and terrorist-financing (ML/TF) risks associated with commercial websites and internet payment systems, providing case studies. Four main recommendations came out of the study.[15] The first is that guidance mechanisms should be developed to detect suspicious transactions. Second, traditional financial institutions should be aware that they still have an important role to play in the detection and monitoring of suspicious internet financial transactions. Third, given the international character of the issues at hand, international cooperation is a key factor in the fight against ML/TF, including the exchange of information and data pertaining to the criminal misuse of commercial websites and internet payment systems. Fourth, it is consequently important that all governments worldwide impose regulations requiring customer identification, due diligence, record keeping and transaction reporting, to avoid certain internet payment service providers choosing the country with the poorest regulations or one that is not at all regulated.

Due diligence/know your customer/correspondent banking

The issues of customer due diligence (CDD) and record keeping are the subject of FATF recommendations 10 and 11. Several countries and jurisdictions have been found deficient in applying the requirements stipulated in the two recommendations. As part of its CDD, FATF prohibits financial institutions from keeping anonymous accounts or accounts in obviously fictitious names and requires them to undertake CDD measures when establishing business relations or carrying out occasional transactions above the applicable threshold, or when there is suspicion of money laundering, terrorist financing, or the veracity of a customer's identification or the beneficiary's. The principle that financial institutions should conduct CDD should be set out in law or enforceable means, depending on specific countries. Additionally, financial institutions should be required to maintain, for at least five years, all necessary records on domestic and international transactions for the purposes of proper record keeping and to enable them to comply swiftly with information requests from the competent authorities.

The relationship with correspondent banks is the subject of recommendation 13. Financial institutions should be required to gather sufficient information about a correspondent institution, assess the correspondent institution's AML/CFT controls, clearly understand the respective responsibilities of each institution, and be satisfied that the correspondent bank has conducted CDD on the customers.

Financial inclusion

FATF's emphasis on financial inclusion is motivated by the objective of protecting the integrity of the global financial system, which requires covering the largest range of transactions that pose money-laundering and terrorist-financing risks. Financial exclusion risks arise when persons have to seek their financial services from informal providers in the cash economy. These risks include financial crimes committed by informal service providers and threats to the integrity of formal financial services, as due diligence inquiries fail when money trails disappear in the cash economy. Thus, ensuring that low income, rural sector or undocumented groups have access to regulated financial services helps to strengthen the implementation of AML/CFT measures. Within this spirit, in June 2011 FATF published a guidance paper which provided support to countries and their financial institutions in designing AML/CFT measures that meet the national goal of financial inclusion. Following the revision of its recommendations in February 2012, FATF adopted an updated version of its guidance on financial inclusion in February 2013.[16] This project was conducted in partnership with the World Bank and the Asia/Pacific Group on Money Laundering (APG), and in consultation with the financial industry. The purpose of the guidance paper is to ensure that AML/CFT controls do not inhibit access to well-regulated financial services for financially excluded and under-served groups. The document provides clarity and guidance on the FATF recommendations that are relevant when promoting financial inclusion and shows how the recommendations can be read and interpreted to support financial access. The guidance reviews the different steps of the AML/CFT process (customer due diligence, record-keeping requirements, reporting of suspicious transactions, use of agents, internal controls), and for each of them shows how the standards can be read and interpreted to support financial inclusion.

Financing proliferation

The FATF mandate was extended in 2008 to include new and emerging threats such as proliferation financing, which means the financing of the proliferation of weapons of mass destruction. In 2010 the FATF issued a document on financing proliferation entitled "Combating Proliferation Financing: A Status Report on Policy Development and Consultation, 2010." This is a status report on the policy work and consultation undertaken to that date in relation to proliferation financing. It develops an understanding of the issues surrounding proliferation financing and provides information that can be used by the FATF to assess the need for policy measures to counter it and to strengthen safeguards against it. In addition, the report outlines a series of options that could be considered by the FATF, and by countries, within the framework of existing United Nations Security Council Resolution 1540 of 2004.

The title of the FATF's forty recommendations of February 2012 has changed to include, in addition to the combating of money laundering, the financing of terrorism and proliferation. Recommendation 7 requires "countries to implement targeted financial sanctions to comply with the United Nations Security Council Resolutions (UNSCRs) relating to the prevention, suppression and disruption of the proliferation of weapons of mass destructions (WMD) and its financing." These resolutions include resolution 1718 and 1737 of 2006, 1747 of 2007, 1803 of 2008, and 1929 of 2010.[17] The first resolution relates to the Democratic People's Republic of Korea, while the remaining four address the case of the Islamic Republic of Iran. FATF had previously issued three guidance papers on this subject matter:[18] in June 2007, *The Implementation of Financial Provisions of UNSCRs to Counter the Proliferation of WMD*; in October 2007 *The Implementation of Activity-Based Financial Prohibitions of UNSCR 1737*; and in October 2008 *The Implementation of Financial Provisions of UNSCR 1803*.

The FATF's efforts in this area are consistent with the needs identified by the relevant United Nations Security Council Resolutions (UNSCRs). In recent years the FATF has published guidance to assist jurisdictions in their implementation of these resolutions. FATF also published a typologies report that identified the issues surrounding proliferation financing and highlighted issues for further consideration. The new guidance of 2013, entitled "FATF Guidance: The Implementation of Financial Provisions of United Nations Security Council Resolution to Counter the Proliferation of Weapons of Mass Destruction," assists countries in implementing, in addition to the targeted financial sanctions, other measures, such as activity-based financial prohibitions and vigilance measures.[19]

As far as banks are concerned, according to the new guidance, a number of additional issues arise where a bank or other financial institution is designated for the purpose of financial sanctions. In this respect, competent authorities should seek to implement financial sanctions as quickly as possible. In so doing, they should take a number of immediate actions: first, regulators should determine whether the designated bank has a presence in their country; second, the authorities should also determine whether the designated bank has accounts in a bank located in its territory; third, regulators should consider whether the designation of the bank will cause concerns relating to the bank's senior management and whether the designation of the bank will cause other regulatory concerns, such as systemic risks (e.g. other banks suffering an adverse effect) or other market impacts (e.g. a run of creditors on the bank or potential disturbances in the payment systems). Such a determination may lead authorities to consider the appointment of an administrator or auditor, or other appropriate action. Fourth, the guidance discusses other issues related to payments made by the designated banks and payments due to the bank, and whether they are due under prior contracts or are extraordinary payments. Fifth, the guidance document discusses cross-jurisdictional cooperation, where countries containing branches or subsidiaries of a designated bank should communicate with each other to ensure that sanctions are being applied in a consistent and effective manner across countries.

Governance/corporate responsibility/ethics

The Basel Committee on Banking Supervision published initial guidance on corporate governance in 1999, with revised principles in 2006 aiming at assisting banking supervisors in promoting sound corporate governance practices. In October 2010 the Committee published the final document, "Principles for Enhancing Corporate Governance." Poor corporate governance is believed to contribute to bank failures, with the possibility of broader macroeconomic implications, such as contagion risk and impacts on payment systems. In addition, poor corporate governance could in turn trigger a bank run or liquidity crisis. Thus, from the perspective of the banking sector, corporate governance involves the allocation of authority and responsibilities, including setting the bank's strategy and objectives, determining its tolerance for risk, protecting the interests of depositors, meeting shareholders' obligations, and taking into account the interests of other recognized stakeholders.

Drawing on the lessons learned during the latest financial crisis, the Committee, in the document "Principles for enhancing corporate governance," sets out best practices for banks in light of the crisis.[20] The key areas in which the principles have been strengthened include the role, qualifications, and composition of the board; the importance of an independent risk-management function monitoring risks; the board's oversight of the compensation systems; its understanding, along with the bank's senior management, of the bank's operational structure and risks; and the importance of supervisors regularly evaluating the bank's corporate governance policies and practices in line with the Committee's principles.

The Basel document also emphasizes the corporate responsibility, values, and code of conduct and ethics that need to be present in financial institutions. Thus, professional and responsible behavior is essential for proper governance. The board should take the lead in establishing and setting professional standards and corporate values that promote integrity for itself, senior management, and other employees. A bank's code of conduct should articulate acceptable behavior by discouraging the taking of excessive risks and by preventing the bank from engaging in any improper or illegal activity, such as financial misreporting, money laundering, corruption, fraud, and bribery. The board should ensure that appropriate steps are taken to communicate throughout the bank the corporate values, professional standards, or codes of conduct, together with supporting policies and procedures. A policy largely relevant to board members relates to conflicts of interest, as these may arise as a result of the various activities and roles of the bank. The board should have a formal written conflicts of interest policy and an objective compliance process for implementing the policy.

According to the document, boards in many jurisdictions ought to establish certain specialized board committees, the number and nature of which depended on the size of the bank and its board, the nature of the business areas of the bank, and its risk profile. For large and internationally active banks an audit committee or equivalent is required, as well as a risk management committee or equivalent responsible for advising the board on the bank's overall current and future risk tolerance and strategy, including strategies for capital and liquidity management, as well as for credit, market, operational, compliance, reputational and other risks.

A major area of interest in the governance of financial institutions is risk management and internal controls. The document recommends that banks have a risk management function that identifies, assesses, measures, and monitors the key risks to the bank to determine whether risk decisions are in line with the board-approved risk tolerance/appetite and risk policy, while reporting to senior management, and the board as appropriate, on such issues. Internal controls are designed to ensure that each key risk has a policy, process or other measure to ensure process integrity, compliance, and effectiveness. Internal controls also place checks on managerial and employee discretion. It is recommended that even in very small banks, for example, key management decisions should be made by more than one person (the "four eyes principle"). Internal control reviews should also determine the extent of an institution's compliance with both company policies and procedures and legal and regulatory policies. Finally, in line with corporate responsibility and proper ethical behavior, the governance of the bank should be adequately transparent to its shareholders, depositors, other relevant stakeholders, and market participants.

Human trafficking/smuggling of migrants

The United Nations Convention against Transnational Organized Crime (UNTOC), which was developed by the United Nations Office on Drugs and Crime (UNODC), adopted by General Assembly resolution 55/25 of 15 November 2000 and entering into force on September 29, 2003, is the main international instrument in the fight against transnational organized crime. The Convention is supplemented by three Protocols, which target specific areas and manifestations of organized crime: the Protocol to Prevent, Suppress and Punish Trafficking in Persons, Especially Women and Children; the Protocol against the Smuggling of Migrants by Land, Sea and Air; and the Protocol against the Illicit Manufacturing of and Trafficking in Firearms, their Parts and Components and Ammunition. Countries must become parties to the Convention itself before they can become parties to any of the Protocols.

The Protocol to Prevent, Suppress and Punish Trafficking in Persons, especially Women and Children, was adopted by General Assembly resolution 55/25 to enter into force on December 25, 2003. It is the first international legally binding document with an agreed definition on trafficking in human beings to facilitate convergence in national approaches that would support efficient international cooperation in investigating and prosecuting cases of trafficking in humans. The Protocol also serves to protect and assist the victims of human trafficking. The Protocol against the Smuggling of Migrants by Land, Sea and Air, adopted by General Assembly resolution 55/25, entered into force on January 28, 2004. A major achievement was the agreement upon a definition of smuggling of migrants for the first time in a Protocol that aims at preventing and combating the smuggling of migrants, as well as promoting cooperation among Member States, while protecting the rights of smuggled migrants. Issues related to these two criminal activities remain some of the main concerns of UNODC, as indicated by major conferences organized by UNODC on Trafficking in Persons in Vienna and on the smuggling of migrants, both in November 2013.

According to UNODC, trafficking in persons and smuggling of migrants are two concepts easily confused, as they have many similarities. However, differences arise in three main issues related to consent, exploitation, and transnationality. The smuggling of migrants involves migrants who have consented to the smuggling. Trafficking victims have either never consented or, if they initially consented, that consent has been rendered meaningless by the coercive, deceptive, or abusive actions of the traffickers. Regarding exploitation, smuggling ends with the arrival of the migrants at their destination, whereas trafficking involves ongoing exploitation to generate illicit profits for the traffickers. Smuggling is always transnational, whereas trafficking need not be. Trafficking can occur regardless of whether victims are taken to another country or are moved from one place to another within the same country.

It is documented that, even after the passage of the two conventions, criminals are increasingly turning to the trafficking of human beings and the smuggling of migrants because of the profitability of these illegal activities. The money generated by such activities finds its way into the financial system. As a result, FATF published a report entitled "Money Laundering Risks Arising from Trafficking in Human Beings and Smuggling of Migrants" in July 2011 in which it addressed these two issues in detail.[21] The key objectives of the report are to assess the scale of the problem, identify different trends in these two criminal activities, determine from case studies the form that money laundering is taking, and inform relevant law enforcement bodies and financial institutions of the results to assist in the suspicious transaction reports and to increase the possibility of identifying and confiscating the proceeds of these criminal activities.

The questionnaires and the case studies developed and addressed in the report identified geographical differences related to the money-laundering processes used. In European countries the traffickers/smugglers make particular use of cash-intensive and money service businesses, cash couriers, hawala systems, front companies, and investments in high-value goods such as cars and real estate; in American countries the use of casinos, import/export companies, cash-intensive (such as car dealership) and money service businesses, wire transfers, and online payments are prevalent; in Asian countries there is considerable commingling of funds with legitimate business proceeds and funds are more likely to be transferred via formal and informal banking systems; in African countries purchase of real estate, investment in clubs or restaurants, offshore investments, informal banking systems, and use of agents/runners to carry cash are the preferred methods.

Red flag indicators to assist financial institutions in their identification of money laundering from human trafficking/smuggling are reported as follows, according to the report's major findings. For banks, these are the usage of a common mobile number, address, and employment references to open multiple accounts in different names; frequent money transfer to "risk" countries, with a concentration of "risk" nationalities among the opening of accounts; money rapidly withdrawn from accounts, from one ATM, or from several ATMs in close proximity; frequent deposits or withdrawals with no apparent business source; third-party cash deposits made at various bank branches and via ATMs; transactions undertaken that appear inconsistent with the customer profile; unusual withdrawals, deposits, or wire activity inconsistent with normal business practices, or dramatic and unexplained change in account activity; and numerous incoming money transfers or personal checks deposited into business accounts for no apparent legitimate purposes. For money service businesses, the red flag indicators are small amounts sent to different recipients; small amounts sent frequently to unconnected persons;

frequent transfers to "risk" countries; and multiple customers conducting international funds transfers to the same overseas beneficiary.

Identity theft/ beneficial ownership

Identity theft, also termed identity fraud, refers to criminal behavior involving wrongfully using another person's personal data, usually to achieve economic gain. Personal data, especially identification cards, bank accounts, credit card and telephone numbers, and home or work addresses, are valuable information that can be used to achieve identity theft. Reports from many countries indicate that unauthorized criminals have taken funds from people's bank or financial accounts, running up debts and committing financial crimes while using their names. In many cases, victims' losses also include additional financial costs in trying to settle the crimes.

In the US the Department of Justice prosecutes cases of identity theft and fraud under a variety of federal statutes, especially the Identity Theft and Assumption Deterrence Act, passed by Congress in 1998.[22] According to this department, statistics show that the average number of US identity fraud victims annually amounts to 11,571,900; 7 percent of US households reported some type of identity fraud; the average financial loss per identity theft incident amounts to $4,930; and the total financial loss attributed to identity theft in 2013 amounted to $21 billion, rising from a figure of $13.2 billion in 2010. The most common types of identity theft are the misuse of credit cards, followed by the misuse of bank accounts and the misuse of personal information.[23]

More recently, identity fraud has grown to include the theft of: cell and landline phone services; cable and satellite television services; power, water, gas, and electricity services; internet payment services; medical insurance; home mortgages and rental housing; automobile, boat, and other forms of financing and loans; and government benefits.

The Huffington Post reports that one of the largest and most sophisticated identity theft cases ever seen in the US, according to Queens (NY) District Attorney Richard Brown, involved a group of 111 people who were arrested for taking part in an operation that netted more than $13 million between July and September 2011.[24] The group would receive information about unknown people from various foreign countries, such as Russia and China, as well as via statewide suppliers— who would use a skimming device to swipe consumer credit card information at retail or food establishments—and illegal identification-gathering websites. "Shoppers" would then be sent out on shopping sprees around the US with counterfeit credit and ID cards manufactured using the stolen information. Shoppers allegedly used the fraudulent cards to stay at five-star hotels and rent high-end cars and even a private jet.

Beneficial ownership is enjoyed by anyone who has the benefits of ownership of an asset, and yet does not nominally own the asset itself. FATF recommendations 24 and 25, dealing with transparency and beneficial ownership of legal persons and arrangements, state that countries should take measures to prevent the misuse of legal persons or arrangements for money laundering or terrorist financing. Countries should ensure that adequate, accurate, and timely information on the beneficial ownership and control of legal persons or trusts can be obtained or accessed in a timely fashion by competent authorities.[25]

Money remittance/currency exchange

Specialized financial businesses provide certain types of services, including money remittance (MR) and foreign currency exchange (CE). The service providers in this field (the "MR/CE sector") are quite diverse and range widely in their complexity. Unless appropriate safeguards are in place, the MR/CE sector may provide significant opportunities for criminals attempting to laundering funds. Risks particular to the sector are related not only to the misuse of MR/CE businesses for laundering money but also to the owning of such businesses by criminal groups and corrupt employees cooperating with criminals. Typologies reports published by the FATF over the years have highlighted money-laundering risks posed by bureaux de change[26] and have examined the vulnerabilities of alternative remittance systems to money laundering and terrorist financing.[27] FATF's last report on the subject matter,[28] entitled "Money Laundering through Money Remittance and Currency Exchange Providers," focuses on non-bank financial institutions that provide at least one of the following services: money remittance, currency exchange/dealing and issuing, and cashing or redeeming of checks/money orders/stored value cards.

In most jurisdictions MR/CE businesses are not defined as banks. National legislation has defined this group of financial service providers in some countries, but not in most. In the US, for example, the term money service business (MSBs), including non-bank financial institutions and MR/CE businesses, has been defined since 1999. The duties of these businesses have also been defined in many countries after the FATF reports to prevent them as far as possible from carrying out money laundering and terrorist financing activities.

The FATF report of 2010[29] both examined how MR/CE businesses may be misused for money-laundering purposes and identified vulnerabilities that may be exploited by criminals, while considering appropriate measures that could be taken to address the identified vulnerabilities. MR/CE providers can be used for money laundering in two ways: either without knowledge of the illegal origin or destination of the funds involved in transactions, or via the direct involvement of the service provider through complicity or the takeover of such businesses by the criminal organization. Several features of the MR/CE sector make them an attractive vehicle, such as the cash character of transactions, their simplicity and certainty, their worldwide reach, the often less stringent customer identification rules that apply to such transactions compared with opening bank accounts, the reduced possibilities for verification of the customer's identification compared with other financial institutions, and the brevity of contacts with the service provider. Also important is that these transactions can be conducted in small denominations with relative ease through structuring, or "smurfing," which appears to remain the most usual money-laundering method of MR/CE providers and the most frequently reported suspicious activity. Structuring occurs when a person carries out several cash transactions in a single day or over a period of days through the same or several agents by breaking funds into smaller amounts in order to avoid the mandatory threshold reporting and/or customer identification requirements.

Information gathered has allowed the money-laundering threat facing MR/CE businesses to be documented. However, there was far less sector-specific information to work with regarding the threat of terrorist financing. The report, then, focused primarily on the range of money-laundering techniques to which MR/CE businesses may be vulnerable, providing a series of illustrative typologies. A non-exhaustive list of indicators of potentially suspicious activity related to transactions or customers has been included in the report to assist policy-makers.

Organized crime

Many of the topics discussed under various headings in this paper, especially ones dealing with corruption, fraud, bribery, human trafficking, the smuggling of migrants, identity theft, and cybercrime, can be considered as part of what is known as organized crime. According to the United Nations Office on Drugs and Crime (UNODC), organized crime threatens peace and human security, violates human rights, and undermines the economic, social, cultural, political, and civil development of societies around the world.

Given that the domestic components of organized crime have been covered and discussed in several other sections, the following analysis will focus on transnational organized crime, which manifests in many forms, including trafficking in drugs, firearms, and even persons, smuggling migrants, and undermining financial systems through money laundering. Products that are illicit in nature are often sourced from one jurisdiction or even continent, trafficked across another, and marketed in a third. Transnational organized criminals operate across borders as well as overcoming cultural and linguistic differences.

The UN, through UNODC, developed and is currently the guardian of the United Nations Convention against Transnational Organized Crime (UNTOC) and the three Protocols—on Trafficking in Persons, Smuggling of Migrants, and Trafficking of Firearms—that supplement it. UNTOC is the only international convention on organized crime that represents the international community's commitment to combating transnational organized crime and acknowledges the UN's role in supporting this commitment. The development of the convention took place in Palermo, Italy, on 12–15 December 2000 (hence its name, the "Palermo Convention") for signature by Member States at a high-level political conference convened for that purpose. Its adoption at the fifty-fifth session of the General Assembly of the UN in 2000 and its entry into force in 2003 reflects the commitment by the international community to counter organized crime. The Convention reflects the recognition by member jurisdictions and nations of the severity of organized crime, as well as of the need to foster and enhance close international cooperation to tackle this criminal activity. By ratifying this Convention states commit themselves to taking a series of measures against transnational organized crime, including the creation of domestic criminal offences (participation in an organized criminal group, corruption, money laundering, and obstruction of justice); the adoption of frameworks for mutual legal assistance, extradition, and law enforcement cooperation; and the promotion of technical assistance and training programs for building or upgrading the necessary capacity of national authorities.

UNTOC does not precisely define the term "transnational organized crime," nor does it list the kinds of crime included within it to allow for its applicability to the new types of crime continuously emerging. However, the Convention defines organized criminal groups to include a group of three or more persons that was not randomly formed and has existed for a period of time. This group acts in concert with the aim of committing at least one crime punishable by at least four years' incarceration for the purpose of obtaining, directly or indirectly, a financial or other material benefit. UNTOC offers member nations and jurisdictions a framework for preventing and combating organized crime and a platform for cooperating in doing so. As such, members of the Convention have committed to establishing the criminal offences of participating in an organized crime group, money laundering, corruption, and obstruction of justice in their national legislation. Member states also have access to a new framework for mutual legal assistance and extradition, as well as a platform for strengthening law enforcement cooperation.

UNTOC deals with transnational crimes covering not only offences committed in more than one country or jurisdiction but also those that take place in one State but are planned or controlled in another, crimes in one State committed by groups that operate in more than one State, and crimes committed in one State that have substantial effects in another State. The implied definition is thus broad, encompassing serious criminal activities with international implications, taking account of global complexities, and allowing cooperation on the widest possible range of common concerns.

The key feature of the UNTOC is its emphasis on international cooperation, especially in criminal matters. Thus, UNODC, in addition to promoting and facilitating cooperation between different countries, liaises between various nations, jurisdictions, and international organizations and facilitates regional networks of cooperation against organized crime around the world. Specifically, UNODC is supporting the establishment and implementation of regional network of central authorities and of prosecutors, such as the West African Network of Central Authorities and Prosecutors (WACAP) and the Network of Prosecutors against Organized Crime (REFCO).

The Protocol to Prevent, Suppress and Punish Trafficking in Persons and the Protocol on the Smuggling of Migrants which supplemented the Palermo Convention were mentioned above. The Protocol against the Illicit Manufacturing of and Trafficking in Firearms, their Parts and Components and Ammunition was adopted by General Assembly resolution 55/255 of May 31, 2001 and entered into force on July 3, 2005. The Protocol, which is the first legally binding instrument on small arms adopted at the international level, aims to strengthen cooperation among Members in order to prevent and combat the illicit manufacturing of and trafficking in firearms, their parts and components and ammunition. In signing the Protocol, Members make a commitment to adopt a series of crime-control measures and implement in their national laws several normative provisions to that effect.

Public–private cooperation/international cooperation/data sharing

A major issue being addressed in the fight against financial and economic crimes is cooperation among public, regulatory, and private sectors, international cooperation between various countries and jurisdictions, and data sharing among all groups concerned. FATF recommendation 2, entitled "National Cooperation and Coordination," states that countries should have national AML/CFT policies that are regularly reviewed and should designate an authority or have a coordination or other mechanism that is responsible for such policies. Countries should ensure that policy-makers, the financial intelligence unit (FIU), law enforcement authorities, supervisors, and other relevant competent authorities at the policy-making and operational levels have effective mechanisms in place which enable them to cooperate and, where appropriate, coordinate domestically with each other concerning the development and implementation of policies and activities to combat money laundering, terrorist financing, and the financing of the proliferation of weapons of mass destruction.

International cooperation is reflected in recommendation 36, which states that countries should take immediate steps to become party to and implement fully the Vienna Convention, 1988; the Palermo Convention, 2000; the United Nations Convention against Corruption (UNCAC), 2003; and the Terrorist Financing Convention, 1999. Where applicable, countries are also encouraged to ratify and implement other relevant international conventions, such as the Council of Europe Convention on Cybercrime, 2001; the Inter American Convention against Terrorism, 2002; and the Council of Europe Convention on Laundering, Search, Seizure and Confiscation of the Proceeds from Crime and on the Financing of Terrorism, 2005.

As such, and in line with the Palermo Convention on organized crime, international cooperation against organized crime should be used as a tool for strengthening sovereignty and security. The United Nations Convention on Transnational Organized Crime (UNTOC) provisions on mutual legal assistance (MLA), extradition, transfer of sentenced prisoners, and asset confiscation make it a practical tool in this area.

Different jurisdictions and countries can use the UNTOC to cooperate at both formal and informal levels. At the formal level it can be used to request and deliver MLA, extradition, and the freezing and confiscation of criminal proceeds. The Convention can also supplement bilateral and multilateral MLA and extradition agreements. Informal cooperation can take place between different authorities, such as law enforcement, witness protection, and financial intelligence, to share criminal intelligence, cooperate in the protection of witnesses, and share information concerning financial crimes respectively. UNODC continuously develops new tools to facilitate international cooperation, including manuals, an online directory of competent national authorities, a mutual legal assistance request writer tool, a legal database, and best practices case law.

Additionally, MLA, in recommendation 37, states that countries should provide mutual legal assistance in relation to money-laundering and terrorist-financing investigations, prosecutions, and related proceedings. In recommendation 38, following, it is stated that countries should ensure that they have the authority to take expeditious action in response to requests by foreign countries to identify, freeze, seize, and confiscate property laundered; recommendation 39 relates to extradition requests, where countries should constructively and effectively execute extradition requests in relation to money laundering and terrorist financing without undue delay. In the case of asset recovery cases, countries require at least one of four legal bases to provide formal MLA. These legal bases are domestic legislation, allowing for international cooperation in criminal cases; bilateral MLA agreements; promises of reciprocity through diplomatic channels; and international conventions containing provisions on MLA in criminal matters.

Tax evasion

The incentive to avoid and evade taxes has been prevalent in all societies owing to the high tax burden in most countries. Thus, people may choose among four options: tax compliance, where all taxes are paid in full; tax avoidance, a legal process in which taxpayers, for example, deposit or invest their funds in tax shelters such as retirement accounts; tax evasion, a process in which the return on investment or deposits is not reported to the home country in order to evade taxes, which is illegal from the home perspective and legal in the haven itself—evasion can also take place in any country by under-declaring income or over-declaring deductions; and, finally, tax fraud, where documents are falsified to hide the return, which is fraudulent and illegal everywhere.

Several countries have historically acted as tax havens, where banking and financial secrecy protects the identity of depositors and investors. The return on deposits or investments in these havens is either tax-exempt or taxed at very low rates in comparison to the tax brackets in the country where the funds originated. Thus, funds are deposited in these havens and their return is not reported to the country of the beneficiary. In March 2010 the US introduced the Foreign Account Tax Compliance Act (FATCA), which stipulates that countries are to sign an agreement with the US through its internal revenue service to report the bank interest income of US citizens to the US government, thus preventing tax evasion. This law targets tax non-compliance by US taxpayers with foreign accounts, focusing on reporting by US taxpayers about certain foreign financial accounts and offshore assets, and by foreign financial institutions about financial accounts held by US taxpayers or foreign entities in which US taxpayers hold a substantial ownership interest.[30]

Tax evasion has also been found in many smuggling and illicit activities. In June 2012 FATF produced a report entitled "The Illicit Trade in Tobacco (ITT)," in which it states that the revenues generated from ITT amount to an estimate of tens of billions of dollars.[31] These revenues are hidden from tax authorities and may also be used to fund other forms of crime and terror. ITT therefore generates significant amounts of criminal proceeds arising from both the trade itself and associated customs and tax offences.

Whistle blowing/reporting/witness protection

There exist several concerns about the disclosure of information by public as well as private employees or agents when they suspect money laundering, financing terrorism or any criminal activity. In 1989 the US developed the Whistleblower Protection Act (WPA) to protect public sector employees from retaliatory action for voluntarily disclosing information about dishonest or illegal activities occurring within a government organization. The law prohibits a federal agency from taking action, or threatening to take action, against these employees for disclosing such information.[32] In 2009 the Whistleblower Protection Enhancement Act (WPEA) was introduced to strengthen the legislation, becoming law in November 2012. The act provides millions of federal workers with the rights they need to report government corruption and wrongdoing safely, and reflects an unequivocal bipartisan consensus, having received the vote of every member in the 112th Congress, passing both the Senate and House of Representatives by unanimous consent shortly before adjournment.[33]

FATF recommendation 20 deals with the reporting of suspicious transactions by stating that if a financial institution suspects that funds are the proceeds of a criminal or terrorist financing activity it should be required, by law, to report its suspicions promptly to the financial intelligence unit (FIU) of its respective country or jurisdiction. Recommendation 21, on "Tipping-off and confidentiality," handles the witness protection issue by stating that the staff of financial institutions are to be protected by law from criminal and civil liability if they report their suspicions in good faith to the FIU, even if they did not know precisely what the underlying criminal activity was, and regardless of whether illegal activity actually occurred; however, these same staff are prohibited by law from disclosing ("tipping off") the fact that a suspicious transaction is being filed with the FIU.

In the report of the Basel Committee on "Principles for Enhancing Corporate Governance," published in October 2010, under corporate values and code of conduct it was stated that staff at all levels, with protection from any type of reprisal, should be encouraged and able to communicate legitimate concerns about illegal, unethical, or questionable practices. It is highly beneficial for banks to establish a policy on adequate procedures for employees to confidentially communicate their concerns. It becomes the duty of the board to determine how and by whom legitimate concerns shall be investigated and addressed, be it an internal control function, an objective external party, senior management, or even the board itself.

The Organized Crime Control Act of 1970 in the US gave grand juries new powers, permitted the detention of unmanageable witnesses, and gave the US Attorney General authorization to protect witnesses, both state and federal, and their families. This last measure helped lead to the creation of WITSEC, an acronym for witness security.[34] Internationally, the United Nations Office on Drugs and Crime (UNODC) states that the cooperation of victims and witnesses is crucial to achieving successful prosecutions of criminal offenders. To help obtain such cooperation, and in accordance with Articles 24 and 25 of the Organized Crime Convention, State parties shall take appropriate measures to provide effective protection to victims and witnesses of crime. Such measures may include establishing procedures to protect witnesses from threats, intimidation, corruption, or bodily injury, and nations and jurisdictions are obliged to strengthen international cooperation in this regard.

Concluding remarks and policy implications

There will always exist politically exposed persons aiming to build global retirement funds outside their jurisdictions and a corrupt component of the private sector seeking secret vehicles to launder its ill-gotten money. This demand side for secrecy necessitates a supply side for the secret market to develop, interact, and flourish. Financial secrecy is fascinating in both its demand and supply components for actors coming out of all segments of life in the pursuit of illicit gains. The variety of the financial and economic crimes addressed in this document represents major issues on both the demand and supply side of criminal activities, with the very few non-covered topics falling largely under the heading of organized crime and corruption. However, the latest criminal activities addressed may not necessarily represent "new wine in old bottles." The criminal vehicles, or the bottles, are also changing, necessitating dynamic policy responses requiring permanent updating, enhancement, implementation, and coordination. According to UNODC, organized crime is not stagnant, but adapts as new crimes emerge and as relationships between criminal networks become both more flexible and more sophisticated, with ever-greater reach around the globe. This underscores the dynamics of the dialectic discussed in the Introduction to this chapter, where regulators need innovation in the rules and market place to remain abreast of and capable of abating crime. On the performance front, these authorities have to a large extent succeeded in developing various conventions and rules to combat ill-gotten money, especially in certain countries. The regulatory model has attempted to combat the supply side of secrecy, as supply in this case motivates its own demand and curtailing it can reduce financial crimes. Limiting the supply through various international coordinated measures is only the beginning, as additional challenges remain in enforcement and implementation. The evidence of the modest success of these measures is in the figures on asset recovery, showing that only minimal amounts were recovered from public and private sector corruption. Fighting a dynamic and evolving enemy gives a new meaning to "more is less," where more standard and deliberate reactions by regulators are lagging behind the adventurous profit-motivated actions of the criminals and perpetrators. As Lewis Carroll, the author of *Alice's Adventures in Wonderland*, stated around 150 years ago in *Through the Looking-Glass*: "It takes all the running you can do to keep in the same place. If you want to get somewhere else, you must run at least twice as fast as that!"

Notes

1 International Symposium on Economic Crime 2011; 2012; 2013; 2014; 2015.
2 FATF 2015a, FATF 2014a.
3 FATF 2015b.
4 FinCEN 2016.
5 FATF 2015b.
6 See Stephenson et al 2011.
7 FATF 2013d.
8 See Stephenson et al 2011.
9 International Symposium on Economic Crime 2011; 2012; 2013; 2014; 2015.
10 FATF 2013c.
11 FATF 2013c.
12 *The Wall Street Journal* 2013.
13 CNN 2013.
14 International Symposium on Economic Crime 2013.
15 FATF 2008.
16 FATF 2013b.
17 See Recommendation 7, FATF 2012a.
18 See FATF 2013a.
19 FATF 2013a.
20 Basel Committee on Banking Supervision 2010.
21 FATF 2011.
22 See Identity Theft and Assumption Deterrence Act 1998.
23 See US Department of Justice Javelin Strategy and Research 2013.
24 *The Huffington Post* 2012.
25 FATF 2014b
26 FATF typologies report, 1996, 1999 and 2001; see FATF 2010a and 2010b.
27 FATF typologies report 2004–2005; see FATF 2010a and 2010b.
28 FATF 2010a, 2010b.
29 FATF 2010a, 2010b.
30 See FATCA 2010.
31 FATF 2012b.
32 See Whistleblower Protection Act 1989.
33 See Whistleblower Protection Enhancement Act 2009.
34 See Organized Crime Control Act 1970.

Bibliography

Basel Committee on Banking Supervision 2010, "Principles for Enhancing Corporate Governance-Final Document," Bank for International Settlement. Available from: http://www.bis.org/publ/bcbs176.htm

CNN 2013, "Germany to send intelligence officials to Washington amid spying uproar," by Laura Smith-Spart and Per Nyberg. Available from: http://edition.cnn.com/2013/10/26/world/europe/germany-us-nsa-spying/

FATCA 2010, *Foreign Account Tax Compliance Act*. Available from: http://www.irs.gov/Businesses/Corporations/Foreign-Account-Tax-Compliance-Act-(FATCA)

FATF 2008, "Money laundering and terrorist financing vulnerabilities of commercial websites and internet payment systems," *Financial Action Task Force (FATF)*. Available from: http://www.fatfgafi.org/topics/methodsandtrends/documents/moneylaunderingterroristfinancingvulnerabilitiesofcommercialwebsitesandinternet-paymentsystems.html

FATF 2010a, "Money laundering through money remittance and currency exchange providers," *Financial Action Task Force (FATF)*. Available from: http://www.fatf-gafi.org/topics/methodsandtrends/documents/moneylaunderingthroughmoneyremittanceandcurrencyexchangeproviders.html

FATF 2010b, "Combating proliferation financing: A status report on policy development and consultation," *Financial Action Task Force*. Available from: http://www.fatf-gafi.org/documents/documents/combatingproliferationfinancingastatusreportonpolicydevelopmentandconsultation.html

FATF 2011, "Money laundering risks arising from trafficking of human beings and smuggling of migrants," *Financial Action Task Force (FATF)*. Available from: http://www.fatfgafi.org/topics/methodsandtrends/documents/moneylaunderingrisksarisingfromtraffickingofhumanbeingsandsmugglingofmigrants.html

FATF 2012a, "International standards on combating money laundering and the financing of terrorism and proliferation: the FATF recommendations," *Financial Action Task Force (FATF)*. Available from: http://ww.fatfgafi.org/media/fatf/documents/recommendations/pdfs/FATF_Recommendations.pdf

FATF 2012b, "Illicit tobacco trade," *Financial Action Task Force (FATF)*. Available from: http://www.fatfgafi.org/topics/methodsandtrends/documents/illicittobaccotrade.html

FATF 2013a, "FATF guidance: The implementation of financial provisions of United Nations security council resolution to counter the proliferation of weapons of mass destruction," *Financial Action Task Force (FATF)*. Available from: http://www.fatf-gafi.org/topics/financingofproliferation/

FATF 2013b, "Revised guidance on AML/CFT and financial inclusion," *Financial Action Task Force (FATF)*. Available from: http://www.fatf-gafi.org/topics/financialinclusion

FATF 2013c, "Best practices paper: The use of the FATF recommendations to combat corruption," *Financial Action Task Force (FATF)*. Available from: http://www.fatf-gafi.org/topics/corruption

FATF 2013d, "Guidance on politically exposed persons," *Financial Action Task Force (FATF)*. Available from: http://www.fatf-gafi.org/publications/fatfrecommendations/documents/peps-r12-r22.html

FATF 2014a, "Risk-Based approach for the banking sector," *Financial Action Task Force (FATF)*. Available from: http://www.fatf-gafi.org/publications/fatfrecommendations/documents/risk-based-approach-banking-sector.html

FATF 2014b, "Guidance on transparency and beneficial ownership," *Financial Action Task Force (FATF)*. Available from: http://www.fatf-gafi.org/publications/fatfrecommendations/documents/transparency-and-beneficial-ownership.html

FATF 2015a, "Guidance for a risk-based approach: effective supervision and enforcement by AML/CFT supervisors of the financial sector and law enforcement," *Financial Action Task Force (FATF)*. Available from: http://www.fatf-gafi.org/publications/fatfrecommendations/documents/rba-effective-supervision-and-enforcement.html

FATF 2015b, "High-risk and non-cooperative jurisdictions," *Financial Action Task Force (FATF)*. Available from: http://www.fatf-gafi.org/publications/high-riskandnon-cooperativejurisdictions/documents/public-statement-october-2015.html

FinCEN 2016, "Advisory on the FATF-identified jurisdictions with AML/CFT deficiencies," FIN-2016-A001, United States Department of the Treasury, January 19. Available from: www.fincen.gov

The Huffington Post 2012, "Largest Identity Theft Case in US History." Identity Theft and Assumption Deterrence Act 1998, Congress of the USA, Public Law 105–318, 112 Stat. 3007. Available from: http://www.ftc.gov/os/statutes/itada/itadact.htm

International Symposium on Economic Crime 2011, "Responsibility for risk," University of Cambridge, 29th Symposium. Available from: http://www.crimesymposium.org

International Symposium on Economic Crime 2012, "Economic crime-surviving the fall, the myths and realities," University of Cambridge, 30th Symposium. Available from: http://www.crimesymposium.org

International Symposium on Economic Crime 2013, "Fighting economic crime in the modern world: the role of the private sector-partners and problems," University of Cambridge, 31st Symposium. Available from: http://www.crimesymposium.org

International Symposium on Economic Crime 2014, "Information-shield, sword and Achilles heel in the fight against economic crime," University of Cambridge, 32nd Symposium. Available from: http://www.crimesymposium.org

International Symposium on Economic Crime 2015, "The limits of law-the role of compliance in the 21st century," University of Cambridge, 33rd Symposium. Available from: http://www.crimesymposium.org

Organized Crime Control Act of 1970, Congress of the USA, Pub.L. 91–452, 84 Stat. 922.

Shahin, W 2013, "Compliance with international regulation on AML/CFT: the case of banks in Lebanon," *Journal of Money Laundering Control*, 16, 2, pp. 109–18.

Stephenson, K, Gray, L, Power, R, Brun, J, Dunker, G., and Panjer, M 2011, "Barriers to asset recovery: an analysis of the key barriers and recommendations for action," *The World Bank, UNODC*, vol. 114.

UNODC n.d., "Conference of the parties to the United Nations convention against transnational organized crime and the protocols thereto," United Nations Office on Drugs and Crime. Available from: https://www.unodc.org/unodc/en/treaties/CTOC/CTOC-COP.html

UNODC n.d., "International cooperation," United Nations Office on Drugs and Crime. Available from: https://www.unodc.org/unodc/en/organized-crime/international-cooperation.html

UNODC n.d., "Organized crime," United Nations Office on Drugs and Crime. Available from: https://www.unodc.org/unodc/en/organized-crime/index.html

UNODC n.d., "Technical assistance," United Nations Office on Drugs and Crime. Available from: https://www.unodc.org/unodc/en/organized-crime/technical-assistance.html

UNODC n.d., "United Nations convention against transnational organized crime and the protocols thereto," United Nations Office on Drugs and Crime. Available from: http://www.unodc.org/unodc/treaties/CTOC/

US Department of Justice Javelin Strategy and Research 2013, *Identity theft/fraud statistics.*

The Wall Street Journal 2013, "Cyber Warfare," Europe Edition. Available from: www.wsj.com

Whistleblower Protection Act 1989, Congress of the USA, Pub. L 101–12.

Whistleblower Protection Enhancement Act 2009, Congress of the USA, WPEA. Available from: http://www.gpo.gov/fdsys/pkg/BILLS-112s743enr/pdf/BILLS-112s743enr.pdf

3 The compliance of worldwide banking systems with evolving international regulatory and supervisory requirements

Facts, challenges and implications

Introduction

In recent years compliance has become a major regulatory and supervisory issue and an essential part of banks' business activities and corporate culture. The term compliance in banking refers, in general, to the compliance of the banking institution with established domestic and international laws, rules, and standards related to the banking profession. The importance and integrity of compliance in banks is fully appreciated given the compliance risk, which is defined by the Basel Committee on Banking Supervision (BCBS) of the Bank for International Settlements (BIS) as: "the risk of legal or regulatory sanctions, material financial loss, or loss to reputation a bank may suffer as a result of its failure to comply with laws, regulations, rules, related self-regulatory organization standards, and codes of conduct applicable to its banking activities." As such, compliance as a concept covers both general and specific matters. Of utmost importance is compliance with anti-money laundering (AML), countering the financing of terrorism (CFT), economic and financial sanctions, and tax evasion regulations, as compliance failure in these areas specifically tend to expose the bank to significant fines and compliance risk (i.e. reputational damage). Obviously, the nature and scale of penalties and charges for non-compliance in other regulatory areas vary from one country to another and could also be substantial in certain cases.

To deal effectively with compliance risk there has to be a dynamic, transparent, and centralized approach to compliance and a board of directors and senior management responsible for both ensuring full compliance with regulations and enforcing the culture of compliance throughout the banking firm. There must also be a compliance function in place originating from a compliance policy, and that function could be organized within other functions, where commonalities exist, or located as a separate function with clear lines of cooperation with other functions on the organizational chart. There could be large differences between banks not only regarding the organization of the compliance function but also when it comes to the responsibilities and activities of its staff. But what matters from a watchdog standpoint is whether the compliance functions in banks and the adopted policies and procedures adhere to the set of international rules and regulations in the area of compliance and compliance-related issues and are consistent with existing best industry practices. Though banks in theory and practice support measures aimed at reducing the compliance risk and avoiding reputational damage, they are also concerned with the uncertainty and burden presented by regulatory complexity, and the substantial direct and indirect costs of compliance to new or modified regulations.

This chapter tries to explore all of these issues in terms of their policy implications, and will focus on compliance with AML/CFT, economic and trade sanctions, and tax evasion regulations. Compliance with other rules and regulations, such as the Basel Agreement on capital and liquidity requirements and main country specific regulations with international ramifications, will be very briefly discussed in this chapter, which is organized as follows. The next section gives an overview of the evolving international regulatory and supervisory framework to highlight and understand the volume of compliance-related requirements and implications. The third section describes the practices adopted by banks in the area of compliance in general and AML/CFT in particular in response to burgeoning domestic and international regulations. This is followed by a discussion of the compliance challenges that most banks face, the costs of regulatory compliance and non-compliance, and the implications or side-effects of "de-risking". The final section concludes with some general remarks and thoughts on the benefits and repercussions of compliance and the available or feasible ways to address and get ahead of the challenges.

The evolving international regulatory and supervisory framework

This section is designed to survey the expansion in the nature and amount of regulations issued by the international standard-setters in the broad area of compliance and particularly in the development and promotion of international policies, principles, and guidelines to combat money laundering, financing of terrorism, sanctions, and tax evasion. For each international standard-setter there is a brief description of its main mission and the content of the main reference documents of interest produced by this party. This section also involves a concise overview of some US and European regulations or legislation with an international dimension, as these are inflicting a heavy compliance burden not only on US and European banks but on banks worldwide. It is designed to clarify the "big picture" of regulatory compliance and facilitate, later on, the description and discussion of related challenges and implications.

Basel Committee on Banking Supervision

The Basel Committee on Banking Supervision (BCBS) was established in 1974 by the central bank governors of the G10 countries in response to disruptions and turmoil in the international financial markets and the associated heavy losses by banks following the breakdown of the Bretton Woods System of managed exchange rates in 1973. It was intended to be a forum for global cooperation (between BIS member countries) on banking supervision matters with a view to boosting international financial stability by working on the enhancing of supervisory proficiency and the quality of banking supervision. The committee is well known today as a leading international standard-setter in the area of prudential regulation and supervision of banks, and originates related standards, guidelines, and sound practices to fortify the regulation, supervision, and practices of banks worldwide. The BCBS is very active and frequently releases working papers and documents; perhaps the best known are those related to the Basel Capital Accord (Basel I, II, and III).

BIS compliance principles

In April 2005 the BCBS issued ten compliance function principles. They are the cornerstones for establishing a sound compliance function in banks and thus deserve a little elaboration in order to serve here as a benchmark in understanding and assessing the principles that banks are adopting and implementing in the area of compliance.

The first four principles of the BIS document relate to the responsibilities of the board of directors and senior management for compliance. The first principle states that the bank's board is responsible for overseeing the management of the bank's compliance risk and the implementation of the bank's compliance policy, which it has to approve. Such a policy should establish, among other things, a permanent compliance function. The same principle also sets out that the board or a committee of the board should assess at least once a year the effectiveness of compliance risk management. The remaining principles of these four emphasize the responsibility of the bank's senior management for the effective management of the bank's compliance risk—in essence, responsibility for:

1   Setting up and passing on a written compliance policy containing the basic guidelines to be followed by management and staff and explaining the main processes for the identification and management of compliance risk at all levels of the organization.
2   Ensuring that the compliance policy is observed in the sense that proper corrective or penal action is taken if violations are identified. Senior management should at least once a year pinpoint and appraise both the main compliance risk issues facing banks and the plans to manage such risks.
3   Reporting to the board (or a committee of the board) on any substantial compliance failure and on the management of the bank's compliance risk to assist board or committee members in evaluating the efficacy of compliance risk management and taking the right decisions.
4   Establishing a permanent and efficient compliance function as an element of the bank's compliance policy.

Principles five through eight are linked to the compliance function in banks, including matters of status, staff, resources, responsibilities, and relationship with internal audit. According to those principles, the compliance function should have an official status with the appropriate authority and independence set out, usually in the bank's compliance policy. This should not prevent a cooperative working relationship between the compliance function and other business units or risk management functions to identify and manage compliance risks at an early stage. There should be also a compliance officer or head of compliance, which may or may not be a member of senior management, with overall responsibility for coordinating the management of the bank's compliance risk and for supervising the activities of the compliance function staff. The head of compliance and other compliance function staff should not be placed in a position where there is a possible conflict of interest between their compliance responsibilities and any other responsibilities they may have in performing non-compliance tasks, and they should have access to the information (records or files) and personnel necessary to carry out their responsibilities. The compliance function staff should have the necessary qualifications, experience, professional and personal qualities, and understanding of compliance laws, rules, and standards to enable them to carry out their duties and understand the impact of the relevant regulations on the bank's operations. Finally, the activities of the compliance function should be subject to periodic review by the internal audit function, implying that compliance risk should be part of the risk assessment methodology of the internal audit function.

Principle nine deals with cross-border issues. Specifically, banks should comply with applicable laws and regulations in all jurisdictions in which they conduct business; that is, they must satisfy the legal and regulatory requirements of the host jurisdiction. In addition, the organization, the structure, and the responsibilities of the compliance function should be consistent with local legal and regulatory requirements. Principle ten, related to outsourcing, states that compliance should be viewed as a main risk management activity within the bank. Specific tasks of the compliance function may be outsourced provided that they are subject to suitable oversight by the head of compliance.

Implementation of the BIS compliance principles

As a follow-up to the above-mentioned principles listed in the document "Compliance and the Compliance Function in Banks," issued in April 2005, in August 2008 the BCBS released another document surveying the implementation of the compliance principles in twenty-one jurisdictions. The survey was intended to both assess the status of the principles' implementation and report compliance-related incidents and challenges. It was found that banks in the survey-participating jurisdictions viewed the compliance function as a vital risk management control function and did manage and supervise this function to different extents in line with the Basel compliance document. No further survey of the implementation of the principles has been issued.

Anti-money laundering (AML) and countering the financing of terrorism (CFT)

In October 2001 the BCBS issued a pioneering paper entitled *Customer Due Diligence for Banks* (*CDD*), which included prudential guiding principles for customer due diligence pertinent to anti-money laundering and countering the financing of terrorism (AML/CFT). The paper outlined standards and offered guidelines that serve as a benchmark for supervisors to set national practices and also help banks to develop their proper due diligence practices, from Know Your Customer (KYC) policies to procedures on new and existing customers, in order to know with whom they are dealing and to protect the safety and soundness of their institutions. This is built on the idea that, without proper due diligence and KYC standards, banks would become subject to serious reputational, operational, legal, and concentration risks, which can lead to substantial financial costs. The main areas covered were customer acceptance policy, customer identification, ongoing monitoring of accounts and transactions, and risk management, all of which are elaborated in the third section of this chapter while discussing the practices adopted by banks.

In February 2003 *Customer Due Diligence for Banks* was reinforced by a paper entitled *General Guide to Account Opening and Customer Identification*, and all the principles laid down in these two mentioned documents have been accepted and adopted by jurisdictions worldwide. The BCBS paper on due diligence remains today a suitable if not the most suitable point of reference for customer due diligence procedures adopted by banks, although the forty recommendations of the Financial Action Task Force (FATF) (described below) reflected to a large extent the set of principles described in *Customer Due Diligence for Banks*. This benchmark's suitability is rooted in the few differences between the *CDD* guidelines and FATF recommendations, as emphasized repeatedly by the BCBS, and these dissimilarities can be summarized as follows. First, the FATF recommendations embrace all financial institutions (banks and non-banks) and some designated non-financial businesses and professions, whereas *CDD* involves only banks. Second, the FATF, by virtue of its mission and goals, concentrates on money laundering and terrorist financing, while *CDD*'s attention is centered on banks' risk management practices. Third, the FATF recommendations are considered and perceived as the minimum standard, whereas *CDD* elaborates on the crucial aspects of KYC standards for worldwide implementation by all banks.

In August 2003 the BCBS issued a related consultative paper, *Consolidated KYC Risk Management*, which was subject to revision to incorporate the feedback and comments received from relevant stakeholders, including the banking industry. The paper explores the essential components for effective management of KYC risks across banks' head offices and all branches and subsidiaries. It focuses on the development by banks of a global risk management program that would encompass coherent policies and procedures for KYC designed to comply with all relevant laws and regulations and, above all, to identify and monitor customer accounts on a group-wide basis across business lines and geographical locations.

Policies and procedures in place must ensure the identification, monitoring, and mitigation of reputational, operational, legal, and concentration risk on a group-wide groundwork. *Consolidated KYC Risk Management* stipulates also that banks' compliance and internal audit units and staff, or external auditors, are responsible for assessing adherence to international KYC standards and evaluating the effectiveness of KYC functions and the requirements for sharing information among group members. *Consolidated KYC Risk Management* was issued in its final form in October 2004.

In January 2014 the BCBS issued a set of guidelines in a new document entitled *Sound Management of Risks Related to Money Laundering and Financing of Terrorism*. The guidelines, which describe the way in which banks should include risks related to money laundering and financing of terrorism within their overall risk management framework, supersede the two above-mentioned publications: *Customer Due Diligence for Banks* and *Consolidated KYC Risk Management*. These risk management guiding principles are also consistent with the *International Standards on Combating Money Laundering and the Financing of Terrorism & Proliferation* issued by the FATF in 2012 and complement their goals and objectives. An earlier version of these guidelines was issued for consultation in June 2013.

The Financial Action Task Force (FATF)

The Financial Action Task Force (FATF) is an independent inter-governmental policy-making body established by the ministers of the Group of Seven (G7) during their Paris summit in July 1989. It was born at that time in response to the growing concern over the increasing threat that money laundering posed to the banking system and to financial institutions. This international task force was initially created to inspect and devise measures to combat money laundering. It was given the task of scrutinizing money-laundering techniques and trends, assessing the actions and measures which had already been taken at national and international levels, and identifying and specifying the measures that still needed to be taken to counter money laundering. The FATF is well known today as an international standard-setter in the development of AML/CFT standards and the support of effective implementation of legal, regulatory, and operational measures for fighting money laundering, terrorist financing, and other related threats to the integrity of the financial system.

In April 1990, around nine months after its inception, the FATF, with its sixteen member jurisdictions, developed its first set of forty recommendations with the intention of supplying concerned authorities with a broad action plan to counter money laundering. The recommendations were revised in 1996, and in 2000 the task force stretched to thirty-one members, following an expansion in membership in 1991 and 1992 to twenty-eight members. In October 2001 the FATF broadened its mandate and mission to include efforts to combat terrorist financing in addition to money laundering, and thus it developed and issued more recommendations, known as the eight special recommendations, to deal specifically with the issue of terrorist financing.

To cope with the ongoing evolution and increasing sophistication of money-laundering means and techniques the FATF comprehensively revised its standards in June 2003, and in October 2004 it added a new special recommendation to the existing eight to further fortify its international standards for combating money laundering and terrorist financing. Recently the 40+9 recommendations were thoroughly reviewed to ensure that they were up to date, relevant, and of universal application, and that they protected the integrity of the financial system. Subsequently, in February 2012 the FATF published the revised recommendations, which both take into account new threats, such as the financing of the proliferation of weapons of mass destruction, and elaborate on transparency and corruption. No new recommendations were added; instead, the nine special recommendations on terrorist financing have been fully integrated within the measures against money laundering to create a stronger and clearer set of standards consisting of forty recommendations aimed at reinforcing global safeguards and helping ensure a level playing field.

The FATF comprises, as of 2016, thirty-four member jurisdictions and two regional organizations (Gulf Cooperation Council and the European Commission) which represent, together, most of the major financial centers in the world. It monitors its own members and other countries' progress in implementing FATF recommendations and the necessary measures and promotes the adoption and implementation of such recommendations and measures worldwide. FATF also reviews both money-laundering and terrorist-financing means and techniques and counter actions or procedures. This is done in collaboration with other international stakeholders.

The forty FATF recommendations of 2012, published in the document entitled *International Standards on Combating Money Laundering and the Financing of Terrorism & Proliferation,* are distributed across seven sections (A–G). They are considered an all-inclusive set of measures for an effective legal and institutional system or framework for fighting money laundering and the financing of terrorism. The recommendations include the requirements for customer identification and due diligence and for suspicious transactions reporting. They involve also asset freezing, seizing, and confiscation mechanisms. In addition, there are recommendations dealing with intensifying international cooperation in the fight against money laundering and terrorist financing, enhancing domestic or national legal systems, and improving the role of the financial sector. To avoid tedious duplication we will outline these recommendations only briefly here, as the details related to their implementation are described in the discussion of the responses of banks and compliance with mounting ongoing regulations (below).

Two recommendations fall within the first section, on AML/CFT policies and coordination, dealing with assessing AML/CFT risks, applying a risk-based approach, and cooperating and coordinating nationally. A further two recommendations in the section on money laundering and confiscation describe money-laundering offences and confiscation measures. The section on terrorist financing and financing of proliferation contains four recommendations that detail terrorist financing offences; targeted financial sanctions related to terrorism, terrorist financing, and proliferation; and the potential abuse of non-profit organisations for the financing of terrorism. The fourth section, on preventive measures, is the largest section and includes fifteen recommendations discussing financial institution secrecy laws; customer due diligence and record keeping; additional measures for specific customers and activities; reliance; controls and financial groups; the reporting of suspicious transactions; and, finally, designated non-financial businesses and professions.

The fifth section, dealing with transparency and beneficial ownership of legal persons and arrangements, includes two recommendations emphasizing that countries should take measures to prevent the misuse of legal persons and legal arrangements for money laundering and terrorist financing. Countries must also ensure that there is adequate, accurate, and timely information on the beneficial ownership and control of legal persons and on express trusts that can be obtained in an appropriate manner by competent authorities. The sixth section, on the powers and responsibilities of competent authorities and other institutional measures, comprises fifteen recommendations that tackle the issues of regulation and supervision of financial institutions, operational and law enforcement, general statistical and non-statistical requirements, and sanctions. The final section, on international cooperation, embraces the final five recommendations, which elaborate on international instruments for cooperation, mutual legal assistance, freezing and confiscation, extradition, and other forms of international cooperation.

FATF periodically reviews AML/CFT measures in place in nearly all countries, providing a report that analyzes the level of compliance with FATF's forty recommendations and the effectiveness of AML/CFT systems. The report provides recommendations on how the system could be strengthened and whether improvements are needed in a number of key areas. FATF also holds a list of the jurisdictions with deficiencies in anti-money laundering and countering the financing of terrorism and a black list of non-cooperative countries or territories (NCCTs). Therefore, failure to comply with FATF recommendations and requests could significantly hurt non-complying countries and banks as they could be, among other things, isolated from international financial markets and institutions.

It is worth noting that in February 2015 FATF published a report on the *Financing of the Terrorist Organization Islamic State in Iraq and the Levant (ISIL)*. The FATF and the FATF-Style Regional Bodies (FSRBs) will use the findings of this report and work together with international organizations to develop new proposals to reinforce counter-terrorism financing apparatus. FSRBs are usually voluntary, independent, and cooperative bodies established by country members sharing the same geographical region, such as the Middle East and North Africa Financial Action Task Force (MENA FATF). FSRBs set their own regional AML/CFT policies and procedures to be adopted and implemented in member countries and cooperate with the FATF and other international organizations to adopt and implement international money laundering and terrorist financing regulations.

Subsequently, in October 2015, FATF issued a new report entitled *Emerging Terrorist Financing Risks*, which analyzed recently identified terrorist financing methods and phenomena, referred to as "emerging TF risks"; this was followed in November 2015 by another report on terrorist financing that summarized the findings on whether 194 jurisdictions have implemented key measures to cut off terrorism-related finance as part of a comprehensive AML/CFT framework.

The International Monetary Fund (IMF)

The International Monetary Fund (IMF), established in 1945, is an organization governed by 188 member countries with the main purpose of securing international monetary system stability or international financial stability in general and promoting international trade and sustainable economic growth around the world. The IMF has long been concerned about the economic and financial effects of economic or financial crimes, particularly money laundering and the financing of terrorism, as they could endanger the stability of a country's financial and external sectors and the broader economy in general. However, only in 2000 did the IMF start to develop its work on AML in reaction to appeals from the international community seeking actions to prevent and combat financial abuse and money laundering. Then, soon after the terrorist attacks of September 11, 2001, the IMF stepped up its AML activities and stretched them to incorporate countering the financing of terrorism (CFT). In 2004 AML/CFT assessments and capacity development activities became a regular part of IMF work in terms of surveillance and financial stability assessment. An AML/CFT strategy or program has been developed, has evolved over the years, and is still subject to modifications and enhancements. The IMF assesses member countries' compliance with the FATF recommendations, which it promotes, and assists countries in their implementation.

The Organization for Economic Co-operation and Development (OECD)

The Organization for Economic Cooperation and Development was established in 1961. It is headquartered in Paris and includes thirty-four member countries. The main mission of the OECD is to promote policies that will improve the economic and social well-being of people around the world. In 2014, in an effort to strengthen international cooperation against tax evasion, OECD and G20 countries developed the *Standard for Automatic Exchange of Financial Account Information in Tax Matters*. The aim is to reduce tax evasion and increase tax revenues or, in other words, to better fight tax evasion and ensure tax compliance. According to the OECD, "The Standard provides for annual automatic exchange between governments of financial account information, including balances, interest, dividends and sales proceeds from financial assets. It covers accounts held by individuals and entities, including trusts and foundations."

The OECD Standard demands that jurisdictions obtain information from their financial institutions for the automatic exchange of such information with other jurisdictions. The Standard consists of three parts and lays down the financial account information to be exchanged, the financial institutions required to report, the different types of accounts and taxpayers covered, and the common due diligence procedures to be followed by financial institutions. By 2016 ninety-four jurisdictions had already committed to implement the OECD Standard, which is open to countries and jurisdictions worldwide, and agreed to launch the first automatic information exchanges in 2017 or 2018.

US regulations with international dimensions (domestic rules which have global impact)

The US Patriot Act

In response to the terrorist attacks of September 11, 2001 on Washington and New York, the US congress reacted swiftly and passed the USA Patriot Act (Uniting and Strengthening America to Provide Appropriate Tools Required to Intercept and Obstruct Terrorism Act) in the fall of that year. This act made a number of modifications to the Bank Secrecy Act of 1970 on combating money laundering, whereby financial institutions were required to report suspicious activity on the part of their customers. The Patriot Act has numerous provisions, but the most relevant to this chapter are related to the requisites that financial service providers (such as banks) ascertain the identity of customers opening new accounts or holding accounts whose terms are changed (by asking, for example, for the customer's ID, social security number, driver's licence or other documents). Service providers are then required both to make sure that the customer's ID does not figure on the government-supplied list of terrorist organizations and individuals and to report any suspicious activity in a customer's account.

Section 311 of the USA Patriot Act is also of utmost importance to banks. It grants the US treasury far-reaching powers to indict individuals and institutions involved in financial crime anywhere in the world by labeling them a "primary money-laundering concern." The accusation, for example, that a certain bank supports financial crime could eventually lock that bank out of the US financial system and prevent it from concluding any transactions denominated in US dollars. The Department of the Treasury's Office of Foreign Assets Control (OFAC) also has the responsibility of naming and listing individuals and entities (Specially Designated Nationals) subject to US sanctions. The assets of Specially Designated Nationals are blocked and US persons and entities are prohibited from dealing with them.

The Foreign Account Tax Compliance Act (FATCA)

The Foreign Account Tax Compliance Act (FATCA) was enacted by the US Congress into US federal law on March 18, 2010. Related regulations were also issued later on January 17, 2013. The law aims, among other things, to reduce offshore tax evasion and enhance government revenues, as it targets "U.S. persons" with financial accounts placed outside the US, who as US tax payers must report their earnings to the Internal Revenue Service (IRS) of the US treasury. "U.S. Persons" includes not only US citizens and legal entities but also Green Card Holders, certain non-US legal entities substantially owned by US individuals, and certain estates or trusts whose beneficial owners in whole or part are US individuals. Under FATCA, Foreign Financial Institutions (FFIs) (i.e. banks, insurance companies, brokers, and other financial institutions outside the US), have the responsibility of identifying US tax payers among their clients and of reporting their names and accounts information to the IRS. FFIs that do not wish to comply with and participate in FATCA will be subject to a 30 percent withholding on all income and sales proceeds from the US. Non-compliant FFIs may also run the risk of being blacklisted by other compliant FFIs and thus could expose themselves to financial, commercial, and reputational risks. Non-compliant FFIs may also face access restrictions to US financial markets.

European Union Regulations and United Nations Conventions

European Union AML/CFT Directives

The EU enforced its first AML Directive in 1991, aiming at preventing the use of EU financial systems for money laundering. A second AML Directive in 2001 repealed the first and extended the scope of the offences initially covered and the range of professions and activities included. The third AML Directive, issued in 2005, revoked the second to incorporate FATF-revised recommendations covering terrorist financing and required, among other things, more measures related to customer identification and verification. A fourth Directive came into force in June 2015 to cover and complement the revised FATF recommendations of 2012. It adds tax evasion to the list of offences, permits Simplified Due Diligence in low-risk situations, and requests the conducting of Enhanced Due Diligence in situations of high risk. In this later Directive, as the previous ones, a Financial Intelligence Unit (FIU), to which suspicious transactions are reported, must be established in each EU country.

It is worth mentioning in this context The Egmont Group, an informal network of worldwide Financial Intelligence Units (FIUs) conceived in 1995 in Brussels. It aims at facilitating international cooperation in the exchange of information, training, and the sharing of expertise to effectively combat money laundering and terrorist financing on an international level. The Egmont Group has five working groups: Legal, Outreach, Training, Operational, and IT.

United Nations Conventions and Resolutions

There exist a number of United Nations Conventions and United Nations Security Council Resolutions aiming at curbing money laundering and the financing of terrorism, including the 1988 United Nations Convention against the Illicit Traffic in Narcotic Drugs and Psychotropic Substances, criminalizing money laundering; and the 2004 United Nations Convention against Transnational Organized Crime and the 2004 United Nations Convention against Corruption, both widening the scope of money laundering offence and calling for the establishment of Financial Intelligence Units (FIUs). In addition to these are the 1999 United Nations International Convention for the Suppression of the Financing of Terrorism, which requests member states to adopt measures to protect their financial systems from being misused by individuals and groups engaged in terrorist activities, and the 2001 United Nations Security Council Resolution 1373, obliging member states to adopt, among other things, the criminalization of terrorism-related activities and the prevention and suppression of the financing of terrorism acts. United Nations Security Council Resolution 1617, of 2005, stresses the importance of the implementation of the FATF recommendations on money laundering and terrorist financing.

Compliance practices adopted by banks and financial institutions

It can be inferred from the above survey of the most important developments in the regulations on combating money laundering, terrorist financing, and tax evasion (representing some but not all developments in the area of international banking regulation and supervision) that the banking industry worldwide has been subject to mounting compliance obligations and intense regulatory inspection over the last two decades. This is particularly true since the 2008 global financial crisis, as a wide array of bank and financial regulations emerged in an effort to address the causes and repercussions of the crisis and to better protect the financial system and all stakeholders. Thus, although international standards, guidelines, and other regulatory requisites started to emerge as early as the 1980s, they have significantly increased recently in response to, among other things, advancements in financial crimes and terrorism, financial crises, financial innovation and sophistication, and loopholes in existing regulations, and thus pose significant challenges to financial and bank regulatory and supervisory authorities and to banks and financial institutions worldwide.

Regulatory and supervisory requirements and the related challenges touched almost all parts and corners of compliance, particularly anti-money laundering and countering the financing of terrorism regulations, economic and trade sanctions, capital markets rules, and tax evasion legislation. The new state of things also drove domestic bank regulatory and supervisory authorities worldwide to become more rigorous and pressured banking entities to enhance compliance management at all levels. Relationships between domestic banks and their global correspondent banks became more complex and demanding, as we shall see later on.

To have a complete picture of the compliance burden affecting banks, however, it is necessary also to consider the compliance obligations related, for example, to the implementation of the International Basel Capital Accord (Basel II or III); in addition, some countries have their own domestic those in excess of those insisted on by others, involving more and more compliance requirements. This is especially true for the US and the UK, where banks have to deal additionally with the requirements of, to mention a couple, the US Dodd-Frank Wall Street Reform and Consumer Protection Act of 2010 and the UK Bribery Act of 2010. But, as mentioned earlier, we will limit the discussion in this section to practices adopted by banks in forming a compliance department, fighting money laundering and terrorism financing, complying with economic and trade sanctions, and identifying tax evasion.

Compliance function

Perhaps the best way to begin elaborating on the compliance practices assumed by banks and financial institutions is to discuss first the formation of a compliance department or function. Domestic regulatory authorities worldwide were started either in the last decade or in the current one to compel banks and financial institutions to establish a compliance department with one or more units in adherence to the BIS principles mentioned above. A first unit could be, for example, a legal compliance unit in charge of identifying, mitigating, and preventing legal risks. A second could be, for instance, an AML/CFT compliance unit in charge of verifying compliance with AML/CFT procedures, laws, and regulations in force, and so forth. In any case, the work of the compliance department is intended to cover the parent bank and all its affiliates both in the country where it is established and abroad. Banks and financial institutions were granted a time limit to comply with the provisions of such regulation.

For the sake of illustration, the compliance department in a typical bank is entrusted according to the regulation with:

1 Identifying and assessing compliance risk associated with the products and activities of the bank.
2 Implementing the compliance procedures to verify compliance with the laws, regulations, procedures, and directives of the regulatory and supervisory authorities and other relevant bodies, on the one hand, and to control, fight, and prevent money laundering and terrorism financing, on the other.
3 Verifying that corrective procedures are taken upon the detection of any violation.
4 Evaluating the efficiency of the adopted procedures to detect any violation or breach.
5 Verifying compliance by the bank's employees with the policies set by the senior management.
6 Advising the senior management on compliance with laws and regulations in force and submitting to it periodic reports (at least twice a year) regarding performed assessment, follow up, and corrections.
7 Reporting to senior management and to the board of directors on any important violation of the laws and regulations in force.

8 Preparing an efficient compliance training program and a compliance guide to help and instruct employees on the implementation of the laws and regulations in force.
9 Following up developments in the laws and regulations in force and proposing the necessary amendments to the bank's policies and procedures.

Compliance regulation in general stipulated that the compliance department must be autonomous and independent in its activities from the other activities and units of the bank, including the internal audit unit and the legal department. It must be granted sufficient power to perform its duties efficiently and must have access to any officer and department in the bank and to the necessary files and information that would help in fulfilling its duties properly. Compliance department employees must have the qualifications and expertise in line with their mission and a thorough understanding of banking and financial laws and regulations. The head of the compliance department must have access to the senior management and the board of directors and must attend the meetings held by the specialized committees and the board committees to be informed of the bank's strategic planning and prospective products and activities, so as to provide early counseling. Compliance regulation also details the role of senior management, which must set a written compliance policy that comprises the essential principles to be adopted by management and employees and the basic procedures concerning compliance with laws and regulations in force.

It follows that the efficiency and effectiveness of the compliance function requires banks' officials, aside from establishing the compliance department in accordance with all the details stipulated in the relevant regulation, to perform a variety of functions and deal with a number of issues. The board of directors and senior management must be convinced, above all, that the compliance function is a crucial ingredient of sound bank management and practices and is thus entrusted, along other business functions, with maintaining the integrity, reputation, and assets of the bank. They must firmly believe as well that it is to their benefit and interest to have and to voice a strong commitment to remaining compliant with all applicable laws and regulations and to stay in conformity with global banking community standards and best practices. Senior management must also be persuaded that promoting a compliance culture at the bank level and among subsidiaries is crucial to remaining a trusted business entity and achieving prosperity goals.

A successful compliance function requires also that risks originating from local and global operations and developments are at all times appropriately identified and managed and the suitable mitigating measures are in place and well implemented. There should also be ongoing efforts and day-to-day monitoring to improve compliance governance, policies, procedures, and assessment in order to successfully face the endless challenges imposed by compliance requirements. A deep and accurate understanding of the applicable laws, regulations, procedures, sanctions, and restrictive measures in each of the jurisdictions in which a bank operates or has a foreign correspondent or subsidiary is also mandatory.

Otherwise, banking firms would be jeopardizing their business activities and reputation in the domestic and international markets and subjecting themselves to potential enormous penalties or fines as a result of partial or non-compliance.

AML/CFT and sanctions practices adopted by banks

The AML/CFT and sanctions practices undertaken by banks worldwide over the last few years are in general compliant (as they have to be) with respective domestic and international regulations. The phrase 'in general' is used as there are definitely exceptions, as illustrated below. The set of procedures and measures developed and implemented by each bank beyond the basic regulatory requirements is not uniform, depending on the management compliance policy, risk philosophy, and business requirements. Still, there are more commonalities among banks in this regard than dissimilarities.

The practices, from procedures to other measures, are built on and motivated by the guiding principles and requirements of the aforementioned set of regulations, ensuring that all adopted policies, procedures, and rules comply with the series of international regulations and guidelines presented in the second section of this chapter. The practices involve different layers or levels and different tasks and activities, from customer acceptance policy and the use of a risk-based approach to implementing customer due diligence and monitoring transactions of different types. Banks have also customer identification and suspicious transactions reporting policies and procedures, in addition to their own rules for record keeping and AML/CFT and sanctions training.

Customer acceptance policy

All banks nowadays implement customer acceptance policies and procedures that are constantly updated and improved to ensure the effective identification of clients who are acceptable or not acceptable to the banking firm. Prohibited customers are usually sanctioned individuals, businesses, and governments; accounts subject to freeze orders; customers of high risk; shell banks; and accounts opened in anonymous or fictitious names. There are clearly defined parameters of risk perception in terms of the nature of business activity, location of customers and their clients, mode of payments, turnover volume, social and financial status, and so on that would allow the categorization of customers into low, medium, and high risk of money laundering and financing of terrorism (ML/FT). Based on this risk categorization, the bank prepares a profile for each customer and collects the necessary documents from the client and other information according to the perceived risk. The bank will not open a new account where it is unable to apply appropriate customer due diligence measures. The nature and extent of due diligence depends in turn on the risk perceived by the AML/CFT officer. Banks also have special policies regarding both non-face-to-face relationships (i.e. accounts opened by proxy or by correspondence), where senior management approval is necessary, and "walk-in customers" and those types of transaction allowed with a specific threshold. The approval of senior management or the AML/CFT special committee is required for high-risk customers.

Risk-based approach

Banks have shifted over the last few years from a tick-box approach to a risk-based approach whereby customers and transactions (products and services) are classified as low, medium, or high risk in terms of money laundering and terrorism financing. To this end, banks instituted the necessary risk parameters to be used for the proper categorization of customers and transactions in relation to money laundering and terrorism financing risk exposure. The level of such risk exposure depends on many elements, most importantly the type of customer and the nature of business; the type of product or service utilized by the customer; the country in which the customer resides or operates; the volume of transactions/chain of transactions; account behavior, and so on. Risk categorization helps banks to establish and apply the right measures, rules, and monitoring approaches to mitigate the identified risks and allocate resources more efficiently. AML/CFT officers at banks use indicative lists that help to identify high-risk customers (where potential for money laundering is believed probable), medium-risk customers (where the possibility of money laundering is deemed less likely than in the case of a customer considered to be high risk), and low-risk customers (not categorized as medium- or high-risk). There are also indicative lists for high-risk and medium-risk products and services.

Customer due diligence

Customer due diligence (CDD) is exerted on all the bank's customers and their related banking transactions. It starts at the time of opening the account, irrespective of its nature, and continues until its closure. It is up to the bank to decide on the proper level of customer due diligence, be that simplified due diligence (SDD) or enhanced due diligence (EDD), depending on the customer risk profile and risk categorization. Customers perceived as being low risk are normally subject to SDD procedures, whereas perceived medium- and high-risk customers are put through EDD measures. It should be clear, however, that the difference between the simplified and the enhanced procedures is not related to the issues of obtaining information on the customers' IDs and addresses, occupation and financial status, sources of funds, the nature of the business, the reasons for intended transactions, and the like; instead it is related, in the case of EDD, to obtaining additional information and documentation on these issues and others, and to imposing a higher degree of monitoring on transactions and obtaining a higher frequency of updates.

Monitoring of transactions

The monitoring of transactions includes, but is not limited to, the monitoring of cash transactions, written checks, point of sale and ATM transactions, wire transfers, trade finance, and transactions across borders. Transactions that appear to have no visible economic or legal purpose or that are large and complex in nature, or represent unusual and non-recurring patterns obviously require closer monitoring. The compliance function or unit is the party generally responsible for making certain that suitable monitoring of customers' transactions has been effected and to assess new products for money laundering and terrorist financing risks prior to their launch. In the case of the detection of a 'non-business as usual' transaction or one with the characteristics that may be correlated with money laundering and terrorist financing, the concerned bank personnel typically turns to the KYC of the client and may update it and possibly request related justification if deemed necessary. Alternatively, the bank employee would report the transaction to the compliance unit if he/she remains unconvinced by the provided justification. The compliance unit will then choose whether or not to report the transaction to the AML/CFT Committee, along with the necessary background and recommendations, depending on the degree of ML/TF suspicion.

Customer identification

The customer identification process consists of collecting the necessary and relevant information about the customer before opening a new account to make sure that the customer is not a person or an entity with a criminal or terrorist background and is not listed on any of the blacklists of the UN, the EU, and the US. Appropriate identification and screening of customers helps risk assessment and attenuation. Know Your Customer (KYC) procedures at banks include in general:

- Purpose and reason for opening an account or establishing a relationship with the bank.
- Details of occupation/employment and sources of wealth or income.
- Expected source of the funds and wealth to be used within the relationship.
- Anticipated level and nature of the activity that is to be undertaken.
- Intention on acting for their own account or for the account of another party.
- Verification of the ultimate beneficial owner.
- Any additional information deemed critical by the bank.

Banks periodically update and verify the data on existing customers. Updates are frequent in the case of high-risk customers and immediate whenever there are any changes in the account behavior or in case of doubt.

Suspicious transactions reporting

It is the responsibility of the designated AML/CFT Officer to report immediately, in writing and using the proper form to the bank's AML/CFT Committee and then usually, based on the senior management decision, to the domestic FIU, any transaction that would bring up serious skepticism and suspicion with regard to its nature, purpose, and relation to money laundering and/or financing of terrorism. The reporting of suspicious transactions generally includes a set of information about the suspicious transaction and the party involved, such as account opening documents, statement of accounts, reasons behind the suspicion, and allegation-supporting documents.

Record keeping

Record-keeping policies and procedures mandate that banks' documents and records related to customers and their transactions are preserved for a set period of time: that is, stored in a safe, secure, and accessible manner in line with the applicable laws and regulations. Internal policies for archiving and safekeeping determine whether records are to be kept at the branch level or at the bank head-quarters. There should also be a designated document controller to ensure that records and files have met the retention period and to oversee their deletion and destruction on due date. However, the destruction process is suspended immediately for customers or transactions undergoing an official investigation or if an investigation appears imminent.

Training

Staff training on AML/CFT policies and procedures is mandated by concerned bank regulatory authorities in most jurisdictions. It is often the responsibility of an AML/CFT Committee at banks to prepare a staff training program, including seminars, workshops, and lectures, to keep employees abreast of the latest AML/CFT methods, procedures, practices, and developments. Employees are trained on a permanent basis in-house, externally, and abroad by domestic and foreign experts in the field, and the training usually covers the following topics:

- The applicable AML/CFT laws and regulations and the adopted policies and procedures.
- Procedures for verifying customer identity and identifying suspicious activity.
- Required forms, record keeping, and reporting requirements.
- Trade-based money laundering.
- Customer due diligence and enhanced due diligence.
- Monitoring of financial transactions and the reporting of suspicious transactions.
- Tipping off.

Cross-border operations

In opening Nostro or Vostro correspondent accounts banks have put in place long lists of measures to ensure the conducting of appropriate and effective due diligence, and determine the candidacy of applicant banks by looking at, among other things, the reputation and establishment, the financial statements, the senior management, and the AML/CFT program, including the policies and procedures of the applicant. The senior management of the bank assessing the application is often involved in screening, assessment of all required documents, and approval of the relationship after obtaining compliance unit clearance. Enhanced due diligence policies and procedures apply for 'high-risk' correspondent accounts or customers. Based on their own risk assessment and types and patterns of conducted transactions, banks also tend to review due diligence and enhanced due diligence carried out on existing correspondent accounts on a periodic basis or when a material change in the risk profile of the correspondent banking customer takes place. High-level data analysis by type of transaction is performed and a deep analysis of the pattern, frequency, routing, and size of wire transfers is often conducted to identify any suspicious activity.

Sanctions

Banks worldwide also screen potential customers against sanctioned individuals, groups, entities, and governments at the stages of customer acceptance and account opening and during all transaction processing, in compliance with the sanction lists issued by the United Nations Security Council (UNSC), the US OFAC Sanctions Programs, the European Union Common Foreign and Security Policy (CFSP), the United Kingdom HM Treasury's Asset Freezing Unit (AFU), and others. They also monitor transactions and periodically check existing customers against updated international sanctions lists in order to take the appropriate action in case any account or operation links to individual, entity, or country under international sanctions. There can be loopholes in implementation or intentional non-compliant behavior, as we will illustrate below. FATF identified that non-cooperative and high-risk jurisdictions are also part of KYC checks and monitoring and are subject to enhanced due diligence.

FATCA practices adopted by banks

In response to the announcement of the Tax Compliance Act and deadlines set by the concerned US authorities for participation in FATCA and the initiation of their respective FATCA compliance programs, Foreign Financial Institutions (FFIs) all over the world, including banks, started to assess the requirements and means of compliance with the new regulation and to design and develop their FATCA compliance frameworks and detailed FATCA policies and procedures manuals accordingly. They also started to prepare for the process of registration with and reporting to the IRS, whether directly or through intergovernmental agreements between sovereign governments of participating banks and the US authorities. FFIs also embarked on designating a senior responsible officer (SRO) with sufficient authority to ensure that the FFI met the FATCA requirements and to certify to the IRS that the information submitted was accurate and complete. Banks had also to raise customer awareness, perform data enhancements of their IT systems, and train staff on the new requirements in order to put into action a successful FATCA compliance framework. Stringent preparations were thus needed on the part of FFIs in order to enter into FATCA disclosure agreements with the US treasury so that they can identify US persons having accounts with them and report identified US persons to the US treasury on an annual basis.

FATCA policies and procedures at banks cover different areas, most of which concern account due diligence and reporting. FATCA regulations demand that banks take certain actions to identify, for individuals and entities, US persons (US citizens and tax payers) and collect associated and relevant information, such as a US address or place of birth, at the time of account opening. In addition, the regulations require all FFIs to identify US persons in their existing customer base. This necessitates undertaking a search of data relating to existing customer accounts, stored physically and electronically, to identify US persons and accounts, and having all the data necessary to confirm a person's US status. There should also be ongoing monitoring of accounts: that is, of changes in the data related to the identified US person. As FFIs are required periodically to report information on US persons to the IRS, banks have set the mechanism for the reporting of information in line with the requested mechanics, including formats and uploading processes.

The challenges, costs, and implications of regulatory compliance

With the rapidly changing regulatory and supervisory environment, compliance challenges and costs have mounted and are expected to remain significant at least over the coming few years. This is especially true for many western countries, which have to comply not only with AML/CFT, sanctions, and tax evasion regulations, but also with a mass of other important legislation and financial reforms, often of unprecedented scope and scale, to address and avert the reoccurrence of the 2008 global financial crisis. An example is the additional challenges and costs to US banks of compliance with and implementation of the US Dodd-Frank Act of 2010, which created many regulatory agencies and examiners, such as the Consumer Financial Protection Bureau, the Financial Stability Oversight Council, and the Office of Financial Research, and included in one of its sections (section 619) the Volcker Rule.[1] UK banks must also confront the burdening requirements of, among other things, the UK Bribery Act of 2010, covering the criminal law relating to bribery, and the Retail Distribution Review (RDR), initiated by the Financial Services Board (FSB) in 2006, which involves a set of investment rules to increase transparency and fairness in the investment industry and affects the way investment products are distributed to retail customers in the UK.[2] Banks in the US and UK, like those in most countries, also have to deal with the Basel III capital and liquidity adequacy rules or requirements and the capital cost of holding higher levels of regulatory capital.[3]

Challenges lie mainly in the uncertainty created by some of the laws and rules and the constrained time management and resources available to accomplish efficiently the multiple tasks, with many regulations coming into force roughly simultaneously. The uncertainty relates specifically to the optimum configuration and implementation of the compliance-related requirements and to ensuring that all the details of compliance are covered. There could be uncertainty associated, for example, with the degree of confidence that all the requirements have been fully met in terms of screening all existing customers and new ones against individuals with a criminal or terrorist background or those listed on any of the blacklists. Uncertainty might also exist when there are interactions or interrelations among various regulations and overlaps, implying both difficulty in assessing both the individual and aggregate effects and costs of all these rules and inaccuracy in cost allocation among the different functions and lines of business in a bank. There are also uncertainties regarding the ability to effect all operational changes, including modifying or upgrading IT and telecommunications systems and software, and to meet all the regulatory requirements within the deadlines, on due time, and with no delay, to prevent the consequences of negative regulatory response. Finally, there could be ambiguity in some texts, making it hard to fully understand the intention and spirit of the regulation and to implement the requirements accordingly. This would necessitate further clarification by regulators on some specific issues and regulations.

As for the cost issue and compliance-related implications, perhaps the best way to see the big picture is to look at the same time at the relative costs of non-compliance or compliance with the new or modified regulations. The former type of costs is best illustrated by examining (below) what the Swiss banking industry and some other reputable international banks have gone through over the last few years in terms of the cost incurred as a result of intentional or accidental non-compliance with certain regulations. The latter is more complex and difficult to measure; there are normally costs to regulators and supervisors related to changes in enforcement and oversight and thus to the additional human and financial resources and time devotion required, and costs to banks and financial institutions. The latter are more likely operational costs related to hiring new compliance staff and training existing ones, modifying and installing new IT and risk-related systems, spending long hours reading and assimilating hundreds of pages of information, coping with new rules and extra regulatory load, and so on. The cost of compliance with regulations could also take the form of modifying or interrupting the business and the relations of the financial services firm with some client banks and non-banks; such repercussions or side-effects of the burdening regulatory compliance are best captured by the notion or practice of "de-risking," on which we shall elaborate below.

Non-compliance cost

The implications and costs of non-compliance with the regulations are not only confined to receiving very large fines or the curbing of some bank activities in certain markets but encompass also the requirements to effect enormous look-back investigations in relation to individual and systemic issues and to revisit and inspect thousands of transactions—surely a tiresome and costly task. The case studies below clarify and exemplify to a large extent what banks are likely to experience as a result of a failure to comply with regulations in the areas of AML/ CFT, sanctions, and tax evasion.

Case study 1: The Swiss banking industry—tax evasion and illegal money transfer issues

Over the past fifteen years there have been striking transformations in the Swiss banking industry and financial markets in response to increasing political and non-political pressures from many regional and international governments and standard-setters. Allegations and controversies relating to tax evasion and the illegal transfer of funds, and the ensuing bilateral and multilateral agreements, undermined to a large extent the Swiss banking secrecy law, which was passed in 1934 and changed dramatically the nature of Swiss banking in terms of the exchange of information on account holders. The Holocaust asset controversy also played a role in these developments. Holocaust survivors who sought to recover deposits made by their families in Swiss banks before World War II had problems trying to retrieve the assets of relatives who had died in concentration camps without possessing relevant death certificates and records of deposits lost in the chaos of the war. This led to a class action lawsuit in 1996 against three major Swiss banks—Union Bank of Switzerland (UBS), Credit Suisse, and Swiss Bank Corporation—and was settled in 2000 for $1.25 billion.[4] In light of this background what follows is a brief description of tax evasion and illegal money transfer accusations made against Credit Suisse and UBS, which together account for half or more of the Swiss banking industry.

Credit Suisse

Credit Suisse Group is the second-largest multinational financial services holding company in Switzerland. It was founded in 1856 in Zurich, acquired over the years many financial services firms, and underwent several corporate restructurings. The group provides, among other things, commercial, private, wealth management, and investment banking. From the early 2000s onwards the group was subject to a lengthy series of investigations by law enforcement authorities in a number of countries—namely, Brazil, Germany, and the US—into whether Credit Suisse accounts, products, and employees were used for money laundering and tax evasion.

In May 2014 the Zurich-based corporation pleaded guilty to years of conspiracy in helping US citizens to hide their actual wealth and evade taxes, having assisted US taxpayers in filing false income tax returns and other documents with the IRS. It agreed to pay a total of $2.6 billion in fines distributed as follows: $1.8 billion to the Department of Justice for the US Treasury, $100 million to the Federal Reserve, and $715 million to the New York State Department of Financial Services.[5] Around three months earlier Credit Suisse also agreed to pay a fine of $196 million in disgorgement, interest, and penalties to the Securities and Exchange Commission (SEC) after one of its businesses violated the federal securities laws and provided cross-border brokerage and investment advisory services to around 8,500 US clients without registering its activities with the SEC. This raised suspicions as to whether it was helping US citizens evade taxes. It was one of fourteen Swiss banks under investigation.[6] Since 2011 there have also been indictments of eight Credit Suisse executives, two of whom have pleaded guilty thus far. Credit Suisse bankers were accused of fraud by the US Justice Department for aiding wealthy US citizens escape taxes.[7]

Earlier in 2009 Credit Suisse AG agreed to pay a penalty of $536 million to the US authorities for violating the International Emergency Economic Powers Act (IEEPA) and New York State law. The bank was charged with illegally conducting transactions involving hundreds of millions of dollars on behalf of individuals and entities from sanctioned countries including Iran and Sudan, and thus assisted those countries in evading US laws. Specifically, wire transfers were falsified to avoid being flagged by removing detectable information so that messages and transactions would pass undetected through both OFAC filters at banks and in the US financial system. Credit Suisse also had to conduct a thorough internal investigation of the delinquency and to improve its compliance programs to be more transparent in terms of international payment transactions.[8]

Aside from US authorities, German prosecutors began in 2013 to investigate employees of Credit Suisse, its private bank subsidiary Clariden Leu, and its German subsidiary Neue Aargauer on suspicion of helping German citizens evade taxes. In 2012 German tax inspectors investigated tax evasion cases related to clients of Credit Suisse Group by way of investing in offshore insurance products that could be used to evade taxes. The investigation focused on about 5,000 clients/citizens who, between 2005 and 2009, bought insurance policies at a Bermuda-based Credit Suisse subsidiary to earn tax-free interest on savings. Credit Suisse presented the defense that clients were told upon buying these policies that they were responsible for talking to their tax advisors and determining their tax obligations and that these practices are legal in Switzerland. Earlier in 2011 the Credit Suisse Group eventually entered into a €150 million settlement with the government to stop German investigations into allegations that bank officials and employees in Germany helped clients in dodging taxes.[9]

Finally, the Brazilian federal prosecutor's office investigated and charged fourteen former and current Credit Suisse employees in 2008 as part of a two-year money laundering and tax evasion probe. Allegations centered on assistance given in the operation of an illegal money transfer scheme and in helping Brazilians evade taxes. The investigation led to arrests in 2008 and 2009, with the federal police detaining nineteen people as part of a larger crackdown on illegal money transfers in Brazil.[10]

Union Bank of Switzerland (UBS)

UBS Group AG is the biggest global financial services holding company in Switzerland. Its origins can be traced back to 1856, the date when one of its earliest precursor banks (Baselr Bankverin) was founded. UBS was formed in 1912 through the merger of two banks and subsequently experienced a series of mergers, acquisitions and restructuring of operations. Perhaps the most well-known merger was with the Swiss Bank Corporation in 1998. The group provides, among other things, commercial, retail, and investment banking, in addition to wealth and asset management services.

In 2004 UBS AG was fined $100 million by the US Federal Reserve for conducting illegal financial transactions with trade-sanctioned countries such as Iran, Cuba, and others. The violation involved the transfer of US bank notes to financial institutions in the mentioned sanctioned economies.[11]

In 2008 US authorities started to probe a multi-million-dollar tax evasion case involving UBS based on communicated revelations accusing UBS, among other Swiss banks, of helping wealthy US citizens to evade taxes through illegal practices and offshore accounts.[12] In 2009 UBS agreed to pay in fines, penalties, interest, and restitution $780 million to US authorities and to reveal the identity of and provide information on 250 account holders in an attempt to avoid US prosecution relateing to accusations that it assisted thousands of wealthy Americans hide accounts from the US Internal Revenue Service (IRS) and evade taxes.

In 2015 UBS AG had to pay the US authorities around $1.7 million for processing 222 transactions between 2008 and 2013 related to US securities held in custody in the US by a customer who was on OFAC's list of Specially Designated Nationals and Blocked Persons under the anti-terrorism regulations. The fine for violating US terrorism sanctions (Global Terrorism Sanctions Regulations) could have been double this amount, but the fine was reduced as UBS cooperated with the investigation and self-reported the transactions, which were thought to be internal transfers not involving external parties, so that no alerts were generated inside the banking institution. The client was not only designated by OFAC but also sanctioned by Switzerland, the UK, the EU, and the UN.[13]

UBS was also involved in German and French tax evasion accusations. It had to pay around €302 million ($406 million) in 2014 to German authorities to settle a probe into tax evasion after it was accused of helping German clients to dodge taxes. Also in that year, UBS was asked to deposit close to $1.48 billion bail in a French tax evasion investigation to cover a possible penalty for laundering tax evasion-related proceeds in France.[14]

Case study 2: British banks and sanctions violations[15]

In November 2015 Barclays Bank, Britain's second-biggest bank, was fined £72 million by the British Financial Conduct Authority (FCA) for weak treatment of financial crime risks. The accusation was that Barclays failed to minimize the risks related to a £1.88 billion transaction that the bank arranged and executed in 2011 and 2012 for a number of high-net-worth politically exposed clients (persons) who should have been the focus of enhanced levels of due diligence and monitoring by the bank. It is worth mentioning that there was no evidence that the transaction actually involved financial crime.[16] Earlier, in 2010 Barclays, had been obliged to pay a $298 million penalty to US authorities against charges of consciously and intentionally violating US sanctions by managing and processing through its New York branch concealed transactions in hundreds of millions of dollars (around $500 million) with banks in prohibited countries such as Cuba, Iran, Libya, Sudan, and Myanmar between 1995 and 2006. The bank agreed also to strengthen its internal procedures, to enhance sanctions-related training and to cooperate with additional investigation by the US authorities.[17]

In December 2012 HSBC, one of the biggest British banks, had to pay a $1.9 billion fine in settlement of US accusations of deliberate failure to implement money-laundering controls and of intentional breach of US sanctions, which allowed Mexican drug-trafficking money to be laundered through the bank's accounts and facilitated transactions in millions of dollars with sanctioned countries. In addition to the mentioned fine, the penalty also required that the bank appoint an independent monitor to gauge reformed internal controls. In fact, HSBC had to spend hundreds of millions of dollars to improve its systems.[18]

Also in 2012, Standard Chartered Bank, another big British bank, was accused by the New York State Department of Financial Services (NYDFS) of hiding $250 billion of transactions with sanctioned country Iran and was thus fined $340 million for failure in anti-money laundering and anti-terrorism controls. The bank also had to identify weaknesses in its systems and procedures and fix them, but it seems that the bank was unable to do so. Two years later, Standard Chartered had to pay a new penalty to NYDFS in the amount of $300 million for failure to improve its money-laundering controls and deal properly with problems spotted in 2012. The penalty of 2014 included the banning of the bank from accepting dollar clearing accounts without the state's approval.[19]

In 2009 Lloyds TSB paid a $350 million fine to the concerned US authorities for infringing US sanctions and dealing with banned countries Libya, Sudan, and Iran. The allegation is that in 1995 the bank removed customer information from wire transfers related to individuals and countries on the US sanctions list so that these transfers would go undetected.[20]

Case study 3: German Commerzbank and weak AML and sanctions controls
In March 2015 the NYDFS declared that one of Germany's biggest banks, the Commerzbank, will pay a penalty of $1.45 billion for violating US anti-money-laundering and sanctions regulations. The accusations of serious wrongdoing and compliance rule breaking included a lack of transparency in SWIFT payment messages from foreign branches to Commerzbank's New York branch, as they did not unveil all the necessary information related to the transactions, including the identity of the remitter or beneficiary. That made compliance processes and controls at Commerzbank's New York branch ineffective and unable to adequately trigger alerts and raise red flags about potential misconduct or suspicious transactions. In addition, wire messages were stripped of information to hide the true identity of the customer and the nature of the payment, allowing the processing of thousands of transactions related to Iranian and Sudanese parties subject to US economic sanctions through New York and the clearing of US dollar payments through the US financial system without detection. Illegal payments processed from sanctioned and banned customers and countries exceeded $250 billion.

The NYDFS accusations also involved weak anti-money-laundering controls and AML compliance deficiencies, which facilitated, through Commerzbank's New York branch, illegal transactions for Olympus Corporation, a Japanese optics and medical device manufacturer, that supported its massive corporate accounting fraud intended to hide away from its auditors and investors millions of dollars in losses. Facilitated illegal transactions surpassed $1.6 billion.

The NYDFS also ordered the termination of the jobs of a number of Commerzbank's employees who had played a fundamental role in the above-mentioned misconduct, both in terms of facilitating transactions for sanctioned individuals and entities and assisting the Japanese firm in falsifying accounts to cover up losses; three former executives were sentenced to jail for their roles in this accounting scandal. The regulator also installed an independent monitor for banking law violations in connection with the improper behavior.[21]

Case study 4: French BNP Paribas and the facilitation of prohibited financial transactions

France's largest bank, BNP Paribas, was forced in 2014 to pay a $9 billion penalty to US authorities (the largest settlement in US history to date) to settle allegations of violation of US sanctions against trade with Cuba, Iran, and Sudan. The bank was charged specifically with deliberately and illegally moving and clearing billions of dollars through the US financial system between 2004 and 2012. The bank had also to fire a number of employees and was prevented from clearing specific transactions in US dollars for one year, starting from 2015.[22]

Case study 5: Dutch ING and breach of US sanctions

In 2012 ING Bank (a member of ING group) agreed to pay to the US treasury $619 million to settle accusations and investigations into US sanctions violations, including non-compliance with sanctions against Iran, Cuba, Myanmar, Sudan, and Libya. Suspicions centered on the deliberate manipulation of information and the deletion of thousands of transactions permitting sanctioned individuals and entities to access and move billions of dollars though the US financial system for more than a decade until 2007.[23]

Case study 6: JPMorgan and the failure to alert suspicious activities

In 2014, JPMorgan, the biggest US bank in term of assets, agreed to pay US federal prosecutors and regulators more than $2 billion in fines in settlement of criminal charges stating that the bank violated the US Bank Secrecy Act in not alerting concerned regulatory authorities to suspicious activities. The accusations were that JPMorgan failed to warn the US authorities about Bernie Madoff's Ponzi scheme and investment activities, enabling Madoff to launder billions of dollars in related proceeds through accounts maintained at the bank, with which he dealt for almost two decades, thus aiding his fraud.[24]

It is important to note at the end of this section on the costs of non-compliance with money-laundering, sanctions and tax-evasion regulation that the fines described above for top European and US banks were imposed mainly by US authorities and do not include fines imposed by the UK, French, German, Swiss, and other authorities in this area.[25] The list of penalties, as mentioned earlier, is not exhaustive but illustrative, as other and perhaps less significant penalties were imposed on many banks all over the world. The listed fines are also confined to money laundering, tax evasion, and the violation of sanctions, and therefore fines related to other issues, such as currency and LIBOR benchmark rigging, trade scandals, and different forms of corruptions and bribery, which could be substantial as well, are not part of this chapter. In order to give the reader a rough idea, fines imposed on only six international banks to settle foreign exchange rigging probes or allegations of manipulation of the London Interbank Offered Rate (LIBOR) exceeded $9 billion at December 2015. In fact, in May 2015 six global banks (Bank of America, UBS, Royal Bank of Scotland (RBS), JPMorgan Chase, Citigroup, and Barclays) were fined a total of $5.7 billion for manipulating foreign exchange markets on top of the previous fines for the same group in the amount of $3.8 billion.[26]

Compliance challenges and costs

As mentioned repeatedly, financial institutions, including banks, are incurring ascending regulatory compliance costs, as novel and amended regulations have implications for the way financial services firms handle data from collection to processing to reporting. There are also IT and human resources implications. In fact, ensuring data quality and traceability, sourcing data across different products and functional areas, and reporting detailed information to supervisors and other concerned parties is at a cost. It is not only time-consuming for existing staff but also necessitates modifying banking processes to be able to deal with the fresh or amended regulatory and standards requirements. An adequate and flexible IT infrastructure or architecture must also be in place to satisfy the needs. As banks have to spend more time on and commit more resources to regulatory compliance, this latter becomes a major expense, with banks continuing to invest millions of dollars in their compliance functions and frameworks and making significant efforts in using adequate evaluation tools to measure their compliance time and cost (i.e. estimates of time spent and wages/salaries paid).[27] Concerns have been raised that the devotion of time, efforts, and resources to compliance leaves less time and fewer resources to conduct business and serve customers and investors, who are likely to enjoy little benefit, if any, from such efforts. However, such an argument misses the point that bank soundness and business performance is supported and enhanced by a demonstrated good reputation involving sound compliance, risk management, and corporate governance practices, and that working on reducing exposure to reputation risk, loss of public trust, and scandals, and on diminishing any possible adverse impact on the bank's standing and international business, is beneficial to banks' shareholders and customers in many ways. Therefore, there must be a trade-off and a balance between excessive and low compliance.

There are many reports and studies on compliance in general and its challenges, costs, and implications in particular. Some of these documents are issued by private companies (including consultants and service providers) and the rest either by bank regulatory and supervisory authorities or by individual banks and associations of banks.[28] As far as private companies are concerned, three reports, from Thomson Reuters, Accenture, and Continuity, are worth mentioning for their reliability, as they are based on surveys involving a large and diverse collection of compliance officers and executives from all over the world.[29]

Thomson Reuters, one of the world's leading sources of intelligent information for businesses and professionals, has so far issued six yearly reports on the cost of compliance and challenges for financial services firms. In each of these reports it posts and analyzes the results of a survey involving the views of hundreds (between 600 and 800) of compliance practitioners, most of whom are heads of compliance or chief executives of banks, brokers, insurers, and other organizations of all sizes across the globe. The 2015 report included four major findings. First, surveyed officers anticipate more regulations to come in the following year and that the expected regulatory changes could be significant. They also express regulatory exhaustion and overburden from ever-increasing regulations and expanding compliance responsibilities. Second, the majority of respondents believe that the personal liability of compliance officers is set to rise in 2015. Third, the bulk of interviewed practitioners foresee an increase in the cost of senior compliance professionals and in compliance budgets in line with growing challenges in the recruitment and retention of skilled and high-quality compliance personnel. Fourth, surveyed individuals noted complaints arising from the increasing amount of time that boards of directors spend on managing and settling regulatory and compliance-related matters.

Reuters' reports covering the years 2012–15 have indicated that tracking and analyzing regulatory developments and amending policies and procedures consume on average, for a compliance officer, one to two days per week (15 percent of weekly time spent on tracking and analysis and 7 percent of weekly time utilized in amending policies and procedures, partly in response to the tracking and analysis). In addition, fewer than two days in a compliance officer's typical week are spent on communicating with other business functions (6 percent of weekly time used for reporting to the board and 16 percent of time devoted to linking with control functions). The remaining 55 percent of the typical week is spent engaged in other compliance tasks, such as monitoring activities, training, and provision of advice and governance.

In 2014 and 2015 the professional services company Accenture issued a compliance risk study based on surveys with compliance officers at 100 to 150 financial services firms (banking, insurance, and capital market firms) across Europe, North America, and Asia-Pacific. One of their key findings is that compliance is a valued function that is gaining in importance, and that its role and stature within organizations is progressing. This is evidenced by the fact that around 31 percent of respondents stated that their compliance programs report directly to the CEO, while another 40 percent report directly to the board of directors. Only 28 percent of surveyed compliance functions report to the head of legal or the head of any other function, who then reports in turn to the CEO. Another key finding is that investment in compliance is not slowing, but instead is anticipated to rise in the coming few years, as additional investment in compliance is necessary to maintain and build upon the compliance frameworks' accomplishments and attain the desired strategic goals. Most respondents expect spending to grow by 10 to 20 percent over the next couple of years and investment to be centered on analytics and risk modeling, which would help in forecasting and extenuating upcoming compliance events. The Accenture study talks also about the challenges. One of these is competition for compliance talent, which is becoming fierce, implying a difficulty in attracting and retaining competent employees that could be a barrier to the success of compliance programs. Competitive hiring is also likely to raise recruitment costs. Another identified challenge relates to compliance performance measurement and the ability to illustrate and communicate the effectiveness of the compliance programs. Additional work is needed in this area to address the expectations of senior management and satisfy their keenness to see both a return on investment and cost control.

Continuity Control, a compliance platform, issues on a quarterly basis a tracking index known as the Banking Compliance Index (BCI), which measures the incremental cost burden on community financial institutions incurred in keeping up with regulatory changes. The latest Banking Compliance Index reports show that there were 329 and 302 regulatory changes in 2015 and 2014 respectively (245 in 2013) that necessitated, respectively, 2,265 and 2,327 additional hours to comply per institution (3,400 additional hours in 2013) and resulted in $153,931 and $147,298 incremental cost per institution in 2015 and 2014 respectively ($150,000 in 2013). According to the same source, total industry regulatory cost was around $1.1 billion in 2013 and $912 million in 2014. Industry cost for the year 2015 was close to $981 million.

It should be noted in this respect that the cost of regulatory compliance in terms of money and time differs from one banking institution to another within the same jurisdiction and from one industry in a given country to another in a different economy. There are many reasons for such discrepancies. First, the cost is a function of the scale and scope of activities undertaken by the banking firm or of the lines of business and products offered. Size matters, in that the larger the number of accounts and the volume of transactions the more time must be spent on due diligence and the more compliance staff are needed. Second, the cost is affected by the bank management philosophy concerning risk and compliance. Firms committed to zero or very low risk tolerances are expected to invest heavily in risk, compliance, and controls functions and to acquire highly skilled professionals, and that is relatively costly. Third, costs in time and money are also related to the level of exposure to domestic and international regulations. We expect financial services firms operating in jurisdictions highly active in issuing domestic regulations and operating in different international markets, where they are requested to adhere to the regulations of the host countries, to have higher costs. Fourth, the tools and methodologies used to measure and compile the cost of compliance and to determine what to include in the calculations are not uniform across individual banks or the sector as a whole, implying non-homogeneous comparability between one source and another. Still, individual or aggregated data on the costs of compliance serve the purpose of both quantifying to some degree the burden of regulatory compliance that banks are confronting in their day-to-day operations and showing recent trends.

De-risking

One of the main implications of more forceful regulatory and related technology obligations, as noted recently by Goldman Sachs's CEO Lloyd Blankfein, is the raising of industry entry barriers to unprecedented levels. According to Mr. Blankfein, given that banking is an expensive business for those with no market share in scale, higher regulatory costs are reducing competition, with many businesses exiting after re-examining their competitive stance and comparative returns. Mr. Blankfein also predicted that, in the longer term, only a few giant financial services firms will be capable of efficiently competing on a global basis, with the opportunity of acquiring even more market share.[30] It would seem, therefore, that more intense regulation and compliance is beneficial for some and detrimental to others, and could result in more consolidation or mergers and acquisitions in the financial services industry in the future.

There are other major implications. Escalating regulatory compliance has recently influenced correspondent banking: that is, the relationship between a domestic bank and its correspondent financial services firm abroad. The threat of prosecutions and substantial fines for non-compliance and the ever-increasing inspection, along with the related mounting costs, drove correspondent banking institutions to respond in one of two ways. First, they strengthened oversight at their institution's level and communicated general and specific obligations to their customer banks and non-banks to comply with international and domestic rules and regulations. Second, they terminated relationships with some client banks and others deemed "high risk," particularly when, under burdening and rapidly changing regulations, the liaison presents more risk and cost than potential yield or return. This latter process or practice is referred to as 'de-risking'.

A global trend consisting of ending correspondent relationships and closing accounts with high-risk customers thus emerged and gained momentum as an inevitable consequence of both intensified and costly regulatory and supervisory requirements, especially in the AML/CFT area, and potential high regulatory penalties and litigation costs from public prosecution and private lawsuits. For the sake of illustration, HSBC terminated more than 326 correspondent bank accounts between 2010 and 2012 and declined to conduct operations in AML/CFT-related high-risk countries such as Angola, Iraq, and Myanmar. In 2003 and 2004 Standard Chartered ended around 70,000 accounts for SMEs and closed hundreds of accounts maintained with banks operating in Latin America and Central Europe. In 2014 JPMorgan Chase terminated more than 100,000 accounts deemed risky in terms of money laundering.[31]

The criteria for de-risking vary from one banking institution to another, but still revolve around the financial firm's risk appetite and cost/return considerations. There is thus no uniformity in the implementation of de-risking across correspondent banks and it is possible for one customer (bank) to have accounts closed by one correspondent bank but maintained with another. It is also natural that those de-risked banks considered and labeled high risk seek accounts with smaller and less reputable correspondent banks able to provide them with similar services. The switch from one correspondent bank to another is possible not only because one or more correspondent banks may have a lower capacity to conduct effective AML/CFT compliance practices but also because the issues determining high-risk customers for one institution may not apply for another, in addition to other bank-specific considerations.

Both positive and negative repercussions may result from de-risking in the financial services industry. On the benefits side, the threat of de-risking tends to force banks across the globe to strengthen their AML/CFT systems in adherence to international regulations and standards and to comply with the rules and regulations affecting and dictating the relationship of correspondent banks with their clients. Addressing correspondents' needs may also require the passing of new laws or modifications to existing ones at home to uphold the credibility of the country and its financial industry among international circles and to strengthen the existing legal anti-money laundering and countering the financing of terrorism framework, thus protecting the work and practice of banks at this level. All of these measures help to protect not only the country's financial system, in terms of banks corresponding with organisations abroad, from being used to launder money and finance terrorists but also the integrity and stability of the international financial system. These actions can also reduce considerably reputational concerns and money-laundering and terrorist-financing risks for banking firms and economies.

On the disadvantages side, and depending on the extent to which it is occurring, de-risking may in certain cases do considerable harm to lawful and rightful customers and their access to essential financial services and markets. Limiting access to correspondent bank accounts abroad will not only harm those banks involved but also their domestic clients and the domestic economy. It can also influence workers' remittances, cross-border wire transfers, and international trade in financial services and goods, where banks are main players in the international channeling of funds and in the financing and guaranteeing of international payments. De-risking with a view to diminishing exposure to potential financial crime by closing accounts of not only correspondent banks but also non-profit organizations, money transfer businesses, and foreign embassies increased financial exclusion and impeded efforts made to promote financial inclusion.[32] De-risking by exiting certain markets and economies can also influence negatively the availability of financing in such places and economic growth, especially if alternative finance providers are absent or weak. Many reports recently have indicated that charities, aid organizations, and other non-governmental organizations in many parts of the world were the victims of de-risking by international financial institutions and had to face restrictions on their access to finance and banking services or were unable to obtain them at all.[33]

Concluding remarks and policy implications

In the last couple of decades the international bank regulatory and supervisory landscape has gone through a drastic but graduated change both in response to political and regulatory concerns and pressures to fight tax evasion, money laundering, terrorism financing, and other types of financial crimes and to protect international economic and financial integrity and stability. The change was more pronounced, however, in the years following the 2008 global financial crisis. In this environment banks and financial institutions found themselves under the threat of a double-edged sword: on one edge, the prohibitive cost and damage of non-compliance with regulations; and, on the other, the soaring cost and repercussions of meeting compliance requirements, including the regulatory cost of constrained revenue avenues and profit opportunities. Thus, cost benefit analysis and other considerations drove some banks at the level of executives or their subordinates to take the risk and partially comply, while others were compelled to fully abide by a mass of often complex and frequently changing regulations involving ascending diverse challenges and both direct and opportunity costs. Examples of compliance unit errors and the 'improper or unacceptable' conduct of a small number of employees or executives are many, and such errors and misconduct could be very harmful to the banking institution at domestic and international levels. Thus, promoting a sincere compliance culture from top to bottom in the banking firm, demonstrating zero tolerance for misconduct, and investing in compliance programs, systems, and control measures are necessities and beneficial to the reputation and growth of the financial services firm. Compliance, though raising operational costs at banks, is therefore a better choice than non-compliance.

The issue for banks is how to cope with burdening and excessive compliance and, if possible, avoid or mitigate some of its undesirable implications, such as business discontinuity or exit pressure. In fact, the new regulatory environment increased demand for compliance officers and experts, and, given their limited supply at least in the short term, created a major difficulty for banks in general, and small ones in particular, in not only recruiting but also retaining compliance staff. Additionally, small banks struggled more in getting the right systems and infrastructure in place and thus their rising regulatory compliance burden threatened not only their competitive position but also their continuity and existence.

There are likely many answers to the issue raised at the beginning of the previous paragraph. One point of view perhaps shared by many is that most banks can and must survive the exorbitant compliance requirements and overcome the anxiety created and the impediments to their continuity and growth by adapting to and managing the imposed shift or evolution, as they have done in the past when faced with similar challenges and changing regulatory environments. A smooth transition to compliance and the outsourcing of some of the compliance tasks could pay a role in this respect. In addition, banks are invited not only to effect the necessary

adjustments in policies and procedures and integrate the compliance requirements in their business-as-usual operations to meet the regulatory demands but
also to create value and business from the whole process. Successful adaptation
to change, therefore, requires taking a fresh look at the issue and making use of
the new technology infrastructure put in place to comply with new regulations, of
data gathering, management, and storage improvements, and of up-scaled internal
organization in order to improve activity and performance and better serve customers. That is, banks are to make use of upgraded KYC procedures and enhanced
data collection to market and provide client-focused and tailored financial products and services. This would allow them to meet compliance needs and expand
their business simultaneously.

Yet, de-risking associated with stepping up compliance, enforcing stronger
risk management practices, and maintaining strong AML/CFT standards at banks
under heightened fear of imposed penalties can lead to unintended and undesirable consequences for some communities and countries. Banks and the financial
sector cannot be the only ones responsible for addressing the issue of the negative
impact of de-risking on particularly economically deprived societies and the possible distressing effects on financial inclusion.[34] Surely financial services firms
have the right to reduce the level of risk to which they are exposed and to decide
whether it is more cost-effective and less troublesome to cease business with
certain customers and in some markets, but perhaps they should be given the necessary incentives to consider the strategy of imposing stronger risk management
and control on high-risk customers and markets, rather than pursuing the strategy
of complete avoidance. Government officials, including regulatory and supervisory bodies, must also play a role in alleviating any adverse side-effects of newly
imposed regulations and must assess carefully the negative impacts of standards'
enforcement with a view to preventing unplanned outcomes. This would not mean
that concerned authorities should lessen global standards and loosen laws, or scale
back regulations and reduce the importance of enforcement. Forcefully compelling compliance with laws and regulations to prevent wrongdoing and protect
financial markets and stakeholders should remain a prime concern, but not to
the point of reaching over-regulation and at the expense of consumer protection.
It is a dilemma in which a trade-off is essential. Research that seeks to throw
further light on this quandary could provide valuable inputs for decision- and
policy-makers on the way to balance between excess regulatory requirements and
protection of banks' clients.

Notes

1 The Dodd-Frank Wall Street Reform and Consumer Protection Act of 2010 aimed at
restoring public confidence in the financial system and markets, improving regulation of financial services firms, protecting depository institutions against failure, and
controlling systemic risk in the financial sector. It concentrated as well on promoting
greater transparency in the flow of information to consumers of financial services. The
Volcker rule, in turn, prohibited insured depository institutions and their affiliates from
engaging in proprietary trading, acquiring and retaining ownership interests in hedge
funds or private equity funds, and sponsoring these funds.

2 See, for example, the 2015 United States Government Accountability Office (GAO) report on the impacts on banks and costs of implementing the Dodd Frank regulations. See also the Retail Distribution Review Post Implementation Review (2014) on the compliance costs and impacts of the Retail Distribution Review regulation.

3 See the Basel Committee quantitative impact studies, estimating, among other things, the additional capital needs resulting from the implementation of the Basel III capital adequacy rules.

4 *The New York Times* 1998; 1999; *The Guardian* 2000.

5 *The New York Times* 2014; Switzerland News.Net 2014.

6 Bloomberg 2014b.

7 See also Bloomberg 2011; *The New York Times* 2011; *The Wall Street Journal* 2012c.

8 US Department of Justice 2009; *The Wall Street Journal* 2009; *The New York Times* 2009.

9 *The Wall Street Journal* 2012b; 2012b; *South China Morning Post* 2013.

10 CBS News 2007; Reuters 2008.

11 *The Wall Street Journal* 2004.

12 Bloomberg 2009; US Department of Justice 2009.

13 FCPA Blog 2015.

14 *The Financial Times* 2014c; Bloomberg 2014c.

15 See also *The Financial Times* 2014b.

16 Financial Conduct Authority 2015a.

17 *The Guardian* 2010.

18 See also on this issue *The Guardian* 2012 and *The Financial Times* 2014a.

19 BBC News 2014b.

20 *The Telegraph* 2009.

21 For more on this issue see BBC News 2013 and New York State Department of Financial Services 2015.

22 BBC News 2014a.

23 *The New York Times* 2012.

24 *The Washington Post* 2014.

25 For example, in the UK, the penalties forced by the Financial Conduct Authority onto regulated institutions and persons was close to GBP 905 million in 2015 and surpassed GBP 1 billion in 2014, compared with almost half this amount in 2013.

26 For more on this issue see *The Guardian* 2015; *The Financial Times* 2015; *Forbes* 2015; *The Wall Street Journal* May 2015; and BBC News 2015.

27 Citigroup, the third-largest US bank, estimated recently that the finance industry may have to spend around $10 billion per year in the future to combat money laundering and keep up with regulation. See Bloomberg 2014a for more information on this issue.

28 The American Bankers Association (ABA) testified in 2012 (before the House Subcommittee on Financial Institutions and Consumer Credit) that the regulatory burden for community banks skyrocketed by ten times in the last decade, with more than 1500 small banks exiting the industry. ABA added that compliance costs for the industry are estimated to be around $50 billion annually, using a conservative approach, tantamount to 12 percent of total operating expenses.

29 There are other reliable reports issued by private firms as good as these three mentioned, but they were excluded from the text because of the different constraints.

30 *The Wall Street Journal* 2015c.

31 *The Wall Street Journal* 2015b.

32 See, for example, Global Center on Cooperative Security 2015 on bank de-risking and its effects on financial inclusion.

33 See, for example, Overseas Development Institute 2015.

34 See also on this issue *American Banker* November 2015.

Bibliography

Accenture 2014, *Accenture 2014 Compliance Risk Study*. Available from: https://www.accenture.com

Accenture 2015, *Accenture 2015 Compliance Risk Study*. Available from: https://www.accenture.com

American Banker 2015, *"Treasury to Banks: Derisking Is Your Problem to Solve."*

American Bankers Association 2012, *ABA Testifies on Impact of Regulatory Compliance Costs on Community Banks*, Press Release, May 9, 2012.

Asset Freezing Unit, HM Treasury, United Kingdom. Available from: www.hm-treasury.gov.uk/fin_sanctions_afu.htm

Bank Secrecy Act 1970, *Currency and Foreign Transactions Reporting Act*, US Congress.

Basel Committee on Banking Supervision 2001, *Customer Due Diligence for Banks*, Bank for International Settlements, Basel, Switzerland.

Basel Committee on Banking Supervision 2003, *General Guide to Account Opening and Customer Identification*, Bank for International Settlements, Basel, Switzerland.

Basel Committee on Banking Supervision 2004, *Consolidated KYC Risk Management*, Bank for International Settlements, Basel, Switzerland.

Basel Committee on Banking Supervision 2005, *Compliance and the Compliance Function in Banks*, Bank for International Settlements, Basel, Switzerland.

Basel Committee on Banking Supervision 2008, *Implementation of the Compliance Principles—A Survey*, Bank for International Settlements, Basel, Switzerland.

Basel Committee on Banking Supervision 2014, *Sound Management of Risks Related to Money Laundering and Financing of Terrorism*, Bank for International Settlements, Basel, Switzerland.

Basel Committee on Banking Supervision, Basel III monitoring. Available from: https://www.bis.org/bcbs/qis/index.htm

BBC News 2013, *Olympus scandal: Former executives sentenced.*

BBC News 2014a, *BNP Paribas to pay $9bn to settle sanctions violations.*

BBC News 2014b, *Standard Chartered to pay fresh penalty to NY regulator.*

BBC News 2015, *Barclays pays extra $150 m penalty for forex misconduct.*

Bloomberg 2009, *U.S. Sues UBS Seeking Swiss Account Customer Names.*

Bribery Act 2010, Parliament of the United Kingdom.

Bloomberg 2011, *Credit Suisse Likely to Settle criminal Tax Probe, Lawyers Say.*

Bloomberg 2014a, *Citigroup sees $10 Billion in Annual Bank Compliance Costs.*

Bloomberg 2014b, *Credit Suisse to Pay $197 Million in SEC U.S. Client Case.*

Bloomberg 2014c, *UBS Net Rises 15%; Bank Settles German Tax Investigation.*

CBS News 2007, *Brazil Arrests 19 In Tax Evasion Scheme.*

Common Foreign and Security Policy (CFSP) of the European Union. Available from: http://eeas.Europa.eu/cfsp/index_en.htm

Continuity, Banking Compliance Index, Q4 2013 Report. Available from: www.continuity.net

Continuity, Banking Compliance Index, Q4 2014 Report. Available from: www.continuity.net

Continuity, Banking Compliance Index, Q4 2015 Report. Available from: www.continuity.net

Dodd-Frank Wall Street Reform and Consumer Protection Act 2010, US congress.

The Egmont Group of Financial Intelligence Units. Available from: www.egmontgroup.org

European Union Council Directive 91/308/EEC of June 10, 1991 on prevention of the use of the financial system for the purpose of money laundering [Official Journal L 166 of 28.06.1991].

European Union Directive 2001/97/EC of the European Parliament and of the Council of 4 December 2001 amending Council Directive 91/308/EEC on prevention of the use of the financial system for the purpose of money laundering [Official Journal L 344, 28/12/2001 P. 0076–0082].

European Union Directive 2005/60/EC of the European Parliament and of the Council of 26 October 2005 on the prevention of the use of the financial system for the purpose of money laundering and terrorist financing [Official Journal L 309/15 of 25.11.2005].

European Union Directive 2015/849 of the European Parliament and of the Council of 20 May 2015 on the prevention of the use of the financial system for the purposes of money laundering or terrorist financing [Official Journal L 141/73 of 5.6.2015].

FCPA Blog 2015, *Compliance department errors cost UBS $1.7 million in OFAC fines.*

Financial Action Task Force (FATF) 1990, *Financial Action Task Force on Money Laundering-Report*, FATF, Paris.

Financial Action Task Force (FATF) 1996, *Financial Action Task Force on Money Laundering-The Forty Recommendations*, FATF, Paris.

Financial Action Task Force (FATF) 2003, *FATF Standards—FATF 40 Recommendations*, FATF, Paris.

Financial Action Task Force (FATF) 2012, *International Standards on Combating Money Laundering And The Financing of Terrorism & Proliferation—The FATF Recommendations*, FATF, Paris.

Financial Action Task Force (FATF) 2015a, *Financing of the Terrorist Organization Islamic State in Iraq and the Levant (ISIL)*, FATF Report, Paris.

Financial Action Task Force (FATF) 2015b, *Emerging Terrorist Financing Risks*, FATF Report, Paris.

Financial Action Task Force (FATF) 2015c, *Terrorist Financing—FATF Report to G20 leaders—Actions taken by the FATF*, FATF report, Paris.

Financial Conduct Authority 2015a, *FCA fines Barclays £72 million for poor handling of financial crime risks*, News.

Financial Conduct Authority, 2015b, *Fines*. Available from: http://www.fca.org.uk/firms/being-regulated/enforcement/fines.

The Financial Times 2014a, "HSBC wrestles with soaring costs of compliance."

The Financial Times 2014b, "Strategies shift as regulators renew scrutiny of bank compliance."

The Financial Times 2014c, "UBS pays €300m to settle probe into tax evasion."

The Financial Times 2015, "Six banks fined $5.6 bn over rigging of foreign exchange markets."

Forbes 2015, *Swiss Bank UBS To Pay $342 Million Currency Manipulation Fine, Plead Guilty On Libor.*

Foreign Account Tax Compliance Act (FATCA) 2010, US Congress.

Global Center on Cooperative Security 2015, *Understanding Bank De-Risking and its Effects on Financial Inclusion*, Research Report.

The Guardian 2000, "Swiss banks agree $1.25bn Holocaust deal."

The Guardian 2010, "Barclays fined $298m for sanction breaking."

The Guardian 2012, "HSBC pays record $1.9bn fine to settle US money-laundering accusations."

The Guardian 2015, "UBS facing £350m in fines as banks hit with fresh sanctions for forex rigging."

International Monetary Fund 2015, *Factsheet—The IMF and the Fight Against Money Laundering and the Financing of Terrorism.* Available from: www.imf.org/external/np/exr/facts/aml.htm

New York State Department of Financial Services 2015, *NYDFS Announces Commerzbank to Pay $1.45 Billion, Terminate Employees, Install Independent Monitor for Banking Law Violations*, Press Release.

The New York Times 1998, "When the Sure-Footed Stumble; Swiss Banks Stagger After Several Investing Missteps."

The New York Times 1999, "Estelle Sapir, 73, Who Fought Bank Over Holocaust Assets."

The New York Times 2009, "Iranian Dealings Lead to a Fine for Credit Suisse."

The New York Times 2011, "U.S. Accuses Four Bankers Connected to Credit Suisse of Helping Americans Evade Taxes."

The New York Times 2012, "ING Bank to Pay $619 Million to Settle Inquiry Into Sanctions Violations."

The New York Times 2014, "Credit Suisse Pleads Guilty in Felony Case."

Office of Foreign Assets Control (OFAC), Available from: https://www.treasury.gov/about/organizational-structure/offices/Pages/Office-of-Foreign-Assets-Control.aspx

Organization for Economic Co-operation and Development (OECD) 2014, *Standard for Automatic Exchange of Financial Information in Tax Matters*, OECD, Paris.

Overseas Development Institute 2015, *UK humanitarian aid in the age of counterterrorism: perceptions and reality*, Research Reports and Studies.

Retail Distribution Review 2006, Financial Services Board, UK.

Retail Distribution Review Post Implementation Review 2014, Europe Economics, London.

Reuters 2008, *Credit Suisse banker arrested in Brazil tax probe.*

South China Morning Post 2013, *German prosecutors probe Credit Suisse tax evasion.*

Switzerland News 2014, *Credit Suisse fined $2.6bn in US tax evasion case.*

The Telegraph 2009, "Lloyds TSB agrees to pay fine of $350 m for sanctions help."

Thomson Reuters 2013, Cost of Compliance Survey 2013. Available from: http://accelus.thomsonreuters.com

Thomson Reuters 2014, Cost of Compliance 2014. Available from: http://accelus.thomsonreuters.com

Thomson Reuters 2015, Cost of Compliance 2015. Available from: http://accelus.thomsonreuters.com

United Nations 1988, *United Nations Convention Against Illicit Traffic in Narcotic Drugs And Psychotropic Substances*, New York.

United Nations 1999, *International Convention for the Suppression of the Financing of Terrorism*, New York.

United Nations 2001, *United Nations Security Council Resolution 1373*, New York.

United Nations 2004a, *United Nations Convention Against Transnational Organized Crime And The Protocols Thereto*, New York.

United Nations 2004b, *United Nations Convention Against Corruption*, New York.

United Nations 2005, *United Nations Security Council Resolution 1617*, New York.

United States Government Accountability Office (GAO) 2015, *Dodd-Frank Regulations: Impacts on Community Banks, Credit Unions and Systemically Important Institutions.*

US Department of Justice, Office of Public Affairs 2009, Press Release, *Credit Suisse Agrees to Forfeit $536 Million in Connection with Violations of the International Emergency Economic Powers Act of New York State Law.*

US Department of Justice 2009, Office of Public Affairs, Press Release, *UBS Enters into Deferred Prosecution Agreement.*

USA Patriot Act 2001, *Uniting and Strengthening America by Providing Appropriate Tools Required to Intercept and Obstruct Terrorism Act*, US Congress.

The Wall Street Journal 2004, "Fed Fines UBS $100 Million For Money-Transfer Violations."

The Wall Street Journal 2009, "Credit Suisse's Secret Deals."

The Wall Street Journal 2012a, "Germany Probes UBS Staff on Tax-Evasion Allegations."

The Wall Street Journal 2012b, "Credit Suisse to Give More Files."

The Wall Street Journal 2012c, "Clients of Swiss Bank Raided in Tax Probe."

The Wall Street Journal 2015a, "UBS Hit With $545 Million in Fines."

The Wall Street Journal 2015b, "Account Closed: How Bank 'De-Risking' Hurts Legitimate Customers."

The Wall Street Journal 2015c, "Regulation Is Good for Goldman."

The Washington Post 2014, "Government extracts $2 billion in fines from JP Morgan in Madoff Case."

Part 2

New policies in the wake of the latest financial crisis

4 The causes and origins of banking crises

A review and critique of theory and evidence

Introduction

The global financial crisis of 2007–8 and the ones that hit many peripheral European countries[1] reignited interest in the topic of financial instability and financial crises among academics, researchers, and policy-makers. Awareness was similarly awakened following the East Asia financial crisis almost ten years earlier, in 1997–8, and other episodes of financial turbulence throughout the current and previous centuries. Financial crises are a recurring phenomenon with a history stretching back long before the Great Depression of 1929. Most crises are similar in many dimensions and can result in serious economic and social costs, often associated with a sharp drop in employment and output. Adverse implications could extend as well to the fiscal situation, the effectiveness of the monetary policy, and the external sector. In an interlinked world economy the damage may not be limited to a single economy, where the crisis originated, and the fear of adverse contagion or spillover effects, with the rapid spread of the crisis across other economies, is a major policy issue. Therefore, understanding the origins of the crisis, where monetary and fiscal policies could have played a contributing role, and identifying the real causes and linkages is of utmost importance in helping monetary and fiscal authorities and financial system regulators and supervisors learn the right lessons to allow them to address existing weaknesses, strengthen the financial system, and limit contagion effects.

This chapter focuses on a branch or type of financial crisis, namely banking sector instability and crises, and not on financial crises in any broader sense, for there is not a single manifestation of financial instability or crisis in the financial system. Financial markets are made up of money and capital markets comprising currency, bond, stock, and financial derivatives markets. Therefore instability and crises in any of these areas could lead to stock market crashes (1987), debt market problems (Mexico 1994), banking panics (East Asia 1997–8), currency crises (EU 1992–3), or capital account crises.[2] Financial distress of all these types, however, can share the same basic elements: they can (i) have common origins, causes, and triggering factors, (ii) be correlated without necessarily implying causality, with linkages running in many directions, and (iii) have banks involved in one way or another along the path to instability and crisis. This serves as partial justification of the thorough analysis of banking crises provided here and the evaluation of the policy lessons and conclusions drawn from several countries' experiences. Another justification for this discussions might be that banking crises have had a longer average recovery time and larger output losses than other crises, particularly currency crises.[3] Laeven and Valencia argue that, for a typical banking crisis, output losses are on average around 37 percent of potential output.[4] It has also been shown that banking and currency crises are likely to occur jointly in most cases and that causation may run in either direction.[5] The focus on banking does not mean, however, that the literature on the turmoil in the sovereign debt and equity markets and on the currency and capital accounts crises will be completely absent in what follows; it will appear when there is an interdependence of such crises and banking problems.

This chapter is intended specifically to review, first, the major approaches to financial crises and banking panics—that is, the academic theories that attempt to explain their origins—as a prelude to surveying, second, the evidence—that is, the empirical research on the determinants of banking problems and crises. The next section offers, therefore, the theoretical background for analysis or empirical assessment in addition to policy options to reduce the adverse effects of crises or the probability of their occurrence. This is followed by a survey of the broad literature dealing with the origins and causes of banking crises and highlights the possible contribution of a number of macroeconomic domestic and external shocks, financial regulation/deregulation, financial innovation, macroeconomic policies, and other elements of banking problems and crises. The final section concludes with some general remarks and policy issues.

The theories

Various theoretical models or approaches have attempted to explain macro and institutional, general and country-specific developments surrounding the onset of a financial crisis and thus to describe how crises are likely to develop and be transmitted. These theories disagree not only on the mechanism by which crises develop and propagate but also on the definition or manifestation of financial instability/crisis and its original source (the financial sector vs real sector).[6] Despite these differences, such mechanisms can be reconciled—or, to be more accurate, the various postulated mechanisms can be seen to all operate in varying proportions and interact to determine the precise nature of each crisis. In what follows we elaborate briefly on two traditional and complete approaches to financial crisis—namely, the business cycle (or financial instability) approach and the monetarist approach. This is followed by a discussion of other main theories that cast further light on certain aspects of the traditional theories—namely, the asymmetric information approach to financial crises and the literature related to the origination of bank runs or panics. We conclude the next section with an attempt to recapitulate on the main differences and commonalities among the competing theories.

The business cycle approach

The business cycle approach, with all its ramifications, holds that financial crises are a key characteristic of the upper turning point of the business cycle and a response to previous "over indebtedness," "financial fragility," or "euphoria and mania."[7] Fundamental elements of this approach are that there are two-way linkages between financial fragility in the non-financial sector and financial fragility in the financial sector, and that financial crises follow and terminate speculative booms or bubbles and crises and asset price bubbles are triggered by shocks.[8] In fact, it is argued that in the build-up to crises, and owing to developing systemic forces, the financial vulnerability to shock in the non-financial sector becomes heightened, which is passed on to the financial system. There is also a reverse causality to non-financial firms' performance once financial institutions are hurt. Any destabilizing shock that follows, such as the deflation of the asset price bubble, would initiate a financial crisis, which could be manifested, among other things, by shifts to money (defined as cash and other bank deposits) and bank runs driven by fears of banks' insolvency. Owing to credit contraction and poor intermediation, crises are likely to contribute to economic downturns.

Fisher associates the upturn in the business cycle with an exogenous shock or event that leads to improved opportunities for profitable investment.[9] This means increased investment in fixed assets and speculation in the real sector and stock market for capital gain, both of which are largely debt-financed through bank loans. Bank credit increases deposits and thus the stock of money and the aggregate price level. In this process the velocity of money also increases, leading to further credit and output expansion. The rise in the aggregate price level reduces the real value of outstanding debt, inciting further borrowing, and as such a state of over-indebtedness is reached in which the probability of insolvency is largely increased.

The financial crisis starts to develop when bank borrowers are no longer able to honour their obligations and refinance their financial positions. In such circumstances, borrowers may be asked by banks to liquidate assets, a process known by "distress selling." Widespread distress selling not offset by a central bank intervention in the market can lead to falling prices and to a decrease in bank deposits, as loans are called when the value of the collateral decreases with falling prices. Deflation increases the real value of outstanding debt and thus the debt burden of borrowers, who will continue to liquidate assets. Falling prices also adversely affect the profits and equity of firms and contribute to loan default. This would lead to an economic depression and trigger bank runs as fears over bank solvency increase. The fall in output and employment is brought to an end only when the wave of bankruptcies eliminates over-indebtedness or an inflationary monetary policy is pursued. The over-indebtedness–deflation cycle then repeats itself.

Minsky builds on Fisher's work in introducing the concept of financial fragility, which is likely to increase during the economic upturn.[10] He focuses on business debt and the ability of firms to either service this debt by generating sufficient revenues (cash receipts) to meet debt payments (cash payments) when due or refinance their positions, which is possible only if expected revenue is deemed to be sufficient. The ability of firms to debt finance new investment is therefore contingent upon the expectation of generating sufficient cash flow from this new investment to repay current debt or refinance it. To Minsky financial crises are endogenously generated events and they occur once the fragile financial structure is shocked by a further increase in interest rates, triggering a sell-off of assets that produces a sharp decline in asset prices. Financial crises are also likely to vary in scale depending on the size of the government sector and the role it plays in the economy. The more the government acts as a lender of last resort, expands budget deficits when demand slackens, and introduces automatic stabilizers, the less significant crises are likely to be. Aborting crises has a price, however, reflected in accelerating inflation.

In his theory of financial instability Minsky argues that, during an economic upswing, new investments, responding to improved profit opportunities, result in an excess demand for funds and thus higher interest rates. New investments are financed by short-term bank loans, long-term debt, and equity, and the excess demand for funds is partly and temporarily offset by an increase in the supply of funds to finance more investment through ongoing financial innovation. Higher interest rates cause a shift from hedge to speculative to Ponzi finance and from long-term to short-term debt. They also increase debt finance and reduce margins of safety for financial firms, thereby creating a fragile financial environment. The differences between hedge, speculative, and Ponzi finance are as follows: hedge finance describes a situation in which cash inflows (receipts) exceed cash outflows (payments) due over a long period; speculative finance entails cash receipts that fall below cash payments due over a short period; and Ponzi finance involves borrowers relying on new debt to meet outstanding commitments for long periods. Minsky argues that a further increase in interest rates can lead to refinancing problems in which firms are unable to roll over their debt, which could initiate a wave of distress selling unless this trend is counteracted by a central bank intervention—that is, when the central bank acts as a lender of last resort to the money markets and supplies reserves on demand to prevent the interest rate from rising in an investment boom. Minsky considers that this cycle repeats itself as memories of previous problems disappear and that it is an intrinsic feature of capitalist economies. The channel for the international transmission of crises is defaults on international loans.

Kindleberger differentiates his work from that of his predecessors in stressing the importance of "euphoria" and "mania" during the economic upturn, rather than Minsky's "fragility" and Fisher's "over-indebtedness".[11] Kindleberger bases his model of financial crises on Minsky's early writings, which attached importance to shocks. The road to a crisis starts with a shock or event that changes the economic outlook and presents new opportunities for profit in one or more important sectors of the economy. Displacement occurs in the economy, with businesses shifting or switching to the perceived profitable sector(s) or market(s), and there will also be newcomers. With increased production and investment a boom fuelled by bank credit will result, expanding the money supply. The boom environment can prompt speculation and a state of euphoria, leading to insufficient risk provisioning at banks and to over-trading and excessive gearing. Speculation then spreads to people, who will act irrationally in buying real or illiquid financial and capital assets, and mania or an irrational speculative bubble ensues as asset prices progress far above the fundamentals. In this manic phase interest rates, the velocity of money circulation, and prices rise.

At the peak of the irrational speculative boom prices level off, as there will be a balance between investors deciding to take profits and sell out and new speculation betting on the continuation of the boom. When the belief that market prices will not increase any further is widespread, there will be an imbalance—which can turn out to be massive—in favor of those who want to sell out in order to preserve existing capital gains. In this environment a state of aversion to certain commodities and securities is likely to develop and banks tend to stop lending on the collateral of such assets; this is similar to the terms "revulsion" and "discredit" in the classical ideas of panics and crashes following speculative bubbles. This state of aversion is followed by a crisis, crash, or panic that tends to feeds on itself. The process comes to a halt only when one of the following events is realized: first, a central bank intervention (acting as lender of last resort) providing a sufficient supply of base money to stop a flight to liquidity; second, a closing of the exchange place where assets in which there has been speculation are traded, or the inhibition of such a trade; and, third, a fall in asset prices to a level where investors are again attracted to less liquid assets. Kindleberger also considers that there are transmission mechanisms of crises internationally in which psychological factors, stock market interconnectivity, and commodity and interest arbitrage play a key role.

The monetarist approach

The monetarist approach[12] disagrees with the idea of the necessary connectivity of crises, with the business cycles viewed (if they exist) as generated by cycles in the real money supply. Monetary shocks are the key sources of cyclical fluctuations. The approach identifies instead financial crises with banking panics related to an exogenous change in the stock of money, such as the actions of the central bank. This line of argument maintains, therefore, that crises are panic-based, as banking panics tend to produce monetary instability, reduce the stock of money, and decrease economic activity. This would happen as a result of a fall in both deposits to currency ratio and deposits to reserve ratio.

A banking panic is usually manifested by the public's willingness to increase its cash holdings and therefore financial crises are associated with a flight to money (including only cash). Given the fractional reserves system, this may lead to a multiple contraction of deposits. A banking panic can lead to widespread bank failures, as banks will have to respond to the rising need for liquidity during sharp deposit conversions into cash by selling assets, leading to a fall in the value of their assets and to their insolvency. This can be offset only by a suspension of deposit convertibility into currency or open market operations undertaken by the monetary authority, increasing the supply of money.

The prime candidate for banking panics is the public loss of confidence in banks' abilities to convert deposits into currency. The loss in banks' credibility is often triggered by the failure of one or more leading financial intermediaries. Prescriptions to avoid runs and panics included the willingness and readiness of the monetary authority to act as lender of last resort and expand the supply of money during crises. In addition to the above mentioned, Cagan provides strong evidence related to the US experience (1875–1960) that panics may not produce a severe economic contraction and may follow peaks in economic activity.[13]

In later work, Schwartz argues that bank insolvency or failures and the ensuing financial instability may be the outcome of unexpected reversals of inflation and excessive monetary tightening.[14] She mentions that both upward and downward aggregate price movements tend to distort lenders' perception of credit and interest rate risks and cause interest rate instability, leading to credit expansion in the rising price situation and poor intermediation in the opposite case. Schwartz also contends that fluctuations in the inflation rate resulting from an altered monetary policy in a contractionary direction make expected return on projects unrealizable, as the underlying price level assumptions originally incorporated in the yield calculations are no longer valid. That would increase the risk level of bank assets and lead to bank failures.

The effects of a monetary policy inadequate to the task of controlling the money supply or the monetary base, resulting in excessive monetary tightening, have been also elaborated by Bruner and Meltzer.[15] Under excessive monetary tightening and in order to obtain needed reserves banks may be forced to sell assets, which reduces the prices of these assets, raises interest rates, contributes to bank insolvency, and undermines confidence in banks. Attempts to respond to the rapid rise in liquidity could cause deterioration in the value of bank assets, force banking institutions into insolvency, and incite bank runs. The separate works of Schwartz and of Bruner and Meltzer suggest a stable and predictable money supply path and a stable price level as a means to escape financial instability. This complements other monetarists' policy prescriptions of lender of last resort facility to avert crises.

Models of deposit runs, banking panics, and contagion

Various models have attempted to explain why banks are vulnerable to runs and panics, particularly in the absence of an adequate deposit insurance scheme and a lender of last resort facility. Though there have been different views on deposit runs or banking panics, three theoretical approaches to the origins of deposit runs are particularly worth examining.[16]

The first is built on the idea that there is something inherent to the functioning of the banking system that could give rise to a deposit run, stemming from, firstly, the financing of long-term illiquid assets with demandable deposits and, secondly, the nature of deposit contracts, particularly the "sequential service constraint," whereby deposits can only be withdrawn sequentially. The implications are that a shock could cause a group of depositors to think that significant amounts of withdrawals by other depositors are likely, which could become a self-fulfilling prophecy. Because of the fractional reserves system and the first-come-first-served principle, those at the end of the sequential service line would be most likely to suffer a loss. Concerns over such potential losses would drive depositors to place themselves at the head of the sequential service line, thus causing a banking panic. This approach is therefore centred on the random behavior of bank agents and is known in the literature as the random deposit withdrawal risk model, first developed by Bryant[17] and by Diamond and Dybvig,[18] where banking panics or bank runs are self-fulfilling predictions unrelated to changes in the real economy and can be traced to illiquidity shocks.[19]

Such models assume that bank clients have indeterminate consumption needs in a situation where banks' long-term investments are expensive to liquidate. Two equilibriums exist. In the first, agents take out their deposits according to their consumption needs in the belief that panic will not take place and that their demand for funds can thus be satisfied without costly assets liquidation. In the second, agents think that other clients will withdraw their savings, all depositors thus realize that it is reasonable to cash in their entitlements, and a panic results.

A major drawback of this approach is that it does not elaborate on what kinds of shock would drive people to think that other people are likely to withdraw their money—that is, there is no account of either actual events that might trigger a crisis or which of the two equilibriums might be selected, but only an explanation of how panics may occur. According to Diamond and Dybvig, any event, including runs on or insolvency of other banks, can provoke runs. The above approach suggests, therefore, that bank panics could be resolved through open market operations conducted by the monetary authority[20] and that banks probably need to design better deposit contracts to avoid runs.[21] To address this drawback, a new literature has recently emerged that studies banking crises using global games, where such an approach seems to offer a kind of selection mechanism relevant to this type of coordination (or incomplete information) game. Carlsson and Van Damme were the first to analyze such games;[22] later, Morris and Shin applied this approach to currency crises,[23] and were followed by Rochet and Vives[24] and Goldstein and Pauzner,[25] who used the same methodology to examine banking crises.

The second line of thinking on deposit runs is based on the idea that shifts in depositors' perceptions regarding the riskiness of banks could lead to these runs. Such shifts take place as a result of concerns over bank solvency. Jacklin and Bhattacharya viewed banking crises as a reaction of bank depositors to the influx of large amounts of negative information on evolving economic conditions.[26] In their view, depositors tend to withdraw their funds from banks in anticipation of financial difficulties in these financial intermediaries when they receive information about looming economic downturn that could lead to a drop in the value of bank assets and thus raise the possibility of banks' inability to meet their commitments. Chari and Jagannathan[27] and Allen and Gale[28] share this analysis.

Gorton associated information on the liabilities of failed businesses incorporated in one of the leading economic indicators in the US in the late nineteenth and early twentieth centuries with the occurrence of banking crises.[29] This encouraged Allen and Gale to build on the empirical work of Gorton and develop their own model arguing that depositors are disposed to keep their deposits in the bank if they receive public information (through a leading economic indicator) about future high returns on bank assets.[30] Conversely, they are willing to withdraw their funds when returns are definitely low, leading to a crisis.

In this approach deposit runs are not limited to the insolvent banking institution, but could be generalized owing to contagious effects and the inability of depositors to obtain information about individual banks' financial situations, instead aggregating information for the entire sector. This would make it difficult for depositors to identify which individual banking institution is likely to face trouble and they may decide, therefore, to withdraw deposits from sound and unsound banks alike. This approach stresses that genuine bank solvency problems could result in a loss in credibility in the affected bank first and then in the banking system as a whole, leading ultimately to deposit runs. This view is consistent with Friedman and Schwartz's explanation of banking panics.[31]

Contagion can result from contractual or informational links (direct and indirect linkages) between banks by means of, for example, interbank loans or balance sheet exposures to common shocks,[32] or from depositors' panics. In contrast, Diamond and Rajan[33] build on their earlier model[34] to show that contagion need not be based on panics or contractual links, but instead can arise from bank failures, which tend to shrink the common pool of liquidity, thus generating or aggravating aggregate liquidity shortages, leading to a rash of failures and the possible breakdown of the system. The authors also argue that banks can fail because of either severe liquidity or solvency problems, which can interrelate in both directions; as the cost of a system meltdown can be substantial, there is a possible role for government intervention.

The third view on deposit runs attaches importance to asymmetric information between banks and depositors in terms of banks' asset management and valuation.[35] It is built on the fact that depository institutions create non-marketable assets that are hard to value while at the same time it is often difficult to monitor the behavior of banks' management. Because of this intrinsic feature, excessive risk-taking at banks is likely to develop, which could lead to periodic losses of confidence or credibility in banks and therefore to runs and panics. According to this line of thinking, therefore, bank panics are induced by asset shocks. This approach does not, however, elaborate on the benchmark against which "excessive risk" is measured—in other words, when does risk become excessive and when is it "acceptable."

Proponents of this approach also argue that although bank panics are short-lived events measured in days they can still have long-term adverse economic effects and are hard to resolve using only monetary policy tools. This is because asset values at individual banks are not under the control of monetary policy.[36] Some have suggested resolving this problem through limiting the risk depositors face via an individual bank action or the government, thus removing the incentive for runs.[37] Others have argued that deposit insurance and similar schemes aiming at insuring depositors could aggravate the problem by adversely affecting the incentives of depositors to monitor banks.

The asymmetric information approach

The asymmetric information approach[38] identifies a financial crisis with a sharp slump in credit extension, as it tends to dislocate the normal functioning of the financial and monetary systems and harm resource allocation and economic activity efficiencies. Asymmetric information models are also referred to as models of credit frictions and market freezes, as they analyze irregularities or resistance in the flow of loans from banks to borrowers, which, once heightened, can result in a market halt and financial crisis.[39] The argument is that, given information asymmetry, the associated adverse selection and moral hazard problems are responsible for generating frictions in the provision of credit; thus, severe asymmetric information contributes to financial instability through credit rationing.

A sharp increase in adverse selection (difficulty in distinguishing between good and bad risk loans), usually associated with rising interest rates or uncertainty, can lead to considerable contraction in lending at the prevailing interest rates (as a means of avoiding these problems) and this may affect mainly low credit quality borrowers, for whom asymmetric information is usually high. An increase in adverse selection problems is also made possible by lower collateral values, which were originally intended as a means to minimize asymmetric information problems. Declining collateral values are often associated with decreasing assets value owing, for example, to stock market crashes.

Advocates of this approach also believe that, given information asymmetry, moral hazard problems (the borrower behaving differently than was agreed upon in the credit contract) would make creditors reluctant to lend to borrowers and that such credit constraints can be magnified when economic conditions deteriorate, with the increase in the level of defaults leading to the financial crisis, as defined above. The incentive to misuse credit in risky activities for abnormal profit-making is usually high when the borrower's net worth is relatively low, as the debtor would have little to lose in the event of default. Therefore, the efficient flow of credit between the two parties necessitates the removal of such incentives to redirect financial resources to the detriment of the creditor by requesting the borrower maintains sufficient stake in the financed project.

In addition, theorists of this approach believe that asymmetric information helps to explain contagious runs on banks, even those that are solvent.

Mishkin defines a financial crisis as a disruption to financial markets, so that these markets are unable to efficiently channel funds to productive investment, causing a decline in economic activity.[40] He argues that financial crises are caused by those asymmetric information problems mentioned above: adverse selection, when potential bad credit risk borrowers are the ones who most actively seek out loans, and moral hazard, when borrowers have incentives to invest in high-risk projects.

Mishkin considers that there are four types of factors that tend to make asymmetric information problems (adverse selection and moral hazard) much worse, thus precipitating a financial crisis. First, a deterioration in financial sector balance sheets implies a substantial contraction in its capital and therefore a decline in overall lending, as it is hard to raise new capital at a reasonable cost; this causes the economy to contract. Severe deterioration in bank balance sheets can lead to bank panics with an even sharper decline in lending, and runs on deposits contagion caused by asymmetric information can spread from one bank to another. Second, increases in interest rates can raise the probability that lenders are granting loans to bad credit risk borrowers; prudent borrowers are likely to see that it is unwise to borrow under such conditions, while those with risky investment projects are more willing to pay higher interest rates. Because lenders are aware of this fact they are likely to react by limiting the number of loans they make. Third, increases in uncertainty reduce the ability of lenders to address adverse selection and moral hazard problems by making it hard to screen out the bad credit risk borrowers. This makes lenders less willing to lend, leading to a decline in lending and economic activity. Fourth, the widespread deterioration of non-financial balance sheets (among borrowers) reduces the ability of lenders to address asymmetric information problems through the use of (i) collateral, the value of which tends to fall if asset prices fall, and (ii) the net worth, the decrease of which increases the incentives for borrowers to commit moral hazard. Because of this, implying reduced protection for banks, lending and economic activity decline.

To Mishkin, fully-fledged financial crises undergo three stages. The first stage is characterized by deterioration in the balance sheets of financial and non-financial firms and could be due to financial liberalization, related risky lending and a considerable increase in leverage in the corporate sector. This stage leads to a second one in which currency crisis occurs, as speculative attacks on the currency are likely to materialize when the banking system is weak and corporations are highly leveraged. This is because investors recognize that the domestic central bank will be reluctant to defend the currency by raising interest rates, as banks' balance sheets will deteriorate further and the cost of financing for other firms is likely to increase. The probability that the currency will depreciate is also increased by the expectation that large fiscal deficits will come from bailing out any collapse in the financial sector. The third stage is the occurrence of further or sharp deterioration in financial and non-financial firms' balance sheets as a result of the currency crisis. The latter can increase actual inflation, expected inflation, and nominal interest rates, as well as the debt burden of domestic firms with foreign currency debt. A sharp deterioration in balance sheets leads to a contraction in lending and to severe economic downturn.

To prevent financial crises Mishkin proposes a set of financial policies covering twelve basic areas:[41] 1) prudential supervision; 2) accounting and disclosure requirements; 3) legal and judicial systems; 4) market-based discipline; 5) entry of foreign banks; 6) capital controls; 7) reduction of the role of state-owned financial institutions; 8) restrictions on foreign denominated debt; 9) elimination of too-big-to-fail in the corporate sector; 10) sequencing financial liberalization; 11) monetary policy and price stability; and 12) exchange rate regimes and foreign exchange reserves.

The role of agency costs or problems in the build-up to the financial crisis can also be viewed from a different angle, as they tend to create bubbles, which are followed by crises once they burst. For example, Allen and Gale observe that there are three separate phases for bubbles in asset prices.[42] The first is marked by an expansion in credit and rising prices for assets (real estate or stocks) induced by financial liberalization, a decision by the central bank to boost lending, or other events. In the second, the inflated bubble bursts and asset prices collapse. Finally, borrowers that acquired assets at overblown prices default. The same authors argue that agency relationships (problems) in the banking sector produce bubbles in asset prices. If banks are incapable of detecting the features of the investment undertaken by borrowers then such investors in real estates and stock markets can exploit funds borrowed from banks to invest in risky assets, resulting in a classic substitution problem.[43] This risk shifting or asset substitution as it is attractive to investors bids up asset prices and leads to assets being priced above their fundamental value, generating a bubble. When the returns are low or the central bank tightens credit, the bubble, which was chiefly determined by the amount of credit granted by the banking system, bursts, leading to a financial crisis. In contrast, McKinnon and Pill[44] and Krugman[45] believe that explicit or implicit government guarantees are conductive to risk shifting and high asset prices.

Summary

This second section of the chapter, which surveyed the theoretical literature on the origins and causes of banking panics and crises, shows clearly that there can be no single definition of financial crises, as each of the approaches to this subject are subject to varying interpretations and sometimes very little clarity. Different theorists have focused on different issues in their treatment of financial crises and the two classical approaches (monetarist vs business cycle) can be reconciled, though they are generally regarded as substitutes.

It is implied by the business cycle approach that financial crises are financial market crashes associated with severe economic recessions or depressions. Financial crises are a natural outcome of speculative booms or asset price bubbles occurring near the peak of the business cycle, but such crises may not occur in all cycles. In this approach the role of forced liquidation, debt deflation, and fragile financial structure is also emphasized, and the financial (banking) system is itself seen as a major source of instability leading to crises, as it encourages over-expansion in the upswing. This latter argument should provide a rationale for regulation.

The monetarist approach considers that financial crises are limited to banking panics that tend to arise out of a public loss of confidence in the ability of banks to convert deposits into currency. These panics, by causing a reduction in the money supply, can have harmful effects on economic activity. Loss of confidence is often triggered by a failure of a prominent financial institution, which could be due to a sharp monetary tightening, increasing the cost burden on borrowers and reducing their profitability. This would increase non-performing loans and lead to bank insolvency.

The two approaches can be reconciled by an assumption that a monetary tightening is responsible for increasing interest rates, which would trigger a crisis in a fragile financial structure. Both the financial fragility approach and the monetarist approach also associate financial crises with a flight or shift to money, and offer therefore a similar policy recommendation: that of a lender of last resort to offset the shift. The term "money," however, is used by monetarists to denote only cash and by financial fragility theorists to refer to cash and other bank deposits. Monetarists' view is that the shift to other bank deposits may not disrupt the payments system (which is seen as an essential characteristic of financial crises) because the recipient banks of inflows can channel the transferred funds back to solvent banks in difficulties.

The empirical literature

Empirical work in this area has attempted to test a particular proposition or theory of individual or system bank failure by focusing on a combination of microeconomic (bank-specific), structural, and macroeconomic variables, for which emphasis has varied within the context of each model. Much of the research relates to a single country experience, while other work involves a panel of countries with a view to assessing wider results and the applicability of hypotheses.

Studies on the possible causes of banking system problems and the conditions under which crises are likely to occur can be subdivided into studies on the potential determinants using, in many cases, logit and probit econometric models, and studies on the "early warning indicators." Among the first category are the studies of Demirguc-Kunt and Detragiache, Eichengreen and Rose, and Hardy and Pazarbasiaglo.[46] Major studies on early warning indicators include those of Demirguc-Kunt and Detragiache, Kaminsky and Reinhart, Kaminsky et al, and Roja-Suarez.[47] Honohan, BIS, Gavin and Hausmann, Caprio and Klingebiel, Goldstein and Turner, and Lindgren et al also contributed substantially to the literature on the causes of banking crises and policy options to prevent their occurrence, reduce their likelihood, or minimize their impact.[48]

Research on the determinants of banking sector problems has identified a list of potential factors falling under three broad categories: macroeconomic, structural, and bank-specific. Although there is a wide variance among academics in the relative weights given to a particular element or sub-element over the others when it comes to systemic crisis, they all agree on the following: unsustainable macroeconomic imbalances and shocks to the economy, unfavorable political and economic conditions and policies, poor risk management and excessive risk taking, regulatory and supervisory loopholes and forbearance, and weak banking system structure are all possible sources of banking industry problems or weaknesses. It has also been observed that many of the identified determinants are interrelated or induce one another, and could commonly be responsible for amplifying the severity of the problem.

Studies on leading indicators of banking crises have examined in turn the behavior of a number of potential macroeconomic early warning indicators shortly before the crisis and contrasted these behaviors to that during "business as usual" times. At any time that one of these indicators or variables crosses a particular threshold it is considered to signal a crisis, and that signal is tested for significance.[49] These studies have shown that forecasting banking crises is more difficult than forecasting currency crises for reasons related to the complexity of their potential determinants, particularly micro-characteristics of the banking industry and the government safety net. According to this literature, the real output, real interest rates, changes in asset prices, changes in export prices, the spread between deposit and lending rates, and the money multiplier are among the best leading indicators of banking crises.

This third section of this chapter is organized as follows. First the role of domestic macroeconomic shocks in the development of a banking crisis is examined, followed by an evaluation of the possible contribution of external macroeconomic shocks to severe banking sector problems. Subsequently the adverse effects of unfavorable economic policy changes and reforms, including financial liberalization, are elaborated upon. The issues of safety net-related banking distress are then highlighted before the way in which the structure of the banking system and government ownership of banks can be a determinant of crises is examined. The effects of poor management, regulation, and supervision on banking system stability are explained and, finally, unclassified determinants of banking weakness are considered.

Domestic macroeconomic instability

Volatile growth rates and sharp contractions in economic activity

Conceptually and empirically, all the reasoning and evidence point to a link between banking fragility and a fall in economic output. How substantial is the weight of this element alone in explaining financial instability remains to be seen; all economies worldwide experience such developments every now and then, with many having their banking system possibly "affected" but not severely "touched." Cyclical output downturn effects on banks can perhaps be seen from two different angles. Low aggregate output and consumption certainly squeeze the profit margin of firms and even cause businesses to incur losses on their operations. This could raise the probability of banks having more non-performing loans on their balance sheet. The other effect is on the demand for loans side, where the reluctance in applying for funds or the undesirability of taking out loans under such circumstances aggravates further the situation through impacting the main source of income to banks and ultimately their profitability.

Hutchison and McDill find that the probability of banking sector distress increases in line with the depth of recession.[50] Demirgüç-Kunt and Detragiache conclude in their studies on the determinants of banking crises in developing and developed countries that low GDP growth relative to previous trends is highly correlated with rising risk to the banking sector.[51] Similarly, Hardy and Pazarbasioglu find, for a sample of thirty-eight countries, that banking distress is associated with a fall in GDP growth.[52] Kaminsky and Reinhart provide evidence that episodes of financial crises occur in a recessionary environment,[53] while Goldstein and Turner state that one of the more robust conclusions of the empirical literature on early warning signals of financial crises is that sharp contractions in economic activity increase the probability of banking crises.[54] Caprio and Klingebiel observe a trend of abrupt changes of growth for countries experiencing systemic banking problems over the period 1960–94, while no such trend was detected for countries experiencing less acute or no banking difficulties.[55] Thus Gavin and Hausmann find that the volatility of growth rates in Latin America (which has experienced banking sector problems) has been substantially larger than in industrial countries.[56]

High and volatile inflation rates

High inflation rates can have adverse effects on banks' balance sheets. Banks are badly affected when high inflation implies reduced real value of capital and forced portfolio adjustments, at least in the short run, in instruments, terms, and conditions, from high-income activities to lower-income ones and from a relatively stable cash flow situation to a speculative one. There is also a common belief that high and changing inflation rates demotivate both borrowers and creditors to engage as before in borrowing and lending activities, meaning less business. This is probably because of future uncertainty and high nominal interest rates, at least before adjusting to high inflation. Negative impacts of high inflation on banks' loan portfolios are also a probability where information on the prices of goods and services and on the creditworthiness of customers used in credit appraisal becomes of low quality. It is significant, however, that high inflation per se would not affect severely banks' balance sheets if all relevant prices rose together. It is argued that it is a change in *relative* prices that presents problems to borrowers and ultimately their banks.

Conversely, banks can gain from moderate inflation when additional income is derived from tax inflation on non-remunerated demand deposits accounts (checking accounts) or on others on which interest paid does not rise with inflation. They can gain also from favorable government regulation, if any, on interest rates and from a favorable gap between interest-sensitive assets and liabilities (depending on the volume of interest-sensitive assets and liabilities, long-vs short-term maturity, and fixed vs variable interest rates). Profits are also generated from the float on payments and foreign exchange speculation. Under such circumstances and in order to lessen the intensity of the impacts of high inflation on their performance, banks may start indexing lending rates and shift into other earning assets, such as foreign exchange and short-term financial instruments whose prices tend generally to precede inflation.[57]

It is argued that these earnings associated with moderate to high inflation are unsustainable, particularly creating difficulties for banks in adjusting to a changing environment when inflation declines. If this fall in the inflation rate is fast and sharp it also poses a problem for enterprises, which will have incorporated high expected inflation in their strategic planning and investment decisions. An unexpected drop in inflation would then leave the forecast targets unmet and undermine enterprises' ability to service their loans. In a nutshell, the effects of high inflation may depend on (i) whether the inflation is anticipated or unanticipated, and (ii) the particular institutional arrangements, such as whether borrowing is largely at fixed or variable interest rates.

On the issue of inflation as a potential determinant of banking sector weakness, Demirguc-Kunt and Detragiache state that high rates of inflation are a potential source of an increased risk of banking sector problems.[58] Hardy and Pazarbasioglu associate banking distress with boom–bust cycles in inflation,[59] while, similarly, Caprio and Klingebiel note that those countries experiencing systemic crises over the period 1960–94 had high and variable inflation rates, compared with price stability for other countries clear of banking difficulties.[60] Goldstein and Turner report that over the period 1980–95 high volatility in GDP growth and inflation was observed for some Latin American countries (Argentina, Brazil, Chile, Columbia, Mexico, and Venezuela), in contrast to the three largest industrial countries (the US, Japan, and Germany).[61] They observe also that those Latin American countries with fluctuating growth and inflation rates were also, in general, the ones with the most volatility in bank deposits and credit to the private sector expressed as a percentage of GDP. Gavin and Hausmann point out that, during the past two decades, inflation rates in some Latin American countries with banking sectors problems were much more volatile than were rates in industrial countries.[62]

High interest rates

Another shock associated with banking sector fragility and increasingly highlighted in the literature is high interest rates. It has been argued that an increase in short-term interest rates may reduce banks' profitability and even make them bear losses, as banks may be pushed to increase the interest paid on deposits (mainly of short-term maturity) before being able to adjust the interest rate charged on loans (mainly of a long-term and fixed-rate nature). It has also been argued that, even if these high rates are passed on to borrowers, high lending rates can make loan repayments more difficult for debtors and increase the share of loan losses at banks. High interest rates during high inflation may exacerbate the moral hazard and adverse selection problems inherent in bank lending.

As a reminder, Minsky argues that high and rising interest rates, induced by excess demand for funds and economic expansion (when investment opportunities present themselves), contribute to the fragility of the financial structure of a given economy.[63] The extent to which this structure becomes fragile depends on a combination of factors. These are related to (i) the weight of speculative and super-speculative finance involved in the total financial structure (direct relationship), (ii) the liquidity of the assets portfolio (inverse relationship) and (iii) the proportion of debt financing in undertaken investments (positive relationship). Once financial structure fragility and insolvency is in place, any shock to the economy (such as a sudden correction in asset prices) would lead to a crisis. This is true when the shock would initiate a situation in which assets are disposed of at a reduced price in a lean market, producing a further decline in asset prices. In Minsky's view, high interest rates drag hedge finance units into speculative and super-speculative units (Ponzi finance), where interest on debts exceeds net income receipts and cannot be serviced without recourse to increased debt. In other words, when the term to maturity of the liabilities of banks/thrift institutions is shorter than that of the assets, then a rise in interest rates increases cash payment commitments without increasing receipts. As these depository institutions have to continually refinance their positions (attract deposits) to meet withdrawals, this creates further difficulties to the extent that interest on cash flow commitments exceeds net income cash receipts, resulting in high vulnerability.

Thus, high domestic interest rates hurt banks not only by damaging their profit margins but also by influencing the quality of their assets portfolio. The severity of these implications depends once more on the term and structure of interest-sensitive assets and liabilities and bank capitalization levels, which should be sufficient to absorb possible losses. A sharp rise in interest rates reduces domestic liquidity as well and can lead to a steep fall in asset prices, which is considered a main contributor to banking sector problems. Against this background, there have been suggestions as part of preventive policy measures to reduce interest rates to ease pressure on banks, as low rates reduce the cost of funding and improve borrowers' creditworthiness. But, then again, a low interest rate environment can lead to rapid credit expansion and high inflation at a later stage, which could also pose a problem for banks, as is explained in elsewhere in this chapter. Demirguc-Kunt and Detragiache provide empirical evidence relating high real interest rates to the likelihood of having banking crises,[64] Hardy and Pazarbasioglu find that banking distress is correlated with rising real interest rates,[65] while Mishkin observes that most banking panics in the US were preceded by an increase in short-term interest rates.[66]

Many factors have been identified as sources for increases in short-term interest rates. Kaminsky and Reinhart mention the need to defend the exchange rate against a speculative attack on the currency as a source of short-term rises in interest rates.[67] Goldstein and Turner indicate that volatility in international interest rates not only affects the cost of borrowing for emerging markets—and increases adverse selection and moral hazard problems—but also alters the relative attractiveness in emerging markets (domestic rates increase with the increase in interest rates).[68] Thus the sharp increase in US interest rates in the early 1980s was considered one of the main culprits behind the Latin American debt crisis. Brock considers inflation stabilization policies to be one of the factors behind high real interest rates,[69] while Galbis observes that financial liberalization and the removal of interest rate control is one of the factors behind short-term interest rate rises.[70] Increases in the rate of inflation and restrictive monetary policies are also among the underlying causes. Some economists would argue, in addition, that weak or insolvent banking institutions could stand behind an increase in interest rates. Shoven et al associate the sharp and sudden increase in real interest rates in the US in the 1980s with the behavior of insolvent Savings and Loan Associations offering relatively high rates on certificates of deposits in competing for funds with treasury securities.[71]

Collapse in asset prices

Sharp negative changes in asset prices (real estate and stocks) following unsustainable asset price bubbles tend also to weaken the solvency and soundness of banks. A fall in asset prices is likely to impact negatively upon the value of the collateral underlying the loan and possibly the bank capital. Declines in stock prices can also hit banks, which are allowed to hold substantial equity positions in the firms to which they lend. The burst of the asset price bubble in Japan in the 1990s, with consequent repercussions for bank soundness, is an example of the negative effect of falling real equity prices. A collapse in asset prices can also raise fears and questions about the safety of banks, possibly encouraging bank runs.

Reinhart and Rogoff observe that house prices soared in the US prior to the onset of the global financial crisis in 2007, and that this is similar to what happened in previous episodes of banking crisis in advanced economies, such as Spain (in 1977), Norway (in 1987), Sweden (in 1991), Finland (in 1991), and Japan (in 1992).[72] Claessens et al argue also that such asset (housing) price bubbles in the US were coupled with a swift growth in credit and were experienced also by other economies hurt by the subprime mortgage crisis (including the UK and Iceland).[73] Dekle and Kletzer argue that loan collateral values declined before the crisis in Thailand, but not in Malaysia and Korea, where real estate values were stable and even rising before the East Asian financial crisis in 1997.[74] Hutchison and McDill find that sharp drops in asset prices increase the likelihood of an episode of banking distress;[75] similarly, Lindgren et al note that real estate price declines, or what is often referred to as the bursting of asset price bubbles, in Brazil, Chile, Indonesia, Mexico, the Nordic countries, the US, and Venezuela were behind banking sector problems in these countries, while Kaminsky and Reinhart[76] point out that sharp declines in equity prices are prime leading indicators of banking crises.[77] However, Mishkin finds equity price declines to be a contributor to financial crises, but not necessary a leading indicator of such events.[78] The BIS reports that over the past decade the volatility of equity prices in emerging economies has been much higher than that in large European industrial countries.[79] Goodhart argues that, of the main financial instability episodes that occurred since 1987, property price bubbles have had the most significant negative effects on real economies.[80]

External macroeconomic volatility

Large sudden changes in international interest rates, large capital inflows, and related credit boom–bust cycles

Large changes in international interest rates affect the cost and amount of foreign borrowing by local banks and the direction and size of private capital flows in general. This is particularly true with increasing market integration and globalization. Many studies have come up with empirical evidence associating the surge in private capital inflows to developing countries in the last four decades with movements in world interest rates.[81] Relatively low international interest rates or sustained declines in these rates tend to induce large capital inflows into emerging markets. International investors may be seeking higher yields and creditworthy domestic borrowers, from which domestic banks may wish to benefit by borrowing at relatively low offshore rates. Financial liberalization and government guarantees of either or both the exchange rate and bank foreign currency deposits, in addition to other factors, can also induce large capital inflows. In this respect, many researchers observe that government guarantees of foreign currency debt (deposits) in the event of devaluation accompany in general a pegged exchange rate regime.[82]

When these inflows are not completely sterilized they tend to increase bank liabilities quickly and drive banks accordingly to increase their lending to the domestic economy, mostly of low credit quality, extensively and in a very short time span. There are several reasons why large capital inflows cannot be allocated/channelled efficiently to creditworthy projects in a short span of time and why lending booms are otherwise associated with banks' assets of low quality. Gavin and Hausmann[83] and Tornell mention three.[84] The first is related to banks' limited capacity to assess and monitor projects; the second concerns both the limited capacity of regulatory institutions to monitor banks and the limited resources available to these regulatory institutions; and the third has to do with the limited number of creditworthy projects. Capital inflows therefore fuel lending and promote output growth, irrespective of domestic savings. There will also be a credit boom if banks are capable of attracting significant savings from domestic and offshore sources. Banking institutions will then be in trouble in a number of situations, resulting mainly in the deterioration of the quality of bank credit: first, when the investment boom and asset price bubble associated with the credit boom collapse; second, when there is exchange rate depreciation in the presence of a large currency mismatch in assets and liabilities of borrowers—that is, when loans are largely denominated in foreign currency while earnings are in the domestic currency; and, third, when the flow of foreign financing is curbed or when unexpectedly capital flows out, driven by a rise in international interest rates or the loss of confidence in the domestic currency or the banking sector. With a hike in world interest rates or a loss of confidence in domestic assets the cost of funds to domestic banks and corporations would rise and increases in interest rates could make adverse selection and moral hazard problems more severe, impacting banking sector stability.[85] Calvo and Reinhart advocate that capital inflow reversal or stoppage can initiate output contraction and severely hurt the financial sector.[86] A sudden withdrawal of bank deposits will also create liquidity problem for banks and force many to liquidate their assets at a relatively high cost, a process often referred to as a "fire sale" of bank assets. Because of the adverse effects of credit overexpansion or boom many have suggested tightening prudential liquidity requirements for banks to cut credit expansion. This may lead in some instances, however, to credit and output contraction. Other authors have suggested monetary policy interventions designed to reduce base money liquidity to banks and consequent credit overexpansion. Monetary tightening, however, may raise interest rates, which could again incite large capital inflows.[87] One could also argue for sterilization as a means to prevent capital inflows from contributing to credit booms and therefore to banking crises.

Irrespective of their origins or drivers, credit booms or fast and prolonged credit expansion characterized numerous episodes of financial unrest, many of which became crises. In this context, following the recent global financial crisis, many have pointed to the role of rapid credit expansion in initiating or aggravating the crisis, as credit booms tend to increase the leverage of borrowers, leading to excessive debt burdens, and are often associated with a decline in lending standards. The International Monetary Fund (IMF)[88] noted that household indebtedness rose sharply in the build-up to the subprime 2007 crisis, though aggregate credit expansion in the US was less noticeable than in past episodes mainly because of slower corporate credit growth. Claessens et al argued that the long-lasting credit increase in the US prior to the 2007–8 crisis is analogous to other experiences with the exception that it was concentrated in the subprime mortgage market and that mortgage-related household debt increased sharply after 2000 thanks to an environment of low interest rates and financial innovation.[89] The same authors note that the ratio of debt service to disposable income attained a record level and the heightened leverage made households susceptible to potential adverse developments such as a fall in housing prices, a retrenchment in credit conditions, and a deceleration in economic activity. They comment that a number of crisis countries exhibited similar patterns and that, in the cases of the UK, Spain, Iceland, and several eastern European countries, credit multiplied rapidly in the pre-crisis stage.[90]

A number of commentators have linked banking crises with lending booms and a strong growth of bank credit, among them Demirguc-Kunt and Detragiache,[91] Courinchas et al,[92] Honohan,[93] Sachs et al,[94] and Gavin and Hausmann.[95] Eichengreen and Rose find in a sample of developing countries that an increase in foreign (international) interest rates raises the probability of banking crises.[96] Krugman argues that, in the wake of their financial crisis, East Asian economies were characterized by over-lending and over-investment in risky projects driven by an over-guaranteed and poorly regulated financial system.[97]

Many studies, of which probably the most important are those of the IMF, BIS and the World Bank,[98] observed that the Asian financial crisis of 1997–8 followed a period of excessive capital inflows into many East Asian countries.[99] According to these studies, large net capital inflows led to very large expansions in credit to the domestic economy through banks and other financial intermediaries; Dekle and Kletzer discuss a strong link between capital inflow and lending for Korea, Malaysia, and Thailand as early as 1994.[100] The ability and capacity of these financial institutions to adequately assess and price the risks associated with the large increases in credit growth by properly screening borrowers was subjected to great stress in this environment of massive capital inflows. This could cause bad loans to increase in the future. The credit boom was also led in some of the Asian countries by the structure of the financial system and discriminatory regulation. Less regulated and supervised non-bank financial intermediaries (such as merchant banks in Korea) and non-bank financial institutions (such as finance companies in Thailand) were allowed to play an important role in the intermediation of incoming capital. This contributed to an increase in competitive pressure on banks and accentuated the credit risk exposure. Capital inflows into East Asian economies were twice as large as the current account deficits of these countries and averaged between 5 and 7 percent of their GDP a few years before the crisis. A large portion of these flows came in the form of bank foreign liabilities. The rest was in the form of portfolio equity and a little in the form of direct equity.

The above-mentioned studies and reports have stressed another important related point, that of international bank lending, as being the most important source or channel of these flows, the majority of which was placed or invested in domestic commercial banks and other financial intermediaries. Much of this short-term lending was extended in the local currency of Asian countries on the Asian interbank markets after being converted from its original denomination in Yen and US dollars to generate a higher spread. The large and sustained international borrowing by domestic (Asian) banks and other financial institutions was lent to domestic corporations in the absence of well-developed capital markets, leading to high leveraged ratios in the corporate sector, thus increasing financial vulnerability. Rising profits associated with large loan portfolios may blur the detection of increasing financial sector fragility during the early stages of a boom.[101] The banking sector exposure to the property or real estate sector was particularly high (between 25 and 40 percent of bank loans) in East Asian countries. The high variability of real estate prices in that region amplified existing risks. The World Bank observes that banking sector exposure to real estate is greater in countries with rates of credit growth exceeding GDP growth rates.[102]

Volatility of the exchange rate, the fixed exchange rate regime, and currency crises

A volatile exchange rate associated with a flexible exchange rate system can undermine banks' strength and soundness. The adverse effects on the banking sector could come through the trade sector, as large exchange rate appreciations may depress exports, at least in the short run, and cause exporting companies financial difficulties, particularly those unable to hedge their positions. Many would argue, however, that flexible exchange rates can be beneficial to banks' stability. Allowing the exchange rate to fluctuate increases the exchange rate risk, which would promote hedging and discourage banks from relying too much on external funding, thus limiting capital flows. Banks can therefore avoid problems related to large capital flows and the subsequent lending boom and excessive risk taking at banks, as discussed above. In addition, many researchers would argue that a flexible exchange rate regime would make room for a monetary policy aimed at stabilization. Therefore, the exchange rate and not the interest rate can be used to absorb adverse external shocks and stabilize output.

The literature also associates pegged exchange rates with banking crises. A fixed exchange rate may lead to surges in capital inflows, as it provides a kind of implicit guarantee against the risk of exchange rate changes. As such, a fixed exchange rate regime can encourage significant dependence on foreign capital, possibly resulting in a credit boom and associated low asset quality at banks. The adverse effects on banks could also result from widespread borrowing in foreign currency, as an unexpected devaluation/depreciation in the presence of a currency mismatch would make domestic currency denominated earnings finance less foreign currency denominated debt. This would apply to banks themselves and bank borrowers. Currency devaluation/depreciation can therefore reduce the creditworthiness of banks with respect to foreign lenders, and can also impair the ability of bank borrowers in foreign currency—whose main cash flow is in the domestic currency—to service foreign exchange denominated loans, thus contributing to the increase in non-performing loans at banks. This would seem to have been the case in Chile (1981), Mexico (1995), the Nordic countries (1990), and Turkey (1994). Under a fixed exchange rate regime borrowers also have much less incentive to hedge their foreign exchange positions.[103]

There could be, however, other reasons or incentives to undertake large-scale foreign borrowing. Goldstein and Hawkins mention four factors applicable to the case of Thailand:[104] much lower interest rates abroad; the belief that the risk of Baht devaluation is low following the long-run stability of the Baht against the dollar; the mandate to borrow abroad in foreign currency for special financial institutions (such as the Bangkok International Banking Facility (BIBF)); and, finally, the belief that the government will intervene to prevent banks failing. Foreign funding is also sensitive to world interest rate shocks. Large-scale foreign exchange exposure characterized the run-up to the recent East Asia turmoil, where many countries in that region did not impose stringent restrictions on foreign borrowing. Even if banks were limited in the amount of foreign exchange exposure they could assume, bank borrowers could still expose themselves to a large exchange rate risk. Therefore, both the banking and corporate sectors were significantly exposed to foreign exchange risks in East Asia. This is especially true when the currency mismatch between the liabilities and assets of either banks or the corporate sector is particularly large. Sudden changes in the fixed or pegged exchange rate (currency devaluation, as happened in the East Asian crisis and in Argentina) can also create difficulties, among which are massive capital outflows undertaken by resident and non-resident investors. Capital outflows can even occur before the devaluation.

There is also an opposing view contending that pegged exchange rates help to maintain banking system stability. Fixed exchange rates constrain expansionary aggregate demand policies and thus lending boom-related problems for fear of jeopardizing the peg and depleting international reserves. In such a situation the central bank needs to have policies consistent with the exchange rate peg, and therefore needs to limit the injection of liquidity to the economy aiming, for example, at supporting banks. Otherwise confidence in the currency peg would be undermined, potentially pressuring the exchange rate. A fixed exchange rate regime can therefore discipline policy-makers and reduce the probability of policy-related banking crises.[105] However, this would also constrain lender of last resort operations, the lack of which could encourage bank runs and panics. There are also other views on how a fixed exchange rate regime can help in reducing the possibility of a banking crisis. Velasco and Cespedes and Calvo[106] see that debt or liability dollarized borrowers present a good case for the adoption of a pegged exchange rate as a nominal currency depreciation can hurt debtors and cause non-performing loans to rise at banks. Domac and Martinez-Peria find, for a sample of eighty-eight developing countries, that fixed exchange rate regimes are correlated with lower probability of crises but with higher costs if a crisis occurs.[107]

The debate over which exchange rate system is better in terms of banking stability extends to the link between currency and banking crises. Attacks on the exchange rate can be a problem for a weak banking sector if the government decides to defend its currency and increase interest rates.[108] Stocker argues that an external shock, such as an increase in foreign interest rates, will result in capital outflows and the loss of international reserves under a commitment to fixed exchange rate parity.[109] If this loss is not sterilized, credit crunch, increased insolvencies, and financial crises will ensue. Velasco provides an explanation for a contrasting causal relationship, running from financial sector problems to currency crises.[110] In this and similar models, currency crises are induced by excessive money creation caused by central bank decisions to bail out financial institutions in trouble. Other models have pointed to the role of exchange rate-based inflation stabilization programs or plans in causing both currency and banking crises. When instituting such a plan there will be a cumulative real exchange rate appreciation as inflation converges to international levels only gradually. Because of the real exchange rate appreciation, there will also be a boom in imports and output financed largely by foreign borrowed funds prompted by the reduced exchange rate risk. This would widen the current account deficit to the point where investors would see that this exchange rate stabilization plan is no longer sustainable, and would start attacking the domestic currency. Under these circumstances capital inflows intermediated largely by banks could become capital outflows and asset markets would tumble, implying banking system instability and failure.

Real exchange rate appreciation

Real exchange rate appreciation, implying a deterioration in international competitiveness, is often cited as one of the developments characterizing the pre-crisis period. It squeezes profit margins or the profitability of tradable sectors and can therefore leave some bank customers unable to repay their debt, suggesting a rise in non-performing loans and banking sector problems. Real exchange rate appreciation also affects the financial position of bank customers through high domestic real interest rates, often associated with the appreciation in the real exchange rate, as they incite locals to borrow in foreign currencies.[111] This would mean more exposure to the exchange rate risk and more trouble for banks, particularly if the currency mismatch is large. It has been mentioned repeatedly in this chapter that currency mismatches expose banks to unanticipated exchange rate movements. Even if foreign currency positions of banks are hedged they can still face problems if their borrowers are unhedged against devaluation. There are many possible reasons for the real exchange rate appreciation, among which are productivity shocks, preference changes, and shifts in economic policies. In fact, an exchange rate-based inflation stabilization plan often leads to real exchange rate appreciation, as has been theoretically and empirically proven.

Kaminsky and Reinhart observe that banking crises are typically preceded by a pronounced real exchange rate appreciation.[112] Gavin and Hausmann point that over the past twenty years the volatility of real exchange rates (in terms of standard deviation of changes) of twenty-two Latin American developing countries has been higher than that of industrial countries (by about two fold).[113]

Unexpected large shifts in the terms of trade

One potential source of banking sector distress is unexpected large shifts or fluctuations in the terms of trade. When the terms of trade (the ratio of export prices to import prices) shifts in favor of foreign countries and against domestic firms, the ability of commodity exporters to service their debts is likely to be impaired because their profitability is likely to be adversely affected. The deterioration of the terms of trade can therefore increase the loan loss portfolio at banks, particularly when depository institutions devote a large share of their loan portfolio to firms in the export sector. In general, large countries capable of maintaining export diversification at high levels are less vulnerable to terms of trade shocks. Conversely, small countries with high export concentration are on average more susceptible to shocks to the terms of trade that could affect the stability of their banking sectors.[114]

Borensztein and Lee mention that terms of trade shocks severely affected the Korean economy before its financial crisis, as exports were concentrated in a few products.[115] Milesi-Ferretti and Razin identify the deterioration of the terms of trade as one of the variables preceding banking crises in a panel of countries,[116] while Hardy and Pazarbasioglu, similarly, find evidence of banking sector distress being associated with adverse trade shocks.[117] Caprio and Klingebiel observe, in studying developing countries with significant banking sector problems, that around three-quarters of these crises were preceded by a fall of not less than 10 percent in the terms of trade.[118] Gavin and Hausmann conclude, in calculating the standard deviation of changes in the terms of trade over the past two decades for a sample of countries, that this deviation from the mean in Latin American countries is nearly on average twice that in industrial countries.[119] Lindgren et al discover, in studying a sample comprising thirty-four countries that have recently experienced significant banking industry fragility, that shifts in the terms of trade have been partly behind banking difficulties in many countries,[120] including Chile, Malaysia, some Eastern and Central European countries, the Baltic region, and the former Soviet Union states. Kaminsky and Reinhart observe that a deterioration of the terms of trade precedes banking crises in small industrial economies and emerging markets.[121]

Global imbalances

In the wake of the global financial crisis of 2007–8 many economists and policy-makers argued that global or external imbalances (large current account imbalances) were to blame in fuelling the financial crisis. This led to the appearance of several studies that attempted to test this hypothesis. Taylor finds a weak association between global imbalances and financial distress relative to financial system variables or predictors of crises.[122]

Unfavorable economic policy changes and reforms

Sharp shifts in monetary and fiscal policies

Many economists have cited shifts from sharp expansionary monetary and fiscal policies to sharp contractionary policies as one of the main reasons behind financial (banking) crises.[123] The rationale is that expansionary monetary and fiscal policies stimulate a credit boom that increases asset prices, notably those of securities and real estate. Sooner or later it becomes necessary to fight the resulting inflation and tighten monetary policy, thus piercing the asset price bubble by making it hard for borrowers to refinance their positions or settle their outstanding debt at higher interest rates. In this changing environment real estate buyers and developers and securities traders who borrowed significant amounts from banks find themselves less able to honour their debt, potentially increasing non-performing loans at banks. In response both to this development and to declining equity and real estate prices and their underlying collateral, banks may reduce their lending activity. This would tighten credit further and reduce more property and securities prices.[124]

As such, a very loose monetary policy could give the go-ahead for rapid expansion of credit by banks, potentially to sectors perceived as being high risk, a process which is often associated with asset price bubbles and inflation—the seed of any potential future banking problems. Easy monetary conditions may also lay the ground for volatile interest rates. On the other hand, a much tightened monetary policy, often used to offset unrestrained fiscal imbalances, increases interest rates and slows economic growth and output, affecting the solvency and liquidity of banks.

Many authors argue that the Savings and Loan crisis in the US was activated by a US monetary contraction policy adopted from 1979. The underlying vulnerability was inherent in the charter of these institutions, which were permitted to operate through extending fixed-rate, long-term residential mortgages against accepting short-term saving deposits subject to regulation Q, which fixed deposit rates to prevent inter-bank interest rate war. Many economists have also argued that the Savings and Loan crisis involved private and public corruption as well, encompassing inadequate accounting practices and provisioning; incompetent, uncontrolled risk-taking and greedy management; regulatory and supervisory forbearance; and political interference.[125]

Policy measures or the deregulation of Savings and Loan undertaken after the initial crisis even exacerbated the problem, rather than mitigating it. The Depository Institutions Deregulation and Monetary Control Act of 1980 and the Depository Institutions Act of 1982—which, among other things, phased out regulation Q—lifted interest rate ceilings on deposits and allowed Savings and Loan to diversify their products and offer variable rate mortgages. However, this deregulation meant for some already insolvent institutions a renewed opportunity to venture again into high-risk projects, but this time armed with the presence of a safety net (lender of last resort and deposit insurance where the new legislation raised the deposit insurance ceiling from US $40,000 to US$100,000) and inefficient supervision. Unfortunately many of these gambles failed and the consequences were great. By mid-1983 additional losses of these institutions were estimated at around US$140 billion.

The Savings and Loan crisis can be compared with that of 2007–8. One can safely say that the global financial crisis of 2007–8 followed a mortgage credit boom associated with rising housing prices many years prior to the crisis. What started and amplified this trend is still a matter of controversy, although it appears that there is some consensus, to varying degrees, on the roles played by homeownership-encouraging government policies; expansionary monetary policies; global imbalances; financial innovation, particularly asset securitization; insufficient regulation and oversight; lenient lending conditions and practices; and attempts to circumvent constraining regulations. All these potential drivers and causes of the crisis are explained in the relevant sections of this chapter, but it is worth mentioning here the blame related to pursuing expansionary monetary policy. Taylor describes how low interest rate decisions by the Fed deviated from the norm (were off the track), arguing that monetary policy was too easy in the period before the crisis.[126] He showed that monetary excesses, or the ultra easy policy, were the main cause of the mortgage credit boom and the resulting bust.

Subsequent to the bursting of the asset price bubble, losses and risks started to spread in the bust period and were difficult to identify and quantify because of the complexity and opacity of certain mortgage-related financial instruments (that is, the asset securitization process). Financial institutions ceased trusting each other and a confidence crisis among market participants erupted that adversely affected the financial system's liquidity. This drove concerned authorities to intervene by, among other things, injecting liquidity into banks and reducing interest rates to a record low.[127]

Unfavorable economic measures and government policies

Unfavorable economic measures include unfavorable tax, exchange rate, and stabilization policies. Potential banking problems are identified with certain tax systems or schemes. Certainly swift, substantial, and poorly thought-out changes in tax rates can affect, directly or indirectly, commodity or asset prices, personal income, and the economic conditions of many sectors.[128] Lindgren et al contend that taxes on bank-provided financial services and transactions place an additional burden on banks and reduce their attractiveness as depository institutions in addition to harming their role in the economy.[129] According to the same authors, banks' soundness may suffer from tax systems that do not allow banks to deduct loan loss provisions from their interest income. This discourages banks from recognizing in a timely manner loan losses on their books, thus further concealing such problems. In addition, systems that do not permit loan losses provision deductions or that include interest accrued on non-performing assets in the bank interest income effectively tax unrealized or non-occurring profit and put more pressure on banks' capital and reserves.

Inadequate exchange rate policies are also blamed for contributing to the deterioration of banks' balance sheets. A prolonged over-valuation of the exchange rate induced by domestic exchange rate policies is damaging to export-dependent sectors, while a prolonged under-valuation harms import-dependent sectors. Many would also point to exchange rate policy effects on the balance of payments, noting that certain policies associated with political uncertainties could bring about capital flight and bank runs.[130] In the case of an exchange rate peg policy, market forces may, at a certain stage and under rising future uncertainty, pressure heavily for the return to a more flexible exchange rate, entailing devaluation. As the expectation of a foreseeable devaluation gains ground, depositors may start redenominating their portfolios in foreign currency or transferring a part or the whole abroad, thus creating a liquidity and solvency problem for banks.

Gavin and Hausmann blame exchange rate pegs and fixed exchange rate regimes for macroeconomic imbalances and associated banking problems.[131] They contend that, more than any other factor, unsustainable exchange rate pegs in Latin American countries have contributed to sharp fluctuations in the GDP growth over the last two decades. They argue also that, under fixed rates regimes, antagonistic shocks will lead to a situation of deficit in the balance of payment, a decrease in the money supply, and an increase in interest rates. Inflexible exchange rates or exchange rate pegs may also contribute to worsening the quality of asset portfolios by encouraging borrowers to ignore exchange rate risk. The potential adverse effects of an exchange rate peg on the stability of the banking system have been detailed previously.

The shift towards a stabilization anti-inflationary policy entails a threat to banks' soundness as well. Garcia observes that macroeconomic stabilization preceded episodes of banking sector weaknesses in many countries, including Chile, Malaysia, and Finland.[132] One of the reasons given is that banks lost income related to inflation tax with all its impact on banks' profitability. It was a question of readjustment to the new reality after banks had successfully adjusted their operations and income to a high-inflation environment. Lindgren et al attribute banking sector problems in twenty-one studied countries (out of their thirty-four-country sample), including Brazil and former Soviet Union states, to a significant reduction in the rate of inflation.[133]

As for unfavorable government policies, it has been noted by many researchers and academics that the US subprime mortgage crisis of 2007 resulted from, among other factors, vigorous government policy pursued over several years aiming at increasing home ownership. Government actions were part of the problem in the sense that government-sponsored agencies such as Fannie Mae and Freddie Mac were strongly supported and incited to grow through their involvement in asset-backed securities, particularly those related to risky subprime mortgages. Earlier, Herring and Wachter had argued that government-subsidized policies have often generated real estate booms resulting in banking crises.[134]

Financial liberalization

Many countries (developing and developed) started as early as the 1970s to liberalize and deregulate their financial systems. The move aimed at reducing direct government intervention in the economy, forcing banks to fund government fiscal imbalances and subsidize priority sectors at low and negative real interest rates, in the belief that this liberalization would promote financial development and economic growth. McKinnon and Shaw argue that "financial repression," created by the government when forcing banks and other financial institutions to acquire funds at low and negative real interest rates, decreases the availability of resources to finance investment as it reduces domestic savings.[135] This would hold provided that there are small foreign capital inflows and the relationship between real interest rates and savings is strong, and would suggest, therefore, a relationship between financial liberalization, domestic savings, and growth. King and Levine advocate that financial liberalization as it promotes financial development can stimulate economic growth by accelerating productivity growth.[136]

Opposing these positive views, other studies have associated financial liberalization with financial fragility and crises that tend to surface a few years after liberalization begins. It is often argued that liberalization and deregulation processes can generate lending booms and asset price bubbles and are likely to breed a financial or banking crisis.[137] This applies particularly to countries with weak or poorly developed institutional environments mainly characterized by ineffective prudential regulation and supervision of financial intermediaries, and ineffective contract and regulations enforcement mechanisms. Ranciere et al point also to credit booms and asset price bubbles caused by large capital inflows as a consequence of capital account liberalization.[138] Therefore, positive and negative views and opinions of financial liberalization have been documented. Furthermore, the connection between financial development and economic growth, on one side, and financial development and financial fragility, on the other, has been highly debatable. The interest here, however, is solely in investigating the relationship between financial liberalization and banking sector problems and crises.

As countries began to liberalize and deregulate their financial system, bank interest rate ceilings, foreign financial entry barriers, and government interference in credit allocation decisions were lifted or eased. Financial liberalization also took the form of the lowering of compulsory reserve requirements at banks and the privatization of many depository and insurance institutions. This would suggest many mechanisms through which financial liberalization may increase banking sector problems, as it drives banks to assume, in general, more risk.[139] A number of conditions heighten the risk element. First, easier access for local banks to new domestic and foreign markets and sectors allows banks to over-lend to a given sector, firm, individual, or risky borrower, as interest rates are now market-determined. Previously banks could not charge a high or market-determined risk premium to high-risk customers, which would have affected their risk/return trade-off and probably induced them to better diversify their portfolios and/or reduce the extension of such risky loans. Second, domestic banks became involved in new risky activities such as derivatives' contracts.[140] Third, competition increased with the lifting of barriers to entry and the removal of ceilings on deposit interest rates. Increased bank competition erodes banks' franchise value (as it constrains monopolistic profits) and contributes to moral hazard and increased risk taking.[141] Fourth, non-trained bank staff have insufficient necessary skills and experience to evaluate and monitor the risk of a bank loan portfolio and manage interest rate risk in this new, less regulated financial system. This is particularly true for banks that have been carrying out one or two activities for years in a very secure environment, such as lending mainly to central government and government-related entities. It is also true for staff not accustomed to interest rates that are likely to be volatile and changing compared with previous fixed rates.

In a nutshell, financial liberalization increases the opportunity for banks to take on additional risks unless alternative effective prudential regulation and supervision is established to prevent this happening. Caprio and Summers and Stiglitz argue that in developing countries some degree of financial regulation is preferable to premature liberalization.[142] It is important to mention, in addition, that it is possible to classify the removal or reduction of controls on international capital movements as financial liberalization (of the capital account). In such circumstances domestic banks may increase risk taking on two fronts. Banks may become exposed to foreign exchange risk by raising foreign currency funds on international markets and more exposed to credit risk by lending those funds to domestic borrowers and intermediating large capital inflows. Studies on capital controls have indicated that their use can be general or selective, inherited from the long past or newly used as a tool for macroeconomic policy purposes.[143] Some would also suggest that controls on capital outflows are more common than controls on inflows.

In describing the mechanism through which the financial crisis in East Asia occurred, Mishkin argues that financial liberalization that lifted interest rate ceilings and the restrictions on the allowed types of lending caused a lending boom, which was supplied by capital inflows.[144] According to Mishkin, excessive risk taking by banks was the result for two reasons. First, there was a lack of expertise in managing risk and banking institutions were unable to acquire well-trained loan officers and risk assessment systems fast enough to manage risk in this new lending environment. Second, there was an implicit safety net that created a moral hazard problem and gave banks an incentive to take on excessive risk. Demirguc-Kunt and Detragiache find, after studying a large data set covering fifty-three developed and developing economies during the period 1980–95, that there is some equivocal evidence that financial liberalization exerts an independent negative effect on the stability of the banking sector.[145] Sundararajan and Balino note, in studying a sample of seven countries (Argentina, Chile, Uruguay, the Philippines, Thailand, Spain, and Malaysia), that the timing and intensity of banking crises and the timing and scope of financial sector reforms varied considerably among the sample countries.[146] They also point out the presence of a lag period between the initiation of the liberalization process and the emergence of banking sector fragility. Also observed is that, during the stage of transition from the old system to the new one particularly, both interest rates and the rate of growth in credits tend to rise. Keely finds a positive correlation among financial deregulation, increased competition and reduction in franchise value of banks, and a rise in the number of bank failures during the 1980s in the US.[147] Diaz Alejandro mentions that banking sector problems in Chile in 1981 followed shortly upon financial sector deregulation.[148] Laeven argues that the period after 1970, during which many countries liberalized their financial markets and capital accounts, has been unmatched in terms of the occurrence and acuteness of banking crises.[149]

The government safety net

All governments establish at least one form of safety net to safeguard the banking system by protecting bank depositors and preventing bank panics. There are many ways in which domestic governments provide a financial safety net for bank depositors. One form is explicit deposit insurance, where in cases of bank failure depositors are paid back a certain amount of funds they have deposited in a bank. Fully insured depositors may thus lack the incentive to run to banks to make withdrawals in times of panic. Another form of safety net is the government's readiness to maintain financial system stability through the lender of last resort facility or by taking over troubled institutions and restoring the public's confidence in the banking system. Being the lender of last resort, central banks may stand ready to lend directly to financial institutions in trouble or to inject liquidity into the financial system through their open market operations. The government may also interfere directly (not through a lender of last resort function) to provide financial support to ailing banks. Governments may also support selected large banks through the too-big-to-fail policy, where governments guarantee insured depositors, uninsured depositors, and other creditors of these banks to prevent the occurrence of a major financial disruption.

It is argued in the literature that this can be a mixed blessing, as the safety net can also increase moral hazard incentives and adverse selection problems, thus harming banking sector stability. Inadequate or underpriced deposit insurance and bank bailouts can increase moral hazard and encourage banks to take excessive risks that may lead to a crisis.[150] Mishkin argues, for example, that because depositors know that their deposits are guaranteed in case of bank failure they tend not to impose market discipline on banks (through withdrawing deposits) when banks take too much risk.[151] It follows that, in the presence of a safety net, banks have an incentive to take on greater risks. For Mishkin, too, risk-taker entrepreneurs might like to take advantage of the provided insurance to depositors and the unwillingness of depositors to impose discipline on the bank to enter the banking industry and engage in highly risky activities. Many would argue also that the too-big-to-fail policy increases moral hazard incentives for banks, as uninsured depositors and other creditors have no incentive to monitor big banks in the presence of such a government guarantee. Large banks may therefore take larger risks than smaller ones, which could make bank failures more likely. Rossi finds for fifteen countries that a bank safety net is positively correlated with bank fragility.[152] Boyd and Gertler provide evidence that large banks in the US have riskier assets (loans) than smaller banks, causing large loan losses for big banks.[153] In what follows we elaborate on the role of deposit insurance.

Deposit Insurance

Following the Great Depression and in order to prevent future bank runs the US established in 1934 its national bank deposits insurance system. Many studies that surveyed deposit insurance around the world, such as those of Kyei, Garcia, and Demirguc-Kunt and Detragiache, agree that the establishment of deposit insurance schemes outside the US started only after World War II and spread particularly during the 1980s and 1990s.[154] Despite its stated benefits in terms of reducing or preventing depositor runs and lowering the cost of funds for banks, deposit insurance can be, under a number of circumstances, a source of moral hazard that encourages banks to finance high-risk projects, potentially leading to systemic banking problems and crises. The arguments for and against deposit insurance remain at present a matter of controversy among academics and policy-makers.

Deposit insurance may increase bank stability by reducing runs on deposits, but may also decrease this stability by encouraging risk taking by banks. Many authors argue that deposit insurance reduces the incentive of depositors to monitor banks' behavior, while others question the desirability and efficacy of depositors' monitoring banks.[155] This could be a valid argument given that deposit insurance is only partial and is usually not honoured at once or upon the desire of depositors. The design features or the nature of such an insurance scheme clearly play an important role in this respect. These features might include limits on the size and nature of covered deposits (whether there are ceilings on the amount covered and whether foreign currency and interbank deposits are covered), premiums paid by banks, and the ownership and management of the deposit insurance scheme. The above statement suggests also the need to have the necessary regulation and supervision to offset the moral hazard problem and the risk taking potential inherent in such schemes as a result of the false sense of security that they provide.

In addition, it is not always clear whether the absence of explicit deposit insurance can prevent risk taking by banks, as there could in some countries be implicit deposit insurance—that is, the government rescues depositors affected by bank failure, or banks are not allowed to fail. The government in many East Asian countries has implicitly guaranteed bank deposits.[156] This made many economists question the added value for countries with formal system of deposit insurance as, in the event of a banking crisis, there will nevertheless be a government bailout or rescue plan. Crises occur in countries both with and without explicit deposit insurance schemes.

Nevertheless, there has been voices calling for a limiting of the extent of coverage of deposits as a means to avoid or reduce the risk incentive related to deposit insurance.[157] Many would advocate also that the moral hazard problem and risk taking could be restrained through adequate prudential regulation and supervision. The World Bank also reviews key issues in deposit insurance design:[158] one suggestion is to limit deposit coverage to one or two times per capita GDP to protect small depositors. Another is to keep the deposit insurance scheme or corporation unfunded to encourage market discipline, but at the same time allow the scheme to have access to funds. A third is to involve the private sector in the management and administration of the deposit insurance company and to enhance market discipline.[159]

Demirguc-Kunt and Detragiache conclude, from an examination of a large panel of countries, that explicit deposit insurance increases the possibility of banking crisis, particularly where bank interest rates are deregulated and the regulatory and supervisory institutional environment is weak.[160] The same authors find also that the correlation between deposit insurance and bank instability tend to increase (i) the higher the fund coverage to depositors and (ii) where the scheme is funded and run by the government. Rossi finds for a sample of fifteen countries that a higher probability of banking crisis is correlated with the level or coverage extent of the safety net, including deposit insurance.[161] Folkerts-Landau and Lindgren mention that the IMF, in its code of practice, supports a limited form of deposit insurance.[162] Kane attributes the US Savings and Loan crisis of the 1980s to the moral hazard created by the deposit insurance, with significant coverage alongside financial liberalization and a weak regulatory framework.[163] Matutes and Vives conclude that explicit deposit insurance has uncertain and undefined welfare effects.[164]

The structure of the banking system and government ownership of banks

The concentration or domination of state-owned banks in a given banking system constitutes a reason for additional concern about the safety and soundness of that system. The rationale is that these banks have traditionally been considered inefficient, overstaffed and non-profit-driven. In addition, their activities are often dictated or influenced by the political objectives and personal interests of those in the public sector and therefore borrowers' creditworthiness plays only a minor role in the credit decision.[165] That is to say, many of these loans would become non-performing. State-owned banks have also fewer incentives to innovate, identify early problem loans, and manage efficiently their cost, as losses are covered by the government. In addition, government-owned banks are not usually monitored by either the public or the private sector.

Contrasting with this view are the many proponents of government ownership of banks on the basis that government can better allocate resources, particularly when bank institutions are not well developed.[166] According to this line of thinking, privately owned banks become involved in "gambling" activities and their actions result in limited access to credit for many sectors and excessive credit concentration. Though large waves of bank privatization have taken place since the 1990s, relatively recent studies show that government ownership or control of banks remains considerable and the market share of these state banks remains substantial. Caprio and Martinez-Peria report for a sample of sixty-four countries that the average share of assets of the top ten banks owned or controlled by the government was still high (33 percent) in 1995, although down from a much higher share (51 percent) in 1970.[167]

There is little empirical evidence for the impact of public (state) ownership of banks on the likelihood of banking crises. There is also little evidence relating to the link between publicly owned banks and financial development, on the one hand, and efficient credit allocation on the other. La Porta et al find that greater government ownership of banks is correlated with slower financial development.[168] Caprio and Martinez-Peria find that the probability of a banking crisis is larger in those countries where the share of bank assets owned by the government is larger than 50 percent.[169] Finding that large-scale public ownership of banks tends to increase the likelihood of banking crises, these authors have suggested a lesser ownership role but a greater role in financial infrastructure and regulation to stimulate financial development and lessen the probability of a banking crisis. Barth et al find no significant effects on banking system stability, but find on average that the larger the share of bank assets controlled by state-owned banks, the lower the level of financial development.[170] Borensztein and Lee investigate whether the financial system in Korea has allocated credit in an efficient way over the last thirty years,[171] finding no evidence that credit flows were directed to relatively more profitable sectors. BIS reports that non-performing loans in countries in which state-owned banks dominate financial intermediation, such as China, India, and Indonesia, have been particularly onerous.[172] Goldstein and Turner make the same observation of Argentina, where one-third of total loans in Argentina's public banks were non-performing at the end of 1994, compared with 10 percent for private banks.[173] It should be noted, however, that there could be reverse causality at work here, in which banking crises cause government ownership of banks as governments respond to banking crises by acquiring the assets of failing banking institutions.

In general, and irrespective of the nature of bank ownership, the higher the level of outside interference in bank affairs the more likely bank profitability and solvency will be at risk and the higher the cost for the government will subsequently be. Such interference could range from directing or underutilizing credits at preferential lending rates—as an instrument for particular sector policy objectives—to obliging banks to hold a substantial amount of bills and bonds at below market interest rates. During periods of financial reform (financial liberalization and deregulation) there also exists the possibility of replacing explicit government interventions with implicit ones. Close relationships among government, banks, and big firms may still allow the government to influence in one way or another credit allocation to priority favored sectors or corporations. "Crony" capitalism—in which the interests of banking institutions, large companies, and political leaders become mixed together—is also associated with banking crises. To Corsetti et al crony capitalism was a characteristic of Korea, Indonesia, Malaysia, and Thailand before the onset of their crises.[174] On the size of government interference and participation in banking activities in many countries, Folkerts-Landau et al mention that in Korea, Malaysia, Indonesia, Thailand, and the Philippines banks were required and even forced to allocate a certain share of their loan portfolios to particular sectors.[175] A survey of 129 countries carried out by the Basle Committee on Banking Supervision[176] reveals that in half the surveyed countries the state participated to a considerable degree in bank capital.

Other structural factors, such as bank specialization, activity restrictions, and strategic preference, could also induce banking weaknesses. The literature in this area has emphasised that the likelihood of experiencing fragility and fail is particularly high for banks that focus their activities on a specific industry or a selected group of clients. Conversely, in countries where the separation between banks and industry is quite well established, in the sense that banking is not under the influence of just one specific industry or group of clients, the probability of such a development is much less. This would suggest that some of the causes of banking weakness are inherent in banks' behavior itself and in the restrictions imposed on banks regarding what they may do and where.

Extending large credits to individual corporations and being dependent on particular companies at the expense of decentralizing the risk via a greater number of smaller credits could be a strategic preference for some banks. In the wake of the Korean financial crisis, for example, the Chaebols (large conglomerates) dominated credit allocation. This makes banks more vulnerable to distress when production and markets turn down. The systemic problem is then judged according to the size and market share of affected institutions. There are times, however, when risk centralization is not a strategic preference. Constraining banks' ability to diversify geographically and by sector could make these institutions more prone to shocks than their less regulated counterparts elsewhere, not to mention that the prohibition of certain activities could also impede banks' ability to evolve and adapt to change. But it is true also that the combination of many economic activities (commercial and investment) and banks' involvement in highly leveraged transactions could also be a major source of banking fragility. It could be, then, that over-diversification, in the sense of high exposure to diverse sophisticated risky financial instruments and contracts, is as bad as under-diversification, and that would depend again on how one would define the optimal degree of diversification.

In addition to all that, many believe that there are country-specific structures with features that tend to reduce asymmetric information problems and other problems related to the debt contract between the bank and its borrower.[177] One of the features that tends to reduce the risk element is the ability of banks to hold equity stakes in corporations and have representatives on their boards. This provides information, risk sharing and bank loan finance to companies, as it promotes close business ties between financial institutions and industry through supervisory boards. Many authors, however, challenge the importance of such a channel in reducing asymmetric information problems and increasing bank financed indebtedness for companies. Instead they argue for increasing risk for banks if they hold debt and equity in the same firm, not to mention the possible issue of conflicts of interest. Davis, for example, argues also that corporate cross holding of equity may not be particularly important, as it is unclear whether supervisory boards have the necessary information to assist in closely assessing the activity of the management board, and most large firms deal with many banks, rather than just one.[178]

Poor and inadequate bank management, regulation, and supervision

Poor management and internal governance

Imprudent or poor managerial practices, often induced by inadequate regulation and supervision, are given a considerable weight in the literature on the origins of banking weaknesses and problems. A survey on "bank failure" issued by the Office of the Comptroller of the Currency of the US in 1988 accuses banks' management practices of being the common factor behind the poor asset quality in banks that failed during the period 1979–87. De Juan also emphasizes the microeconomic causes of banking crisis,[179] identifying poor management as an important source of banks' illiquidity and insolvency. To De Juan, poor management encompasses, first, the over-extension of lending relative to the bank's equity or deposit base, domestically and abroad; second, over-diversification of products to include sophisticated risky instruments and contracts; third, rapid balance sheet growth through aggressive lending with less stringent criteria or through aggressive, highly remunerated deposit collecting; fourth, poor lending manifested by loan concentration in a small number of borrowers or a given segment of the economy, in addition to connected lending and term/currency mismatching; fifth, poor internal controls, such as poor credit valuation and follow-up systems, internal audit mechanisms, and management information systems; sixth, poor disclosure, comprising the hiding of the truth from the public and the supervisors by means of inadequate provisioning and reporting on loan losses and other practices; and seventh, diverse fraudulent activity. De Juan argues also that banking problems would have been avoided or reduced in intensity had the regulatory authority set the appropriate limit on these above-mentioned practices and the supervisory authority put in place the appropriate mechanisms to ensure full and timely compliance with established regulations.

But it could be argued that even if regulation is very effective, and supervision is forceful and farsighted, problems related to bank-specific factors would still exist. This is the case with, for example, "evergreens," when doubtful loans are rolled over or refinanced by new credit and classified as current in order to hide bad debt. It is also the case with insider lending (loans extended to bank owners and managers) or lending to related parties (subsidiaries) because in related lending on preferential terms the people or entities involved are disposed to be reluctant in servicing their loans, and, where objectivity in assessing credit risk is almost absent, the rise of non-performing loans would become more problematic. Though prudential practices limit and constrain insider lending or lending to related parties in most countries, such practices may still take place through complex off-balance-sheet activities and offshore transactions. They may also take place under fictitious names and dummy accounts that makes it both hard to trace these loans and easier to hide losses.[180] If connected lending is done on a large scale then the failure of a group of large borrowers can erode a bank's capital. Related lending—that is, bank loans to firms controlled by the bank's owners— has received some attention in the banking literature. Lindgren et al, Sheng, De Juan, Sanhueza, Laeven, and La Porta et al provide evidence associating connected lending with large loan losses and banking problems in Argentina, Brazil, Mexico, Chile, Spain, Russia, Bangladesh, Indonesia, Malaysia, and Thailand.[181] La Porta et al conclude for Mexico that related lending is a manifestation of looting and does not enhance information sharing.[182]

This would suggest, therefore, that poor internal governance of banks,[183] including the misuse of bank resources, is one of the culprits behind banking sector problems. Poor internal governance also includes (i) the inability or unwillingness to set appropriate rules, procedures, and policies for controlling risk and minimizing the organizational hazards, (ii) the absence of adequate incentives for directors and managers to operate the bank in a safe or sound manner, and (iii) the willingness of owners/managers to hide problems.[184]

Fraudulent activities have also been at the origin of many bank collapses, some of which ended in banking crises.[185] Examples of bank fraud, especially at important systemic banks, are many. Laeven mentions that in the two bank swindle cases of Venezuela in 1994 and the Dominican Republic in 2003 insiders diverted depositor funds at systemically important banks and that the fraud-related closure of Bank of Credit and Commerce International had a widespread effect in some African countries where it had a substantial presence.[186] More recent large bank losses ascribed to fraud are many, among which the case of the French bank Societe Generale in 2008 is notable.

Accounting fraud could also play a part in the failure of banking institutions. A recent example is that of the US investment bank Lehman Brothers, which filed for bankruptcy in 2008. It is widely believed that its breakdown distressed international banking markets because of the large exposures of many banks to Lehman and the fear of market players that other banks might have been involved in similar accounting or management misbehavior. The firm was accused of overstating its value by utilizing repurchase agreements to temporarily remove securities from its balance sheet at each record date.

Inadequate bank regulation

In this chapter bank regulation is defined as the set of laws, decrees, and rules that govern the entry/exit of banks and the scope and scale of their activities. For each country, some of this regulation is established in the law while the rest is delegated to an administrative authority (such as the central bank), which issues rules and decrees as needed in line with changing circumstances. Bank regulations establish the supervisory authority that oversees and controls the behavior of depository institutions.

To strengthen internal governance, adequate prudential regulations are essential. These could involve forcing banks to comply with international capital, loan classification, and accounting standards. Regulations dealing with appropriate disclosure rules and provisioning for non-performing loans should also be in place. The same applies to regulations restricting foreign exchange exposure and insider lending. Regulators should also properly design entry and licensing rules and procedures to ensure, first, that domestic banks do not become vulnerable to insolvency when competition is introduced and, second, that banks' owners, managers, and directors are the right people in place.[187]

A number of issues relating to bank regulation have received a great deal of attention, as "bad" or "inadequate" regulation can contribute to banking problems. This is because regulation in general determines the competitive structure of the banking industry and such regulation varies across countries, depending on many elements, including economic and institutional factors. The issues that have received attention include licensing, allowed activities, internal governance, and market discipline.

It is often argued that countries need to properly design their licensing procedures or rules, as both liberal and excessively restrictive entry rules can harm the banking sector. Free entry rules bring more competition to the market, which is good for customers but problematic for many domestic banks. Customers will benefit from lower costs, but poorly managed or undercapitalized banks will have to compete for funds by offering above market rates to depositors and then cover their higher cost of funds with risky lending activities. On the other hand, excessively restrictive entry rules create a protected environment in which banks can generate significant economic rents but corporate governance may be poor. Furthermore, this would make banks highly vulnerable to problems resulting from unexpected changes in this operating environment, especially if the protection period is relatively long. The suggestion is therefore for licensing rules that aim, among other things, at ensuring the soundness of the bank wishing to enter the market and the proper qualification of its owners and managers. Ownership ties to other financial and non-financial firms should also be clearly defined.

The importance of the scope of activities issue stems from the fact that the range of allowed activities can expose banks to either more or less risk, suggesting that regulation should avoid inappropriate restrictions on bank activities. There are many researchers who would suggest that diversified portfolios at banks geographically and by sector are less risky, while banks exposed to cyclical fluctuations or commodity and real estate price changes are more so. Others consider that banks assume excessive risk if they are allowed to become involved in non-traditional banking activities, such as holding large equity positions. In such a case the bank becomes more vulnerable to asset price shocks. One cannot say that universal banks are in a better or worse position than other banks, as has been mentioned previously.

Regulatory restrictions on the activities of banks relate to the degree to which a country's regulatory system allows banks to engage in non-traditional activities in the areas of securities and insurance underwriting and selling, in addition to investment and non-financial firm ownership and control. The importance of this issue lies in the possible connectivity between relatively restrictive regulatory systems (in terms of allowed banking activities) and both poor bank performance and a higher probability of banking crises.

In fact, there are at least two different views concerning this connectivity issue. The first argues that there is a direct relationship between regulatory restrictions and banking fragility.[188] According to those authors, this could be due to one of two forces. Narrower banking activities or narrower powers would imply less diversification in operations, which would increase the likelihood of bank failures.[189] Restriction is also likely to lower franchise value by limiting or increasing the variability of profits. The second view advocates that stricter restrictions on non-traditional activities limit excessive risk taking by banks, as they make allowable bank activities easier to monitor by supervisory authorities and market participants and therefore reduce the probability of crisis. Some would suggest in this respect as well that imposing restrictions (such as deposit interest rate ceilings) could lead to a higher franchise value and therefore to a more robust banking system.[190]

A third issue under regulation is corporate or internal governance. Regulation must ensure that the "right" owners or managers are in place and that the level of bank capital is adequate and the quality of risk management and control systems is high. Sound banking requires that the roles and responsibilities of directors and management be clearly defined and the competency of those people verified. In this respect regulatory authorities are often delegated the responsibility to approve shareholders and the appointment of directors and senior management of a bank when licensing or whenever there is a change in ownership. Corporate governance of banks is also enhanced when capital standards or capital adequacy regulations ensure that the capital is sufficiently large to cover a part of credit, market, and operational risks undertaken by banks. Capital adequacy is also needed to incentivize owners to protect their shares and avoid taking excessive risk and possible losses, as they could lose their investment or be required to re-capitalize whenever the bank becomes undercapitalized. Equally important is the setting of appropriate loan valuation, classification, and provisioning standards and international accounting practices. Inadequate loan classification, provisioning, and accounting have contributed in many cases to the reporting of unreal positive capital and earnings for insolvent banks that were making losses even when these results were verified by honest external audits.

Corporate governance of banks is improved also when regulations allow and encourage banks to establish appropriate internal risk management and control systems to restrict or set the appropriate levels of exposure to insider lending, maturity mismatch, and foreign exchange positions. Allowing banks to set appropriate levels of credit, liquidity, exchange rate, and interest rate risk is a relatively recent trend and contrasts with the traditional approach, in which regulators specify through prudential regulation the levels of exposure or set certain standards. It would make the bank management more involved in risk management and control, however. Better internal governance is also achieved when banks are required to have clearly defined internal audit functions with externally audited annual accounts. This would help managers, directors, and owners detect failures or weaknesses and act accordingly.[191]

The fourth and last issue under regulation is market discipline. The argument is that regulation should promote the disclosure of financial information by banks to the public so that market participants can assess the position of banks and take action (in the form of sanctions) if needed. Adequate disclosure helps the public to distinguish between poorly and well-run institutions, which could help, in turn, in reducing potential systemic risk. Proper disclosure of information should be on a consolidated basis that takes into account the positions of subsidiaries, affiliates, and other related entities, and should involve trading and off-balance-sheet activities. Market discipline is also strong when the legal framework clearly defines the rights and obligations of both banks and clients, so that the latter can protect their interests. The patterns of sharing or distributing assets in the event of bank failure—on a pro rata basis or according to certain priorities—should be made clear also.

Recently the Basle Committee on bank supervision has placed a great deal of emphasis on the issue of transparency and disclosure of bank information to facilitate market-imposed discipline. The idea is that public disclosure of information about banks' risk exposure may induce the market (depositors) to monitor banks' performance and penalize risk-taking behavior by banks in the absence of an explicit or implicit deposit insurance scheme or when this insurance is limited to small sums. That would lessen banks' risk-taking incentives.[192] Some have argued strongly for "free banking," a concept based on an overt reliance on creditors' monitoring of banks and manifested in full disclosure of information and the elimination of bank regulation and deposit insurance schemes.[193]

The issue of the need to enhance the dissemination of banking information has been investigated in terms of banks' risk-taking incentives and to establish to what extent dissemination should take place and how. In this respect there have been studies on the impact of disclosing information on the probability of bank failures to the public, the outcome of which suggested that there could be benefits and pitfalls of information disclosure, depending on whether or not banks control their risk exposure. Cordella and Yeyati argue that public disclosure of banks' information reduces the probability of banking crises only when banks have control over their risk exposure.[194] Conversely, when banks do not control their risk exposure, informing depositors may increase the probability of bank failures. According to these authors, the rationale is that when a bank is able to choose its portfolio risk then a penalty imposed by informed depositors demanding a deposit rate in line with the associated risk may induce the bank to move to a lower-risk strategy. This cannot be the case when risk is exogenous, as disclosure may not affect risk-taking behavior by banks but instead induce massive runs. Kane and Rice document and explain banking stress in African countries during the 1980s and 1990s.[195] They show that depositors are vulnerable to loss because of the difficulty of obtaining timely and reliable information on their banks' position to mitigate their risk exposure. They point also to the fact that regulatory policy-makers do not efficiently address this issue because of limited fiscal capacity and incentive conflicts.

Poor bank supervision

A strong, skilled, and independent supervisory authority is also a must for reinforcing internal governance at banks. Supervisors have to ensure banks' compliance with regulations, enforce corrective actions, provide inputs into legislation and regulations, and analyze or evaluate the consistency and accuracy of financial reports.[196] Sufficient on-site and off-site inspection is necessary in this respect.

Supervision deals, therefore, with bank compliance with regulations and is monitored through the off-site analysis of reports that are submitted by banks to the supervisory authority and on-site verification of the accuracy and reliability of reports and the quality of internal controls. Supervisors also have the means to enforce compliance with regulations and are qualified to warn banks of any decline in the quality of assets, and may demand that they take actions such as increasing collateral. Enforcement actions may range from cease-and-desist orders and fines to bank liquidation. External auditors with increased responsibilities can make the work of supervisory authorities much easier by evaluating the consistency of accounting methods, the accuracy of financial reports, and the adequacy of internal risk management systems.

One of the issues related to supervision is the speed with which supervisors take corrective actions in the event that a bank faces liquidity or solvency problems in order to prevent such problems from becoming systemic. It is often argued that the continued operation of weak and troubled banks can weaken other banks and that banking laws should provide supervisors with the power to act swiftly to close and liquidate the problematic bank. Supervisors need not only the authority to take rapid actions to enforce corrective measures but also independence, as political interference can hinder their work. Tuya and Zamalloa argue that greater independence of supervisory actions is generally achieved by supervision not being a part of the government.[197]

Another issue relating to supervision is supervisory laxity and forbearance: that is, a lack of supervisory firmness and speed in enforcing rules and regulations. Lax standards and supervisory forbearance characterized the East Asia crisis.[198] It is often argued that this supervisory weakness is rooted in the incentive structure for supervisors.[199] In many countries supervisors are implicitly promised a well-renumerated job with a private bank when their supervisory contracts are terminated. That would incite many to pursue "friendly" supervision in order not to lose the promised job, essentially receiving a penalty for the tough enforcement of rules and regulations. In addition, in some countries supervisors can be sued by banks for their actions and held personally liable. This, too, would encourage supervisory laxity and forbearance. Recommendations in this respect are focused on ensuring sufficient compensation for supervisors, providing immunity to supervisors from civil liability for their actions, and confiscating supervisors' pensions in cases where malpractice is discovered during or subsequent to their supervisory careers.[200]

A third issue in this field is the capacity of supervisors to fulfil the required work efficiently—that is, the availability of the necessary human and financial resources. As their tasks in assessing bank operations and systems are diverse, supervisors need to have highly qualified employees that are provided with the necessary training, equipment, and facilities.

Mishkin argues that the rationale for prudential supervision (prudential regulation in the context of this chapter) is to prevent the excessive risk taking by banks that the presence of a government safety net might create.[201] He considers that there are nine basic forms of prudential supervision: first, restrictions on asset holdings such as common stocks and activities considered to be outside the core banking business; second, the separation of the banking and other financial industries, such as securities, insurance, or real estate; third, restrictions on competition, as increased competition could lead to declining profitability and hence a lower franchise value, therefore increasing moral hazard incentives for banks. Competition could be restricted by ceilings on rates charged on loans and deposits, restrictions on branching and on the entry of foreign banks, and the separation of banking and non-banking business; fourth, the imposition of capital requirements, as large capital implies more to lose from taking risks; fifth, the institution of risk-based deposit insurance premiums priced to properly reflect the amount of risk taken by a bank. These could be based on capital adequacy levels; sixth, the disclosure of information related to the risks taken by banks and the quality of their assets to enhance the evaluation and monitoring of banks—that is, market discipline; seventh, the establishment of bank chartering based on the quality of banks' management and its plans for carrying out business; eighth, the examination of banks to ensure that they are complying with regulations; and, ninth, the adoption of a supervisory versus regulatory approach where bank examiners focus less on compliance with capital requirements and restrictions on asset holdings and more on the soundness of banks' management practices with regard to controlling risk.

Thus, as far as regulation and supervision are concerned, the absence of any or a combination of the above-mentioned elements or the presence of any gaps, loopholes, or forbearances in the two regulatory and supervisory systems constitute a source of banking sector weakness. There is a large body of evidence that the banking systems of East Asia crisis countries were poorly regulated and supervised in the period preceding the crisis.[202] Insufficient regulation and inadequate oversight of "shadow banking" and financial innovation has also been cited as one of the factors behind the recent global financial crisis. It would seem that regulators and supervisors underestimated the risks and potential massive problems of the mechanism of loan origination and loan sale, better known as the originate-to-distribute model, and many finance companies, commercial banks, and investment banks conducted their activities out of line with existing regulations to varying degrees.[203]

Others

Interbank funds payment and settlement systems can trigger financial difficulties and threaten the stability of banks, the payment system, and the real economy. This is the case when these systems are poorly designed and implemented and participants' credit and liquidity exposures are high.[204] Thus the vulnerability of the banking system to systemic risk—the risk of many participants failing to meet their obligations when due because of the failure of one participant to meet its obligation in due time—should be addressed and kept at a minimum. Therefore, firm interdependencies arising from interbank loans and payment and settlement relationships increase systemic risk.[205] Financial consolidation, or the creation of large and complex financial institutions, can also increase systemic risk, as these institutions have significant on- and off-balance-sheet activities and participate extensively in large value payment and settlement systems.[206]

Some scholars have pointed to the role played by regime changes in heightening the vulnerability of the banking system. Honohan argues that regime shift could alter the nature, scale, frequency, and correlation pattern of shocks to the economic and financial system by modifying the incentives for banks, increasing the risks of operations, and introducing new and inexperienced players.[207]

Volatility not only of asset prices but also of commodity prices is associated with banking crises. Sharp upward movements in commodity prices are no less of a threat to banks, especially when this shift has an international dimension. Lindgren et al mention that the rise in oil prices in the 1970s and early 1980s damaged oil-import-dependent businesses, countries, and banks.[208] Output downturns, deteriorating assets quality, and bank failures were observed also in many oil-exporting countries, such as Nigeria and Norway, in the late 1980s following a sharp decline in oil prices in that period. The same happened to some mineral-exporting countries, such as Chile, in 1981, on the eve of the collapse in the price of copper.[209]

Concluding remarks and policy implications

Financial crises, particularly banking crises, have a long history and appear to be, irrespective of their different magnitudes, chronic and inevitable developments affecting single or multiple economies anywhere in the world and at any time. They often produce significant economic and social problems and losses, and the adversities and costs could also extend to the performance and efficacy of monetary and fiscal policies. Thus, identifying and dissecting the causes and origins of instability and crisis are of utmost importance to law- and policy-makers in general, and to monetary and fiscal authorities and bank regulators and supervisors in particular, in order to address any weaknesses and loopholes in existing rules and regulations and take additional measures to fortify the financial system and reduce potential vulnerabilities. This would ensure the protection of savings, the efficient allocation of credit to the economy, the design and effectiveness of economic policies and other issues— at least for a variable period of time before the onset of a new episode of financial instability.

The literature on the determinants of banking crises has identified a number of factors that adversely affect the quality of assets at banks and therefore contribute to their weakness. Many of these factors operate mainly by causing or inciting excessive risk taking by banks. Such factors are poorly designed safety nets and financial liberalization processes, a poorly regulated and supervised banking sector, and certain exchange rate and inflation stabilization policies. These potential causes of banking crises demand from policy-makers attempts to address these issues and forge the "right" solution based on policy recommendations given the peculiarity of each economy and its characteristics. Other determinants of banking crises have been found to directly impact upon the financial position of borrowers and eventually of banks. These include cyclical economic downturns, high inflation and real interest rates, shifts in the terms of trade, real exchange rate appreciation, currency mismatches and crises, and collapses in asset prices.

In a nutshell, the potential direct causes or origins of crises are many and often interlinked, and the economic and regulatory operating environments under which crises are likely to occur can vary from one economy or crisis episode to another. This implies that there is not a single cure to be prescribed to all economies and at all times, but commitments to regularly strengthening global capital and liquidity rules for banks in line with market developments and financial innovation, on the one hand, and commitments to price and financial stability, on the other, are important issues in promoting banking system stability and resilience.

Notes

1 The Icelandic financial crisis (2008–2011), the Irish banking crisis (2008–2014), the Spanish financial crisis (2008–2014), the Greek government debt crisis (2009–2012), the Portuguese financial crisis (2010–2013), and the Cypriot financial crisis (2012–2013).

2 For a survey of the literature on currency crises see, for example, Flood and Marion 1999; Krugman 2000; and Dooley and Frankel 2003. For a review of sovereign debt crises see Sturzenegger and Zettelmey 2007.

3 International Monetary Fund 1998.
4 Laeven and Valencia 2010.
5 See Kaminsky and Reinhart 1999 on the interdependence of banking and currency crises.
6 For a survey of the theoretical literature on banking crises see Calomiris and Gorton 1991; Allen and Gale 2007; Allen et al 2009.
7 The main contribution is attributed to Fisher 1932; Minsky 1977; Kindleberger 1978.
8 For an overview of the theories on how bubbles can develop see Tirole 1982; 1985; Camerer 1989; Allen et al 1993; Allen and Gorton 1993; Brunnermeier 2001; Abreu and Brunnermeier 2003; Scheinkman and Xiong 2003; Brunnermeier and Nagel 2004; Hong et al 2008.
9 Fisher 1932; 1933.
10 Minsky 1977; 1982.
11 Kindleberger 1978.
12 Friedman and Schwartz 1963; Cagan 1965.
13 Cagan 1965.
14 Schwartz 1987.
15 Bruner and Meltzer 1988.
16 For a review of the theoretical and empirical work on the origins of banking panics and crises, see Calomiris and Gorton 1991; and Calomiris 2010.
17 Bryant 1980.
18 Diamond and Dybvig 1983.
19 See also Donaldson 1993.
20 Champ et al 1991.
21 Alonso 1996.
22 Carlsson and Van Damme 1993.
23 Morris and Shin 1998.
24 Rochet and Vives 2004.
25 Goldstein and Pauzner 2005.
26 Jacklin and Bhattacharya 1988.
27 Chari and Jagannathan 1998.
28 Allen and Gale 1998.
29 Gorton 1998.
30 Allen and Gale 1998.
31 Friedman and Schwartz 1963.
32 Bhattacharya and Gale 1987; Allen and Gale 2000b.
33 Diamond and Rajan 2005.
34 Diamond and Rajan 2001.
35 See Calomiris and Gorton 1991; Calomiris and Kahn 1991; Calomiris and Schweikart 1991; Bhattacharya and Thakor 1993; Kaufman 1994; and Calomiris and Mason 1997.
36 Mishkin 1991a; Calomiris 1994.
37 Calomiris and Mason 1997.
38 Gorton 1998; Jacklin and Bhattacharya 1988; Mishkin 1991a.
39 Goldstein and Razin 2013.
40 Mishkin 1991b.
41 Mishkin 1994.
42 Allen and Gale 2000a.
43 On risk shifting and assets substitution see Jensen and Meckling 1976; and Stiglitz and Weiss 1981.
44 McKinnon and Pill 1998.
45 Krugman 1998.

46 Demirguc-Kunt and Detragiache 1997; 1998; 1999; 2000; Eichengreen and Rose 1998; Hardy and Pazarbasioglu 1998.
47 Demirguc-Kunt and Detragiache 1999; Kaminsky and Reinhart 1996; 1999; Kaminsky et al 1997; Rojas-Suarez 1998.
48 Honohan 1997; Bank for International Settlements 1996; Gavin and Hausmann 1995; Caprio and Klingebiel 1996a, 1996b; Goldstein and Turner 1996; Lindgren et al 1996.
49 Event study techniques, or the approach of identifying systematic differences between tranquil periods and periods surrending the crisis, have been followed by, among others, Cerra and Saxena 2008; Reinhart and Rogoff 2009; Reinhart and Reinhart 2010; Claessens et al 2010; Gourinchas and Obstfeld 2011; Schularick and Taylor 2012; and Reinhart et al 2012.
50 Hutchison and McDill 1999.
51 Demirguc-Kunt and Detragiache 1998, 1999.
52 Hardy and Pazarbasioglu 1998.
53 Kaminsky and Reinhart 1996; 1999.
54 Goldstein and Turner 1996.
55 Caprio and Klingebiel 1996a.
56 Gavin and Hausmann 1995.
57 See Lindgren et al 1996.
58 Demirgüç-Kunt and Detragiache 1998; 1999.
59 Hardy and Pazarbasioglu 1998.
60 Caprio and Klingebiel 1996b.
61 Goldstein and Turner 1996.
62 Gavin and Hausmann 1995.
63 Minsky (1977, 1982, 1986)
64 Demirgüç-Kunt and Detragiache (1998, 1999a)
65 Hardy and Pazarbasioglu 1998.
66 Mishkin 1996.
67 Kaminsky and Reinhart 1996.
68 Goldstein and Turner 1996.
69 Brock 1995.
70 Galbis 1993.
71 Shoven et al 1992.
72 Reinhart and Rogoff 2008.
73 Claessens et al 2010.
74 Dekle and Kletzer 2001.
75 Hutchison and McDill 1999.
76 Kaminsky and Reinhart 1996.
77 Lindgren et al 1996.
78 Mishkin 1994.
79 Bank for International Settlements 1996.
80 Goodhart 1995.
81 See Calvo et al 1993; 1996; Dooley et al 1994; Goldstein 1995; Hausmann and Gavin 1996; Khan and Reinhart 1994; Taylor and Sarno 1997; and International Monetary Fund 1997.
82 See, for example, Mishkin 1996 and Obstfeld 1998.
83 Gavin and Hausmann 1995.
84 Tornell 1999.
85 See Mishkin 1996 on the links between interest rates, adverse selection and moral hazard problems and financial crises.
86 Calvo and Reinhart 1999.
87 Honohan 1997.
88 International Monetary Fund 1998.

89   Claessens et al 2010.
90   Claessens et al 2010.
91   Demirguc-Kunt and Detragiache 1999.
92   Gourinchas et al 1999.
93   Honohan 1997.
94   Sachs et al 1996.
95   Gavin and Hausmann 1995.
96   Eichengreen and Rose 1998.
97   Krugman 1998.
98   International Monetary Fund 1998; Bank for International Settlements 1998; World Bank 1998.
99   See also Goldstein and Hawkins 1998.
100 Dekle and Kletzer 2001.
101 World Bank 1998.
102 World Bank 1998.
103 Eichengreen and Hausmann 1999; Burnside et al 1999.
104 Goldstein and Hawkins 1998.
105 Eichengreen and Rose 1998.
106 Velasco and Cespedes 1999; Calvo 1999.
107 Domac and Martinez-Peria 2000.
108 Rojas-Suarez and Weisbrod 1995; Obstfeld 1994.
109 Stocker 1994.
110 Velasco 1987.
111 See Goldstein and Turner 1996.
112 Kaminsky and Reinhart 1996; 1999.
113 Gavin and Hausmann 1995.
114 See Caprio and Klingebiel 1996a; Gavin and Hausmann 1995.
115 Borensztein and Lee 1999.
116 Milesi-Ferretti and Razin 1998.
117 Hardy and Pazarbasioglu 1998.
118 Caprio and Klingebiel 1996b.
119 Gavin and Hausmann 1995.
120 Lindgren et al 1996.
121 Kaminsky and Reinhart 1996.
122 Taylor 2013.
123 See Schwartz 1997.
124 See, for example, Kindleberger 1978; and Gavin and Hausmann 1995.
125 See Guttentag and Herring 1982; Kaufman 1994; and Herring 1998.
126 Taylor 2009.
127 For a comprehensive account of the events that took place before, during and after the crisis see Gorton 2008; Laeven and Valencia 2008; Brunnermeier 2009; and Adrian and Shin 2010.
128 See Drees and Pazarbasioglu 1995.
129 Lindgren et al 1996.
130 See Lindgren et al 1996.
131 Gavin and Hausmann 1995.
132 Garcia 1995.
133 Lindgren et al 1996.
134 Herring and Wachter 2003.
135 McKinnon 1973; Shaw 1973.
136 King and Levine 1993; Levine 1997.
137 Drees and Pazarbasioglu 1998; Kaminskyamd Reinhart 1999; and Allen and Gale 2000a.
138 Ranciere et al 2008.

139 See also Park and Kim 1994.
140 See Goldstein and Turner 1996.
141 Caprio and Summers 1993; Hellmann et al 1994; 2000.
142 Caprio and Summers 1993; Stiglitz 1994.
143 See Johnston and Tamirisa 1998.
144 Mishkin 1999.
145 Demirguc-Kunt and Detragiache 1998.
146 Sundararajan and Balino 1991.
147 Keely 1990.
148 Diaz-Alejandro 1985.
149 Laeven 2011.
150 Boot and Greenbaum 1993; Bhattacharya and Thakor 1993; Laeven 2002; Hovakimian et al 2003; Demirguc-Kunt et al 2008.
151 Mishkin 2000.
152 Rossi 1999.
153 Boyd and Gertler 1993.
154 Kyei 1995; Garcia 1999; Demirguc-Kunt and Detragiache 2000.
155 Stiglitz 1985; 1992; 1994; Hellmann et al 2000.
156 See Park 1994 and Dekle and Kletzer 2001.
157 Garcia 1999.
158 World Bank 2001.
159 On the principles for effective deposit insurance systems see Bank for International Settlements 2009.
160 Demirguc-Kunt and Detragiache 1998; 2000.
161 Rossi 1999.
162 Folkerts-Landau and Lindgren 1998.
163 Kane 1989.
164 Matutes and Vives 1996.
165 See Goldstein and Turner 1996.
166 Gerschenkron 1962.
167 Caprio and Martinez-Peria 2000.
168 La Porta et al 1999.
169 Caprio and Martinez-Peria 2000.
170 Barth et al 1999.
171 Borensztein and Lee 1999.
172 Bank for International Settlements 1996.
173 Goldstein and Turner 1996.
174 Corsetti et al 2000.
175 Folkerts-Landau et al 1995.
176 Bank for International Settlements 1996.
177 See Cable 1985; Cable and Turner 1985; Mayer 1988; and Davis 1995.
178 Davis 1995.
179 De Juan 1995.
180 Davis 1995.
181 Lindgren et al 1996; Sheng 1996; De Juan 1995; Sanhueza 2001; Laeven 2001; and La Porta et al 2002.
182 La Porta et al 2002.
183 On the quality of governance of banks see also Saunders et al 1990; Caprio et al 2007; and Laeven and Levine 2009.
184 See Lindgren et al 1996.
185 Caprio and Honohan 2010.
186 Laeven 2011.
187 See Lindgren et al 1996.
188 Barth et al 1999.

189 See also Caprio and Wilson 1997 on the relationship between diversification and bank failure.
190 Hellmann et al 2000.
191 For a detailed description of best corporate governance practices at banks see Bank for International Settlements 2010.
192 For details on the issue of market discipline refer to pillar III, Basel II Capital Accord issued in its final version in June 2006 (Bank for International Settlements 2006).
193 See Dowd 1996.
194 Cordella and Yeyati 1998.
195 Kane and Rice 2000.
196 See Dowd 1996.
197 Tuya and Zamalloa 1994.
198 Dekle and Ubide 1998; Lindgren et al 1999; Dekle and Kletzer 2001.
199 See World Bank 2001.
200 World Bank 2001; Caprio and Martinez-Peria 2000.
201 Mishkin 2000.
202 See, for example, International Monetary Fund 1998; Ito 1998; Organization for Economic Co-operation and Development 1998; and Pomerleano 1998.
203 See, for example, Claessens et al 2010.
204 See Bank for International Settlements 1997.
205 See Group of Ten 2001.
206 De Nicolo and Kwast 2002.
207 Honohan 1997.
208 Lindgren et al 1996.
209 See Lindgren et al 1996.

Bibliography

Abreu, D and Brunnermeier, M 2003, "Bubbles and crashes," *Econometrica*, 71, pp. 173–204.

Adrian, T and Shin, H 2010, "Liquidity and leverage," *Journal of Financial Intermediation*, 19, pp. 418–37.

Allen, F and Gale, D 1998, "Optimal financial crises," *Journal of Finance*, 53, pp. 1245–84.

Allen, F and Gale, D 2000a, "Bubbles and crises," *The Economic Journal*, 110, pp. 236–55.

Allen, F and Gale, D 2000b, "Financial contagion," *Journal of Political Economics*, 108, pp. 1–33.

Allen, F and Gale, D 2007, *Understanding Financial Crises*, Clarendon lecture series in finance, Oxford University Press.

Allen, F and Gorton, G 1993, "Churning bubbles," *The Review of Economic Studies*, 60, pp. 813–36.

Allen, F, Morris, S and Postlewaite, A 1993, "Finite bubbles with short sale constraints and asymmetric information," *Journal of Economic Theory*, 61, pp. 206–29.

Allen, F, Babus, A and Carletti, E 2009, "Financial crises: theory and evidence," *Annual Review of Finance and Economics*, 1, pp. 97–116.

Alonso, I 1996, "On avoiding bank runs," *Journal of Monetary Economics*, 37, pp. 73–87.

Bank for International Settlements 1996, "Dott.Padoa-Schioppa examines developments in the field of banking supervision," *BIS Review. Principles for enhancing corporate governance*, vol. 74.

Bank for International Settlements 1997, "Financial stability in emerging market economies," mimeo, Bank for International Settlements.

Bank for International Settlements 1998, "Report of the working group on international financial crises," mimeo, Bank for International Settlements.

Bank for International Settlements 2006, *Basel Committee on Banking Supervision. International convergence of capital measurement and capital standards*, Basel Committee Publications.

Bank for International Settlements 2009, *Basel Committee on Banking Supervision. Core principles for effective deposit insurance system*, Basel Committee Publications.

Bank for International Settlements 2010, *Basel Committee on Banking Supervision. Principles for enhancing corporate governance*, Basel Committee Publications.

Barth, J, Caprio, J and Levine, R 1999, "Financial regulation and performance: cross-country evidence," World Bank Policy Research Working Paper 2037, The World Bank. Available from: http://elibrary.worldbank.org/doi/abs/10.1596/1813–9450–2037

Bhattacharya, S and Gale, D 1987, "Preference shocks, liquidity, and central bank policy," in eds W Barnett and K Singleton, *New Approaches to Monetary Economics*, Cambridge University Press, pp. 376.

Bhattacharya, S and Thakor, A 1993, "Contemporary banking theory," *Journal of Financial Intermediation*, 3, pp. 2–50.

Boot, A and Greenbaum, S 1993, "Bank regulation, reputation, and rents: theory and policy implications," in eds C Mayer and X Vives, *Capital Markets and Financial Intermediation*, Cambridge University Press, pp. 380.

Borensztein, E and Lee, JW 1999, "Credit allocation and financial crisis in Korea," Working Paper 20, International Monetary Fund.

Boyd, J and Gertler, M 1993, "U.S. commercial banking: trends, cycles and policy," *NBER Macroeconomics Annual*, pp. 319–68.

Brock, PL 1995, "High interest rates and bank recapitalizations," Policy Research Working Paper 1683, The World Bank.

Brunner, K and Meltzer, AH 1988, "Money and credit in the monetary transmission process," *American Economic Review*, 78, 2, pp. 446–51.

Brunnermeier, M 2001, *Asset pricing under asymmetric information: bubbles, crashes, technical analysis and herding*, Oxford University Press, pp. 264.

Brunnermeier, M 2009, "Deciphering the liquidity and credit crunch 2007–2008," *Journal of Economic Perspectives*, 23, pp. 77–100.

Brunnermeier, M and Nagel, S 2004, "Hedge funds and the technology bubble," *Journal of Finance*, 59, 5, pp. 2013–40.

Bryant, J 1980, "A model of reserves, bank runs, and deposit insurance," *Journal of Banking and Finance*, 4, pp. 335–44.

Burnside, C, Eichenbaum, M and Rebelo, S 1999, "Hedging and financial fragility in fixed exchange rate regimes," Working Paper 7143, National Bureau of Economic Research.

Cable, R 1985, "Capital market information and industrial performance: the role of West German banks," *The Economic Journal*, 95, pp. 118–32.

Cable, R and Turner, P 1985, "Asymmetric information and credit rationing: another view of industrial bank lending and Britain's economic problem," in ed D Currie, *Advances in Monetary Economic*, Croom Helm.

Cagan, P 1965, "Determinants and effects of changes in the stock of money 1875–1960," *Studies in Business Cycles* 13, National Bureau of Economic Research, Columbia University Press.

Calomiris, C 1994, "Is the discount window necessary? A Penn central perspective," *Federal Reserve Bank of St Louis Review*, 76, pp. 31–55.

Calomiris, C 2010, "The great depression and other 'contagious' events," in ed A Berger, P Molyneux and J Wilson, *The Oxford Handbook of Banking*, Oxford University Press, pp. 721–36.

Calomiris, C and Gorton, G 1991, "The origins of banking panics: models, facts and bank regulation," in ed R Hubbard, *Financial Markets and Financial Crises*, National Bureau of Economic Research, University of Chicago Press, pp. 109–74.

Calomiris, C and Kahn, C 1991, "The role of demandable debt in structuring optimal banking arrangements," *American Economic Review*, 81, pp. 497–513.

Calomiris, C and Mason, J 1997, "Contagion and bank failures during the great depression: the June 1932 Chicago banking panic," *American Economic Review*, 87, 5, pp. 863–83.

Calomiris, C and Schweikart, L 1991, "The panic of 1857: origins, transmission, and containment," *Journal of Economic History*, 51, pp. 807–34.

Calvo, G 1999, "Fixed versus flexible exchange rates: preliminaries to a turn-of-millennium rematch," mimeo, University of Maryland.

Calvo, G and Reinhart, C 1999, "Capital flow reversals, the exchange rate debate and dollarization," *Finance and Development*, pp. 13–5.

Calvo, G, Leiderman, L and Reinhart, C 1993, "Capital inflows and real exchange rate appreciation in Latin America: the role of external factors," Staff Papers 40, International Monetary Fund, pp. 108–50.

Calvo, G, Leiderman, L and Reinhart, C 1996, "Inflows of capital to developing countries in the 1990s," *Journal of Economic Perspectives*, 10, 2, pp. 123–39.

Camerer, C 1989, "Bubbles and fads in asset prices," *Journal of Economic Surveys*, 3, 1, pp. 3–41.

Caprio, G and Honohan, P 2010, "Banking crises," in eds A Berger, P Molyneux and J Wilson, *The Oxford Handbook of Banking*, Oxford University Press, pp. 700–20.

Caprio, G and Klingebiel, D 1996a, "Bank insolvencies: cross-country experience," Policy Research Working Paper 1620, The World Bank.

Caprio, G and Klingebiel, D 1996b, "Bank insolvency: bad luck, bad policy, or bad banking?" Annual World Bank Conference on Development Economics, The World Bank.

Caprio, G and Martinez Peria, M 2000, "Avoiding disaster: policies to reduce the risk of banking crises," Working Paper 47, The World Bank.

Caprio, G and Summers, L 1993, "Finance and its reform: beyond laissez-faire," World Bank Policy Research Working Paper 1171, The World Bank.

Caprio, G and Wilson, B 1997, "On not putting all the eggs in one basket: the role of diversification in banking," paper presented at the World Bank/IMF Annual Meetings held in Hong Kong.

Caprio, G, Laeven, L and Levine, R 2007, "Governance and bank valuation," *Journal of Financial Intermediation*, 16, pp. 584–617.

Carlsson, H and Van Damme, E 1993, "Global games and equilibrium selection," *Econometrica*, 61, pp. 989–1018.

Cerra, V and Saxena, S 2008, "Growth dynamics: the myth of economic recovery," *The American Economic Review*, 98, 1, pp. 439–57.

Champ, B, Smith, B and Williamson, S 1991, "Currency elasticity and banking panics: theory and evidence," Report 9109, University of Western Ontario.

Chari, V and Jagannathan, R 1988, "Banking panics, information, and rational expectations equilibrium," *Journal of Finance*, 43, pp. 749–60.

Claessens, S, Dell' Ariccia, G, Igan, D and Laeven, L 2010, "Lessons and policy implications from the global financial crisis," Working Paper WP/10/44, International Monetary Fund.

Cordella, T and Yeyati, EL 1998, "Public disclosure and bank failures," Staff Papers 45, 1, International Monetary Fund, pp. 110–31.

Corsetti, G, Pesenti, P and Roubini, N 2000, "Fundamental determinants of the Asian crisis: the role of financial fragility and external imbalances," Federal Reserve Bank of New York.

Davis, EP 1995, *Debt, Financial Fragility, and Systemic Risk*, Oxford University Press.

De Juan, A 1995, "The roots of banking crises: micro-economic issues and issues of supervision and regulation," paper presented to the IADB/G-30 Conference on Banking Crises in Latin America, World Bank.

De Nicolo, G and Kwast, M 2002, "Systemic risk and financial consolidation: are they related?" Working Paper 55, International Monetary Fund.

Dekle, R and Kletzer, K 2001, "Domestic bank regulation and financial crises: theory and empirical evidence from East Asia," Working Paper 63, International Monetary Fund.

Dekle, R and Ubide, A 1998, "Korea: financial sector development and reform," mimeo, International Monetary Fund.

Demirguc-Kunt, A and Detragiache, E 1997, "The determinants of banking crises—evidence from developing and developed countries," Working Paper 106, International Monetary Fund.

Demirguc-Kunt, A and Detragiache, E 1998, "Financial liberalization and financial fragility," Working Paper 83, International Monetary Fund.

Demirguc-Kunt, A and Detragiache, E 1999, "Monitoring banking sector fragility: a multivariate logit approach," Working Paper 147, International Monetary Fund.

Demirguc-Kunt, A and Detragiache, E 2000, "Does deposit insurance increase banking system stability? An empirical investigation," World Bank.

Demirguc-Kunt, A, Kane, E and Laeven, L 2008, *Deposit insurance around the world: issues of design and implementation*, MIT Press.

Diamond, D and Dybvig, P 1983, "Bank runs, deposit insurance, and liquidity," *Journal of Political Economy*, 91, pp. 401–19.

Diamond, D and Rajan, R 2001, "Liquidity risk, liquidity creation and financial fragility: a theory of banking," *Journal of Political Economics*, 109, pp. 2431–65.

Diamond, D and Rajan, R 2005, "Liquidity shortages and banking crises," *Journal of Finance*, 60, pp. 615–47.

Diaz-Alejandro, C 1985, "Good-bye financial repression, hello financial crash," *Journal of Development Economics*, 19, pp. 1–24.

Domac, I and Martinez-Peria, MS 2000, "Banking crises and exchange rate regimes: is there a link?" mimeo, The World Bank.

Donaldson, G 1993, "Financing banking crises: lessons from the panic of 1907," *Journal of Monetary Economics*, 31, pp. 69–95.

Dooley, M and Frankel, J 2003, "Managing currency crises in emerging markets," Proceedings, National Bureau of Economic Research," conference March 28–31, Chicago, University of Chicago Press.

Dooley, M, Fernandez-Arias, E and Kletzer, K 1994, "Recent private capital inflows to developing countries: is the debt crisis history?" Working Paper 4792, National Bureau of Economic Research.

Dowd, K 1996, "The case for financial laissez-faire," *The Economic Journal*, 106, pp. 679–87.

Drees, B and Pazarbasioglu, C 1995, "The Nordic banking crises: pitfalls in financial liberalization?" Working Paper 61, International Monetary Fund.

Drees, B and Pazarbasioglu, C 1998, "The Nordic banking Crisis, pitfalls in financial liberalization," Occasional Paper 161, International Monetary Fund.

Eichengreen, B and Hausmann, R 1999, "Exchange rates and financial fragility," Working Paper 7418, National Bureau of Economic Research.

Eichengreen, B and Rose, A 1998, "Staying afloat when the wind shifts: external factors and emerging-market banking crises," Working Paper 6370, National Bureau of Economic Research.

Fisher, I 1932, *Booms and Depressions*, Adelphi

Fisher, I 1933, "The debt deflation theory of great depressions," *Econometrica*, 1, pp. 337–57.

Flood, R and Marion, N 1999, "Perspectives on the recent currency crisis literature," *International Journal of Finance and Economics*, 4, pp. 1–26.

Folkerts-Landau, D and Lindgren, CJ 1998, "Toward a framework for financial stability," IMF World Economic and Financial Surveys.

Folkerts-Landau, D, Schinasi, G, Cassard, M, Reinhart, C and Spencer, M 1995, "Effects of capital flows on the domestic financial sectors in APEC developing countries," eds MS Khan and C Reinhart, *Capital Flows in the APEC Region*, International Monetary Fund, pp. 31–57.

Friedman, M and Schwartz, A 1963, "A monetary history of the US 1867–1960," working paper?National Bureau of Economic Research.

Galbis, V 1993, "High real interest rates under financial liberalization: is there a problem?" Working Paper 7, International Monetary Fund.

Garcia, G 1995, "Lessons from bank failures worldwide," paper presented at the conference on Regulating Depository Institutions, Koc University, Istanbul.

Garcia, G 1999, "Deposit insurance: a survey of actual and best practices," Working Paper WP/99/83, International Monetary Fund.

Gavin, M and Hausmann, R 1995, "The roots of banking crises: the macroeconomic context," eds R Hausmann and L Rojas-Suarez, *Banking Crises in Latin America*, John Hopkins University Press, pp. 27–63.

Gerschenkron, A 1962, *Economic backwardness in historical perspective: a book of essays,* The Belknap Press of Harvard University Press.

Goldstein, I and Pauzner, A 2005, "Demand-deposit contracts and the probability of bank runs," *Journal of Finance*, 60, pp. 1293–327.

Goldstein, I and Razin, A 2013, "Three branches of theories of financial crises," Working Paper 18670, National Bureau of Economic Research.

Goldstein, M 1995, "International financial markets and systemic risk," mimeo, Institute of International Economics.

Goldstein, M and Hawkins, J 1998, "The origin of the Asian financial turmoil," Research Discussion Paper 9805, Reserve Bank of Australia.

Goldstein, M and Turner, P 1996, "Banking crises in emerging economies: origins and policy options," Economic Papers 46, Bank for International Settlements.

Goodhart, C 1995, "Price stability and financial fragility," in eds K Sawamoto, Z Nakajima and H Taguchi, *Financial Stability in a Changing Environment*, St Martin's Press.

Gorton, G 1998, "Banking panics and business cycles," *Oxford Economic Papers*, 40, pp. 751–81.

Gorton, G 2008, "The panic of 2007," Working Paper 14358, National Bureau of Economic Research.

Gourinchas, PO and Obstfeld, M 2011, "Stories of the twentieth century for the twenty-first," Working Paper 17252, National Bureau of Economic Research.

Gourinchas, PO, Valdes, R and Landerretche, O 1999, "Lending booms: some stylized facts," mimeo, Princeton University.

Group of Ten 2001, "Report on consolidation in the financial sector," mimeo, Bank for International Settlements.

Guttentag, J and Herring, R 1982, "The insolvency of financial institutions: assessment and regulatory disposition," in ed P Wachtel, *Crises in the Economic and Financial Structure*, Lexington Books.

Hardy, D and Pazarbasioglu, C 1998, "Leading indicators of banking crises: was Asia different?" Working Paper 91, International Monetary Fund.

Hausmann, R and Gavin, M 1996, "The roots of banking crises: the macroeconomic context," in eds R Hausmann and L Rojas-Suarez, *Banking Crises in Latin America*, IADB/ Johns Hopkins University Press.

Hellmann, T, Murdock, K and Stiglitz, J 1994, "Addressing moral hazard in banking: deposit rate controls vs. capital requirements," mimeo, Stanford University.

Hellmann, T, Murdock, K and Stiglitz, J 2000, "Liberalization, moral hazard in banking, and prudential regulation: are capital requirements enough?" *The American Economic Review*, 90, 1, pp. 147–65.

Herring, R 1998, "Banking disasters: causes and preventative measures, lessons derived from the U.S. experience," in eds G Caprio, W Hunter, G Kaufman and D Leipziger, *Preventing Bank Crises: Lessons from Recent Global Bank Failures*, Federal Reserve Bank of Chicago and Economic Development Institute of the World Bank.

Herring, R and Wachter, S 2003, "Bubbles in real estate markets," in eds W Hunter, G Kaufman and M Pomerleano, *Asset Price Bubbles: The Implications of Monetary, Regulatory, and International Policies*, MIT Press, pp. 217–30.

Hong, H, Scheinkman, J and Xiong, W 2008, "Advisors and asset prices: a model of the origins of bubbles," *Journal of Financial Economics*, 89.

Honohan, P 1997, "Banking system failures in developing and transition countries: diagnosis and prediction," Working Paper 39, Bank for International Settlements.

Hovakimian, A, Kane, E and Laeven, L 2003, "How country and safety net characteristics affect bank risk shifting," *Journal of Financial Services Research*, 23, pp. 177–204.

Hutchison, Ml and McDill, K 1999, "Are all banking crises alike? The Japanese experience in international comparison," Working Paper 7253, National Bureau of Economic Research.

International Monetary Fund 1997, *Interim assessment of the world economic outlook-regional and global implications of the financial crisis in Southeast and East Asia*, Washington, DC.

International Monetary Fund 1998, *World Economic Outlook*, Washington, DC.

Ito, T 1998, "The development of the Thailand currency crisis: a chronological review," mimeo, Hitotsubahi University.

Jacklin, C and Bhattacharya, S 1988, "Distinguishing panics and information-based bank runs: welfare and policy implications," *Journal of Political Economics*, 96, pp. 568–92.

Jensen, M and Meckling, W 1976, "Theory of the firm: managerial behavior, agency costs and ownership structure," *Journal of Financial Economics*, 3, 4, pp. 305–60.

Johnston, B and Tamirisa, N 1998, "Why do countries use capital controls?" Working Paper 181, International Monetary Fund.

Kaminsky, G 1999, "Currency and banking crises: the early warnings of distress," Working Paper 178, International Monetary Fund.

Kaminsky, G and Reinhart, C 1996, "The twin crises: the causes of banking and balance-of-payments problems," International Finance Discussion Paper 544, Board of Governors of the Federal Reserve System.

Kaminsky, G and Reinhart, C 1999, "The twin crises: the causes of banking and balance-of-payments problems," *The American Economic Review*, 89, 3, pp. 473–500.

Kaminsky, G, Lizondo, S and Reinhart, C 1997, "Leading indicators of currency crises," Working Paper 79, International Monetary Fund.

Kane, E 1989, *The SandL Insurance Mess: How Did It Happen?* Urban Institute Press.

Kane, E and Rice, T 2000, "Bank runs and banking policies: lessons for african policymakers," Working Paper 8003, National Bureau of Economic Research.

Kaufman, G 1994, "The US banking debacle of the 1980s: an overview and lessons," Working Paper 6, Center for Financial and Policy Studies, Loyola University of Chicago.

Keely, MC 1990, "Deposit insurance, risk, and market power in banking," *The American Economic Review*, 80, pp. 1183–200.

Khan, M and Reinhart, C 1994, "Macro-economic management in maturing economies: the response to capital inflows," International Monetary Fund Issues Paper.

Kindleberger, C 1978, *Manias, Panics and Crashes*, Basic Books.

King, R and Levine, R 1992, "Financial indicators and economic growth in a cross section of countries," PRE Working Paper 819, The World Bank.

King, R and Levine, R 1993, "Finance and growth: Schumpeter might be right," *Quarterly Journal of Economics*, 108, pp. 717–37.

Krugman, P 1998, "Saving Asia: it's time to get radical," *Fortune*, September 7, pp. 74–80.

Krugman, P 2000, "Currency crises," *National Bureau of Economic Research Conference Report*, University of Chicago Press.

Kyei, A 1995, "Deposit protection arrangements: a comparative study," Working Paper 134, International Monetary Fund.

La Porta, R, Lopez-de-Silanes, F and Shleifer, A 1999, "Government ownership of commercial banks," mimeo, Harvard University.

La Porta, R, Lopez-de-Silanes, F and Zamarripa, G 2002, "Related lending," Working Paper 8848, National Bureau of Economic Research.

Laeven, L 2001, "Insider lending and bank ownership: the case of Russia," *Journal of Comparative Economics*, 29, pp. 207–29.

Laeven, L 2002, "Bank risk and deposit insurance," *World Bank Economic Review*, vol. 16, pp.109–37.

Laeven, L 2011, "Banking crises: a review," *The Annual Review of Financial Economics*, 3:4.1–4.24.

Laeven, L and Levine, R 2009, "Bank governance, regulation and risk taking," *Journal of Finance and Economics*, 93, pp. 259–75.

Laeven, L and Valencia, F 2008, "Systemic banking crsises: a new database," Working Paper 08/224, International Monetary Fund.

Laeven, L and Valencia, F 2010, "Resolution of banking crises: the good, the bad, and the ugly," Working Paper 10/146, International Monetary Fund.

Levine, R 1997, "Financial development and growth: views and agenda," *Journal of Economic Literature*, 35, pp. 688–726.

Lindgren, CJ, Garcia, G and Saal, M 1996, "Bank soundness and macroeconomic policy," International Monetary Fund.

Lindgren, CJ, Balino, T, Enoch, C, Gulde, AM, Quintyn, M and Teo, L 1999, "Financial sector crisis and restructuring: lessons from Asia," Occasional Paper 188, International Monetary Fund.

McKinnon, R 1973, "Money and capital in economic development," The Brookings Institution.

McKinnon, R and Pill, H 1998, "International overborrowing: a decomposition of credit and currency risks," mimeo, Stanford University.

Matutes, C and Vives, X 1996, "Competition for deposits, fragility, and insurance," *Journal of Financial Intermediation*, 5, pp. 184–216.

Mayer, C 1988, "New issues in corporate finance," *European Economic Review*, 32, 5, pp. 1167–83.

Milesi-Ferretti, GM and Razin, A 1998, "Current account reversals and currency crises: empirical regularities," Working Paper WP/98/89, International Monetary Fund.

Minsky, H 1977, "A theory of systemic fragility," in eds E Altman and A Sametz, *Financial Crises*, Wiley.

Minsky, H 1982, "The financial instability hypothesis, capitalist processes and the behavior of the economy," in eds CP Kindleberger and JP Laffargue, *Financial Crises, Theory, History and Policy*, Cambridge University Press, pp. 13–29.

Minsky, H 1986, *Stabilizing an Unstable Economy*, Yale University Press.

Mishkin, F 1991a, "Asymmetric information and financial crises: a historical perspective," in ed R Hubbard, *Financial Markets and Financial Crises*, University of Chicago Press.

Mishkin, F 1991b, "Anatomy of a financial crisis," Working Paper 3934, National Bureau of Economic Research.

Mishkin, F 1994, "Preventing financial crises: an international perspective," Working Paper 4636, National Bureau of Economic Research.

Mishkin, F 1996, "Understanding financial crises: a developing country perspective," Working Paper 5600, National Bureau of Economic Research.

Mishkin, F 1999, "Lessons from the Asian crisis," Working Paper 7102, National Bureau of Economic Research.

Mishkin, F 2000, "Prudential supervision: why is it important and what are the issues?" Working Paper 7926, National Bureau of Economic Research.

Morris, S and Shin, H 1998, "Unique equilibrium in a model of self fulfilling currency attacks," *American Economic Review*, 88, pp. 587–97.

Obstfeld, M 1994, "The logic of currency crises," *Cahiers Economiques et Monetaires*, 43, pp. 189–213.

Obstfeld, M 1998, "The global capital market: benefactor or menace?" *Journal of Economic Perspectives*, 12, pp. 9–30.

Office of the Comptroller of the Currency 1988, "Bank failure: an evaluation of the factors contributing to the failure of national banks."

Organization for Economic Co-operation and Development 1998, OECD Economic Outlook.

Park, YC 1994, "Korea: development and structural change of the financial system," in eds H Patrick and YC Park, *The Financial Development of Japan, Korea, and Taiwan: Growth, Repression, and Liberalization*, Oxford University Press.

Park, YC and Kim, DW 1994, "Korea: development and structural change of the banking system," in eds H Patrick and YC Park, *The Financial Development of Japan, Korea, and Taiwan: Growth, Repression, and Liberalization*, Oxford University Press.

Pomerleano, M 1998, "The East Asia crisis and corporate finances—the untold micro story," *Emerging Markets Quarterly*, Winter, pp. 14–27.

Ranciere, R, Tornell, A and Westermann, F 2008, "Systemic crises and growth," *Quarterly Journal of Economics*, 123, pp. 359–406.

Reinhart, C and Reinhart, V 2010, "After the fall," Working Paper 16334, National Bureau of Economic Research.

Reinhart, C and Rogoff, K 2008, "Banking crises: an equal opportunity menace," Working Paper 14587, National Bureau of Economic Research.

Reinhart C and Rogoff, K 2009, *This Time is Different: Eight Centuries of Financial Folly*, Princeton University Press.

Reinhart, C, Reinhart, V and Rogoff, K 2012, "Debt overhangs: past and present," Working Paper 18015, National Bureau of Economic Research.

Rochet, J and Vives, X 2004, "Coordination failures and the lender of last resort: was Bagehot right after all?" *Journal of the European Economic Association*, 2, pp. 1116–47.

Rojas-Suarez, L 1998, "Early warning indicators of banking crises: what works for emerging markets," paper presented at the meetings of the Allied Social Sciences Association, Chicago. Inter-American Development Bank, Washington DC.

Rojas-Suarez, L and Weisbrod, SR 1995, "Financial fragilities in Latin America—the 1980s and the 1990s," Occasional Paper 132, International Monetary Fund.

Rossi, M 1999, "Financial fragility and economic performance in developing economies: do capital controls, prudential regulation and supervision matter?" Working Paper 66, International Monetary Fund.

Sachs, J, Tornell, A and Velasco, A 1996, "Financial crises in emerging markets: the lessons from 1995," *Brookings Papers on Economic Activity*, 1, pp. 147–98.

Sanhueza, G 2001, "Chilean banking crisis of the 1980s: solutions and estimation of the costs," Working Paper 104, Central Bank of Chile.

Saunders, A, Strock, E and Travlos, N 1990, "Ownership structure, deregulation, and bank risk taking," *Journal of Finance*, 45, pp. 643–54.

Scheinkman, J and Xiong, W 2003, "Overconfidence and speculative bubbles," *Journal of Political Economy*, 111, pp. 1183–219.

Schularick, M and Taylor, A 2012, "Credit booms gone bust: monetary policy leverage cycles, and financial crises, 1870–2008," *The American Economic Review*, 102, 2, pp. 1029–61.

Schwartz, A 1987, "The lender of last resort and the federal safety net," *Journal of Financial Services Research*, 1, pp. 77–111.

Schwartz, A 1997, "Comment on debt deflation and financial instability: two historical explorations," in eds B Eichengreen, R Grossman, F Capie and G Wood, *Asset Prices and the Real Economy*, St Martins Press.

Shaw, S 1973, *Financial Deepening in Economic Development*, Oxford University Press.

Sheng, A 1996, "Bank restructuring—lessons from the 1980s," The World Bank.

Shoven, J, Smart, S and Waldfogel, J 1992, "Real interest rates and the savings and loan crisis: the moral hazard premium," *Journal of Economic Perspectives*, 6, pp. 155–67.

Stiglitz, J 1985, "Credit markets and the control of capital," *Journal of Money, Credit, and Banking*, 17, pp. 133–52.

Stiglitz, J 1992, "SandL bail-out," in eds JR Barth and R Dan Brunbaugh Jr, *The Reform of Federal Deposit Insurance*, Harper Collins.

Stiglitz, J 1994, "The role of the state in financial markets," in eds M Bruno and B Pleskovic, *Proceedings of the World Bank Annual Conference on Development Economics*, The World Bank.

Stiglitz, J and Weiss, A 1981, "Credit rationing in markets with imperfect information," *American Economic Review*, 71, pp. 393–410.

Stocker, J 1994, "Intermediation and the business cycle under a specie standard: the role of the gold standard in English financial crises, 1790–1850," mimeo, University of Chicago.

Sturzenegger, F and Zettelmeyer, J 2007, *Debt Defaults and Lessons from a Decade of Crises*, MIT Press.

Sundararajan, V and Balino, T 1991, "Issues in recent banking crises," in eds V Sundarajan and T Balino, *Banking Crises: Cases and Issues*, International Monetary Fund, pp. 1–57.

Taylor, A 2013, "External imbalances and financial crises," Working Paper WP/13/260, International Monetary Fund.

Taylor, J 2009, *Getting Off Track: How Government Actions and Interventions Caused, Prolonged, and Worsened the Financial Crisis*, Hoover Institution Press.

Taylor, M and Sarno, L 1997, "Capital flows to developing countries, long- and short-term determinants," *World Bank Economic Review*, 11, 3, pp. 451–70.

Tirole, J 1982, "On the possibility of speculation under rational expectations," *Econometrica*, 50, pp. 1163–81.

Tirole, J 1985, "Asset bubbles and overlapping generations," *Econometrica*, 53, pp. 1499–528.

Tornell, A 1999, "Lending booms and currency crises: empirical link," mimeo, University of Harvard.

Tuya, J and Zamalloa, L 1994, "Issues on placing banking supervision in the central bank," in eds T Ballino and C Cottarelli, *Frameworks for Monetary Stability*, International Monetary Fund.

Velasco, A 1987, "Financial crises and balance of payments crises: a simple model of the Southern cone experience," *Journal of Development Economics*, 27, pp. 263–83.

Velasco, A and Cespedes, LF 1999, "Exchange rate arrangements: a developing country perspective," unpublished manuscript.

World Bank 1998, *East Asia: The Road to Recovery*, The World Bank.

World Bank 2001, "Finance for growth: policy choices in a volatile world," World Bank Policy Research Report.

5 Bank lending during the financial crisis of 2008

An empirical investigation

Introduction

This chapter empirically examines the effects of the global financial crisis in 2008 on total bank lending to retail and corporate customers in selected countries, as declining bank credit is one of the major causes of economic slowdown or recession. In many cases, bank credit could also decline as a result of the slowdown. The goal of the chapter, therefore, is to first investigate whether the global credit crisis and ensuing world economic recession resulted in a decline in bank private sector credit. Second, the study addresses whether this decline, if any, was supply- or demand-driven by bank borrowers. The former could be the case if bank credit to the private sector was constrained by a decline in deposits, an increase in non-performing loans, and issues of risk aversion by banks reflected in adverse selection and moral hazard mechanisms, whereas the latter could result from an increase in unemployment, a decline in business opportunities, and risk aversion by borrowers regarding investment profitability. To test whether there has been a contraction of bank credit following the global credit crisis and whether it came from a shift in the demand or a shift in the supply or both, we build on the methodologies commonly used in the literature addressing both the determinants of bank lending and the means to disentangle the shift of loan supply from the shift of loan demand. We first develop a credit theoretical model in line with the existing models in the literature. Then we rely on empirical methodology to estimate with panel data the overall impact on banks' loan extension using a comprehensive quarterly International Financial Statistics data set of banking sector claims on the private sector for eight countries for the period January 1995–December 2013. We divide the data into two sub-periods: before the crisis and after the crisis. An OLS analysis is conducted to identify the determinants of bank credit to the private sector. The credit demand and supply functions used in our econometric estimations include some supply and demand variables and are derived from the theoretical model. As such, if there are supply-side or demand-side effects on bank lending they are likely to be equally important for both retail and corporate customers. The distinction in the cause of credit slowdown or retreat has important policy implications. If the credit decline is related to weak demand for bank loans, whether due to pessimistic economic perspectives, deteriorations in borrowers' balance sheets, excessive leverage, or other factors, then policies aiming at stimulating aggregate demand could be effective. If, on the other hand, the decline is due to banks' inability and reluctance to lend because of a decline in bank deposits, of capital losses (related to loan losses or asset price collapse), and increased riskiness, then other sets of measures, including easy monetary policy, are needed to revive bank lending and foster investment. The chapter is organized as follows. The next section discusses the financial crisis of 2008 and its possible impact on the selected countries. The third section reviews the literature that has examined the impact of financial crises in general on credit and examines the conclusions reached concerning the demand and supply causes. This is followed by a section highlighting the testing methodology and the results reached in the current study, while the next section reports the estimation results. The final section concludes with policy recommendations.

The impact of the financial crisis of 2008 on selected countries

The financial crisis of 2008 is widely believed to be the second worst crisis in history, after that of 1929, and has caused an unprecedented global recession not seen since the 1929 recovery. The crisis started in the US and the financial systems of the advanced economies and quickly spread to the rest of the world, including the emerging and developing countries. Amazingly, the crisis affected banking systems, financial debt, equity, and foreign exchange markets simultaneously. This section summarizes the possible channels of the transmission mechanism of the crisis to the rest of the world. Three major channels of transmission and several secondary ones are believed to have taken effect.[1] The first is a trade channel, as world demand for exports, especially those of countries with negative terms of trade, declined. Countries in the ESCWA (Economic and Social Commission for Western Asia) region witnessed a decline in both their imports and their exports during the crisis. Total imports declined from $560.9 billion in 2008 to $454.1 billion in 2009, while total exports declined from $825.7 billion to $520.2 billion for the same years.[2] The decline in exports figures reflect, in addition to the decline in oil prices, the deteriorating macroeconomic conditions in ESCWA's major trading partners, namely the EU and the US. However, Intra-Regional ESCWA member countries' trade also declined between 2008 and 2009, as intra-regional exports fell from $73.3 billion to $54.5 billion and intra-regional imports declined from $78.9 billion to $58.7 billion. This fact reflects the deterioration in the macroeconomy of ESCWA countries as a result of the crisis.

The second channel is commodity prices. A change in these prices—a decline, in this case—reduced export revenues for many developing and emerging economies relying on commodity exports. The third channel relates to financial transmission mechanisms. This channel comprises several aspects, such as asset prices, exchange rates, interest rate spreads, and credit availability. We will focus on the impact of the financial crisis on credit, in line with the topic of this chapter. Financial crises usually affect both the demand and supply side of credit. The supply side is influenced by a decline in residents' and non-residents' deposits, an increase in non-performing loans, and risk aversion by banks reflected in information asymmetries leading to the agency problems of adverse selection and moral hazard. On the demand side, credit could be curtailed by uncertainty about the profitability of investments and borrowers' risk aversion in crisis times.

The empirical research, as we will see in the next section, has centered around determining, first, whether there is a credit slowdown and, second, whether this slowdown is supply or demand driven. In order to select a group of countries to be used in our empirical methodology, we observed a sample of fourteen countries in the Middle East and North Africa region (MENA). Casual empiricism or anecdotal evidence showed that eight of them witnessed a decline in credit during the financial crisis (2008–9). The selected countries, all outside the American and European continents, were Jordan, Egypt, and the six Gulf Cooperation Council (GCC) countries, Saudi Arabia, Qatar, Oman, Kuwait, Bahrain, and the United Arab Emirates (Figure 5.1).[3] We will confine the study to this group of countries to determine the impact of the financial crisis on credit availability and to test the credit crunch hypothesis.

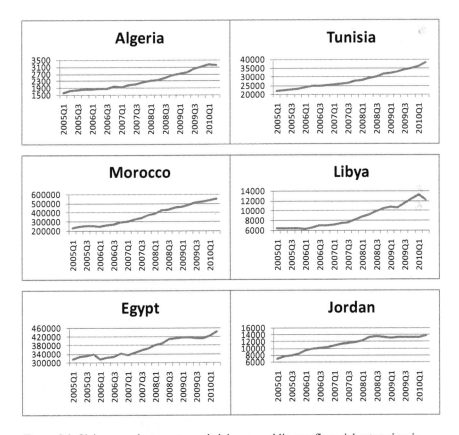

Figure 5.1 Claims on private sector and claims on public non-financial enterprises in millions/billions of domestic currency during the crisis of 2008–9.

(Continued)

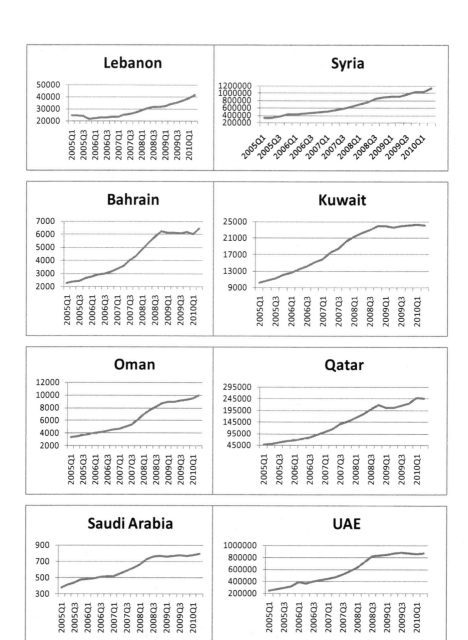

Figure 5.1 Claims on private sector and claims on public non-financial enterprises in millions/billions of domestic currency during the crisis of 2008–9. (Continued)

Note: Only Algeria, Lebanon, and Saudi Arabia are presented in billions of domestic currency; other countries are in millions.

Source: International Monetary Fund, *International Financial Statistics*, various issues

Literature review of the impact of various financial crises on credit

The literature examining the impact of financial crises on credit is very wide. Several studies examine the impact on credit of various crises, including the Mexican crisis, the Asian crisis, and the Russian crisis. These studies were largely regional, as many financial crises and their effects were confined to specific areas. For example, after the Mexican crisis of 1994 studies were developed examining the impact on some Latin American countries.[4] The same applies to East Asia after 1997.[5] Currently, the 2008 financial crisis is a worldwide one affecting the whole global environment. Studies highlighting the impact of the current crisis are thus expected to be conducted across the whole world or across specific regions, such as the MENA countries. Additionally, the literature includes several studies that have examined the impact of a crisis on the credit conditions in a particular country, such as, for example, Morocco,[6] Japan,[7] and Finland.[8] Empirical research has also examined the impact of a crisis in a set of countries on those countries specifically.[9] Finally, a number of studies have examined the impact of the latest financial crisis of 2008 on credit.[10]

It is widely believed that when financial crises affect the credit market the impact may occur on both the demand and supply sides of this market. In this sense, a reduction in the amount of loans, or total lending, may result from a decline in credit availability or the willingness to borrow. A decline in the supply of credit is referred to as the credit "crunch," where credit is unavailable at existing interest rates. Studies in this area have attempted to identify the causes of the decline in credit using demand for and supply of credit in a disequilibrium analysis framework. This section highlights some of the conclusions reached in the literature.

Studies conducted on the impact of the East Asian crisis used various empirical methodologies to address the issues. Ghosh and Ghosh used a disequilibrium framework, defining credit crunch as a situation in which interest rates do not equilibrate the credit market with the aggregate amount of credit being supply constrained, showing the presence of credit rationing.[11] The study was conducted on Indonesia, Korea, and Thailand, using monthly data covering the period 1992–8. The results showed that in Indonesia there was a sharp contraction in the supply of credit in 1997, with an increase in credit demand. Later on, credit demand began to decline, making credit supply no longer a constraining factor. In Thailand there was excess demand for credit in late 1996 that later began to decline, outstripping the decline in real credit supply. In Korea there was excess demand throughout 1996 and part of 1997, but little evidence of a credit crunch since. The authors conclude, therefore, that while the supply of real credit declined, estimated demand for real credit fell even more sharply, suggesting that quantity rationing was not an issue. The result for Thailand was challenged in several studies, particularly Ito and Silva, that used survey data from commercial banks to argue in favor of a credit crunch in Thailand during the period extending from mid-1997 to early 1998.[12] By contrast, Dollar and Hallward-Driemeier found little evidence of a credit crunch in Thailand.[13] Along the same lines, Dwor-Frecaut et al,[14] using survey data from 3,700 firms for Indonesia, Korea, Malaysia, the Philippines, and Thailand, concluded that the fall in credit in these five countries was demand driven. Finally, Chen and Wang,[15] assessing the impact of the Asian financial crisis on Taiwan, showed that both the demand and the supply of loans were responsible for the credit slowdown, with the shrink in supply being more drastic.

The literature on the impact of the Mexican financial crisis on neighboring countries, as reflected in Argentina, shows that, in a manner similar to many crises before, the outflow of deposits explains most of the contraction in credit to the private sector from December 1994 to the first half of 1995. In the second half of 1995 the recovery of credit capacity was partly offset by issues of adverse selection and informational constraints. The demand side was constrained by relatively high interest rates and unemployment, the slow growth of private sector borrowing in the first half of 1996 thus being explained mainly by demand factors.

Studies conducted on specific countries provide mixed results. For Finland, Pazarbasioglu,[16] employing a disequilibrium model of credit supply and demand following the banking crisis of 1991–2, shows that the reduction in bank lending was mainly demand driven likely because of borrowers' high levels of indebtedness. It was also shown that banks were less willing to supply credit in periods of deteriorating asset quality and that there was a need to increase capital adequacy levels. For Japan, Woo found that the decline in credit in 1997 was supply driven in a year when the Japanese financial system was changed fundamentally.[17] For Morocco, Allain and Oulidi,[18] also using a disequilibrium approach, examined the reasons for the slow credit growth during the rapid expansion of liquidity during the first half of the decade from 2000. Their results do not support the credit crunch hypothesis. Barajas and Steiner examined the marked slowdown in bank credit in eight Latin American countries in the few years before their study.[19] The credit crunch hypothesis was tested for three countries, Columbia, Mexico, and Peru, to show that while both supply and demand factors seem to have played key roles, their relative importance has varied across countries.

Lately, several studies have been conducted on the impact of the latest financial crisis using disequilibrium analysis. Ivashina and Scharfstein show that new lending declined across all types of loan, with some of this decline reflecting a drop in demand as firms reined back expansion plans during the recession.[20] There is also a supply effect as well, as banks with poorer access to deposit financing and more revolving line exposure reduced their lending more than other banks. In another study, Puri et al examine the impact of the US financial crisis on retail lending in Germany by distinguishing between affected and non-affected banks.[21] Demand for loans is found to decrease across banks. However, a supply-side effect is also strongly present, in that the affected banks reject substantially more loan applications than non-affected ones. Poghosyan examined the case of Jordan using a disequilibrium model.[22] The results show that there was a credit crunch, as the decline in credit was largely driven by the supply side, even though demand-side factors had a modest impact. Agur analyzes how different types of bank funding affect the extent to which banks ration credit to borrowers, and the impact that capital requirements have on that rationing.[23] Unsecured wholesale finance that surged in the pre-crisis years is shown to amplify the credit market impact of capital requirements compared with funding by retail depositors. Kapan and Minoiu examine the role of bank balance sheet strength in the transmission of financial sector shocks to the real economy to estimate the impact of exposure to market freezes during 2007–8 on the supply of bank credit.[24] Their results suggest that banks with strong balance sheets were better able to maintain lending during the crisis. Banks that were more dependent on market funding and had lower structural liquidity reduced the supply of credit more than other banks. Chen and Wu deal with bank ownership and credit growth in emerging markets during and after the latest financial crisis.[25] Their results show that credit growth of domestic banks was higher than that of foreign banks in Asia in 2009 and in Latin America and emerging market countries in Europe in 2010. Additionally, inside the group of domestic banks, credit growth of state-owned banks grew faster than that of private banks during the crisis in Latin America and emerging Europe, and after the crisis in Latin America. An IMF working paper uses the case studies of Latvia, Lithuania, Montenegro, Poland, and Romania to examine whether supply or demand drove the credit cycle in these countries during the financial crisis.[26] Using panel data analysis, supply factors on average were shown to be more important than demand ones in explaining credit movements. Lithuania and Montenegro showed similar results, whereas the experiences of the other three countries were heterogeneous. Thus, the credit crunch literature suggests that both supply- and demand-side effects are prevalent. However, a difference exists in the magnitude of each across countries, regions, and financial crises.

The model and estimation methodology

Like the studies listed in the previous section examining supply- or demand-driven credit market slowdown, this paper builds on the work of Maddala and Nelson[27] and Laffont and Garcia[28] in the estimation of a disequilibrium model of a system of equations for the supply of and demand for bank credit to the private sector in the selected countries. The chapter draws also on the relevant existing literature in specifying or modeling the credit demand and credit supply functions, taking into account the peculiarities of the countries studied along with data quality and availability.[29] According to the disequilibrium framework of Laffont and Garcia,[30] imperfect flexibility in interest rates can lead to a temporary disequilibrium in the credit market, with either excess supply or demand, implying that the observed (actual) drop in credit could be attributed to declining credit supply, credit demand or both. To identify the issue and solve the problem a switching regression framework is used, whereby a priori exclusion restrictions are imposed on the supply and demand functions (e.g., a given explanatory variable such as resources or liquidity availability at banks affects the supply of credit but not demand for credit). The model consists thus of three equations: the supply equation, the demand equation, and a third equation relating the two. We will describe first the determinants of credit supply and credit demand and then explain the model components of the estimation method.

The credit supply equation

A main determinant of credit supply is resources availability, which in turn determines the lending capacity of a depository institution. The reasoning is based on the portfolio management framework within which, given expected yields on different asset classes, bank management decides on the amount of loans to supply after considering, among other things, the available sources of funds. Knowing the nature of banking in the selected countries, available resources are best represented by the amount of total deposits and capital accounts on the liabilities side of the balance sheet. No attempt was made, however, to manipulate the amounts of reported total deposits and capital of banks, as some other studies did, to better reflect and measure the lending capacity through subtracting required reserves from total deposits and using the excess capital over the minimum required regulatory capital (i.e. measuring lending capacity after complying with reserve requirements and minimum capital standards). The motives are many and related mainly to measurement complications and potential inaccuracy. In fact, despite the fact that reserve requirements are not uniform across the selected countries and have recently changed greatly for many of these economies, reserves at the central bank often include legal and excess reserves in addition to liquidity requirement, with none of these sub-items being reported separately. In addition, a part of the required reserves is often freed against certain types of credit extended by banks to sectors that the government wishes to encourage. As for capital, data on capital adequacy is not frequently available. Nevertheless, the available resources or lending capacity variable, as defined in this paper, is expected to be positively correlated with credit supply.

It is also worth mentioning that no other measures were used to assess the ease with which banks can raise liquidity and new capital to fund credit, as a few other authors did, by relying on data on bank share performance on the stock market (i.e., market assessment of creditworthiness and profitability). The reason is that stock markets in the selected countries are in general not well-developed, mature, and transparent, and only a limited number of banks (and other corporations) are listed. This would imply that data on prices and stock market capitalization may not reflect the true picture and could be misleading. This fact also prevented us from including, as did Blundell-Wignall and Gizycki,[31] the variance of bank share prices (σ) relative to the market average to reflect risks specific to the banking sector and where a higher σ, denoting higher banking risks, is expected to negatively affect the willingness of banks to extend credit to the private sector. It should be mentioned as well that low frequency and interrupted data on the ratio of problem loans to total credit prevented us from using this variable in our specification, as banks' risk aversion is likely to increase when the ratio of problem loans in total credit increases.

Other independent variables used in specifying our credit supply equation include the lending interest rate, the spread between the lending rate and the deposit rate, expected inflation, and expected real economic activity or growth. The average lending rate is anticipated to have a positive effect on the supply of credit, as higher interest rates, up to a certain point, tend to increase return or banks' profitability from lending activities. But we are also aware that lending rates could be negatively correlated with credit supply, as adverse selection can occur as a result of loan pricing where rates or prices above a certain threshold level will decrease the expected return for a bank because the most risky borrowers will commonly stand ready to accept a loan at a very high rate. To account for perceived higher lending risk, the intermediation spread, or the difference between the lending and borrowing interest rates, is used. The higher the loan rate relative to the deposit rate the higher the risk, and this would represent a binding constraint on credit.

In this context, we need to mention that some studies on individual countries included in their supply equation an independent variable that would capture the collateral available to banks, such as the net worth of corporations proxied by the market capitalization of the corporate sector, or a measure of real estate prices, when the importance of real estate as collateral for bank loans is high, on the basis that adequate collateral availability should facilitate the expansion of bank credit and therefore be a positive sign. We did not attempt to include such a variable in our work, mainly because we are dealing with many non-homogeneous countries where market capitalization does not necessarily reflect the capitalization level of the corporate sector for reasons already mentioned, and the types of collateral used and the importance of each differ greatly from one country to another.

The expected inflation variable appears in our supply equation as a measure of economic uncertainty, as the higher the expected inflation rate the greater the uncertainty and thus the more cautious or reluctant banks would be in extending credit. This explanatory variable is anticipated, therefore, to be inversely related to credit supply and thus be a negative sign. Another related variable used in our supply equation specification, which intends to measure the economic outlook or prospects, is the growth in real output measured by GDP volume index at constant prices, as banks are willing to expand credit supply when economic prospects are positive. Thus, this variable is expected to capture firms' ability to repay and to be a positive sign. It should be mentioned that some research papers investigating the credit crunch in a particular country during a certain period used, rather, an industrial production index with a distributed lag to capture future economic prospects. We also used this approach, employing an industrial or a petroleum production index whenever data on the GDP volume index was missing or interrupted.

In light of the above, the specification for the credit supply equation used for estimation purposes is as follows:

$$S_t^c = \beta_0 + \beta_1 AR_{t-1} + \beta_2 r_t^l - \beta_3 (r_t^l - r_t^d) - \beta_4 I_t^e + \beta_5 RGDP_t^e + \varepsilon_t^s \tag{1}$$

Where:

S_t^c Denotes supply of credit at time t

AR_{t-1} = Available resources of deposits and capital at time t-1

r_t^l = Lending rate at time t

$r_t^l - r_t^d$ = Lending rate minus deposit rate at time t

I_t^e = expected inflation rate at time t

$RGDP_t^e$ = Expected real growth in GDP at time t

ε_t^s = Error term

The credit demand equation

In modeling credit demand we assume that demand for bank credit is a function of the cost of credit (lending interest rate), expected inflation, and level of economic activity. We anticipate demand for credit to be negatively related to the lending rate and to depend positively on the expected rate of inflation. Given expected inflation, one can predict lower and delayed investment when lending rates are increasing. Conversely, as higher inflation reduces the nominal debt value, higher demand for credit is likely to be associated with rising expected inflation. The last variable used in our demand equation specification captures expected growth in economic activity, as this influences firms' decisions to expand their businesses and operations and is proxied by the expected growth in real output or the level of industrial or petroleum production. We therefore expect a positive effect for this variable.

As such, the credit demand equation used for estimation takes the following form:

$$D_t^c = \alpha_0 - \alpha_1 r_t^l + \alpha_2 I_t^e + \alpha_3 RGDP_t^e + \varepsilon_t^d \tag{2}$$

Where:

D_t^c Denotes demand for credit at time t

r_t^l = Lending rate at time t

I_t^e = Expected inflation rate at time t

$RGDP_t^e$ = Expected real growth in GDP at time t

ε_t^d = Error term

The model

As mentioned earlier, the model can be written in its simplest form after simplifying equations (1) and (2) as such:

$$S_t^c = \alpha_1 X_{1t} + u_{1t}, \tag{3}$$

$$D_t^c = \alpha_2 X_{2t} + u_{2t}, \text{ and} \tag{4}$$

$$A_t^c = \min (S_t^c, D_t^c) \tag{5}$$

Where:

S_t^c represents the unobserved quantity of bank credit supplied at period t

D_t^c denotes the unobserved quantity of bank credit demanded at period t

X_{1t} and X_{2t} are the group of explanatory variables that affects supply and demand respectively

α_1 and α_2 are the parameters, u_{1t} and u_{2t} are the residuals, and A_t^c is the actual (observed) quantity of credit at period t

Equation (5) states that the actual (observed) amount of credit is the minimum of credit supplied and credit demanded, and not the equilibrium amount. This is the case when the interest rate fails to fulfill its market clearing function in the presence of rigidities.

Following Maddala and Nelson,[32] and assuming that u_{1t} and u_{2t} are independently and normally distributed random variables with variances σ_1 *and* σ_2 respectively, the maximum likelihood method of estimation is appropriate and used for this class of models.

The maximum log likelihood function (ML) is defined as follows:

$$ML = \sum_{t=1}^{n} log \,[f_1\,(A_t^c) * F_2\,(A_t^c) + f_2\,(A_t^c) * F_1\,(A_t^c)], \tag{6}$$

Where:

$$f_1\,(A_t^c) = \frac{1}{\sqrt{2\pi}\sigma_1} \exp\left[-\frac{1}{2\sigma_1^2}\,(A_t^c - \alpha_1 X_{1t})^2\right]$$

$$f_2\,(A_t^c) = \frac{1}{\sqrt{2\pi}\sigma_2} \exp\left[-\frac{1}{2\sigma_2^2}\,(A_t^c - \alpha_2 X_{2t})^2\right]$$

$$F_1\,(A_t^c) = \frac{1}{\sqrt{2\pi}\sigma_1} \int_{A_t^c}^{\infty} \exp\left[-\frac{1}{2\sigma_1^2}\,(S_t^c - \alpha_1 X_{1t})^2\right] dS_t^c$$

$$F_2\,(A_t^c) = \frac{1}{\sqrt{2\pi}\sigma_2} \int_{A_t^c}^{\infty} \exp\left[-\frac{1}{2\sigma_2^2}\,(D_t^c - \alpha_2 X_{2t})^2\right] dD_t^c$$

f_1 and f_2 are the probability density functions, whereas F_1 and F_2 are the cumulative density functions.

We optimize the log likelihood function shown in equation (6) using the Marquardt iterative procedure and obtain maximum likelihood estimates based on quarterly data for the group of eight countries (Egypt, Jordan, Oman, Kuwait, Saudi Arabia, UAE, Bahrain, and Qatar) from 1995 to 2013. Table 5.1 displays variables definition and data sources.

Estimation results

The estimation results of our disequilibrium model of bank credit for the selected eight countries, using quarterly data for the period Q1 1995–Q4 2013 (a potential sample of 608 observations) are displayed in Table 5.2. It appears that the results for most exogenous variables used are in line with expectations—that is, the majority of the supply and demand equation coefficients are significant and have the expected signs.

For the credit demand equation, the real lending rate is significant and has the expected negative sign, implying that higher real lending rates are associated with lower real credit demand. Higher expected output, denoting good or improving economic prospects, is also associated with greater credit demand, as predicted, but inflation did not have the expected explanatory power and thus did not have an effect on the demand for loans. This suggests that higher demand for loans for this

Table 5.1 Variables definitions and data sources.

A_t^c	Actual real credit to the private sector: logarithm of nominal credit to the private sector by banks deflated by CPI	International Monetary Fund *International Financial Statistics*
r_t^l	Real lending interest rate: weighted average lending rate deflated by CPI	International Monetary Fund *International Financial Statistics*
AR_{t-1}	Real available resources or lending capacity: logarithm of total commercial bank deposits plus capital accounts deflated by CPI	International Monetary Fund *International Financial Statistics*
$RGDP_t^e$	Expected economic activity: logarithm of either GDP volume index or industrial/petroleum production index	International Monetary Fund International Financial Statistics
$r_t^l - r_t^d$	Real interest rate spread: Weighted average lending rate minus weighted average deposit rate deflated by CPI	International Monetary Fund *International Financial Statistics*
I_t^e	Consumer price inflation: $\Delta\ln$ CPI	International Monetary Fund *International Financial Statistics.* Central bank bulletins of sample countries

Table 5.2 Estimation results.

	Parameter estimate	t-stat
Demand equation		
Constant	7.24	18.51
Lending interest rate	−0.03	−6.21
Real output /industrial production	0.62	7.79
Inflation	4.10	1.39
Supply equation		
Constant	8.51	6.23
Lending interest rate	0.05	4.10
Real output/industrial production	3.49	8.96
Lending capacity	0.54	3.91
Inflation	−5.08	−2.83
Interest rate spread	−0.04	−2.71
Log likelihood	360	
Number of observations	564	

specific sample of countries is unrelated to rising expected inflation and ensuing lower nominal debt amount.

For the credit supply equation, the banks' available resources or lending capacity variable is significant and has the expected positive sign, with strong elasticity of supplied credit to potential to lend, reinforcing the fact that deposits are the main bank funding instruments in the selected countries and that money market debt plays only a minor role as a source of funds and liquidity. The real lending rate has a strong positive impact on the real credit supply and the effects of expected inflation and output on the credit supply function are significant, with the expected negative and positive signs respectively. This indicates that economic uncertainty increases risk aversion and affects the willingness of banks to lend, irrespective of their ability to extend credit given resources availability. It shows also that the elasticity of credit demand to economic activity is strong. The real interest rate differential, or the spread between the lending rate and the deposit rate, also has the expected significant negative coefficient, reflecting the adverse effects of credit risk on lending decisions.

The estimates of credit demand and supply obtained from the disequilibrium model were used to plot predicted credit demand and credit supply series and calculate deviations from observed lending values with a view to identifying excess demand or supply periods. Our results indicate that the period before Q3 2008 was one of rapid credit expansion, with alternating periods of excess supply and excess demand, and that the trend was reversed from Q3 2008 until end 2009 or early 2010, when credit extension flattened or declined. The results also suggest that, during this specific period, the recent credit slowdown in the selected countries was mainly driven by slow credit supply affected most likely by liquidity shortage and heightened risk, although it would seem that credit demand was influenced as well by the recent global financial crisis, but to a lesser extent, for reasons probably related to the global economic recession and regional slowdowns in economic activity.

Concluding remarks and policy implications

The term "crisis" in the Chinese language is "Wei Ji," meaning risk (Wei) and opportunity (Ji). So each crisis, if analyzed and assessed properly, can bear the seeds needed to make the necessary reforms to prevent its reoccurrence and to adjust policies to reverse its trajectory. Therefore, the challenge is to properly understand the impact of every crisis. Thus, this chapter aimed, first, at examining the impact of the financial crisis of 2008 on credit availability in eight selected countries. The results show that there was a credit decline after the crisis. Second, in line with the literature on credit crunch using disequilibrium analysis, the analysis addressed the effects of the crisis on the demand for and supply of credit. The identification of the cause of credit slowdown or retreat has important policy implications. If the credit decline is related to weak demand for bank loans, whether due to pessimistic economic perspectives, deteriorations in borrowers' balance sheets, excessive leverage, or other factors, then policies aiming at stimulating aggregate demand could be effective. If, on the other hand, the decline is due to banks' inability and reluctance to lend because of a decline in deposits, capital losses (related to loan losses or asset price collapse), and increased riskiness, then other sets of measures, including easy monetary policy, are needed to revive bank lending and foster investment. The results obtained here suggest that the recent credit slowdown in the eight countries studied was largely caused by credit supply factors. Banks seem to have been mainly affected by liquidity shortage and heightened risk. The results also show that credit demand was influenced as well, for reasons probably related to the global economic recession and regional slowdowns in economic activity. However, the demand impact was less significant. The results are in line with many studies in the literature, especially ones that have addressed the impact of the latest financial crisis, such as those from Puri et al, Poghosyan, and the IMF.[33] Such results suggest that, in order to motivate credit, policy-makers must emphasize policies aimed at stimulating credit supply, with an eye also on affecting loan demand.

Notes

1 European Economy 2009.
2 International Monetary Fund, *World Economic Outlook.*
3 Fourteen countries were considered in total, including, in addition to the eight mentioned countries: Algeria, Lebanon, Lybia, Morocco, Syria, and Tunisia, as shown in Figure 5.1. These six countries happened to have witnessed an increase in credit

defined as claims on the financial sector and on non-public enterprises over the crisis period and were thus excluded from the sample.

4 Catao 1997.
5 Chen and Wang 2008; Agenor et al 2000; Ghosh and Ghosh 1999; Ito and Silva 1999; Dwor-Frecaut et al 1999; Dollar and Hallward-Driemeier 1998.
6 Allain and Oulidi 2009.
7 Woo 1999.
8 Pazarbasioglu 1997.
9 Barajas and Steiner 2002.
10 International Monetary Fund 2015; Chen and Wu 2014; Agur 2013; Kapan and Minoiu 2013; Poghosyan 2010; Puri et al 2011; Ivashina and Scharfstein 2008.
11 Ghosh and Ghosh 1999.
12 Ito and Silva 1999.
13 Dollar and Hallward-Driemeier 1998.
14 Dwor-Frecaut et al 1999.
15 Chen and Wang 2008.
16 Pazarbasioglu 1997.
17 Woo 1999.
18 Allain and Oulidi 2009.
19 Barajas and Steiner 2002.
20 Ivashina and Scharfstein 2008.
21 Puri et al 2011.
22 Poghosyan 2010.
23 Agur 2013.
24 Kapan and Minoiu 2013.
25 Chen and Wu 2014.
26 International Monetary Fund 2015.
27 Maddala and Nelson 1974.
28 Laffont and Garcia 1977.
29 See, for example, Pazarbasioglu 1997; Catao 1997; Ghosh and Ghosh 1999; Baek 2005; Allain and Oulidi 2009; and Poghosyan 2010.
30 Laffont and Garcia 1977.
31 Blundell-Wignall and Gizycki 1992.
32 Maddala and Nelson 1974.
33 Puri et al 2011; Poghosyan 2010; International Monetary Fund 2015.

Bibliography

Agenor, PR, Aizenman, J and Hoffmaister, A 2000, "The credit crunch in East Asia: what can bank excess liquid assets tell us?" Working Paper 7951, National Bureau of Economic Research.

Agur, I 2013, "Wholesale bank funding, capital requirements and credit rationing," Working Paper WP/13/30, International Monetary Fund.

Allain, L and Oulidi, N 2009, "Credit market in Morocco: a disequilibrium approach," Working Paper WP/99/53, International Monetary Fund.

Baek, EG 2005, "A disequilibrium model of the Korean credit crunch," *The Journal of the Korean Economy*, 6, 2, pp. 313–36.

Barajas, A and Steiner, R 2002, "Credit stagnation in Latin America," Working Paper WP/02/53, International Monetary Fund.

Blundell-Wignall, A and Gizycki, M 1992, "Credit supply and demand and the Australian economy," Reserve Bank of Australia Research Discussion Paper RDP9208, Economic Research Department, Reserve Bank of Australia.

Catao, L 1997, "Bank credit in Argentina in the aftermath of the Mexican crisis: supply or demand constrained?" Working Paper WP/97/32, International Monetary Fund.

Chen, G and Wu, Y 2014, "Bank Ownership and Credit Growth in Emerging Markets During and After the 2008–2009 Financial Crisis—A Cross-Regional Comparison," Working Paper WP/14/171, International Monetary Fund.

Chen, NK and Wang, HJ 2008, "Financial crisis and the effects on bank credits – the evidence from Taiwan," *Southern Economic Journal*, 75, 1, pp. 26–49.

Dollar, D and Hallward-Driemeier, M 1998, "Crisis, adjustment, and reform in Thai industry," unpublished, The World Bank.

Dwor-Frecaut, D, Hallward-Driemeier, M and Colaco, F 1999, "Corporate credit needs and corporate governance," unpublished, The World Bank.

European Economy 2009, "Impact of the global crisis on neighboring countries of the EU," Occasional Papers 48, European Commission, Directorate-General for Economic and Financial Affairs.

Ghosh, Atish R and Ghosh, Swati R 1999, "East Asia in the aftermath: was there a crunch?" Working Paper WP/99/38, International Monetary Fund.

International Monetary Fund, *Annual Reports*, various issues.

International Monetary Fund, *International Financial Statistics*, CD-ROM.

International Monetary Fund 2015, "Does Supply or Demand Drive the Credit Cycle? Evidence from Central, Eastern, and Southeastern Europe," Working Paper WP/15/15, International Monetary Fund.

International Monetary Fund, *World Economic Outlook*, database.

Ito, T and Silva, LP 1999, "The credit crunch in Thailand during the 1997–98 crisis," unpublished, the WORLD Bank.

Ivashina, V and Scharfstein, DS 2010, "Bank lending during the financial crisis of 2008," *Journal of Financial Economics*, 97, 3, pp. 319–38.

Kapan, T and Minoiu, C 2013, "Balance sheet strength and bank lending during the global financial crisis," Working Paper WP/13/102, International Monetary Fund.

Laffont, JJ and Garcia, R 1977, "Disequilibrium econometrics for business loans," *Econometrica*, 45, 5, pp. 1187–204.

Maddala, G and Nelson, F 1974, "Maximum likelihood methods for models of market disequilibrium," *Econometrica*, 42, 6, pp. 1013–30.

Pazarbasioglu, C 1997, "A credit crunch? Finland in the aftermath of the banking crisis," *Staff Papers*, 44, 3, International Monetary Fund.

Poghosyan, T 2010, "Slowdown of credit flows in Jordan in the wake of the global financial crisis: supply or demand driven?" Working Paper WP/10/256, International Monetary Fund.

Puri, M, Rocholl, J and Steffen, S 2011, "Global retail lending in the aftermath of the US financial crisis: distinguishing between supply and demand effects," *Journal of Financial Economics*, 100, 3, pp. 459–684.

Woo, David, 1999, "In search of 'capital crunch': factors behind the credit slowdown in Japan," Working Paper WP/99/3, International Monetary Fund.

6 Corporate governance in the banking industry and Basel III challenges and implications

Introduction

Since the early 1990s corporate governance has been receiving much and increasing attention and contemplation by international standard-setters, domestic law-makers and regulators, and all domestic and external stakeholders in general with the rising awareness of its importance for and impact on the soundness and performance of financial and non-financial companies and on certain economic outcomes. The ongoing pressure to adhere to constantly updated international standards in this area and to related applicable domestic laws and regulations and mounting conviction on the part of shareholders and investors of the positive efficiency, profitability, and sustainability signals that adequate corporate governance can send to the markets have been the main drivers for the board and senior management of banks and non-banks to incorporate the best corporate governance practices into their daily operations and decision-making.

There is no single definition of corporate governance, yet it is commonly known to be a set of structures, systems, policies, and procedures by the means of which corporations are managed and controlled. The Organization for Economic Co-operation and Development (OECD) has one of the best definitions, which mentions that corporate governance "specifies the distribution of rights and responsibilities among the main participants in the corporation—including shareholders, directors and managers—and spells out the rules and procedures for making decisions on corporate affairs. By doing this, corporate governance provides the structure through which company objectives are set, implemented and monitored."

The commitment to and the adoption of good corporate governance practices in reference to well-known international standards differ from one company, industry, and country to another. This is because such practices are decided in part by companies and dictated to a large extent by laws and regulations. So, in addition to the regulatory and legal considerations, there are other factors that play a role in divergence in practices, including the size, complexity, and risk-taking culture of the firm and the political, institutional, social, and cultural environment. Nevertheless, a company devoted to sound corporate governance has a clearly described shareholders' role and equal rights, an empowered board of directors with well-determined responsibilities to exercise management and oversight, strong internal controls and accountability, and high levels of transparency and disclosure.

A corporate governance framework of guiding principles and practices is exceptionally momentous in the banking industry given the role played by banks in the economy and the functions performed, which are central to financial market development and economic growth. The importance of corporate governance in the banking sector is also related to the fact that weak corporate governance and poor management and oversight can lead to bank failures and heighten systemic risk, potentially destroying savings and necessitating costly bail-outs by governments.[1] Proper corporate governance framework at banks thus requires both well-established laws and regulations and the strong commitment of bank shareholders and management to the implementation of the best practices.

The section following this introduction looks at the international developments and trends in corporate governance guidance and regulation and provides some background information on the reasons behind the interest in corporate governance and the motivation for its current importance as a discipline for corporations in general and banks in specific. The third section deals with the corporate governance practices undertaken by banks in compliance with the related international standards and domestic regulations. It also discusses the challenges and implications of adopting and implementing the best practices. The fourth section discusses the challenges and implications of implementing the Basel III global regulatory framework for more resilient banks and banking systems; this new framework focuses on risk management and governance since corporate governance of banks is enhanced when capital standards ensure that capital is sufficiently large and covers a good part of the credit, market, and operational risks undertaken by financial services firms. Capital adequacy is also needed to incentivize bank owners to protect their shares and avoid taking excessive risk, as they can lose their investment or are required to recapitalize whenever the bank becomes undercapitalized. The fifth section briefly surveys the literature on corporate governance in banking and highlights some specific areas of corporate governance research to illustrate various aspects of corporate governance from different angles and to enrich the understanding of the pros and cons of the diverse features of governance in financial services firms and other companies as well. The final section concludes with some general remarks and policy issues.

Background and prevailing guidelines, standards, and regulations

The policies and practices adopted by banks in the area of corporate governance are largely built on the guidelines and standards set by international standard-setters and comply with the relevant national laws and other rules and regulations issued by domestic bank regulatory and supervisory authorities, whether in line with or complementary to the international guidance. This section, therefore, will briefly describe the prevailing international guidelines and regulations pertaining to sound corporate governance as a point of reference to assist in an understanding and evaluation of what banks have been doing in the last fifteen years or so in this area. The survey of reference documents is not intended to be exhaustive, given the different constraints, nor detailed, as many of the guiding principles and sub-principles concisely described below are better clarified and elaborated in the third section of the chapter, where they reappear in discussions of the corporate governance structures, policies, and procedures assumed by banks worldwide.[2]

To start with, it can be inferred from the survey of the relevant literature (summarized in the 'Important areas of governance research' section below) that the attention given to the various aspects of corporate governance dates back many decades and even centuries, irrespective of its size and scope.[3] The awareness of the necessity and importance of sound corporate governance became more pronounced and prevalent, however, in the early to mid-1990s, in the wake of a wave of dismissals of chief executive officers (CEOs) of well-established and reputable US companies by their board of directors and the emergence of a new trend of warm relationships between the CEO and the board (encompassing the uncontrolled issuance of stock options) at the expense of shareholders.[4] There were also concerns in the UK at that time about the proper working of the corporate sector or system arising from the widening perception that accounting standards were loose and that a clear framework for effective board accountability for a number of matters was absent, thus contributing to a low level of confidence in financial reporting and in the ability of auditors to provide the expected protection. These worries were also amplified by a number of corporate scandals and unanticipated failures of prominent UK companies.[5] These developments raised awareness of the urgent need to take action to improve governance standards and clarify responsibilities.

In this respect, and as a reaction to, among other things, scandals and public outcry, a committee was created in May 1991 in the UK by the Financial Reporting Council, the London Stock Exchange, and the accountancy profession to deal with the financial features of corporate governance (such as the way in which the board sets financial policy and oversees its implementation) and to improve the standard of corporate governance in financial reporting and auditing. This committee published its final report, entitled *The Report of the Committee on the Financial Aspects of Corporate Governance* and later known as the Cadbury Report in recognition of the committee chairman Sir Adrian Cadbury, in December 1992. The report came up with recommendations and actions that need to be taken in the field of financial reporting and accountability, hoping that these would contribute to the process of establishing corporate standards. Though the committee's recommendations focused on the control and reporting functions of the board and the role of auditors, they also covered other issues and were, as a whole, intended to promote a system of good corporate governance. Recommendations relating to the structure and responsibilities of boards of directors were summarized in a Code of Best Practice based on the principles of openness, integrity, and accountability and ensuring high standards of corporate behavior. The other recommendations mainly tackled the rights and responsibilities of shareholders, the role of auditors, and accounting profession issues. Companies listed on the London Stock Exchange (LSE) and registered in the UK were required as part of the obligation of listing to state whether they complied with the Code of Best Practice and to justify any non-compliance in any of its areas. The ninety-page Cadbury Report was a landmark in corporate governance standards setting, though it was not an attempt to reform corporate governance in its totality.

The Cadbury Report mentioned in one of its parts that a new committee should review the extent to which its findings had been implemented and thus, in January 1995, a second committee, known as the Greenbury Committee, was set up and chaired by Sir Richard Greenbury in an effort to come up with good practice with regard to executives' remuneration. Again, the work of this committee was not intended to deal with the different aspects of corporate governance but to focus on identified weaknesses in corporate governance in the UK and tackle, like the previous committee, specific corporate governance problems. The Greenbury Report, properly entitled *Directors' Remuneration*, was issued few months later in July 1995 and contained a code of best practice for directors' remuneration focusing on related accountability, transparency, and linkage to performance. The Greenbury Report again suggested that another committee should review the state of implementation of its recommendations.

In November 1995, and based on the initiative of the chairman of the UK Financial Reporting Council (FRC), the Committee on Corporate Governance was established, chaired by Sir Ronald Hampel, with the objective of re-examining the role of directors, shareholders, and auditors in corporate governance, reviewing the Cadbury and Greenbury Codes and their implementation, and passing judgment on whether they served their purposes. The Hampel Committee dealt, in fact, with the entire range of corporate governance and produced a preliminary report in August 1997 and a final report in January 1998.[6] The main outcome of this committee was a draft document including a set of corporate governance principles and a code, which incorporated the work of this committee and of the two previous ones (Cadbury and Greenbury). These combined efforts, sent to the LSE for feedback and inputs, led ultimately to the issuing of the Combined Code in June 1998, consisting of two parts, the first of which contains the principles of good governance and the second the code of best practice.[7] The Combined Code was then appended to the LSE listing rules and listed companies were thus required to mention whether they apply the principles set out in this Code and provide explanations of any non-compliance. A new version of the Combined Code was issued by the FRC in July 2003 after taking into account the recommendations of the Higgs Report of January 2003, which focused on and reviewed the role and effectiveness of non-executive directors. The Higgs review was initiated by the UK government. The Combined Code of 2003 set a standard for director's duties in the UK and laid out best practice for directors, remuneration, accountability and audit, and relations with shareholders.

Shortly after the Combined Code of 1998 came the *OECD Principles of Corporate Governance* and the Basel Committee on Banking Supervision guidelines, *Enhancing Corporate Governance for Banking Organizations*, both published in 1999. The driving force behind and the content of these principles and guidelines are elaborated upon below. Public, political, and regulatory interest in regulating corporate governance continued to grow in the early 2000s, following the massive collapses of large corporations and the series of corporate scandals involving accounting fraud and other forms of misconduct.[8] In response to the widespread manipulation of financial reports and additional types of misdemeanor at the expense of market investors, and in order to restore confidence in corporate sector governance, the US Congress enacted the Sarbanes–Oxley Accounting Standards Act of 2002. US lawmakers attempted through this Act to legislate many of the Cadbury and OECD principles and recommendations and shape, through a set of requirements, corporate governance in the US.

The Sarbanes–Oxley law, which inspired similar legislations in many economies, formally regulated the previously self-regulating auditing profession by establishing the Public Company Accounting Oversight Board (PCAOB) with the aim of imposing higher standards in the accounting vocation and supporting accurate and unbiased audits of the financial reports of public financial and non-financial companies. The Act also placed auditors in charge of examining the financial statements of companies and expressing their opinions regarding the accuracy and reliability of such statements' contents, and required both the CEO and the Chief Financial Officer (CFO) to attest to the financial statements so that they cannot claim not to have viewed or reviewed such financial information. To ensure the delivery of an independent opinion on the accuracy and reliability of financial statements and avoid potential conflicts of interest, external audit firms are not allowed under this Act to provide specific types of consulting services and must alternate their lead partner every five years. The US law also obliged corporations to have independent board committee members, at least one of whom is a financial expert, to be disclosed if present and, if absent, such absence to be justified. Sarbanes–Oxley encouraged powerful and independent corporate boards, required stronger and stricter internal control mechanisms, and forced hundreds of companies to restate their financial results to reflect better objectivity and accuracy.

The period running from 2004 until 2015 was mainly characterized by the amendment and updating of the most relevant international standards for sound corporate governance issued by the Organization for Economic Co-operation and Development (OECD) and the Basel Committee on Banking Supervision (BCBS). It should be noted here that many European countries and non-European economies during this period, and even before, had developed their own codes and reports on corporate governance, but these are not the subject of this chapter.

The principles of the Organization for Economic Co-operation and Development (OECD)

The OECD, established in 1961 in Paris, France, is well known for the advance of policies aiming, among other things, at achieving sustainable economic growth and employment and maintaining financial stability in member countries. OECD policy-makers have long thought that good corporate governance contributes to financial market stability, investment, and economic growth. To this end, in 1999 the OECD published its first version of the *Principles of Corporate Governance* in reply to appeals from its member countries and council to conceive a set of corporate governance standards and guidelines in association and cooperation with national governments, international organizations, and the private sector. These principles have constituted the foundation for good corporate governance schemes and frameworks in OECD and non-OECD economies alike, as they represent explicit guidance for governance related legislative, institutional, and regulatory initiatives and improvements in these countries. The original and updated OECD principles on corporate governance are also considered an international yardstick for policy-makers, investors, stock exchanges, corporations, and other involved parties, and they are adopted by the Financial Stability Board/Forum as one of its twelve key standards for sound financial systems.[9] The principles also support the corporate governance part of the Observance of Standards and Codes (ROSC) reports of the International Monetary Fund (IMF).[10]

Subsequently the 1999 corporate governance principles were carefully examined and reviewed to take into consideration developments, challenges, and experiences in corporate governance in OECD and non-OECD countries and to profit from consultations with and feedback from main international institutions (such as the World Bank, the IMF, and the Bank for International Settlement (BIS)) and private sector experts. The revised principles were issued in 2004. The six new non-binding *OECD Principles for Corporate Governance* concentrated on financial and non-financial public trading companies but were also useful and applicable to non-traded companies. In addition, they were not intended to be a substitute for but to complement initiatives of local government and the private sector, and best practices in this area. The improved principles stress that the corporate governance framework should protect the rights of shareholders and ensure their equitable treatment, irrespective of minority or foreign status. The corporate governance framework must also respect the role and rights of stakeholders and ensure the transparency and timely and accurate disclosure of relevant information. The principles deal also with the board's oversight responsibilities and accountability to shareholders, and with the need to have a corporate governance structure that supports transparent and efficient markets. The six principles, along with the sub-principles, have been embedded in six chapters or sections, which are: (1) Ensuring the Basis for an Effective Corporate Governance Framework; (2) The Rights of Shareholders and Key Ownership Functions; (3) The Equitable Treatment of Shareholders; (4) The Role of Stakeholders in Corporate Governance; (5) Disclosure and Transparency; and (6) The Responsibilities of the Board.

Recently, the 2004 principles were in turn reviewed and amended to become the *G20/OECD Principles of Corporate Governance*, published in 2015. The G20 countries were invited to participate, along with the previously mentioned parties, in the review. The updated principles maintained the six-chapter structure and the bulk of the recommendations or sub-principles of the previous versions (although some were expanded and more fully elaborated), introduced new issues, and clarified or emphasized others to be in line with trends and developments in the marketplace and to address shortcomings in corporate governance that were apparent during the global financial crisis of 2007–8. Elements of novelty involved, among other things, merging the contents of chapters 1 and 3, mentioned above, into one chapter (chapter 2) and creating a new chapter (chapter 3) entitled "Institutional Investors, Stock Markets and Other Intermediaries". This new chapter emphasizes that institutional investors should also disclose their corporate governance and voting policies relating to their investments and unveil how they manage material conflicts of interest that might arise.

The principles of the Basel Committee on Banking Supervision (BCBS)

The Basel Committee on Banking Supervision (BCBS), an international standard-setter and one of the very active committees of the Bank for International Settlements (BIS) housed in Basel, Switzerland, firmly believes that sound and effective corporate governance is crucial for promoting public and market confidence in the banking system and for maintaining its safety and soundness and its proper functioning, along with that of the economy as a whole. Both the market and the public are considered to be highly sensitive to problems emanating from corporate governance weaknesses in financial intermediaries and, subsequently, corporate governance should be of utmost significance both to individual banks and to the international financial system as a whole, which warrants global supervisory guidance. Against this background, the BCBS has long sought to provide through a set of guiding principles an adequate corporate governance framework that would assist both supervisors in advancing the adoption of sound corporate practices by banking organizations operating in their jurisdictions or under their authority and banks in their own development of their corporate governance structure, policies, and procedures.

In September 1999 the BCBS issued a fourteen-page document entitled *Enhancing Corporate Governance for Banking Organizations* in the belief that establishing sound corporate governance at banks tends to facilitate the work of bank supervisors across the globe and can contribute to a positive two-way working link and cooperation between bank management and bank supervisors. The guidance on corporate governance in banks aimed essentially at assisting bank supervisors in implementing the *Core Principles for Effective Banking Supervision* (a document issued by the Basel Committee), particularly insofar as it encourages the adoption in their countries of sound corporate governance practices by banking firms.[11] It came also as part of the hard work on the part of the BCBS to reinforce risk management and disclosure procedures in banks and to emphasize for financial services firms the importance of the 1999 OECD principles.

The sound corporate governance practices included at that time the setting of strategic objectives and corporate values to be conveyed across the whole bank and the implementation of clear lines of responsibility and accountability throughout the banking firm. They also involved the need to have qualified board members well aware of their role in corporate governance and senior management exercising appropriate oversight. The practices deal as well with the importance of the control function and the work provided by the internal and external auditors, and other issues, such as (i) compensation policies and practices, which should be consistent with the bank's corporate culture and objectives; and (ii) corporate governance transparency. The 1999 document had, in addition to the chapter on sound corporate governance practices (of which there were seven), a chapter on the role of supervisors and another on ensuring an environment supportive of sound corporate governance.

A revised version of the 1999 paper was issued in February 2006 to take into account the content of the OECD revised corporate governance principles in 2004 and to address failures and introduce improvement in corporate governance at banks. The new thirty-page *Enhancing Corporate Governance for Banking Organizations* aimed, like the previous edition, at aiding banking firms in improving their corporate governance frameworks and helping supervisors in quality control and evaluation of those governance structures. It included, as had the previous document, a chapter on sound corporate governance principles (which expanded to eight and were more elaborated), a chapter on the role of supervisors, and a chapter on promoting an environment supportive of sound corporate governance. The newly introduced principle required the board and senior management to better understand the bank's operational structure—"Know-Your-Structure"—including where the bank operates in jurisdictions or through complex structures (e.g. special purpose vehicles, corporate trusts) that obstruct transparency and thus impede effective board and senior management oversight. This can also create financial, legal, and reputational risks for the banking firm.

The Basel Committee reviewed and revised the 2006 principles and guidance once more following the global financial crisis of 2007–8, during which a number of corporate governance failures and omissions came to light and deficiencies became more apparent. The crisis demonstrated that, in many cases, there were, among other things, inadequate board oversights of senior management, deficient risk management, and overly complex or non-transparent organizational structures and activities. The principles outlined in earlier versions continued to be relevant, but were further elaborated and expanded into a set of fourteen principles in the new *Principles for Enhancing Corporate Governance* of October 2010, falling under one chapter and distributed across six areas: board practices; senior management; risk management and internal controls; compensation; complex or opaque corporate structures; and disclosure and transparency. The two chapters of the previous versions on the role of supervisors and the supportive environment for sound corporate governance continued to be maintained.

More recently, in July 2015, the BCBS issued a revised set of the principles published in 2010. The revised guidance includes thirteen principles which are briefly described below, widening the assistance and advice on the role and responsibilities of the board and stressing the importance of risk governance within the overall corporate governance framework. The thirteen principles summarize the efforts made by the BCBS in this area of corporate governance from 1999 until

2005, and their abstracts, given below, assist in an understanding of the discussion in the coming section on what banks have been doing to comply with these guidelines and international standards.

The first three principles in the 2015 version of the Corporate Governance Principles for Banks are about the Board's overall responsibilities, qualifications and composition, and own structure and practices.

Principle 1 details the Board's overall and ultimate responsibility for the bank. It has to authorize and watch over senior management's putting into action the bank's business strategies and objectives; organizational structure; governance framework and practices; risk management, policies and limits; compliance policies and obligations; internal control systems; and corporate culture and values.

Principle 2, on Board qualifications and composition, argues that in order for the Board to exercise effectively its responsibilities of governance and oversight it must include sufficient independent directors and members with relevant and diverse qualifications (knowledge, skills, experience, background, reputation, and so on) in the different areas (capital markets, financial analysis, information technology, strategic planning, regulation, and so on).

Principle 3, related to the Board's own structure and practices, says that in order to perform effectively its supervisory role and the range of responsibilities held, the Board must delineate an adequate governance structure, practices, and procedures (involving its own structure and the committee's structures), which must be periodically assessed and reviewed to make any necessary changes and improvements. It also describes the role, required qualifications, and responsibilities of the Chair. The Chair is preferably an independent or non-executive Board member for checks and balances considerations. Principle 3 also mentions that the Board must watch over the formulation and execution of policies on conflicts of interest arising from the bank's diverse activities and roles.

Principle 3 also recommends the creation of a number of specialized board committees by the authorization of the full board for the sake of enhancing efficiency and concentration in key specific areas. One of the five recommended committees is the Audit Committee, comprised solely of independent or non-executive board members and individuals with experience in audit practices, financial reporting, and accounting, with the main responsibility of devising policies on internal audit and financial reporting and providing oversight. Another specialized board committee is the Risk Committee, which is given the task of, among other things, discussing and reviewing risk strategies and policies and advising the board on such issues and on the bank's overall risk appetite. It also has the responsibility of interacting with and overseeing the Chief Risk Officer (CRO). The Risk Committee is made up of members the majority of whom are independent and have experience in risk-management issues and practices. Like the audit committee, the Chair has to be an independent director and not the Chair of the Board or of any other committee. The third committee is the Compensation Committee, which is involved in evaluating compensation policies and practices adopted by the bank and the incentives created by the remuneration system, thus assisting the Board in controlling the remuneration system's configuration and functioning and making sure that the remuneration system is suitable and in agreement with legal and regulatory requirements and with the bank's culture and other issues. The Chair of this committee, like any other board committee Chair, should be an independent non-executive board member. There are also the Nomination/Human Resources/Governance Committee, which is involved, among other things, in the nomination and recommendation of new board members and senior management and in overseeing human resources policies, and the Ethics and Compliance Committee, which deals with compliance with laws, regulations, and internal rules.

Principle 4 relates to senior management responsibilities, most of which involve running and managing the activities of the bank under the direction and oversight of the Board and in a way compatible with its approved policies concerning business strategies, risk appetite and risk management and control, compliance with laws and regulations, remuneration, and so on. Members of senior management are responsible and accountable to the Board for the reliable and cautious daily management of the bank and for the implementation of the laid-out policies and should possess the required experience, competencies, and integrity for the position in question in order to manage the banking firm and supervise the work of subordinate employees. To ensure the effective management of the bank there should be clarity and transparency regarding the role, authority, and responsibility of the different positions within senior management, including that of the CEO. Senior management should supply the Board with the necessary information to perform its responsibilities in supervising it and assessing its performance and in dealing with legal, regulatory, internal control, and performance concerns.

Principle 5 focuses on the governance of a group structure where the Board of the parent company has to be conscious about the risks and forces that might impinge on the bank as a whole and its subsidiaries, and has to ensure the formation and functioning of a comprehensible governance framework with clearly outlined roles and responsibilities suitable to the group structure and to the business, and to the risks of the group and its affiliated entities. The Board of the parent company also has the duty of conducting appropriate oversight over subsidiaries independently and aside from the legal and governance responsibilities exercised by subsidiary boards.

Principles 6 through 8 discuss risk issues, including the creation and role of a risk-management function and risk identification, monitoring, control, and communication.

Principle 6 talks particularly about the risk-management function that should be established in a bank. This function should have the authority and be effective and independent of the business units, with the responsibility of supervising or controlling risk-taking activities across the banking firm, including identifying, assessing, monitoring, mitigating, and reporting risks. The risk-management function should be headed by a Chief Risk Officer (CRO) and should have the necessary number of experienced and qualified employees in the risk discipline, with expertise in risk regulation, management, and control; the staff should also have the right to receive regular training. The CRO ought to possess, in addition to the requisite skills, the authority and the appropriate organizational stature to perform his/her diverse responsibilities and must have the right of entry to any information deemed necessary to carry out his/her duties, which should be independent and distinct from other executive functions. The CRO must have access to the Board and should be the one to oversee the bank's risk-management activities and the development of risk-management systems, policies, and processes that would support the strategic objectives of the bank.

Principle 7 relates to risk identification, monitoring, and control. It says that existing and emerging risks to the bank must be identified, assessed, monitored, and controlled on a bank-wide level (including subsidiary banks and affiliates) and individual entity basis, and that risk identification and measurement should be based on both quantitative and qualitative information and analysis, utilizing stress tests and scenario analysis. Policies, procedures, and processes must be devised in a way that guarantees that risk identification, monitoring, and mitigation means are appropriate in relation to the bank's size, activity sophistication, and risk exposure. The bank's risk management and internal control infrastructure must keep pace with alterations in industry practices and the bank's risk profile.

Principle 8 deals with risk communication. Prioritized and to the point risk information and risk-related key issues (involving risk exposures, risk/return relationships, risk appetite, and deficiencies) should be passed onto the Board and senior management in a timely and precise manner to enable them take the appropriate decisions and measures. Banks—through their Boards, senior management, and control functions—must also ensure and encourage the effective sharing or communication of risk information and issues, particularly the risk strategies adopted across the banking firm to advocate robust risk culture and risk awareness.

Principle 9 is about compliance risk and function. It reiterates the duties of the Board in overseeing the management of the bank's compliance risk and in instituting a compliance function. The bank's senior management responsibility lies in setting up a compliance policy that must be approved by the Board and that contains basic principles and processes for identifying, assessing, monitoring, and reporting compliance risk. The compliance function is in charge of ensuring that the bank operates in compliance with applicable laws, regulations, standards, and internal policies and should advise and inform both the Board and senior management on compliance and on any developments in this area. It must have enough authority, adequate resources, and independence from the bank's management in order to prevent unnecessary pressure or impediments, and must enjoy direct access to the Board.

Principle 10 relates to the internal audit function, which should be independent of the other functions of the bank, liable to the Board, and have complete or absolute access to records, data, and other material to carry out its duties effectively and objectively. The tasks and responsibilities of the audit function involve analyzing and reporting on the efficacy and quality of the bank's governance, risk management, and internal control systems and processes in order to assist the

Board and senior management in protecting the reputation and soundness of the banking firm. Internal auditors are expected to have the necessary skills and to abide by domestic and international professional standards.

Principle 11 elaborates on compensation. It is the responsibility of the Board or its delegated compensation committee to (i) supervise the senior management's implementation of the whole bank remuneration system, (ii) evaluate whether this system is generating the best incentives for managing risk, capital, and liquidity through regularly monitoring and reviewing remuneration plans, processes, and outcomes, and (iii) approve the compensation of senior executives (CEO, CRO and head of internal audit). The remuneration structure has to be aligned with the bank's strategies, objectives, and interests, and must mirror risk taking and effects.

Principle 12 tackles disclosure and transparency, emphasizing that transparency and the timely and accurate disclosure of relevant and useful information provide shareholders, depositors, and other stakeholders, in addition to market participants, with the material necessary to allow them to effectively monitor the activities of a bank, gauge the efficacy of its board and senior management in governing the firm, and hold them accountable. Information disclosed through annual reports or other periodic publications should include, among other things, the bank's objectives, its organizational and governance structures and policies, major share ownership and voting rights, risk exposures and risk-management strategies, incentive and compensation policies, and related party transactions.

Principle 13 discusses the roles of bank supervisors, the first of which is to give guidance in strong corporate governance at banks by requesting the latter to have sound corporate governance policies and practices in harmony with both the thirteen principles laid down in this BIS document and the industry best practices. Supervisors also have the role of evaluating the effectiveness of a bank's corporate governance through the various well-known types of on- and off-site monitoring and through regular communication with the senior management and the Board to assess the processes and mechanisms in place for executing the relevant oversight responsibilities and to foster corporate governance. Supervision of corporate governance at banks requires regular interaction and dialogue on a range of strategic, management, and risk issues, not only with Board members and senior management but also with people responsible for risk management, compliance, and internal audit functions, in addition to external auditors. Bank supervisors should also have the authority and the means to require governance improvement and to compel corrective actions or, alternatively, to impose sanctions and penal measures when there is a need. Remedial actions may include changes in adopted policies and practices at banks or changes in the composition of the Board of Directors or senior management. Finally, supervisors must cooperate and share corporate governance information with other relevant public authorities and with host supervisors of cross-border banking entities.

The implementation of best practices at banks and related challenges and implications

The adoption of international standards

Banks in general and internationally active ones particularly provide regular updated information on their corporate governance framework and practices adopted at their institutions through their annual reports and websites. The description outlined below of the development or evolution in practices undertaken by banks in the area of corporate governance and standards implementation over the last few years is largely built on such information aggregated from an indicative sample of banks and personal experience. It is not intended, therefore, to be exhaustive nor fully reflective of each and every individual bank around the globe. The practices should be viewed, therefore, as those of a typical bank, considering that the sophistication and diversity in corporate governance frameworks and codes at financial services firms are a function of, among other things, the structure, size, complexity, and business model of the firm and the jurisdiction regulating and supervising the bank and dictating the scale and scope of its activities, as has been mentioned above.

Recently a commitment to sound corporate governance and to the implementation of its principles has intensified, with the boards of directors of banks giving considerable weight to sound corporate governance practices, to monitoring development in governance regulations and standards, and to initiating the necessary changes in their own frameworks or codes, sometimes beyond compliance requirements. Relatively new initiatives have included the formalization of the functions and responsibilities of the board; changes to board members; the nomination of independent directors; the creation and/or the modification of board committees and their charters, where these committees report directly to the board, which acts on their recommendations; and the adoption of new policies or the updating of existing ones regarding compensation and benefits, management performance, and so on. Written policies and procedures regarding, for example, board practices and committee structure, compliance, internal control, risk, and ethics have become more common. A number of core policies and procedures have been prepared, including (i) Codes of Ethics and Conduct designed to increase translucency around moral values; (ii) by-laws relating to internal control, audit committee, dividend policy, corporate conflict and so on; and (iii) compliance and risk manuals. The development of and regular revisions and updates of corporate governance codes were adopted and communicated throughout the bank to make the governance structure more transparent, demonstrate commitment to sound corporate governance, and foster the confidence of all stakeholders, including investors, shareholders, and employees. Frequent training for board members and executives also emerged as a new trend in raising information awareness and keeping them informed of the latest developments in banking rules and regulations, financial accounting, strategy, and other subjects. The issue of disclosure and transparency has been thoroughly addressed as well, so that potential investors and other interested parties can easily access information not only on the financial performance or position of the bank but also on the bank's management, operations, and risks through public annual reports and the internet. Many boards also had to ensure that their bank's governance framework adhered to the related regulations and guidelines and was tailored to the needs and expectations of its internal and external stakeholders. Many banks broadened their shareholder base to expand their narrow ownership structure for better corporate governance, and formalized certain procedures to protect shareholder rights and to communicate effectively with stakeholders, whether through a public or investors' relations officer, press releases and conferences, annual reports, or other means.

Shareholder rights

In many jurisdictions efforts have been intensified to treat all shareholders (minority and majority, domestic and foreign) equally with respect to voting rights, subscription rights, and transfer rights, and to improve communications with shareholders in terms of the notification of and the results of general shareholders' meetings by taking advantage of advancements made in information and telecommunication technologies. Shareholders should be informed of such meetings, including time, place, and agenda, more than twenty days ahead of their scheduled date, and not only through the press but also through other means, such as mail, in line with international best practices. The practice of sending financial information, external auditors' reports, and other documents is also becoming more common, as is the release to the wider public of the main outcomes of such meetings through the press, through the bank's website, or through mail. Proportional voting remains a mechanism for protecting shareholders' rights and clear policies have been developed with respect to treatment in changing of controlling stake. Minority shareholders have also been encouraged to attend general shareholders' meetings to express, like other shareholders, their views on issues such as nomination, election of board members, and the remuneration of board members and executives, including the equity component, and to provide their approval or disapproval. A written dividend policy has also been among the new practices that would make current and potential shareholders aware of potential future cash inflow and enable them to take the proper decisions regarding their investments.

Board and senior management's roles and responsibilities

The board's traditional roles of defining the bank's mission or objectives and overall business strategy, directing and monitoring senior management, ensuring adequate control, and assuming the whole responsibility for the operational and financial soundness of the bank have always been respected to a large extent and undertaken by most board of directors of banks, even before the emergence of the related international standards. A number of issues, however, were not addressed or clearly defined by many banks. One of these was that, in many cases, divisions in the different roles and responsibilities of the board, the chairperson, and management were not always plainly described. This necessitated establishing throughout the bank cloudless lines of responsibilities and accountability and effective channels of communications and making boards more active in monitoring management.

Another issue is that many boards were totally or largely dominated by executives, making them incapable of exercising independent and objective judgment in the absence of non-executive board members in terms of tasks where there was a potential for conflicts of interest. They were also in a poor position to evaluate their own performance and determine their remuneration based on their qualifications and work contributions. These banks needed to attract gradually more independent directors. In addition, board evaluation and training have been given the needed attention. Board members' compensation (for executive and non-executive directors) had to be proportionate to their different skills, qualities, and input to the board. Previously, the remuneration of board members was largely based on a periodical (monthly, quarterly, or annual) flat rate and thus not linked to the bank's long-term performance in line with international best practices. Though the skills of board members (education, experience, reputation, and knowledge) have been adequate, they lacked, in many cases, the necessary skills variations in different areas of banking, finance, economics, information technology, and law that would allow them to make better contributions to the effectiveness of the board.

A third point to consider is that a large number of banks lacked board-level committees believed to play an important role in the governance of the bank, such as risk, corporate governance, nomination and/or remuneration, and audit committees. Furthermore, when present, an audit committee is usually composed exclusively of board members, with no or few independent directors. This necessitated, for most banks, the formation over the years of risk, audit, corporate governance and nomination, and remuneration committees composed mostly of independent directors. The risk committee has the duty of helping the board in carrying out its risk-related responsibilities through outlining and recommending the bank's risk policies and risk appetite to the board for approval and assessing and monitoring risk-management effectiveness and risk profiles for all types of risk to which the bank is exposed. The audit committee is to assist the board in exercising its oversight role and responsibilities regarding the autonomy and efficacy of the internal audit function; the suitability of accounting, financial reporting, internal control, and compliance policies and procedures; the integrity of the financial statements and the honesty of financial and non-financial information disclosure; and the independence, qualifications, and effectiveness of the external auditors. The corporate governance and nomination committee is to aid the board in securing a successful corporate governance framework for the bank and the best possible board composition and arrangements. Finally, the remuneration or compensation committee is to assist the board in adopting a set of values and incentives for the bank's executives and employees that center on performance and loyalty, among other issues. It proposes recommendations to the board regarding compensation and benefit policy consistent with the bank's culture, long-term objectives and strategies, and legal or regulatory requirements.

A fourth element relates to the Senior Management Committee (SMC), which includes executive directors and other senior management officials. Though most banks had an SMC in place, its role and responsibilities (including planning, advising, supervising, monitoring, and decision making) had not been clearly defined in a large number of financial services firms and formal succession planning policies for its members were lacking. Many SMCs did not report to the board and not all boards approved SMC member election and dismissal. In many cases, SMC members did not have liability insurance and their salaries were not disclosed. Incentive-based compensation linked to long-term performance and formal assessment of SMC members were lacking as well. In some cases, internal audit was appointed to the committee, jeopardizing its independence. These concerns had to be addressed in line with best practices in order to ensure that the SMC reports to the board are treated in the same way as those of any other committee and its role and responsibilities are formally defined and clarified in a document.

Control mechanisms

To ensure that adequate internal control mechanisms are in place banks have been required, in order to have a better independent oversight, to form an independent audit committee made up of independent auditors and reporting directly to the board, and an internal audit function reporting to this board audit committee (and to the board). Substantial efforts were made in many places to secure these requirements, albeit gradually, as it is not easy to find suitable and trustworthy independent committee members or directors in order to develop an audit committee composed of a majority, if not an entirety, of independent executives. Furthermore, it initially seemed difficult to assimilate the proposed changes within the lines of responsibilities and reporting. In any case, audit committees and the internal audit functions at banks nowadays assume a range of responsibilities and tasks, including monitoring compliance with laws and regulations and ensuring that risk-management systems and operational processes are well established and implemented. The audit committee has to ensure also that the internal audit meets the guidance and standards set by the Institute of Internal Auditors (IIA). Training of personnel involved in the internal control process also became more prevalent.

Proper external control is the duty of independent external auditors, who are recommended by the audit committee of the board and who should be rotated according to international guidance and best practice, particularly in the case of the lead audit partner. Given the inconveniences and costs of rotating audit partners and firms and the ambiguity surrounding the benefits, many banks are still hesitant about changing external auditors every few years. The bank's relationship with the external auditor has to be managed by the audit committee, which monitors the independence (which can be impaired by their providing non-audit services) and the professional and technical competence of external auditors and other relevant issues.

Risk management

Since the recent global financial crisis risk-management practices in banks have been given more attention and strengthened, with boards and senior management gaining better understandings of the financial, non-financial, strategic, and operational risks faced by their institutions and devoting more time to risk management. Risk is being managed on a corporate-wide basis and both risk management and risk appetite are aligned with the corporate strategy. Boards also took measures to reduce incentives for excessive risk-taking, such as stopping options for top executives. Risk managers were also brought close to management; they are nowadays considered a fundamental element in putting into practice the bank's strategy and are involved in senior management decision making.[12]

Transparency and disclosure

The international and domestic guidance on enhancing corporate governance encouraged banks worldwide to develop proper disclosure policies pertaining to financial and non-financial information, on the basis that more and better disclosure is often associated with an improvement in the bank's attractiveness to potential investors. Transparency is also essential in allowing shareholders and market participants to appropriately monitor and hold accountable the board and senior management. Banks thus began to reveal—mainly through their annual or interim reports—timely and reliable information that previously they had been unenthusiastic about disclosing publicly, as many financial services firms had previously unveiled only information required by the regulatory and supervisory authorities and related mainly to their financial statements or financial position. Information divulged to the general public involves, nowadays, among other aspects, biographical and background information on board and senior management committee members, the bank's organizational chart, and information about major shareholders and their share ownership. Disclosure of information on risk management, the bank's operations, all related party transactions and those exceeding 5 percent of the bank's assets, board member and senior management remuneration policies, amounts and types to shareholders became more common. In addition, financial statements are increasingly prepared in accordance with International Financial Reporting Standards (IFRS), thus enhancing the reliability and comparability of reporting and improving the capacity to gain a deep and accurate understanding of banks' performance.

Challenges and implications

There are obviously challenges related to the state authorities' formulation, promotion, and overseeing of corporate governance guidelines or best practices and other regulations concerning the implementation by financial institutions of the occasionally revised and updated principles and standards or the devising of their own complementary governance practices. That is to say, there are legal challenges on top of those confronted by banks' regulators and supervisors and faced by banking institutions.

In fact, it is difficult for some provisions or principles in the international standards and guidelines to be adopted by local authorities fully or partially (as they are) and incorporated into domestic laws and regulations. The issue of the compatibility of international regulations with existing domestic legislations and rules is a serious one, as compliance with international best practices may demand on the national level new legislation or legislative and financial reforms, or modifications to existing laws and regulations that could be substantial in certain cases and could perhaps initiate a nationwide debate about the pros and cons taking years to be concluded. The reforms and modifications proposed to achieve adherence to international guidelines and standards entail a thorough review and examination of the legal and regulatory framework pertaining to the corporate governance of banks and non-bank companies in each country and of the specificities of each economy. This partly explains why some countries can move faster in devising and implementing corporate governance standards and in complying nearly fully with international best practices than can others. Legal impediments regarding cooperation, communication, and information sharing among relevant authorities (regulatory, supervisory, monetary, judiciary, and others) within countries and between local authorities and others in other jurisdictions could arise from, among other issues, conflicting legal and regulatory requirements across the different jurisdictions or an absence of relevant agreements of cooperation between one country and another or between one country and a group of countries. This, in turn, could weaken the official supervision of corporate governance policies and practices, at least for a while, before conflicts are resolved and convergence to international best practices becomes possible and simplified.

As far as domestic bank regulatory and supervisory authorities are concerned, they have to keep up with a highly dynamic and evolving banking or financial system and the rapidly changing and complex operating environment for banks and financial institutions. To adequately perform their roles and effectively exercise their duties in the area of corporate governance in making sure that banks practice sound corporate governance consistent with the applicable domestic rules and regulations and the international principles and guidelines, concerned authorities must be able to satisfy a number of requirements. Regulators and supervisors need to secure adequate financial, human, and capital resources and have the necessary tools at hand to establish good guidance and rules; evaluate banks' corporate governance policies and practices, including control mechanisms and the qualifications of board members and senior management; conduct proper on-site inspections and off-site monitoring; and relate the corporate governance structure to the risk profile of the bank. Supervisors must be adequately trained to keep up and assess the corporate governance framework that each bank has adopted and need to have a good understanding of the risks that emanate from the sophistication of products and services offered by banks and the innovation in financial services instruments, provision, and delivery channels. The introduction of innovative financial tools and the expansion in new financing structures to circumvent constraining regulation or for any other reason necessitates understanding properly the governance implications and risks to the financial firm and perhaps imposing different and more vigorous governance approaches, arrangements, and practices. Failure to deal with this complexity of operations and risks may result in weakened supervisory oversight of corporate governance practices by banks, which could incur excessive risk and in certain cases burden the government and taxpayers. Supervisors must also have the ability to deal with the demanding task of overseeing banking groups with active cross-border operations and that are growing in size, and should have also the authority to oblige banks to take the proper remedial actions within the necessary time frame to address corporate governance deficiencies. Such authority, in turn, may demand changes in relevant laws, which suggests that there could be many impediments before the necessary results are achieved.

The challenges to the industry are also many. The adoption of international best practices and the implementation of related domestic laws and regulations may often require changes to existing policies and practices to make internal rules consistent with standards and regulations, which could involve substantial costs in time and money to effect systems, policies, and procedures change, produce the necessary documentation, and improve monitoring and control capabilities. There could also be additional education and training costs at all levels of the financial services firm in adherence to certain provisions of international bank guidance. The creation of new functions and new board committees at banks and the requirement to have independent directors with diversified and supplementary qualifications also entail an expansion in operating expenses, not to mention an exhausting and time-consuming hunt for competitive and skilled personnel and executives. Even if the necessary qualified directors and employees are found and recruited, this does not guarantee in itself excellence in corporate governance. Nothing can ensure that this or that board composition is ideal given the business and risk profiles and whether or not a particular composition of independent and expert people understands fully the different types of risks and vulnerabilities, is heavily committed to sound practices, and is definitely conducive to the optimum governance outcomes. This is especially true for large financial groups operating in many jurisdictions and offering a diverse range of products and services, from traditional to complex, where, in addition to the challenge of managing the different and complicated types of operation and the multiple lines of responsibility and accountability, there is also the challenge of managing distant employees with different cultures, habits, personal interest, and goals. Another related challenge could be the timely implementation of sound corporate governance practices throughout the group or the holding company, especially if the latter is spread across many countries, possibly leading to challenges of compliance with different local jurisdictions and global requirements at the same time and to issues with potentially conflicting rules in different operating environments. With the rising role and responsibilities of the board, there could also be a partial diversion in attention away from the main business activity of the bank and the potential profit opportunities given the time constraints and the need to allocate work time to discussing and deciding on continuously increasing duties and tasks. Mounting roles and responsibilities means also an increase in the potential liabilities of board members, entailing reviewing and upgrading the remuneration package in line with the additional burden and the broadening of tasks and duties to retain the already attracted talent that is able to adapt to changes in the banking and operating environments through acquiring more knowledge, expertise, and skills.

Basel III standards: challenges and implications

In the period before the Basel Accord of 1988 banks were generally asked to keep a total capital to asset ratio of at least 6–8 percent of their total assets. There was no mention of risk-adjusted assets, irrespective of the risk component of the assets. Thus, bank capital was not tied to bank risk. However, examinations of banks' balance sheets addressed risk issues and regulated asset holdings. Regulations provided for prompt corrective action (PCA) based on capital ratio thresholds. The level of these ratios, though slightly different across countries, provided early warning signals. Therefore, for banks that are deemed well-capitalized, regulators were not required to take any action, while supervisory intervention in under-capitalized banks became marked as capital positions deteriorated. Often, these banks became restricted in their activities, while severely undercapitalized ones were subject to early closure. Bank examiners used six factors in evaluating the safety and soundness of commercial banks. Based on the score in each of these factors, an overall rating was assigned to each bank in a ranking system framework known by the acronym CAMELS: C for capital adequacy, A for asset quality, M for management quality, E for earnings record, L for liquidity position, and S for sensitivity to market risk. Some bank examiners add the letter I to CAMELS, reflecting the importance of information technology in sound bank management, especially in offering online services.

The Basel agreement on new bank capital standards, named after the city in Switzerland where it was signed in July 1988, had been phased in by January 1993. The purpose of the Basel Accord was mainly twofold: to ensure the tying of bank capital to bank risk by adjusting assets to their respective risk (risk-adjusted assets) and the holding of capital against off-balance sheet activities. Additionally, the Accord aimed at benchmarking capital requirements in different countries against a common set of rules and accounting for the financial innovation revolution in the marketplace. Thus, according to Basel I, for a bank to qualify as adequately capitalized current capital requirements ought to include: the ratio of core capital Tier 1 (comprised of common stock and surplus undivided profits, qualifying noncumulative preferred stock, minority interests in the equity accounts of consolidated subsidiaries, selected identifiable intangible assets less goodwill, and other intangible assets) to total risk-weighted assets must be at least 4 percent; the ratio of total capital (Tier 1 + Tier 2) to risk-weighted assets must be at least 8 percent, with Tier 2 including all remaining items considered as capital, most importantly allowance for loan and lease losses, subordinated debt capital instruments, and equity notes; additionally, the amount of Tier 2 capital was to be limited to 100 percent of Tier 1 capital.

After serious evaluation of Basel I, Basel II was introduced in 2004 and a revised and comprehensive version was later released in 2006 to correct some of the weak points of Basel I by emphasizing three pillars. First, minimum capital requirements for each bank are to be based on the bank's estimated risk exposure—that is, against credit risk as well as a newly introduced operational risk or the risk of losses resulting from inadequate internal processes, people and systems, and/or external events. Several basic and advanced approaches were provided for banks to use in their estimation of minimum capital requirements. Second, a supervisory review was introduced to assess each bank's internal risk procedure. Third, greater public disclosure of banks' true financial conditions was adopted to enhance the role of market discipline.

Basel III was introduced in 2010 as a result of and response to the financial crisis of 2008. Further additions, clarifications, and adjustments were later made to the new framework in 2011, 2013, and 2014. According to the Bank for International Settlement (BIS), the implementation of Basel III will considerably increase the quality and required level of bank capital and reduce systemic risk and bank contagion effects. The quality will be enhanced by placing greater focus and a stricter definition on common equity, as it represents the highest-quality component of a bank's capital. The addition to capital will be reflected in the increase of the minimum common equity requirement to 4.5 percent (2 percent under Basel II). The Tier 1 minimum capital requirement will be increased to 6 percent (4 percent under Basel II), with total capital remaining at 8 percent (Tier 2 at 2 percent). Banks will be required to hold a capital conservation buffer of 2.5 percent of common equity to withstand future periods of stress. Thus, the new common equity requirement becomes 7 percent (4.5 percent + 2.5 percent), the Tier 1 requirement is 8.5 percent (6 percent + 2.5 percent), and total capital 10.5 percent (8 percent + 2.5 percent), after adding the conservation buffer. Reducing systemic risk or risk of financial system disruption that could destabilize the macroeconomy can take place by reducing the pro-cyclicality of Basel II and by taking into account the interlinkages among financial institutions. Basel III will promote the build-up of buffers that can be drawn down in periods of stress. A counter-cyclical buffer in a range of 0–2.5 percent is to be created. This capital would be released in a downturn of the cycle.

As far as transitional arrangements to Basel III are concerned, the minimum common equity and Tier 1 requirements increased from 2 percent and 4 percent to 3.5 percent and 4.5 percent respectively at the beginning of 2013. They were 4 percent and 5.5 percent respectively starting in 2014 and 4.5 percent and 6 percent beginning in 2015. The 2.5 percent capital conservation buffer will be phased in progressively, starting in 2016, to be fully effective by 1 January 2019. In January 2013 the Liquidity Coverage Ratio and Liquidity Risk Monitoring Tools were introduced. To promote the short-term resilience of a bank's liquidity risk profile the Basel Committee developed the Liquidity Coverage Ratio (LCR). This standard aims to ensure that a bank has an adequate stock of unencumbered high-quality liquid assets (HQLA) consisting of cash or assets that can be converted into cash at little or no loss of value in private markets to meet its liquidity needs for a thirty-calendar-day liquidity stress scenario. The LCR stipulates that the value of the stock of HQLA over the total net cash outflows over the next thirty calendar days is to exceed or be equal to 100 percent. Banks are expected to meet this requirement on an ongoing basis and hold a stock of unencumbered HQLA as a defense against the potential onset of liquidity stress. During a period of financial stress, however, banks may use their stock of HQLA, thereby falling below 100 percent. Specifically, the LCR was introduced as planned on 1 January 2015, but the minimum requirement began at 60 percent, rising in annual steps of 10 percentage points to reach 100 percent on 1 January 2019. This graduated approach is designed to ensure that the LCR can be introduced without disruption to the orderly strengthening of banking systems and the ongoing financing of economic activity. The other required liquidity ratio introduced by Basel III is the Net Stable Funding Ratio (NSFR), which requires the available amount of stable funding to exceed the required amount of stable funding over a one-year period of extended stress. Basel III also introduced a minimum 3 percent leverage ratio (capital to total on- and off-balance-sheet assets) to become effective in January 2018 as a supplement to risk-based measures of regulatory capital and implemented without taking into account the risks related to the different categories of assets (i.e. measured on a gross and unweighted basis). The remainder of this section will address the main challenges and implications of the Basel III capital and liquidity standards facing the banking industry.

The main potential effects of the full implementation of Basel III on individual banks and the industry as a whole can be summarized as follows. Banking institutions are likely to incur additional and thus higher regulatory compliance costs, including the cost of carrying out a major revision and update to their IT infrastructure to meet the new capital adequacy, liquidity, leverage, and risk-management requirements. To handle and reinforce the new stipulated rules and standards there must be fresh investments in time and money for data sourcing, collection and traceability systems, and in banking processes for effective liquidity and risk management and reporting and for the enhancement of the bank's reputation and credibility in general. Basel III requirements may also increase the cost of bank credit and reduce credit availability or lending capacity—that is, it may negatively influence financial intermediation. Higher interest rates could then contribute to slower economic activity and growth, depending on a number of factors, particularly elasticity of demand for credit. New capital and liquidity standards can also raise the operating costs at banks and lower their profitability, and could ultimately encourage mergers and acquisitions. There are definitely other implications and challenges related to Basel III implementation but, given the multiple constraints, we will elaborate briefly below on only two possible repercussions: (i) the higher cost of financial intermediation and poorer credit availability, and (ii) higher operating costs and lower profitability for banks.[13] It should be mentioned also that the gradual implementation of Basel III over a period up to 2019 was intended to give banking institutions enough time to comply with the new requirements and to mitigate and smooth out the potential impacts mentioned above. This is why there could be a smaller negative influence than the significant impact that is currently expected.

Cost of financial intermediation and availability of credit

It is well known, based on the theory and practice, that in order to meet and maintain the minimum regulatory capital ratios banks can rely, among other things, on one or more of the following strategies or alternatives. First, they can increase the volume or level of capital by issuing new equity tools or securing high retained earnings. Second, they can reduce the level or the volume of assets (risk-weighted assets) or shift portfolios from high-risk assets to lower-risk categories. Given that raising capital externally is considered in general expensive and difficult, especially for small banks, which have a problem in easily tapping the markets for funds, in making higher profits, and in retaining more of net earnings, then some financial services firms may opt for adding this supplementary cost to loans and/or contracting the volume of credit, thus affecting the financial intermediation function and possibly influencing economic activity and growth. Therefore, one potential outcome of higher capital requirements is that some banks are inclined to extend less credit than before and/or re-price loans upwards and deposits downwards to counterbalance for securing and maintaining higher capital. A credit contraction could ensue, negatively affecting investment, output level, and growth, suggesting the necessity to equilibrate between the level of economic activity and the soundness of the banking system. But many scholars believe that the average cost of capital (cost of debt and equity) is minimally or insignificantly affected by capital requirements and that, therefore, variations to the capital structure are unlikely to affect lending rates and economic activity. According to this strand of thought, although equity is more expensive than debt more equity will be associated with lower equity risk and cost, with no major effect on the overall cost of capital. This is rooted in the Modigliani–Miller theorem,[14] linking the increase in capital to better protection of shareholders' investments and a reduction in their risk. Therefore, when investing in better capitalized banks, shareholders will demand a lower expected return. But to have a tiny cost of capital effect there has to be a perfect and efficient capital market with no distortions and frictions, so that the increased volume of capital is offset by the lower cost of equity.[15] In any case, the issue of the potential effects of more capital on the risk and cost of bank equity and the overall cost of capital has been investigated by a large number of researchers, many of whom have attempted to examine whether better-capitalized banks are perceived by the market as being less risky and more able to withstand possible losses, leading to the return demanded by shareholders' being lower, in line with the level of riskiness of the bank. Brogi and Langone could not strongly confirm in their study that well-capitalized banks are perceived as low risk by market participants and that the required rate of return by shareholders was consequently lower.[16] Baker and Wurgler found, using US data, that the equity of better-capitalized banks has lower systematic risk and idiosyncratic risk and that lower-risk banks have higher stock returns.[17] This suggests to those authors that the capital requirements effects on the cost of capital could be significant, and not minor as the standard theory predicts. It was found that a ten percentage-point increase in the required Tier 1 capital to risk-weighted assets ratio is likely to increase the overall cost of capital by as much as 90 basis points.

In addition, we need to say that the issue related to the optimum choice between raising new capital internally or externally and adjusting risk-weighted assets may not be a main concern to some well-capitalized banks with excess capital adequacy surpassing the requirements. Thus, another outcome of this discussion is that the impact of additional capital requirements on financial intermediation hinges upon, among other things, the existing capitalization level[18] and the net cost of raising equity,[19] and not all banks will necessarily respond to additional capital requirements, at least in the short run, by raising rates and constricting credit to remain within the stipulated capital levels.

Nevertheless, several empirical studies have recently attempted to examine the link between higher and toughened capital requirements and increased costs of intermediation, or the impact of capital requirements on credit activity and economic growth. The literature is mixed in terms of the size and magnitude of the potential effects, with much research considering them substantial, while others view them as moderate to insignificant. Brogi and Langone analyzed a sample of large European listed banks for the period 2007–13 and found no evidence associating higher capital requirements (imposed by Basel III) with a credit crunch; instead they found an increase in total loans in the period under consideration.[20] Maredza found for South African banks that capital requirements are associated with increased costs of intermediation, with a 1 percent increase in the former leading on average to a 12–14 basis point increase in the latter during the period 2001–12.[21] The US Government Accounting Office investigated the likely effects of Basel III implementation on US banks[22] and came to the conclusion that raising capital requirements has a fairly small influence on the cost and availability of credit. That is, there could be slight increase in loan rates and a minor decrease in credit extension. Such a conclusion is shared by Miles et al, who argue that the costs of stricter capital requirements are fairly small.[23] Sutorova and Teply attempted to measure the impact of Basel III on lending rates using a large sample of EU banks for the period 2006–11.[24] Their results showed, in contrast to the studies mentioned above, that there was a significant and positive correlation between common equity and bank lending rates, with a 1 percent increase in the former provoking on average an 18.8 basis point increase in loan interest rates.

The issue of whether capital obligations are costly for society and can negatively shape the loans market was also examined by Admati et al.[25] The authors came to the conclusion that bank equity is not socially (economically) expensive and that the argument relating the increase in capital requirements to lower economic activity and slower growth is fallacious, as the impairment to the economy comes from under- or inadequately capitalized banks and a fragile system. Martin-Oliver et al used data on Spanish banks to investigate the effects of equity capital ratios on lending rates at banks[26] and found that interest rates on loans rise with equity capital and that the increase is more manifested during the adjustment period than in the steady state. The study, across the period 1992–2007, showed specifically that a 1 percent increase in the capital ratio is correlated with around a 7 basis point increase in lending interest rates. Allen et al also examined the impacts of the Basel III framework and argued that reforms to banking regulations could constrain the availability of credit and lower economic activity but not as a result of higher capital and liquidity requirements but instead owing to difficulty in managing compliance with and adapting to new rules, which could lead to severe shortages of funding.[27] Slovik and Cournede examined the potential relationship between Basel III capital requirements and economic growth using data from the period 2004–6 pertaining to the US, Japan, and the euro area.[28] Their study indicated that Basel III capital requirements are likely to lower GDP growth in the three studied economies on average by 0.05 percent annually, which would total 0.23 percent after five years of implementation (2015–19). Another finding is that a 1 percentage point increase in the ratio of capital to risk-weighted assets lifts up, on average, bank lending spreads by 14.4 basis points. Cosimano and Hakura assess banks' actions in reacting to Basel III requirements and argue that the implementation of this new capital and liquidity regulation would demand, on average, that the world's top 100 banks raise their equity to assets ratio by 1.3 percentage points.[29] This could imply an augmentation of 16 basis points in the lending rate and a drop of 1.3 percent in the growth of loans in the long term.

Finally, in August 2010 the Basel Committee on Banking Supervision (BCBS) published a document that assessed the long-term impact of stronger capital and liquidity requirements and found that there are clear net long-term economic benefits from introducing Basel III with a view to improving the safety and soundness of the global banking system. According to the assessment, the benefits, coming from lowering the probability of financial crisis and the related output losses, exceed the potential output costs. Also in that month, the Macroeconomic Assessment Group (MAG), established by the Financial Stability Board (FSB) and the BCBS, issued a report in which it, too, evaluated (in collaboration with the International Monetary Fund (IMF)) the macroeconomic transition costs of Basel III. The interim report, entitled "Assessing the macroeconomic impact of the transition to stronger capital and liquidity requirements," believes that such a transition will have most likely a modest impact on aggregate output.[30] It has been estimated that each 1 percentage point increase in banks' actual ratio of tangible common equity to risk-weighted assets would reduce the annual GDP growth rate by an average of 0.04 percentage points over a 4.5-year period (as higher requirements are phased in over this time). Kashyap et al argue also that as long as capital requirements for significant financial institutions are adequately phased in their impact on loan rates for households and corporations is likely to be modest and in the range of 2.5 to 4.5 basis points for a 1 percentage point increase in capital requirements.[31]

Operating costs and profitability

The potential impact of the implementation of Basel III on the operating costs and profitability of banks can be seen from different angles. The introduction of the thirty-day Liquidity Coverage Ratio (LCR) to ensure that banks have adequate high-quality liquid assets to meet expected short-term liquidity needs and withdrawals, and therefore improve the stability of the banking system, will force many banks to change their funding strategies or their assets/liabilities management and hold more liquid and low-yielding assets to satisfy the requirements. Thus, higher liquidity requests could lower profitability in certain cases. The introduction of the Net Stable Funding Ratio (NSFR) to encourage banks to use more stable and long-term sources of funds to finance assets expansion and activities and reduce reliance on short-term volatile wholesale funding is also likely to result in higher funding costs. A more stable bank funding mix would shift to maturities exceeding one year, and given that the appetite of creditors to hold longer term bank debt could be low, this could breed higher costs of funding in a narrow market, the need to compete for stable funds leading to competitive rates on higher maturities for depositors and other creditors. In conclusion, new liquidity requirements and standards involving securing short-term and long-term liquidity ratios may cause a shift in banks' assets and liabilities management and in their funding strategies, favoring long-term over short-term liquidity arrangements. This could have negative effects on the cost of funds and the margins at financial services firms. Karel and Blahova showed that the implementation of Basel III LCR will lead to a change in a bank's liquidity allocation and thus to allocation ineffectiveness, in addition to less effective and more costly funding and restrictions on credit provision.[32] The authors conclude that adaptation to LCR will restructure the balance sheets of banks, raise the cost of meeting regulatory requirements, and lower the amount of resources used for extending loans. Balasubramanyan and VanHoose showed that imposing an LCR constraint has ambiguous effects on optimal dynamic loan and deposit (or balance sheet) paths.[33]

Given that the implementation of the Basel III standards requires improvements in the quality and quantity of the capital base at banks and imposes a leverage ratio of capital to assets of 3 percent implemented on a gross and unweighted basis, we would expect, on average and other things being constant, the new capital regulation on banks' profitability to have a negative effect. The requirements to increase the common equity Tier 1 ratio from 2 percent to 4.5 percent (more than double) and to hold a capital conservation buffer of 2.5 percent, and the need to compensate for the reduction in the eligible capital by additional capital, are elements that could negatively impact the return on equity.[34] Another factor is that the implementation of the new capital and liquidity framework may also result in considerable augmentation in the volume of risk-weighted assets for some banks, depending on their assets/liabilities management strategies and types of business undertaken, especially in the trading book, and that would mean higher capital requirements, influencing, in turn, shareholders' return.

To meet additional capital requirements, specifically Tier 1 capital made up mostly of common stock and retained earnings, some banks may need to retain more profits and distribute fewer dividends. This is a main concern, as lower earnings distributions would send a negative signal in the market and would make investment in banks' debt and equity instruments less attractive. Lower bank profitability and the ensuing decline in the attractiveness of bank-issued securities of bonds and equity to investors could, in turn, affect the borrowing capacity of some banks from debt sources or from stockholders. Another outcome of Basel III obligations could be more or more intense pressure on "weak" or "fragile" banks to sell a part of the whole business, exit the industry, or continue to operate through other financial entities. There could be, therefore, increased consolidation and vigorous merger and acquisition operations driven by the increasing difficulty some banks experience in complying in general and raising the required capital and funding under the new framework. To mitigate the impact of capital deductions on capital ratios, or to make the best possible capital calculation, banks may also pursue undesirable or unfavorable strategies, such as selling some of their stakes in some financial institutions or the pure exit, implying possible reorganization of banks at the group level.

Important areas of corporate governance research

The theoretical and empirical literature on corporate governance in corporations in general and its diverse aspects is rich and varied and has a long history. One governance issue much studied revolves around the ownership structure or the separation of ownership and control in large corporations and the resulting agent–principal problem, or agency costs. Another topic that has gained substantial importance is executive compensation: if inappropriate this can also lead, among other things, to agency problems and excessive risk taking, whereas, if designed properly, it can have the opposite effects. Other areas of research involve examining the macroeconomic implications of corporate governance or focusing at the micro level on the relationship between corporate governance and the firm's performance and value. There are also other areas or fields of study no less important, such as those on large shareholdings or large blocks and corporate performance; the effects of shareholder activism on profitability; governance under controlling shareholders; the quality of corporate governance and foreign direct investment; and corporate governance and politics.[35]

Between parentheses, the hypothesis that good corporate governance contributes to good economic outcomes has been tested over the years by many scholars. Many researchers have examined the real effects or the macroeconomic implications of corporate governance by investigating the relationship between corporate governance quality or adequacy level and the performance of certain economic and financial variables, including stock or capital market performance, economic development or growth, and foreign investment into the country, or capital inflows. One of the premises is that firms with improved governance (i.e. improved investor protection) can attract and have access to domestic and foreign funds at lower cost and that could increase the supply of credit and foster investment and growth. For example, La Porta et al found that in countries with good shareholder protection equity markets are broader and more valuable than in countries with poor shareholder protection.[36] De Nicolo et al found positive and significant impacts of improvement in corporate governance quality on GDP growth, productivity growth, and the ratio of investment to GDP.[37] Bebchuk and Neeman pointed out, however, that there could be a correlation or causation running in the reverse direction, in the sense that the stage of investor protection may depend at least partly on a developed stock market or strong economic growth, or an advanced level of economic development.[38] Leuz et al investigated, using a very large sample of firms, whether foreigners invest less in poorly governed countries.[39] They found that foreigners do in fact invest less in companies that reside in countries with poor outside protection and disclosure and with ownership structures contributing to governance problems. Poor governance can thus restrict the ability to draw capital from foreign investors and thus can limit capital inflows.

The literature on corporate governance in banking institutions sometimes differs to a certain extent from that on corporations, yet much commonality exists in some of the subjects dealt with. It concentrates on the possible connection between certain features of corporate governance, on the one hand, and risk taking, performance, and the value of the banking firm on the other. As such, it is convenient to divide the literature review in this chapter into four topics. These involve the relationship between risk and performance, from one side, and ownership structure, board composition, executive compensation, and corporate governance in general, or some of its specific aspects, from the other. We will focus in what follows on these four potentially interlinked areas. There are further fields of research definitely worth examining, but given various limitations they are not surveyed here. This does not mean that we are entirely excluding some of the literature on corporate governance incorporations in general, especially given that banks are, after all, companies that have much in common with other non-financial services firms. There are other reasons for this exception, related to comparisons drawn with the findings regarding non-financial services firms and to obtaining a better picture of the whole issue of corporate governance. Therefore, the literature review in what follows is selective and is not intended to be, nor can it be, comprehensive. It aims at shedding more light on the importance of corporate governance at banks and at allowing the reader to relate, where possible, some of the above-mentioned international best practices and their rationale to the work of a large number of scholars and their findings.

Ownership structure

A good start for the literature review could be with Adam Smith, who claimed that the objectives of firm's owners will probably be weakened rather than achieved whenever the firm is controlled by individuals other than the owners.[40] Much later, the seminal work of Berle and Means argued that the structure of US corporate law in the 1930s imposed the separation of "ownership" and "control," giving the management and directors the possibility of running the company to their own benefit without effective shareholders' inspection.[41] The authors called for establishing voting rights for all shareholders and inserting greater transparency and accountability. Thereafter, Jensen and Meckling developed a theory of ownership structure built on elements of the theories of agency, property rights, and finance.[42] Their paper focused in part on the agency costs inherent in the corporate form, which are real as any other costs, the level of which depends on the statutory and common law and on human ingenuity in devising contracts. Agency costs are related to the separation of ownership and control issue and arise when the principal (e.g. shareholders) delegates some decision-making authority to the agent (e.g. corporate management) who will not necessarily act in the best interest of the principal. The authors also commented on the importance of efficient monitoring in controlling the agency problem, but did not investigate ways to achieve it.

There have been many attempts subsequently to explain how to control the agency problem resulting from the separation of ownership and control. Fama argued that the separation of ownership and control in big companies can be an effective type of arrangement,[43] controlled by means of internal policies and procedures set up for efficiently monitoring the performance of managers— mechanisms that are forced by the market and competition from other firms. Fama and Jensen contended that the separation of ownership and control or decision- and risk-assuming functions endures in large corporations due to the payback of specialization in these two functions and to the efficient method of controlling the agency problems resulting from the separation of decision and risk bearing.[44] Such an effective approach is manifested by contract structures that separate decision control (approval and monitoring of decisions) from decision management (initiation and implementation of decisions), such segregation being at both the top and the lower levels of the firm's hierarchy.

The literature on ownership structure or owner–manager agency problems and risk in banking firms is notable. It is mixed, as some studies highlight the role of bank owners in intensifying risk while other blame the management for too much risk taking. Saunders et al investigated the relationship between bank ownership structure and risk taking and found that stockholder-controlled banks demonstrated greater risk-taking behavior than managerially controlled banks during the period of relative deregulation 1979–82.[45] Gorton and Rosen linked increased risk taking at banks in the 1980s with the owner–manager agency problem.[46] Their argument is that, confronted with diminishing projections for future profits, bank managers turned to high risk in their portfolios in order to mask the weak profit prospects from shareholders. According to the authors, the behavior of the US banking industry, which became less profitable and riskier in the 1980s, is explained by managerial entrenchment more than, as many have thought, moral hazard associated with deposit insurance. Demsetz et al found that ownership structure and franchise value interact and affect risk at banks, as owner–manager agency problems affect the choice of risk for banks with low franchise value and no insider holdings.[47] They also argue that managerial risk aversion in the presence of owner–manager agency problems may counterbalance excessive risk taking generated by moral hazard. Laeven and Levine examined the relationship between risk taking by banks and ownership structure and bank regulation.[48] Bank risk taking was found to be positively related to the comparative power of shareholders within the corporate governance structure. That is, bank risk taking depends on the bank's corporate governance structure. The authors particularly found a significant positive relationship between institutional ownership and a number of riskiness measures. Berger et al analyzed the role of corporate governance in bank failures during the recent global financial crisis by studying the impacts of bank ownership and management structures on the default risk or probability of default of US commercial banks.[49] It was found that the bank's ownership structure could have a positive or negative effect on defaults. Shareholdings of outside directors and chief officers (CEO, CFO, etc.) seemed to have no direct effect on the probability of default but high shareholdings of lower-level management (vice presidents, etc.) augment default risk considerably. The explanation given is that moral hazard incentives related to elevated stakes in the bank encourage lower-level management to take risks that could lead to bank default. The authors also found that aligning the incentives of Chief Officers and lower-level management is also likely to increase the probability of default.

Board composition

Another strand of the literature looked at some other aspects of corporate governance: that is, board composition and characteristics and how they relate to bank risk taking, stability, or failure. It mainly investigates the effects of board size and board composition, including the percentage of outside directors to inside directors, on the bank's performance and value. The literature is mixed, in that some authors argue that large boards are value reducing owing to free rider problems or other reasons, while others contend that large boards with a strong representation of outside directors can bring stronger monitoring and increase performance and value. There are also studies that found no evidence of a positive or a negative relationship between the variables of board composition and performance. Other than the issue of board composition, the characteristics of outside or independent directors, including their experience, seemed to have either a positive or negative role on performance and value. Fernandes and Fich examined close to 400 US banks during 2006–7 with a view to relating the board's financial experience with credit crises.[50] It was found that the financial experience of external directors is positively related to the performance of financial firms' stock return during the credit crisis and inversely related to the likelihood of bank failure. Pathan investigated the influence of bank board structure on bank risk taking using a large sample of more than 200 US bank holding companies over the period 1997–2004[51] and found that small and less restrictive boards are associated with bank risk taking, whereas CEO power negatively affects bank risk taking. Faleye and Krishnan examined the impact of bank governance on risk taking in commercial lending and found that more effective boards with board-level credit committees are less likely to lend to risky borrowers in periods of distress in the banking industry.[52] Minton et al investigated the issue of board composition or characteristics and its link with risk taking and firm value for financial firms.[53] Among their findings related to the issue of directors' independence is that financial firms with a higher ratio of outside directors to inside ones did not fare better during the financial crisis, whereas their findings related to the issue of directors' experience highlighted that the experience of outside or independent directors plays a role in risk taking, as it is positively correlated with volatility. Adams and Mehran used data for bank holding companies over almost a four-decade period (1959–99) to investigate the connection between corporate performance and board structure in the banking industry,[54] and found no evidence that large board size correlates with poorer performance and value reduction compared to peers. They argue that performance is not linked to the ratio of outside directors to inside directors; instead, the performance of bank holding companies is poorer when the board contains directors or executives who serve on other boards or as directors of other companies as well. Interlocking also negatively affects banks' performance. Erkens et al examined the effects of corporate governance in financial firms on performance during the 2007–8 global financial crisis using a large data set of close to 300 firms from thirty countries.[55] The main finding is that directors' independence and institutional shareholding seemed to have a negative influence on performance, as financial firms with more independent boards and higher institutional ownership experienced worse stock returns during the crisis period, as they took more risk before the crisis and raised more equity during its occurrence.

For the sake of comparison with similar literature, but dealing with companies in general or with non-financial services firms, Bhagat and Black, for example, examined the relationship between board composition and firm performance and found no convincing evidence that greater board independence correlates with greater firm profitability and faster growth.[56] They also found that firms with more independent boards do not perform better than other firms.[57] Yet, other empirical research indicated that directors' independence or outside directors have an effect on certain internal managerial and operational issues such as CEO resignation,[58] CEO compensation decisions,[59] and the occurrence of financial fraud.[60]

Executive compensation

A great part of the literature on corporate governance in financial firms examined specifically the relation between executive compensation arrangements and practices and risk taking. But, before elaborating on this essential topic, it is important to mention that research in the field of executive compensation in corporations (banks and non-banks) is in itself varied and wide. One of the investigated topics is the relationship between compensation arrangements and the agency problem. There are two opposing views, one arguing that executive compensation schemes can help in addressing or reducing the agency problem arising from the separation of ownership and control, while the other sees that executive compensation arrangements in publicly traded companies can be part of the agency problem itself. The advocates of the first view, better known as the "optimal contracting approach,"[61] assume that boards devise compensation systems that give managers efficient incentives to maximize shareholder value, which would lessen, as much as possible, the agency problem. Advocates of the second approach, labeled the "managerial power approach,"[62] argue, however, that compensation arrangements can be structured below optimum, resulting in weak or bad incentives, and can therefore constitute an element of the problem and not a remedy. Jensen et al argue that, while executive compensation can be a powerful tool for reducing the agency conflicts between managers and the firm, compensation can also be a substantial source of agency costs if it is not managed properly.[63]

It is also worth mentioning that interest in executive pay has been revived following the global financial crisis of 2008–9, though it was considerable prior to this period and during the waves of corporate scandals and failures mentioned earlier in the chapter.[64] The observations and lessons drawn from the stated developments and crisis, and the growing public awareness of the compensation levels of top executives, incited more research in this field and prompted concerned authorities and regulators around the globe to re-examine existing measures and introduce new ones to improve corporate governance in the area of compensation. Poor incentives for executives at banks were hypothesized as one of the fundamental causes of the global credit crisis, and there were widespread suspicions of misalignments between pay and long-term performance. This ignited discussions on the need to modify or change compensation practices and give shareholders a better say on executive pay.

Houston and James examined whether executive compensation in banking is structured to promote risk taking.[65] Their results showed that compensation policies do encourage risk taking in banking. Also among the findings is that, on average, bank CEOs receive less cash and a smaller percentage of their compensation as options and stock than CEOs in other industries and that there is a positive and significant relationship between the importance of equity-based incentives and the value of the bank's charter. De Young et al investigated the relationship between executive compensation and risky policy decisions or choices between 1994 and 2006 at US commercial banks[66] and found strong evidence that bank boards' modification of CEOs' compensation to prompt them to search for new growth opportunities increased risk-taking incentives for executives, who reacted by taking more risk. This relationship is more pronounced under deregulation and technological change that increased banks' scope and ability for risk taking. Chesney et al inspected the link between risk-taking incentives for CEOs and other governance issues in the period before the 2008 financial crisis and the losses of US financial institutions incurred during the crisis.[67] It was found that financial services firms in which the CEOs had strong risk-taking incentives, weak ownership incentives, and independent boards ended with the most elevated writedowns, whether in absolute terms or in relation to their total assets. Fahlenbrach and Stulz explored the relationship between CEO incentives before the global financial crisis and bank performance during it,[68] finding no evidence that banks in which CEO incentives were better aligned with the interests of shareholders performed better; however, there was little evidence that they performed worse.

The authors also found that banks with higher cash bonuses and options compensation for their CEOs did not have an inferior performance during the crisis and that bank CEOs did not trim down their holdings of shares in anticipation of or during the crisis. Cheng et al studied the relationship between pay and risk among financial firms focusing on whether misaligned compensation (from shareholders' value) because of managerial entrenchment drove financial firms to take more risk before the financial crisis of 2008, as many have claimed.[69] The authors argued that a strong correlation between pay and risk can arise naturally in a classical principal–agent setting without entrenchment and with exogenous firm risk, as the principal–agent theory predicts that riskier firms have to offer higher total compensation for the extra risk in equity stakes assumed by risk-averse managers in order to provide the same incentives for a risk-averse manager as less risky firms. Pay and risk are interrelated, therefore, for these reasons and not because misaligned compensation leads to more risk taking. Residual compensation—that is, compensation unexplained by firm size—is strongly correlated with risk taking and institutional shareholding.

Apart from the mixed results in the banking industry-related research, as shown above, there have been during the last twenty years many studies dealing with the level, structure, and growth of executive pay in the corporate sector in general, with attempts to explain the underlying reasons. Bebchuk and Grinstein examined the growth of US executive pay during the period 1993–2003 and noticed that the substantial increases seen in compensation could not be justified by changes in firm size, performance, and industry classification, and that the considerable growth in equity-based compensation did not come at the expense of reducing non-equity pay (cash compensation).[70] Kaplan tried to examine whether the high pay of CEOs in the US is appropriate and largely a market phenomenon, or instead is provoked by the power of the CEO and the weakness of the board.[71] He concluded that high CEO pay is largely a market phenomenon likely driven by the increased scale of technological change.[72]

Corporate governance in general

The fourth element of the literature looks into the liaison between corporate governance in general, or some of its aspects (other than the ones discussed above), and firms' risk and performance. Beltratti and Stulz studied the factors that could have contributed to the poor performance of banks during the global financial crisis, including governance, short-term capital market funding, and high leverage.[73] The study found that poor bank governance, contrary to many expectations, was not a major cause of the crisis and that banks with better governance performed worse than other banks during the crisis and were not less risky before its occurrence. Adams used a large sample of data on financial and non-financial firms for the period 1996–2007 to examine the link between governance and the financial crisis.[74] The author documented that financial firms (banks and non-bank financial institutions) are better governed than non-financial firms and that directors of the latter earned significantly more compensation than their counterparts in financial firms. The main finding is that measures of governance for policies use are insufficient to describe governance failures attributed to financial firms. Anginer et al used an international sample of banks during the 2003–11 period to investigate the association between corporate governance and bank capitalization and stability.[75] The authors found that good corporate governance, in terms of banks acting in the interest of their shareholders, created lower levels of bank capital, which could be bad for bank stability and might involve higher social costs. Also among the findings is that capitalization rates increase with CEO overall compensation (including cash income, options, and stock wealth invested in the bank), possibly implying that high executive compensation attached to the bank drives executives to raise capitalization levels in order to diminish the riskiness of their income and wealth. But, at the same time, these higher levels of income and wealth tied to the bank are likely to lead to riskier payout strategies, as related banks had a greater tendency to continue payouts to stock investors even if the bank was performing poorly. Ellul and Yerramilli constructed a risk-management index that would measure the strength and independence of risk-management functions at bank holding companies to relate its level to the level of risk exposure before and during the latest global financial crisis.[76] The main finding is that a strong and independent risk-management function can restrain tail risk exposure at banks as financial services firms with a large risk-management index had lower exposures to different types of risky asset. The authors also found a significant positive relationship between institutional ownership and many measures of riskiness.

As such, it seems that there could be positive or negative connections between corporate governance and the performance or stability of the financial firm. The literature in this area is also mixed concerning the advantages and disadvantages of good or sound corporate governance. For the sake of comparison, Gompers et al, for example, examined corporate governance and equity prices for a sample of 1500 large firms and found that firms with strong shareholder rights had, among other things, higher sales growth, higher profits, and higher firm value.[77] Bebchuk et al used an index of selected corporate governance metrics reflecting to a large extent shareholders' rights and found an association between poor performance of the six selected provisions in the index, on the one hand, and significant reductions in firm valuation and large negative abnormal returns on the other.[78]

Concluding remarks and policy implications

Corporate governance at banks could be regarded as one form of financial safety net and an extension to the existing forms established by governments—that is, an explicit deposit insurance scheme and a lender of last resort function created initially with the intention of protecting bank depositors and other creditors, preventing bank failure, and safeguarding the banking system. This additional private sector element of the safety net, like the public sector elements, can be a mixed blessing, as an inappropriately designed or inadequate net can also increase moral hazard incentives or incentives to take on greater risks, thus harming banks' performance and banking sector stability. Therefore, adequate corporate governance structures can reduce banking institutions' risk of failure and thus the risks of government bail-outs and burdening taxpayers. Conversely, a poorly thought-out or ineffective corporate governance framework can result in excess risk that could weaken public confidence and perhaps contribute to the failure of financial firms. This would mean that the bank regulatory and supervisory authority has a crucial role to play in ensuring that banks, which they regulate and supervise, have effective boards with strengthened practices, roles, and responsibilities, and strong senior management oversight. Strong, skilled, and independent supervisory authority is also a must for reinforcing what is perceived as adequate and strong internal governance. Supervisors have to ensure banks' compliance with corporate governance regulations, enforce corrective actions, and provide inputs into legislation and regulations. Boards and senior management, for their part, must also assume the responsibility of translating regulatory guidelines and bank management policies and rules into operational practices, show strong commitment, and reflect periodically on the effectiveness and relevance of the governance arrangements and practices in place, in line with the changes in the scale and scope of the business and changing operating environment. It seems, therefore, that the governance of banks will always remain a dynamic and difficult issue, under constantly changing financial and operating environments, in spite of the progress that has been made over the last two decades. In fact, many governance practices become less useful with the passage of time in a rapidly changing world, and it would seem that there is always a race between risk-taking and risk-prevention measures and therefore between stability and instability.

Nevertheless, the commitment to efficient corporate governance will always remain an important issue for banking system stability, and, by promoting sound governance practices, countries also promote financial stability. Corporate or internal governance must ensure that the appropriate owners or managers are in place and that the quality of risk-management and control systems is high. Sound banking requires that the role and responsibilities of directors and management be clearly defined and the competency of those people be verified. In this respect, regulatory authorities are often delegated the responsibility to approve shareholders and the appointment of directors and senior management of a bank when licensing or whenever there is a change in ownership. Corporate governance of banks is improved also when regulation allows and encourages banks to establish appropriate internal risk-management and control systems to restrict or set appropriate levels of exposure to different types of risk. Letting banks set the appropriate level of credit, liquidity, exchange rate, and interest rate risk is a recent trend compared with the traditional approach, in which regulators specify through prudential regulation the levels of exposure or set certain standards. Setting appropriate rules, procedures, and policies for controlling risk and minimizing the organizational hazards would make the bank management more involved in risk management and control. Better internal governance is also achieved when banks are required to have clearly defined internal audit functions with externally audited annual accounts. This would help managers, directors, and owners to detect failures or weaknesses and act accordingly. Sound internal governance requires, in addition, ensuring adequate incentives for directors and managers to operate the bank in a safe or sound manner and preventing any willingness of owners–managers to hide problems.

The Basel III Accord on capital adequacy required by banks in light of the latest financial crisis seems to present many challenges to banks, largely relating to raising more capital, improving the quality of capital, and meeting the liquidity capital requirements on coverage ratio and liquidity requirement tools. At a time when many worldwide banks are still trying to meet the Basel II capital adequacy requirements, banks are asked to address the composition and quality of their capital as well as create buffer capital zones to address pro-cyclicality. Specifically, it is very challenging for banks that are not operating as public ones to raise the share of common stock in their Tier 1 capital and apply the stricter definition of this equity. It is additionally difficult to create a capital conservation buffer of common equity to withstand future periods of stress. Such requirements are believed to influence the way banks do business in most countries, especially if Basel III has effects on financial markets and on monetary policy implementation. The literature on the impact of the new Accord shows that, for the most part, raising more capital and holding more liquidity, as required by Basel III, seem to cause a rise in the cost of financial intermediation, a decline in the availability of credit, an increase in operating costs, and a reduction in profitability. However, the true impact cannot be predicted with certainty, as many countries have yet to attempt application and enforcement of the new capital standards.

Notes

1 See also Adams and Mehran (2003) for a discussion on the difference in the governance of banking firms and of non-financial firms.
2 Among the corporate governance principles and codes issued by international organizations and private sector associations and which are not covered in this chapter are "Guidance on Good Practices in Corporate Governance Disclosure," issued by the United Nations Conference on Trade and Development (UNCTAD) in 2006, and "Corporate Governance—the Foundation for Corporate Citizenship and Sustainable Business," released by the International Finance Corporation (IFC) and the United Nations Global Compact in 2009.
3 See, for example, the early work of Adam Smith (1776) and Berle and Means (1932) on the separation of ownership and control in corporations.
4 In the first half of the 1990s, the boards of IBM (a US multinational technology and consulting corporation), Kodak (a US technology company), and Honeywell (a US multinational conglomerate involved in commercial and consumer products, engineering services, and aerospace systems), to name a few, dismissed their CEOs.
5 High-profile corporate failure in 1990 and 1991 included, for example, the collapse of Polly Peck (a British textile company), Bank of Credit and Commerce International (an international bank), and Maxwell Group (a publishing company).
6 Committee on Corporate Governance 1998a.
7 Committee on Corporate Governance 1998b.
8 Corporate scandals and accounting fraud in the US involved, for example, Enron corporation (a US energy company), which went bankrupt in December 2001, and WorldCom (one of the largest US telecommunication corporations), which filed for bankruptcy in July 2002. There were also scandals in other countries, such as Italy,

where Parmalat (a multinational dairy and food corporation) filed for bankruptcy in December 2003. For more on this issue refer to *The Economist* 2002; *The Guardian* 2002; and Bloomberg 2004.

9 The Financial Stability Board (FSB) is an international organization established in 2009 as the successor of the Financial Stability Forum. It focuses on promoting and strengthening international financial stability. The FSB has twelve key standards for sound financial systems distributed across three policy areas. The first area is macro-economic policy and data transparency, under which there are three standards issued by the IMF on monetary, fiscal and financial policy transparency, and data dissemination. The second area is financial regulation and supervision, with another three standards on banking, securities and insurance regulation, and supervision. The third area is institutional and market infrastructure, encompassing six standards, one of which is on corporate governance and its principles issued by the OECD.

10 The reports on the Observance of Standards and Codes issued by the IMF (International Monetary Fund 2016) summarize the extent to which countries respect a number of internationally recognized standards and codes in twelve areas. One of these areas is corporate governance, while the others are: accounting; auditing; AML/CFT; banking supervision; data dissemination; fiscal transparency; insolvency and creditor rights; insurance supervision; monetary and financial policy transparency; payments systems; and securities regulation.

11 Basel Committee on Banking Supervision 2012. *Core Principles for Effective Banking Supervision* was originally published by the Basel Committee on Banking Supervision in 1997 then reviewed twice in 2006 and 2012. Its principles are considered the minimum standards for sound prudential regulation and supervision of banks and banking systems. The version of September 2012 includes thirteen principles addressing supervisory powers, responsibilities, and functions, and stressing effective risk-based supervision in addition to urging early intervention and timely supervisory actions. The other sixteen principles deal with the supervisory expectations of banks, underscoring the importance of good corporate governance, risk management, and compliance with regulatory standards.

12 See Organisation for Economic Co-operation and Development 2014 for a review of the corporate governance practices relating to risk management in the private sector and state-owned enterprises in twenty-seven jurisdictions participating in the OECD corporate governance committee. See also Financial Stability Board 2013 on the progress in measures taken to improve regulatory and supervisory oversight of risk governance in financial institutions.

13 See KPMG 2011 for a thorough discussion for the issues and implications of Basel III.

14 Modigliani and Miller 1958.

15 e.g. Baker and Wurgler 2013.

16 Brogi and Langone 2016.

17 Baker and Wurgler 2013.

18 e.g. VanHoose 2007 and Jensen-Laerkholm 2013.

19 e.g. Cosimano and Hakura 2011.

20 Brogi and Langone 2016.

21 Maredza 2015.

22 Government Accounting Office 2014.

23 Miles et al 2013.

24 Sutorova and Teply 2013.

25 Admati et al 2013.

26 Martin-Oliver et al 2013.

27 Allen et al 2012.

28 Slovik and Cournede 2011.

29 Cosimano and Hakura 2011.

30 Macroeconomic Assessment Group 2010.
31 Kashyap et al 2010.
32 Karel and Blahova 2016.
33 Balasubramanyan and VanHoose 2013.
34 Under Basel III, eligible capital reduction is likely to occur as banks are required to deduct fully from capital those capital components with little loss-absorption capacity, such as minority interests, holdings in other financial institutions, and deferred tax assets.
35 See Bebchuk and Weisbach 2009 for a rich review and comment on the state and areas of corporate governance research in recent years. See also Jassaud 2014; Aoyagi and Ganelli 2014; Ivaschenko and Brooks 2008; and Odenius 2008 for an evaluation of whether corporate governance reforms which have been undertaken in Italy, Germany, the EU, and Japan were successful in achieving the desired objectives.
36 La Porta et al 1999.
37 De Nicolo et al 2006.
38 Bebchuk and Neeman 2009.
39 Leuz et al 2009.
40 Smith 1776.
41 Berle and Means 1932.
42 Jensen and Meckling 1976.
43 Fama 1980.
44 Fama and Jensen 1983.
45 Saunders et al 1990.
46 Gorton and Rosen 1995.
47 Demsetz et al 1997.
48 Laeven and Levine 2009.
49 Berger et al 2012.
50 Fernandes and Fich 2009.
51 Pathan 2009.
52 Faleye and Krishnan 2010.
53 Minton et al 2010.
54 Adams and Mehran 2010; 2012.
55 Erkens et al 2012.
56 Bhagat and Black 1999.
57 Bhagat and Black 2002.
58 e.g. Weisbach 1988.
59 e.g. Chhaochharia and Grinstein 2008.
60 e.g. Beasley 1996.
61 e.g. Holmstrom 1979.
62 e.g. Bebchuk and Fried 2003; 2004.
63 Jensen et al 2004.
64 See Murphy 1999 for a summary of the empirical and theoretical research on executive compensation and description of pay practices for CEOs in the period before the 2000s. See also Core et al 2003 for a survey on equity compensation and incentives until the early 2000s.
65 Houston and James 1995.
66 De Young et al 2010.
67 Chesney et al 2010.
68 Fahlenbrach and Stulz 2011.
69 Cheng et al 2015.
70 Bebchuk and Grinstein 2005.
71 Kaplan 2008.
72 See also Jensen and Murphy 1990 on the historic CEO pay and performance relation.
73 Beltratti and Stulz 2012.

74 Adams 2012.
75 Anginer et al 2013.
76 Ellul and Yerramilli 2013.
77 Gompers et al 2003.
78 Bebchuk et al 2009.

Bibliography

Adams, RB 2012, "Governance and the financial crisis," *International Review of Finance*, 121, 1, pp. 7–38.

Adams, RB and Mehran, H 2003, "Is corporate governance different for bank holding companies?" *Economic Policy Review*, 9, 1, pp. 123–42.

Adams, RB and Mehran, H 2010, "Corporate performance, board structure and their determinants in the banking industry," mimeo, Federal Reserve Bank of New York.

Adams, RB and Mehran, H 2012, "Bank board structure and performance: Evidence for large bank holding companies," *Journal of Financial Intermediation*, 21, pp. 243–67.

Admati, AR, DeMarzo, PM, Hellwig, MF and Pfleiderer, P 2013, "Fallacies, irrelevant facts, and myths in the discussion of capital regulation: why bank equity is not socially expensive," Stanford University Graduate School of Business Research Paper 13–7.

Allen, B, Chan, KK and Milne, M 2012, "Basel III: Is the cure worse than the disease?" *International Review of Financial Analysis*, 25, pp. 159–66.

Anginer, D, Demirguc-Kunt, A, Huizinga, H and Ma, K 2013, "How does corporate governance affect bank capitalization strategies?" Policy Research Working Paper 6636, World Bank.

Aoyagi, C and Ganelli, G 2014, "Unstash the cash! Corporate governance reform in Japan," Working Paper WP/14/140, International Monetary Fund.

Baker, M and Wurgler, J 2013, "Do strict capital requirements raise the cost of capital? Banking regulation and the low risk anomaly," Working Paper 19018, National Bureau of Economic Research.

Balasubramanyan, L and VanHoose, DD 2013, "Bank balance sheet dynamics under a regulatory liquidity-coverage-ratio constraint," *Journal of Macroeconomics*, 37, pp. 53–67.

Basel Committee on Banking Supervision 1988, *International convergence of capital measurement and capital standards (Basel Capital Accord)*, Bank For International Settlements.

Basel Committee on Banking Supervision 1999, *Enhancing Corporate Governance for Banking Organizations*, Bank for International Settlements.

Basel Committee on Banking Supervision 2006a, *Enhancing Corporate Governance for Banking Organizations*, Bank for International Settlements.

Basel Committee on Banking Supervision 2006b, *Basel II: International Convergence of Capital Measurement and Capital Standards, A Revised Framework Comprehensive Version*, Bank For International Settlements.

Basel Committee on Banking Supervision 2010a *An assessment of the long-term economic impact of stronger capital and liquidity requirements*, Bank for International Settlements.

Basel Committee on Banking Supervision 2010b, *Basel III: A global regulatory framework for more resilient banks and banking systems*, Bank For International Settlements.

Basel Committee on Banking Supervision 2010c, *Principles for enhancing corporate governance*, Bank for International Settlements.

Basel Committee on Banking Supervision 2011, *Basel III: A global regulatory framework for more resilient banks and banking systems*, Bank For International Settlements.

Basel Committee on Banking Supervision 2012, *Core principles for effective banking supervision*, Bank for International Settlements, Basel, Switzerland.

Basel Committee on Banking Supervision 2013, *Basel III: The liquidity coverage ratio and liquidity risk monitoring tools*, Bank For International Settlements.

Basel Committee on Banking Supervision 2014, *Basel III: the net stable funding ratio*, Bank For International Settlements.

Basel Committee on Banking Supervision 2015, *Corporate governance principles for banks*, Bank for International Settlements.

Beasley, MS 1996, "An empirical analysis of the relation between the board of director composition and financial statement fraud," *Accounting Review*, 71, pp. 443–55.

Bebchuk, LA and Fried, J 2003, "Executive compensation as an agency problem," *Journal of Economic Perspectives*, 17, pp. 71–92.

Bebchuk, LA and Fried, J 2004, *Pay without Performance*, Harvard University Press.

Bebchuk, LA and Neeman, Z 2009, "Investor protection and interest group politics," *Review of Financial Studies*, 23, 3, pp. 1089–1119.

Bebchuk, LA and Weisbach, MS 2009, "The state of corporate governance research," Working Paper 15537, National Bureau of Economic Research.

Bebchuk, LA and Grinstein, Y 2005, "The growth of executive pay," *Oxford Review of Economic Policy*, 21, pp. 283–303.

Bebchuk, LA, Cohen, A and Ferrell, A 2009, "What matters in corporate governance," *Review of Financial Studies*, 22, pp. 783–827.

Beltratti, A and Stulz, R 2012, "The credit crisis around the globe: Why did some banks perform better?" *Journal of Financial Economics*, 105, 1, pp. 1–17.

Berger, AN, Imbierowicz, B and Rauch, C 2012, "The roles of corporate governance in bank failures during the recent financial crisis," European Banking Center Discussion Paper, pp. 2012–23.

Berle, AA and Means, Gardiner C 1932, *The Modern Corporation and Private Property*, MacMillan.

Bhagat, S and Black, B 1999, "The uncertain relationship between board composition and firm performance," *The Business Lawyer*, 54, pp. 921–63.

Bhagat, S and Black, B 2002, "The non-correlation between board independence and long-term firm performance," *Journal of Corporation Law*, 27, pp. 231–73.

Bloomberg 2004, "How parmalat went sour," January 12.

Brogi, M and Langone, R 2016, "Bank profitability and capital adequacy in the post-crisis context," *Contributions to Economics*, 214, 95–109.

Cheng, I, Hong, H and and Scheinkman, JA 2015, "Yesterday's heroes: compensation and risk at financial firms," *The Journal of Finance*, 70, 2, pp. 839–79.

Chesney M, Stromberg, J and Wagner, A 2010, "Risk-taking incentives, governance, and losses in the financial crisis," Swiss Finance Institute Research Paper Series 10–18, Swiss Finance Institute.

Chhaochharia, V and Grinstein, Y 2008, "Executive compensation and board structure," Working Paper, Cornell University.

Committee on Corporate Governance 1998a, *Final Report* (Hampel Report), Gee Publishing Ltd.

Committee on Corporate Governance 1998b, *The Combined Code*, Financial Reporting Council.

Committee on Corporate Governance 2003, *The Combined Code on Corporate Governance*, Financial Reporting Council.

Committee on the Financial Aspects of Corporate Governance 1992, *The Report of the Committee on the Financial Aspects of Corporate Governance* (Cadbury Report), Gee and Co. Ltd.

Core, JE, Guay, WR and Larcker, DF 2003, "Executive equity compensation and incentives: a survey," *Economic Policy Review*, 9, pp. 27–50.

Cosimano, TF and Hakura, D 2011, "Bank behavior in response to Basel III: a cross-country analysis,' Working Paper No. 11/119, International Monetary Fund.

De Nicolo, G, Laeven, L and Ueda, K 2006, "Corporate governance quality: trends and real effects," Working Paper WP/06/293, International Monetary Fund.

De Young, R, Peng, EY and Yan, M 2010, "Executive compensation and business policy choices at U.S. commercial banks," Research Working Papers RWP 10–02, The Federal Reserve Bank of Kansas City.

Demsetz, R, Saidenberg, M and Strahan, P 1997, "Agency problems and risk taking at banks," Working Paper, Federal Reserve Bank of New York Banking Studies Department.

Department of Trade and Industry 2003, *Review of the Role and Effectiveness of Non-Executive Directors* (Higgs Report), UK Government.

The Economist 2002, "Enron: the real scandal," January 17.

Ellul, A and Yerramilli, V 2013, "Stronger risk controls, lower risk: evidence from U.S. bank holding companies," *The Journal of Finance*, 68, 5, pp. 1757–803.

Erkens, DH, Hung M and Matos, P 2012, "Corporate governance in the 2007–2008 financial crisis: evidence from financial institutions worldwide," *Journal of Corporate Finance*, 18, 2, pp. 389–411.

Fahlenbrach, R and Stulz, R 2011, "Bank CEO incentives and the credit crisis," *Journal of Financial Economics*, 99, pp. 11–26.

Faleye, O and Krishnan, K 2010, "Risky lending: does bank corporate governance matter?" Paper, 23rd Australasian Finance and Banking Conference 2010.

Fama, EF 1980, "Agency problems and the theory of the firm," *The Journal of Political Economy*, 88, 2, pp. 288–307.

Fama, EF and Jensen, MC 1983, "Separation of ownership and control," *Journal of Law and Economics*, 26, 2, pp. 301–25.

Fernandes, N and Fich, E 2009, "Does financial experience help banks during credit crises?" Available from: ftp://ftp.cemfi.es/pdf/papers/wshop/WPM$60DE.pdf

Financial Stability Board (FSB), *Key standards for sound financial systems*. Available from: http://www.financialstabilityboard.org/what-we-do/about-the-compendium-of-standards/key_standards/table-of-key-standards-for-sound-financial-systems/

Financial Stability Board (FSB) 2013, *Thematic review on risk governance peer review report*. Available from: http://www.financialstabilityboard.org/2013/02/r_130212/

Gompers, Paul, A, Ishii, JL and Metrick, A 2003, "Corporate governance and equity prices," *Quarterly Journal of Economics*, 118, pp. 107–55.

Gorton, G and Rosen, R 1995, "Corporate control, portfolio choice, and the decline of banking," *The Journal of Finance*, 50, 5, pp. 1377–420.

Government Accounting Office 2014, "Bank capital reforms: initial effects of Basel III on capital, credit and international competitiveness," United States Government Accounting Office, GAO-15-67.

The Guardian 2002, "WorldCom goes bankrupt." Holmstrom, B 1979, "Moral hazard and observability," *The Bell Journal of Economics*, 10, 1, pp. 74–91.

Houston, JF and James, C 1995, "CEO compensation and bank risk: is compensation in banking structured to promote risk taking?," *Journal of Monetary Economics*, 36, 2, pp. 405–31.

Institute of International Auditors (IIA), *International professional practices framework*. Available from: https://na.theiia.org/standards-guidance/Pages/New-IPPF.aspx

International Finance Corporation (IFC) and United Nations Global Compact 2009, "Corporate governance—the foundation for corporate citizenship and sustainable business," Washington, DC.

International Financial Reporting Standards (IFRS) 2016, "Access the unaccompanied Standards," Available from: http://www.ifrs.org/IFRSs/Pages/IFRS.aspx

International Monetary Fund 2016, "Reports on the observance of standards and codes (ROSCs)," Available from: http://www.imf.org/external/NP/rosc/rosc.aspx

Ivaschenko, I and Brooks, PK 2008, "Corporate governance reforms in the EU: do they matter and how?" Working Paper WP/08/91, International Monetary Fund.

Jassaud, N 2014, "Reforming the corporate governance of Italian banks," Working Paper WP/14/181, International Monetary Fund.

Jensen, MC and Murphy, KJ 1990, "Performance pay and top management incentives," *Journal of Political Economy*, 98, pp. 225–64.

Jensen, MC and Meckling, WH 1976, "Theory of the firm: managerial behavior, agency costs, and ownership structure," *Journal of Financial Economics*, 3, 4, pp. 305–60.

Jensen, MC, Murphy, KJ and Wruck, EG 2004, "Remuneration: where we've been, how we got to here, what are the problems, and how to fix them," Working Paper Series in Finance 44, European Corporate Goverance Institute.

Jensen-Laerkholm, T 2013, "The cost of financial stability: how increased capital requirements to banks impact firm growth," University of Copenhagen and Denmark's Nationalbank.

Kaplan, S 2008, "Are U.S CEOs overpaid?" *Academy of Management Perspective*, 22, pp. 5–20.

Karel, B and Blahova, N 2016, "Systemic liquidity shocks and banking sector liquidity characteristics on the eve of liquidity coverage ratio application—the case of the Czech Republic," *Journal of Central Banking Theory and Practice*, 5, 1, pp. 159–84.

Kashyap, AK, Stein, JC and Hanson, S 2010, "An analysis of the impact of 'substantially heightened' capital requirements on large financial institutions," Harvard University working paper.

KPMG 2011, *Basel III: Issues and implications*, KPMG LLP.

La Porta, R, Lopez-de-Silanes, F and Shleifer, A 1999, "Corporate ownership around the world," *Journal of Finance*, 54, 2, pp. 471–517.

Laeven, L and Levine, R 2009, "Bank governance, regulation, and risk taking," *Journal of Financial Economics*, 93, pp. 259–75.

Leuz, C, Lins, K and Warnock, F 2009, "Do foreigners invest less in poorly governed firms?" *Review of Financial Studies*, 22, 8, pp. 3245–85.

Macroeconomic Assessment Group 2010, "Assessing the macroeconomic impact of the transition to stronger capital and liquidity requirements," Interim Report, Bank for International Settlements.

Maredza, A 2015, "Do capital requirements affect cost of intermediation? Evidence from a panel of South African banks," ERSA Working Paper 541, Economic Research Southern Africa.

Martin-Oliver, A, Ruano, S and Salas-Fumas, V 2013, "Banks' equity capital frictions, capital ratios, and interest rates: evidence from Spanish banks," *International Journal of Central Banking*, 9, 1, pp. 183–225.

Miles, D, Yang, J and Marcheggiano, G 2013, "Optimal bank capital," *The Economic Journal*, 123, 567, pp. 1–37.

Minton, BA, Taillard, J and Williamson, R 2010, "Board composition, risk taking and value: evidence from financial firms," mimeo, Ohio State University.

Modigliani, F and Miller, M 1958, "The cost of capital, corporation finance and the theory of investment," *American Economic Review*, 48, pp. 261–97.

Murphy, KJ 1999, "Executive compensation," in eds A Orley and D Card, *Handbook of Labor Economics, Volume 3*, Elsevier.

Odenius, J 2008, "Germany's corporate governance reforms: has the system become flexible enough?" Working Paper WP/08/179, International Monetary Fund.

Organisation for Economic Co-operation and Development 1999, *OECD Principles of Corporate Governance*, Paris.

Organisation for Economic Co-operation and Development 2004, *OECD Principles of Corporate Governance*, Paris.

Organisation for Economic Co-operation and Development 2014, *Corporate Governance— Risk Management and Corporate Governance*, Paris.

Organisation for Economic Co-operation and Development 2015, *G20/OECD Principles of Corporate Governance*, Paris.

Pathan, S 2009, "Strong boards, CEO power and bank risk-taking," *Journal of Banking and Finance*, 33, 7, pp. 1340–50.

Sarbanes-Oxley Accounting Standards Act 2002, US Congress.

Saunders, A, Strock, E and Travlos, NG 1990, "Ownership structure, deregulation, and bank risk taking," *The Journal of Finance*, 45, 2, pp. 643–54.

Slovik, P and Cournede, B 2011, "Macroeconomic impact of Basel III," OECD Economics Department Working Papers 844, OECD Publishing.

Smith, A 1776, "An inquiry into the nature and causes of the wealth of nations," eds W Strahan and T Cadeli, in the Strand, London.

Study Group on Directors' Remuneration 1995, *Directors' Remuneration* (Greenbury Report), Gee Publishing Ltd.

Sutorova, B and Teply, P 2013, "The Impact of Basel III on lending rates of EU banks," *Journal of Economics and Finance*, 63, 3, pp. 226–43.

United Nations Conference on Trade and Development (UNCTAD) 2006, "Guidance on good practices in corporate governance disclosure," United Nations.

VanHoose, D 2007, "Theories of bank behavior under capital regulation," *Journal of Banking and Finance*, 31, 12, pp. 3680–97.

Weisbach, MS 1988, "Outside directors and CEO turnover," *Journal of Financial Economics*, 20, pp. 431–60.

Part 3

Central banks in the new era of quantitative easing, monetary unions without fiscal unions, and the holding of foreign reserves

7   Monetary policy in an era of quantitative easing

Introduction

The environment and conduct of monetary policy have drastically changed in this century with the establishment of monetary unions and the adoption of unconventional policies of quantitative easing aimed at combating the financial crisis. Specifically, quantitative easing by the US and the UK, and potentially by the European Central Bank, came immediately in the aftermath of the financial crisis to address its recessionary and deflationary impacts and restore economic growth and price stability. This book analyzes these two new developments in the financial environment and the conduct of monetary policy and their impact on administration and strategy in two chapters. Chapter 8 deals with monetary policy conduct in monetary unions without fiscal unions, emphasizing the monetary policy of the European Central Bank. It also examines central banks' holdings of foreign currency reserves for precautionary reasons in the wake of the global financial crisis. Meanwhile, the current chapter analyzes the monetary policy of quantitative easing adopted with the advent of the financial crisis to address and reverse its recessionary and deflationary environments. This involves an analysis of the new and unconventional monetary policy, including its background and description; its strategy of instruments–targets–goals; its channels of transmission mechanisms; the experiences of the US and the UK, which were the first two countries to adopt it after the crisis; the assessment of its success based on empirical evidence; and, finally, various exit strategies from quantitative easing on the road to policy normalization. The analysis also addresses the nature of monetary policy when short-term interest rates are zero bound using a money demand and velocity framework. The chapter is organized as follows. The next section describes quantitative easing and its application in the US and the UK. The third section evaluates the transmission mechanisms of unconventional monetary policy, adding the forward guidance and signaling channel to the discussion and providing empirical evidence on various channels. The fourth section adds empirical evidence based on casual empiricism and econometric studies addressing the macroeconomic impacts of the policy on the wider economy to the discussion of the decision to adopt quantitative easing. This is followed by a section dealing with monetary policy when interest rates are zero bound, based on the recent experience of the US with money demand and velocity. The sixth section discusses exit strategies from quantitative easing and monetary policy normalization, and the last section contains concluding remarks and policy implications.

Quantitative easing in the aftermath of the latest financial crisis and its applications in the United States and the United Kingdom

Chapter 4 analyzed the financial crisis that started in 2008 and addressed its possible causes and impacts on various world economies. Central banks responded to the crisis by resorting to conventional and unconventional monetary policy strategies and tactics. The conventional policy adopted in many countries aimed at reducing short-term interest rates to zero or near zero, as will be discussed in the 'Evidence on quantitative easing' section below. Once interest rates become zero bound it becomes difficult to stimulate the economy through further short-term interest rate manipulations, which necessitates different adjustments in expansionary monetary policy other than interest rate tools. This phenomenon led to the adoption of unconventional monetary policy which took two forms: liquidity programs and quantitative easing. Liquidity programs or provisions are reflected in short-term collateralized lending funded by reserve creation and money printing. These programs have not, for the most, been adopted before, thus being termed "unconventional," with the central bank acting as a lender of last resort on a large scale. These lending programs were based on the premise that the shortage of liquidity in the market place had to be reversed to get the economy out of its crisis. Thus, these programs needed to be more creative than the existing practice of single discount window lending to banks. A case in point is the experience of the Federal Reserve Bank of the US, which will be discussed in the next section.

The second type of unconventional monetary policy took the form of asset purchase programs, which became known afterwards as quantitative easing (QE). Simply put, unlike the conventional central bank practice of open-market operations with government securities, particularly short-term ones, this policy aims at increasing reserves and liquidity in the economy through the purchase of unconventional assets such as mortgage-backed securities and long-term Treasury securities, as was the case in the US. QE thus effects changes in the composition of a central bank's balance sheet away from some types of traditionally held asset, and in its size, which is the result of injecting liquidity and easing credit conditions in the economy. QE policies aim at expanding the monetary base by creating new base money with the intention of increasing various monetary aggregates. In addition to combating recession and assisting in exiting the financial crisis, QE also has the objective of preventing deflation, as inflation rates fell during the crisis in many countries to levels well below the ones compatible with the objective of price stability. The decrease in inflation rates, especially when they become negative in the presence of deflation, can raise real interest rates even when nominal ones are near zero, countering the stimulating impact of zero bound interest rates on the real sector. Providing liquidity and credit easing was thus supposed to keep inflation rates at positive levels in order to maintain near zero or zero real interest rates. QE policies started as early as 2001, when the Bank of Japan, between 2001 and 2006, bought long-term government bonds and asset-backed securities. However, with the advent of the financial crisis of 2008 QE was officially planned and adopted from 2008–9 in two major countries witnessing recession, namely the US and the UK. Japan reactivated its QE policies in 2010 by buying, between 2010 and 2013, in the amount of 80 trillion yen per year Japanese government bonds, Treasury discount bills, corporate bonds, commercial paper, exchange-traded funds, and real estate investment trusts.[1] More recently, the European Central Bank announced the adoption of QE policy effective from 2015. The experience of the US and the UK, the first two countries to embark on QE immediately after the latest financial crisis, will be addressed in detail next, while the decision of the European Central Bank to embark on QE and other monetary policy strategies and conduct in a monetary union environment will be addressed in Chapter 8.

The remainder of this section thus addresses the practice of QE by two central banks, namely the US Federal Reserve System (the Fed) and the UK's Bank of England (the BoE), in the aftermath of the financial crisis of 2008. The purpose is to shed some policy light on the process and experience of QE, explaining in detail the steps that were pursued by different countries, the type of instruments used in the QE process, and the quantities of funds injected into the market place. Both countries' experience of the impact of QE on long-term government bond rates, other financial markets interest rates, and other asset prices will be analyzed in the next section, on the transmission mechanisms of monetary policy. The impact of QE on various economic indicators in the US and UK will be assessed and analyzed in Section 4, which deals with the empirical evidence, especially the possible effects on monetary aggregates, output growth, employment, and inflation rates.

Quantitative easing in the United States

As was stated in the previous section, QE was put into effect after the Fed reduced the federal funds rate, which is its implicit policy anchor, to near zero (see Figure 7.9). Additionally, the Fed initially adopted a wide array of collateralized lending programs which have been described as liquidity programs funded by reserve creation or the printing of money. Such programs were temporary in nature and thus not perceived as an inflationary threat, especially given the lower rate of inflation prevailing during the financial crisis. QE by the Fed thus implied the additional aggressive asset-purchase program also funded by reserve creation with more persistent Fed balance-sheet effects possibly causing a medium-term inflationary consequence.[2] An evaluation of the various possible macroeconomic impacts of these liquidity and QE programs will be conducted after their description.

The liquidity programs in the US were partly motivated by the indicator known as the LIBOR-OIS spread. The London Inter-Bank Offered Rate (LIBOR) is the rate at which banks borrow unsecured funds from other banks in the London wholesale money market. The holder of an Overnight Indexed Swap (OIS) receives a fixed rate of interest on a notional amount. This spread reflects the liquidity conditions in markets with a higher spread (high LIBOR), reflecting a tighter market liquidity and thus a decline in the willingness of major banks to lend. In August 2007, for example, the spread was around 10 basis points, rising to 85 basis points in September and reaching a then all-time high of 108 basis points in December. However, as of October 2008 the spread had reached 365 basis points, indicating a severe credit crunch following the failure of Lehman Brothers.[3] These liquidity programs are based on the lending of last resort function and are temporary in nature, thus being priced in such a way as to make them unattractive to markets upon the beginning of the recovery. Some of these programs were authorized under some of the provisions of the Federal Reserve Act of 1913, allowing the Fed to lend to banks and depository institutions in unusual circumstances with collaterals, including a wide array of private assets deemed satisfactory by the Fed. The allowable collaterals included issues of the US government or ones guaranteed by it or any of its agencies.[4] The liquidity programs that were initiated between December 12, 2007 and November 25, 2008 and were ended in March 2010, except for The Term Asset-Backed Securities Loan Facility (TALF), took the following forms:[5] (i) the Term-Auction Facility (TAF), which involved extending short-term fully collateralized loans of fixed amounts to depository institutions at rates determined by competitive auctions rather than by the Fed; (ii) the Terms Securities Lending Facilities (TSLF), which was aimed at collateralized lending of Treasury securities to primary dealers to provide enough of these securities to act as collateral in credit markets; (iii) Central Bank Liquidity Swaps, involving granting US dollars by the Fed to a host of central banks in return for receiving foreign currency with an agreement to reverse the transaction at a future date. The aim was to ensure dollar liquidity to foreign commercial banks and thus businesses needing to conduct transactions in US dollars. The process involved determining the notional amount of the swap, the maturity, the interest rate, and the exchange rate; (iv) the Primary Dealer Credit Facility (PDCF), involving overnight collateralized lending to banks and brokerage firms that trade US government securities to improve their ability to provide financing to participants in securitization markets and borrow on terms similar to those granted to banks at the discount window; (v) the Asset-Backed Commercial Paper Money Market Mutual Funds Liquidity Facility (AMLF), which involved lending primary dealers the funds to purchase asset-backed commercial paper (ABCP) from money market mutual funds. The funds paid a lower interest on the loan than the one earned on the ABCP. The funds can sell the paper later on to meet redemption by their investors; (vi) the Commercial Paper Funding Facility (CPFF), set up by the Fed to finance the purchase of commercial paper from issuers through a special purpose vehicle paying back the loans to the Fed after the commercial paper mature; (vii) the Money Market Investor Funding Facility (MMIFF), which involved lending to special purpose vehicles to buy money market mutual funds assets; (viii) the Term Asset-Backed Securities Loan Facility (TALF), which involved lending to issuers of asset-backed securities against these securities. In addition to the eight liquidity programs, the Fed provided lending of $30 billion to JPMorgan to buy Bearn Sterns and loans to AIG of $85 billion.

QE, which relied on unconventional measures, was first referred to as the large-scale asset purchase program announced on November 25, 2008. This program quickly eased monetary conditions. The QE program involved buying three types of instrument: namely mortgage-backed securities (MBS) owned by government-sponsored enterprises (GSEs); GSE bonds; and long-term Treasury securities.[6] The beginning of the easing program was called QE1 and the initial quantity purchased amounted to $500 billion of MBS from GSEs and $100 billion of GSE bonds or direct obligations. On March 18, 2009 a decision by the Federal Open Market Committee (FOMC) was made to purchase an additional $750 billion of MBS, making the total amount purchased equal to $1.25 trillion, and also to purchase an additional amount of GSE debt of $100 billion, to a total of $200 billion. Additionally, the FOMC decided to purchase up to $300 billion of long-term Treasury securities, initially to be effective in six months but tapered down to the end of October 2009 and then to the end of October 2010. The second phase, QE2, started in November 2010, when the FOMC stated its intentions to purchase a further $600 billion of long-term Treasury securities by the end of the second quarter of 2011, or around $75 billion per month. The third phase, QE3, started in September 2012, when the FOMC agreed to purchase additional MBS at a pace of $40 billion per month, and continued to extend the average maturity of its holdings of securities. The purpose of all three QE programs was to stimulate economic activity, reduce unemployment, improve the outlook for labor market conditions, promote the resumption of sustainable economic growth, preserve price stability, and support the functioning of financial markets.

Regarding the exit strategy from various liquidity programs and QE, the Fed adopted two approaches. First, in March 2010 it closed all special liquidity facilities except for the TALF. Second, regarding QE, the FOMC started gradually tapering off its purchases of MBS and of long-term Treasury securities around the end of 2013 owing to the progress towards maximum employment. Thus began the reduction in the pace of asset purchases. In the meeting of the FOMC of September 17, 2014 a policy normalization plan and principles were announced, a move viewed by many as the ending of QE in the US effective October 2014.[7]

Quantitative easing in the United Kingdom

After the intensification of the financial crisis of 2007–8 and to prevent the economy from falling further into recession and deflation, the Bank of England (BoE) provided the groundwork for QE by setting up an Asset Purchase Facility (APF) in January 2009 as an additional tool of monetary policy that the Monetary Policy Committee (MPC) could use to improve liquidity in the credit markets by buying high-quality assets, initially financed by the issuance of Treasury Bills but later on by the creation of new money, when this APF was to be used to conduct unconventional monetary policy.[8] On March 5, 2009 the MPC was authorized to use the APF for monetary policy purposes and thus began the purchase of gilts (UK government securities) in the secondary market and high-quality private sector assets such as corporate bonds and commercial paper. Thus, QE in the UK started in March 2009, when the MPC started to inject money directly into the economy by purchasing financial assets. This policy began after the BoE had reduced the bank policy rate to 0.5 percent. As is shown in Figure 7.10, the MPC had reduced the bank rate by 3 percentage points in the last quarter of 2008 and by 1.5 percentage points in early 2009 to 0.5 percent, where it has remained since March 5, 2009. This was coupled with inflation falling to around 1 percent, way below its target of 2 percent in the medium term. Like the process in the US that had started few months before, in November 2008, QE in the UK took effect after the bank rate was reduced to near zero to prevent deflation. Given that deflation raises real interest rates, it was necessary to provide markets with the necessary liquidity to boost economic activity. This is in line with the BoE strategy on price stability, which is still the same six years after the first QE scenario. In a Remit for the MPC addressed to the Governor of the BoE, Mark Carney, from the Chancellor of the Exchequer George Osborne on 18 March, 2015 it was reiterated that the inflation target of 2 percent applied at all times, reflecting the primacy of price stability and the inflation target in the monetary policy framework.[9] In the Remit it was stated that the inflation target was symmetric, as deviations below the target are treated in the same way as deviations above in order to prevent the deflationary bias in the framework, given the risk this bias could pose to achieving policy objectives.

Strategies to conduct expansionary monetary policy by the BoE started before March 5, 2009, specifically on January 19, when a decision was made to purchase up to £50 billion in high-quality private sector assets. These asset purchases were financed by the sale of short-term gilts by the BoE rather than by reserve creation. As a result, the monetary base measured by some of the liabilities of the BoE did not initially increase. Therefore, these operations were not termed QE, but were more in the nature of the BoE acting as market maker of last resort. In the same spirit, the BoE also purchased corporate bonds through a reverse auction and commercial paper, restoring market functioning rather than reserve creation, as its holdings of private sector assets reached only £3 billion out of the £50 billion announced in January 2009. In fact, the commercial paper facility was ended in November 2011 owing to improved market conditions, while the corporate bonds and the secured commercial paper are still in effect. Thus QE1 effectively started on March 5, 2009, when the BoE announced and started buying up to £75 billion of assets through the APF. The purpose as stated was to increase the monetary base by this amount, boost money supply, and bring about a level of nominal demand to meet the medium-term inflation targets. On May 7, 2009 the program was expanded to £125 billion and on November 5 the target ceiling reached £200 billion. These assets were composed largely of medium- and long-dated gilts held by the private sector at the time and constituting around 14 percent of annual nominal GDP. The gilt market seems to have been characterized by enough depth, breadth, and resiliency to accommodate the volumes of purchases deemed necessary. This target size lasted until October 6, 2011, when QE2 started with the expansion by the BoE of the QE program by £75 billion to £275 billion.

QE3 started on February 9, 2012, when the BoE expanded the asset purchase program to £325 billion. The amount was raised again on July 5 to £375 billion. All the asset purchases in the three QE programs were financed by issuing money or central bank reserves in order to increase the monetary base and thus money supply. The latest increase in the QE3 program was made because the growth rate declined from the last quarter of 2011 to the first quarter of 2012, as Figure 7.6 shows. The growth rate had been increasing before this period, and its slowdown necessitated further stimulus. Figure 7.7 shows that the unemployment rate was not declining during this period and needed an economic boost to start declining. In fact, based on casual empiricism, an improvement in both events took place following the implementation of QE3.

The nature and size of assets purchased amounted over the three QE periods to £379 billion, equivalent to around $596 billion based on the average exchange rate for the period considered. This amount consisted mostly of £375 billion in gilts ($590 billions), £1.97 billion in commercial paper ($3.1 billion) and £1.6 billion in corporate bonds ($2.52 billion). The total amount of £379 billion represented 26.3 percent of UK GDP, which stood at £1,441 billion at the end of the QE3 period. As noticed, gilts of long-term denominations represent practically all the QE assets purchased. In fact, in a Remit sent by the Chancellor of the Exchequer, George Osborne, to the Governor of the BoE, Mervyn King, dated November 29, 2011, the ceiling on private assets purchase was lowered from £50 billion to £10 billion, emphasizing the concentration on gilts for reserve creation.

Currently, the BoE is pursuing its QE programs. In its meeting of August 2015 the MPC voted unanimously to maintain the £375 billion target and so to reinvest the £16.9 billion of cash flows associated with the redemption of the September 2015 gilt held in the APF.[10] There is no exit strategy in sight, as various Remits addressed to the MPC confirm that the APF created in January 2009 will remain in place for the financial year 2015–16, which reinforces the signaling factor and the forward guidance transmission mechanism channels of monetary policy.

Transmission mechanism of quantitative easing: an additional forward guidance channel?

One of the most important issues to be addressed in the QE literature centers on the transmission mechanism through which a monetary policy strategy based on QE transmits to the real economy. Understanding how QE transmits to the wider economy by affecting output, employment, and inflation becomes necessary in evaluating the effectiveness of QE as an unconventional policy option to be used in times of financial crisis. This section first highlights various types of transmission mechanisms of monetary policy and the financial and regulatory environment necessary for their success. It then analyzes and discusses the most plausible mechanisms of QE given short-term interest rate levels approaching zero. The arguments will be supported by empirical evidence from the literature that has addressed the impact of QE policies on long-term interest rates and other asset prices in various financial markets and countries.

Transmission mechanisms of monetary policy are usually classified under three broad headings: the liquidity view, or the cost of capital channel; the credit view; and other asset price channels.[11] Initially, this policy operates in each channel through one or more of the following variables: nominal and real interest rates; asset prices; and bank deposits. Additionally, the second and third steps inside these channels following the three mentioned variables show that monetary policy effectiveness depends largely on its impact on exchange rates and bank loans and on agency theory effects of moral hazard and adverse selection. Thus, we can summarize the five main transmission mechanisms of monetary policy: nominal and real interest rates; bank loans; exchange rates; stock prices; and moral hazard and adverse selection.

Given that QE policies have been clearly announced with full transparency, an additional mechanism could be added, which operates through several forward guidance channels. These channels, as stated,[12] work as follows: forward guidance affects expectations both about short-term policy rates with continuous announcements about the size of QE and about the decision to keep these rates zero bound. Transparency in this guidance reduces uncertainty about the path of short-term market interest rates. Forward guidance may, in addition, reduce term premia, as uncertainty is reduced even for longer horizons, and could also boost several asset prices by impacting the level and volatility of short-term risk-free rates. Lowered expectations about the possibility of short-term rates increasing and a reduction in term premia could also act to lower long-term rates. A policy signaling effect may come into play here, as continuing asset purchases from QE1 to QE3 may signal the determination of various monetary authorities to boost the macroeconomy, causing economic agents to revise down their short-term expectations about policy rates.

An efficient and well-developed financial and regulatory environment is necessary for the effectiveness of various transmission mechanisms of monetary policy.[13] In the liquidity view, there is a need to have flexible market-determined interest rates; full or partial price stickiness; a large degree of central bank autonomy, transparency, and operational independence; efficient primary and secondary markets for government securities with proper institutional and regulatory arrangements, and the presence of many tools of monetary policy, such as repurchase and discount window operations. In the credit view, it becomes necessary to have highly developed loan markets and credit facilities with dominant firms' indirect external finance, and the ability to reduce information asymmetries and agency costs. In the asset prices view, it is of primary importance for the economy to be characterized by flexible de facto exchange rate regimes with efficient spot, forward, and currency derivative arrangements, a central bank's ability to predict real exchange rate appreciation and stock price bubbles, a wide range of public firms, and well-developed financial markets with high capitalization.

To analyze the possible transmission mechanisms of monetary policy in a QE environment we examine the effectiveness of various channels given the asset purchase programs. The new form of unconventional monetary policy started after reducing various short-term interest rates to historically low levels nearing zero. Thus, this new form was not aimed at bringing short-term interest rates further down as much as it was pumping enough reserves in the economy to motivate its activity and prevent deflation. The expansionary policies aimed at preventing deflation also reduced real interest rates to unprecedented levels, largely aiming at 2 percent inflation, such as in the UK and the EU, at a time when nominal interest rates were nearing zero. This adds to the fact that QE policies were not relying on lowering nominal or real short-term interest rates further after reversing deflation as much as keeping them at historically low levels and stimulating the economy through the increase in liquidity. This, however, does not neutralize or nullify the liquidity view, as policy-makers also aimed through their QE strategy to lower long-term interest rates. Time and again, QE in countries such as the US and the UK was conducted mainly through the purchase of long-term securities to reduce long-term rates, as will be shown in the next section. This is referred to as the portfolio balance effect of QE. Empirical evidence of the success of these policies took two main forms: event studies and more reliable and technically sophisticated econometric evidence. Event studies results have been summarized by Martin and Milas.[14] Several studies show that for QE1 in the US ten-year government bonds yields were reduced by 100 basis points after the March 18, 2009 announcement that a major expansion of QE in the amount of $1.15 trillion would be undertaken. The decline in the five-year government bond rate was around 85 basis points. For QE2, evidence from event studies in the US is mixed, but there is no indication of a large impact. In the UK differing estimates of the impacts of QE1 were reported, ranging between 40 and 100 basis points on the long-term gilt yields. However, the QE2 program did not reduce government bond rates, while the QE3 program had very small effects on the twenty-, ten-, and five-year UK government bond rates. The results, then, show that, initially, in both the US and the UK, QE1 had an impact on long-term government bond rates. However, these rates increased back again, reflecting the temporary impact of QE. When more QE measures were taken the impact as shown in events studies became much smaller and sometimes insignificant, casting doubt on the size and period of the impact of QE.

Results found in econometric studies were based on the belief that long-term rates are reduced because many assets with long maturities and duration are removed from the market place.[15] The decrease in the duration risk causes a reduction in the required premium to hold these long-term risky assets. The econometric evidence is found to be mixed, as will be shown. In addition, those studies that have shown QE to have some effect, especially in terms of QE1's impact on long-term government yields, report a smaller impact than do the event studies. For example, Gagnon et al, inferring the impact of the $1.75 trillion in the US QE1 program, find that the US ten-year bond rate was reduced between 38 and 82 basis points.[16] Using an example from the UK experience, Joyce et al found the impact of QE1 on gilt yields to be significant, at around 85 basis points, with the effect being reduced to 32 basis points after six months.[17] The evidence also suggests, again, that the impact of QE1 on long-term government bonds rates was stronger than that of QE2 and QE3. Martin and Milas attribute this fact in their analysis to three main issues:[18] first, the second and third QE programs were announced and anticipated by the markets and already affected bond rates through the effects of expectation; second, more rapid portfolio adjustments took place in the second and third rounds, causing the prices of government bonds to be translated more rapidly on to the prices of other assets; third, before QE1, government bond rates in both the US and UK were higher than before QE2 and QE3. It is possible that the higher bond rates are the more effective unconventional policies may be in reducing them.

However, the significant portfolio balance effects of both event studies and, to a lesser extent, econometric research were challenged in other, sometimes more recent, studies. Thornton, for example, examines the relationship between long-term yields and the supply of public debt in the US.[19] Several measures of the public's debt holdings and various yields were used in the empirical investigation. The results reached have been consistent with some of the literature[20] in reflecting no statistical significance and providing no support for the portfolio balance channel. The insignificance is attributed to the fact that, in the US, the amounts of long-term asset purchases by the Fed are too small—"a drop in the bucket"—relative to the outstanding amount of these securities. Thus, it was suggested that the effects of purchases on long-term yields could possibly be present through the forward guidance that they signal. This remains a possibility owing to the theoretical relationship between forward guidance and expectations about the path of short- and long-term interest rates.

Given the mixed impact of the liquidity view based on the historically low nominal and real short-term interest rate levels, which have not necessarily activated the economy, and the results of the portfolio balance effects, which measure the impact of QE on long-term government bond yields, the expansionary effects of QE could possibly be felt more through the credit view and the asset price channels. Regarding the credit view, the impact of QE is to transmit to credit activity in two ways. Traditionally, excess funds at banks are channeled to bank-dependent borrowers, increasing the quantity of loans and, thus, investment and consumption spending. In this view, the QE strategy will definitely increase the size of the central bank's balance sheet and thus the monetary base. However, whether this translates into an increase in money supply depends on the impact of the increase in bank excess reserves, accumulated through asset sales to the central bank, on bank loans and bank deposits. However, asset purchases from the non-bank public tend initially to increase the level of broad money, especially if funds are translated into bank deposits and transformed into further bank lending. This view was examined in a recent study by Butt et al,[21] who tested whether QE boosted traditional bank lending in the UK by using two approaches to determine if variations in deposits affected individual banks' balance sheets and reinforced lending. The results were insignificant, because QE gave rise to several very short-term deposits (flighty deposits), reducing the ability of banks to transform them into loans and thus diminishing the traditional bank lending channel. Additionally, the higher level of deposits and liquidity, which could in principle work towards facilitating the process of lending to the public, was slowed down by the strain on the financial system at that time and the resulting pressure on banks to reduce the lending portfolio, fearing loan defaults and capital holdings against some types of loan. Thus, QE operated, in the authors' opinion, through a portfolio balance channel when potential depositors traded their long-term securities for initially very short-term deposits. This result does not, however, preclude QE from operating through other credit channels, such as the second transmission mechanism in the credit view, which relates to agency theory and information asymmetries. A reduction in agency costs through a reduction in adverse selection and moral hazard reduces the spread between the cost of internal finance and external finance such as bank lending. QE increases consumer confidence in the future of the economy and banks' confidence both in the ability of consumers to repay and in loan recovery. Principals and agents thus interact in a scenario of available funds and lower agency costs, causing an increase in money supply.

As far as the asset price channels are concerned, QE works through its impact on the exchange rates and other asset prices. The excess funds generated by QE can cause a decline in the value of domestic currency and an increase in net exports. This channel found support in the US and the UK. A study by Neely shows that QE1 led to the depreciation of the US dollar by 4–11 percent, depending on the currency.[22] Glick and Leduc found that QE1 in the UK also impacted the value of the sterling by causing it to depreciate by 1.5–3.5 percent, depending on the currency.[23] Other asset prices beside those of debt instruments may also increase as a result of QE impacting investment, household liquidity, firms' balance sheets, and household wealth.[24] Several studies conducted on the impact of QE on asset prices other than government bonds found significant results for the US[25] and the UK.[26] In general, the empirical evidence on the link between monetary policy and stock prices is mostly inconclusive, as movements in these prices seem to be more influenced by economic fundamentals and economic expectations. However, the QE policies of asset purchases seem to have increased liquidity in the portfolio of the non-bank public, causing it to increase spending on different asset categories, driving asset prices and thus financial wealth up. Higher asset prices reduce yields and borrowing costs; thus, higher spending would be generated by the increase in financial wealth and lower yields. In addition, agency theory comes into play in the transmission mechanism to the economy through a reduction in agency costs caused by the increase in private financial wealth and the reduction in adverse selection and moral hazard. In summary, the transmission mechanisms of unconventional monetary policy seem to be many, depending on various studies and countries. Most of these mechanisms seem to lend support to the impact of QE policies, although to varying degrees.

Evidence on quantitative easing

The evidence on QE is largely based on empirical studies that have examined the impact of unconventional policies on three broad issues: government bond yields in all their maturities, other asset prices, and the wider macroeconomy, especially growth, unemployment, and inflation rates. These studies were conducted on countries having adopted QE as a result of the latest financial crisis, such as the US and UK. A few studies have included Japan, which adopted QE for the periods 2001–6 and 2010 onwards. Before discussing the findings of these studies, we will analyze some of the casual empiricist data collected for the US and UK to show some trends and developments in their macroeconomies since the financial crisis. This anecdotal evidence will be based on eight series for both countries, including the monetary base, money supply, nominal gross domestic product (GDP), inflation rates, growth rates, unemployment rates, interest rates, and velocity. The first six variables will be analyzed in this section and the last two in the next one, dealing with monetary policy when interest rates are zero or near zero.

The impacts of QE on the monetary base in the US and UK have been examined in various studies.[27] As far as the US is concerned, total assets held by the Fed increased from $891 billion in December 2007 to $4,498 billion in December 2014, increasing more than four times the size of the Fed's balance sheet. These assets increased from 6.1 percent to 25.3 percent of GDP. Decomposing the increase in the asset size shows that it increased to $2,026 billion by June 2009 during QE1, representing 14.1 percent of GDP.

In terms of the size of the monetary base composed of currency and reserves, currency outstanding amounted to $792 billion and reserves to $4.2 billion, or 0.5 percent of total Fed liabilities in 2007. In December 2014 currency increased to $1,299 billion, while bank reserves outstanding and repurchase agreements accounted for 64.2 percent of total FED liabilities, as the amount of currency in circulation was considerably below the amount needed to finance the expansion in the FED's assets.

For the change in the monetary base to affect the economy, it has first to impact the monetary aggregates. If asset purchases in a QE scenario were made from non-banks and/or if banks used the excess reserves held to extend lending or buy other assets from the non-bank sector, operations by the Fed would cause an increase in money supply. Figure 7.1 shows the growth of money supply M2, which, though positive, declined at the beginning of the financial crisis from around 8 percent to slightly over 2 percent, increasing once more in the middle of QE1 and reaching levels close to 9 percent after QE2—one of the highest growth rates since 1990—before falling back to 6 percent in 2015. This shows that QE policies coincided with an increase in the monetary aggregates in the same period. However, Figure 7.12 shows that the level of M2 relative to GDP increased at the beginning of the crisis and declined slightly later on for a short period before resuming its increase from 2010. The trend in these series reflects the fact that monetary aggregate growth is larger than nominal GDP growth, which has been continuously increasing since the middle of 2009. This may be due to possible increasing trends in money demand and, thus, declining velocity, which will be analyzed in the next section of this chapter. The increase in M2 does not seem to fully translate into a full increase in GDP.

In terms of the other observations of the impact of QE on the macroeconomy, the US real GDP growth rate shown in Figure 7.2 recorded a negative

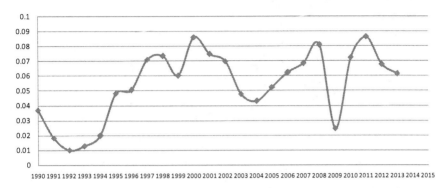

Figure 7.1 US M2 growth rate, annual, seasonally adjusted.

Source: http://research.stlouisfed.org/fred2

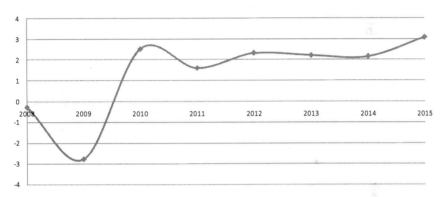

Figure 7.2 US growth rate.

Source: imf.org

performance at the beginning of the crisis, reflecting the early recession, with the recovery starting in the middle of 2009 and continuing to 2015, when the growth rate reached a level of over 3 percent. These rising growth rates coincided with declining unemployment rates (Figure 7.3) from the middle of 2009, from a high point of 10 percent to less than 6 percent in 2015. Annual inflation rates dropped significantly in the early period of the crisis, from a high of 4 percent to negative levels in the middle of 2009, before deflation was reversed. A major increase in the inflation rate to a period high of over 3 percent occurred at the end of 2011, before stabilizing at levels slightly above 1.5 percent in early 2015 (Figure 7.4).

In the UK QE started in March 2009, four months after the beginning of the asset purchase program in the US. Between March 2009 and January 2010 monetary policy measures, including QE, increased the size of the BoE's balance sheet relative to GDP by three times compared with the pre-crisis period.[28] The

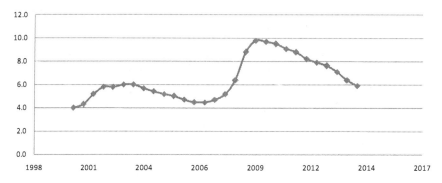

Figure 7.3 US unemployment: civilian unemployment rate, percent, semiannual, seasonally adjusted.

Source: http://research.stlouisfed.org/fred2

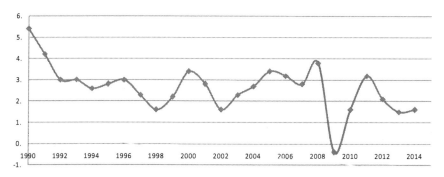

Figure 7.4 Annual inflation rate in the US from 1990 to 2014.

Source: Bureau of Labor Statistics, bls.gov

quantity of purchased assets alone over the mentioned period represented around 14 percent of nominal GDP. Nevertheless, money supply growth rates fell, as Figure 7.5 shows, from over 14 percent in 2007, before the crisis began, and slightly below 10 percent when the asset purchase program started, all the way to negative 2 percent, until reaching 0 percent in early 2011. Negative levels were reached again in 2013. As far as other macroeconomic variables are concerned, the UK witnessed a major recession from 2007 until late 2009 before growth resumed to 2014, with the level reaching slightly less than 4 percent (Figure 7.6). This was coupled with a decline in the unemployment rate from around 8 percent in the middle of 2010 to around 6 percent in 2014 (Figure 7.7). The inflation rate stabilized at around 1.5 percent at the end of 2014 after reaching a high of 4.5 percent in 2011, before its major drop (Figure 7.8). Based on this casual coincidental evidence, five years after the beginning of QE the UK economy did not imply anything about causation or even simple correlation at a 4 percent growth rate, 6 percent unemployment rate and 1.5 percent inflation rate.

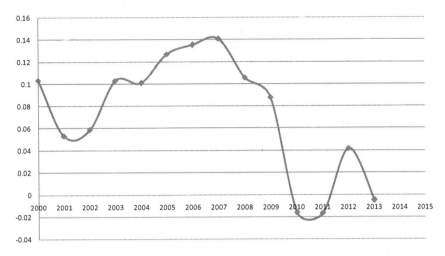

Figure 7.5 UK M3 growth rate.

Source: https://data.oecd.org/money/broad-money-m3.htm

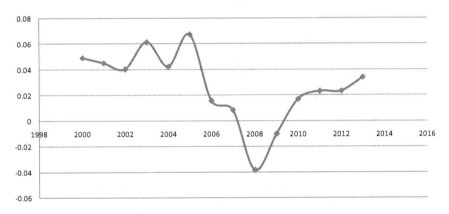

Figure 7.6 UK growth rate.

Source: www.oecd.org

Empirical evidence, as was stated above, addressed the impact of QE on government bond yields, other asset prices, and the wider real economy. The first two issues were analyzed in the third section of this chapter. The remainder of this section surveys the empirical literature that has addressed the impact of QE on the real economy, with special emphasis on the US and UK. Studies of the empirical evidence relating to the eurozone economy will be addressed in the next chapter. Examining the impact of QE on the real economy, as eloquently stated by Joyce et al,[29] is challenging in the sense that many other contributing factors may exist, such as expansionary fiscal policy and spillover effects from other countries adopting similar policies. In addition, unlike event studies, the

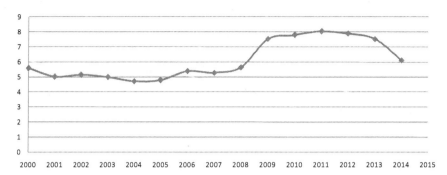

Figure 7.7 UK unemployment rate, total, % of labor force.

Source: https://data.oecd.org/unemp/unemployment-rate.htm

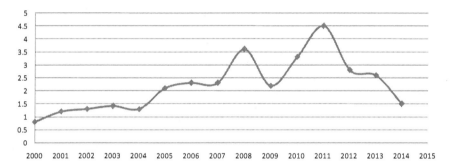

Figure 7.8 UK inflation rate.

Source: https://data.oecd.org/price/inflation-cpi.htm

wider economic effects may involve long and variable lags with many factors that must be controlled for. Thus, constructing model-based policies and no-policy counterfactuals becomes necessary, especially since QE involves new, unconventional policies, meaning that the results reached are heavily qualified. Despite these possible shortcomings, a literature is being developed from a wide list of studies, some of which will be discussed below. The results reached in these studies differed in terms of methodologies, impacts, magnitudes, and countries. Some studies used case analysis, while others relied on dynamic stochastic general equilibrium models, vector auto regression models, and so on. The results of the impact on the real sector also depend largely on counterfactuals related to what would have happened to the real sector in the absence of unconventional policies. A number of these studies will be briefly listed here chronologically and their macroeconomic findings reported.

   In one of the earliest studies on the subject, Baumeister and Benati use time-series estimates of US and UK quarterly data in a counterfactual framework to show that monetary policy actions in these two countries had an immediate impact, preventing risks of major output declines and deflation.[30] Specifically, they found that in the absence of QE output growth in the US would have declined to –10 percent, compared with an actual –3 percent, while in the UK this figure would have fallen to –14 percent. This shows the importance of QE programs in countering the recessionary shocks associated with the early financial crisis, with the strongest impact showing in the first quarter of 2009, when QE started in the UK and a few months after it had begun in the US. Results on inflation show that, in the absence of QE, inflation would have been negative in the US and close to –4 percent in the UK. Thus, these results show the effectiveness of monetary policy actions on both variables and in both countries. A second study by Bridges and Thomas used several monetary models to estimate the effects of QE, first on money supply in the UK and then on growth and inflation.[31] The results show that M4 increased by around 8 percent. This estimate of the increase in the money supply is applied to two econometric models, one of them being a set of sectoral money demand systems, with the aim of calculating how total spending and asset prices need to adjust to re-equilibrate the money market. The effects of the impacts of unconventional monetary policy are simulated by choosing shocks that affect M4 by 8 percent effective the first quarter of 2009. The effect on output is modest in the sense that it starts to increase in the middle of 2009, causing a growth rate of a maximum of 1.5 percent by the beginning of 2010 and becoming negligible by the middle of 2011, which necessitates further and consecutive increases in the amount of QE and money supply growth. The impact on inflation is positive, as its rate starts to increase from early 2010, reaching a high of around 2 percent before declining but remaining positive. In another study by Chen et al,[32] QE was shown to be less effective than in other studies. This study aimed at determining the effects of QE2 in the US, assuming that interest rates remain at their near zero level for at least one more year. The results reached using simulation show that output growth caused by unconventional monetary policy reaches close to 0.4 percent only with minimal inflationary impact. A fourth study by Chung et al[33] using a Federal Reserve Bank model for the US economy augmented with a portfolio balance model and calibrated to be consistent with QE1 shows that unconventional monetary policy was successful in the US in terms of reducing the unemployment rate and preventing deflation. A combination of QE1 and QE2 periods show that such policies raised output growth to 3 percent and lowered unemployment by 1.5 percent. They also show that inflation is 1 percent higher than it could have been in the absence of unconventional policies. Additionally, the study shows that the impact on the three macroeconomic variables is similar to a cut in the federal funds rate of around 300 basis points given the period of 2009–12. The last study highlighted here is by Kapetanios et al[34] and uses counterfactual analysis based on three different models allowing for structural change in one model, parameters change at a particular time to capture regime changes in the second model, and an assessment of the general time variation in parameters in the third model. The purpose of using different models that vary in their emphasis on data, according to the authors, is to increase the likely robustness of the conclusions. The study aims to examine what would have happened to the wider economy of the UK had unconventional monetary policy not been undertaken. Results from various models suggest that, in the absence of QE, real GDP would have declined more dramatically during 2009 and inflation would have been lower or even negative. Specifically, QE had a peak upward effect of 1.5–2.0 percent on real GDP and 0.75–1.5 percentage points on CPI inflation. Given that real GDP fell by 4.9 percent in 2009, this implies that the growth rate would have been around –7 percent had it not been for QE1. The conclusion reached is that QE was effective in preventing the UK economy from falling into deeper recession and deflation.

The results of the reviewed studies, except that by Chen et al,[35] show that for the most part unconventional monetary policy had a major impact on output growth, inflation, and unemployment. However, these results are to be viewed with caution for reasons discussed at the beginning of the analysis of empirical evidence, as well as in some other studies, such as that of Martin and Milas.[36] In this last study, the authors state that other policy measures, such as fiscal and regulatory policies, could have also impacted the macroeconomic variables considered, and recommend the use of alternative estimates based on different models and methodologies to widen the existing evidence.

Monetary policy when interest rates are zero bound: the role of velocity in the recent US experience

QE began after various monetary authorities brought their short-term interest rates to near zero levels, as discussed above. Such reductions are perceived to be a conventional monetary policy aimed at stimulating economic activity through the liquidity channel of transmission mechanism. In addition, however, unconventional monetary policy measures such as QE were pursued in order to reverse the impact of the 2008 recession on the economy. Even though QE led to major increases in the monetary base and, to a lesser extent, in money supply, the growth rates in nominal GDP were not always consistent with money growth rates, falling behind throughout the crisis in the US. A major explanation of this fact centers around the behavior of the velocity of circulation, which is based on the impacts of the QE policy on the holdings of money. The interest rates decrease had broad consequences for the demand side of the money market that may slow down the impact and magnitude of QE, affecting the supply side. This decrease in interest rates has a direct impact on velocity. There is strong evidence that money demand will increase in response to increasing risk premia, defined, for example, as the difference between the spread on corporate bonds and long-term Treasury yields due to flight to quality funds. Holding money will also become more prevalent with decreasing opportunity cost of money versus long-term bond yields, as they tend to fall. This increase in money demand tends to reduce velocity, complicating the interpretation of movements in money supply through QE and possibly slowing down the impact and magnitude of QE. This section, using a money demand framework, will formalize the relationship between interest rates and velocity. We utilize actual data from the US's latest experience with QE to study the figures on the interest rate, velocity, and money supply to GDP ratio and infer linkages based on casual empiricism. In support of our arguments, we rely on a recent study by Anderson et al[37] to provide strong empirical evidence for the links described.

We first base the analysis on the Quantity Theory of Money, where $MV = PY$ and where M, V, P, Y, and PY stand for money supply, velocity, aggregate price level, output, and nominal GDP respectively. We express money demand as $MD/P = f(y, i)$, where i stands for the short-term interest rate and y for real income. Assuming money market equilibrium, inversing the money demand function and multiplying both sides by Y, following Mishkin,[38] gives $PY/M = Y/f(y, i)$ or $V = Y/f(y, i)$, based on rearranging the Quantity Theory of Money. Thus, a decrease in i increases the quantity of money demanded and lowers velocity. Expressing the Quantity Theory in percentage changes allows us to rewrite it as $m + v = p + y$, where m, v, p, and y represent the growth rates of money, velocity, aggregate price level, and output respectively. An increase in m through QE translates into a larger increase in GDP when v is positive and a lower one when v is negative. In a system of declining though positive velocity, the growth rate of velocity becomes negative. In this situation, $m/(p + y)$ increases, showing a stronger impact of QE on the growth of money supply than GDP.

Considering data for the US economy allows us to make the following observations. Figure 7.9 shows the decline in the US federal funds rate to zero bound levels (between 0 and 0.25 percent) during and after the crisis. Figure 7.11 traces the movements in velocity for the latest period, showing a decline in its level and thus a negative velocity growth rate. Based on the previous analysis, Figure 7.12 shows how the ratio of M2 monetary aggregate to GDP increases, showing that the growth rate in M2 (m) was increasing by more than the growth rate in nominal GDP (p + y), largely owing to the possibility of an increase in money demand and alluding to a negative v. The decrease in interest rates and in the M2 velocity, causing the increase in money M2 to GDP ratio, are more convincing given proper empirical evidence. Anderson et al[39] build on a broad money demand model for the US economy dating from 1929, or before the Great Depression, and all the way to what they refer to as the current great recession, to estimate money demand and velocity determinants. The model, according to the authors, remedies the shortcomings of previous models, which failed to include all determinants of money demand found significant in the current study and the interactions among them, namely the traditional opportunity cost of M2, long-run declines in transactions

Figure 7.9 US federal funds rate.

Source: http://www.federalreserve.gov/releases/H15/data.htm

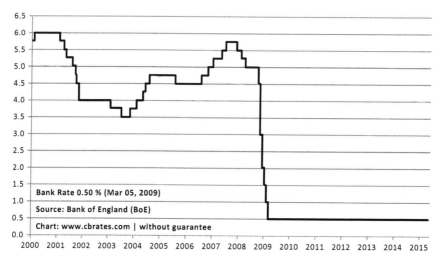

Figure 7.10 UK bank rate.

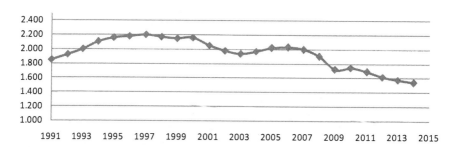

Figure 7.11 US velocity of M2.

Source: http://research.stlouisfed.org/fred2/help-faq

costs using M2 substitutes, and a measure of the perceived risk of financial market participants. The results reached show that M2 velocity is indeed influenced by interest rates risk premia, major banking regulations, and financial innovation. The results also confirm what we stated in our casual empirical analysis, that the average 6.5 percent growth in M2 since 2007–2008 did not translate into GDP growth because risk premia effects and reforms to the financial sector lowered velocity by increasing money demand. Their model also uses coefficient estimates to forecast that velocity will soon increase in 2016 and 2017 to levels where a 4 percent M2 growth instead of the current average of 6.5 percent implies low to moderate nominal GDP growth consistent with a price stability objective of inflation rates standing slightly below 2 percent. A growth rate in M2 in line with its current one will cause inflation to rise by more than 2 percent a year. The implications of their results are twofold, according to our analysis of QE. First, in considering further economic stimuli through QE, the fact of a declining velocity and its

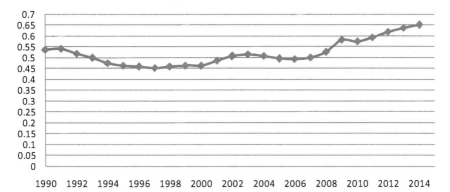

Figure 7.12 US M2/GDP ratio.

Source: http://research.stlouisfed.org/fred2

negative growth rate should be accounted for by monetary authorities in increasing the amount of reserves creation to create larger increases in M2. Second, in considering an exit strategy from QE when the economy returns to some degree of normalcy, and given that, according to their results, velocity is expected to rise soon, the decision on the growth rate of money in conventional terrains should consider the expected fall in money demand in order to ensure that inflation does not exceed its policy objectives.

An exit strategy from quantitative easing and monetary policy normalization

After entering into a new policy scenario to reverse a crisis or at least prevent it from worsening, monetary authorities usually decide to adopt an exit strategy when one of three outcomes resulting from the entry happens: first, the outcome of the policy fulfilled the aims of the entry; second, the policy was moving in an effective direction but had side-effects endangering other policy objectives, such as restoring growth and reducing unemployment at the expense of price stability; finally, the new policy turned out to be ineffective in achieving the desired outcome. The last option is ruled out, as counterfactual evidence suggests that QE had successful impacts, preventing further major losses in output growth and more severe deflation in the US and UK. The second option is not under consideration yet as the current inflation rates are still below the peak levels acceptable for the objective of price stability. The first option has been treated differently by three of the central banks adopting QE. Ending QE has been mooted but not yet achieved in the US; on September 17, 2014 the Federal Open Market Committee (FOMC) announced its "Policy Normalization Principles and Plans," in which it mentioned that it will raise its overnight interest rate target when there is no more need for monetary accommodation and that it will reduce the size of the Fed's balance sheet to the levels existing before the crisis when Treasury Bills and mortgage-backed securities held by the Fed start maturing.[40] In fact, the federal funds rate was raised in December 2015 from a range of 0–0.25 percent to a range of 0.25–0.5 percent owing to improvements in labor market conditions in 2015, as judged by the Federal Open Market Committee, which also stated that it is reasonably confident that inflation will rise, over the medium term, to its 2 percent objective. It is worth mentioning that the US had started tapering off QE at the end of 2013 by reducing the pace of asset purchases and, as clearly stated by the then Chairperson of the Board of Governors of the FED, Ben Bernanke: "We have been pushing down on the accelerator pedal more and more in previous months but in months to come, we will push on it a bit less but this is not like applying the brakes."[41] In the UK, and based on the several Remits of the BoE discussed earlier, especially in March 2015, it was stipulated that monetary policy will remain accommodative and QE will continue unabated for the year 2015–16 with no mention of exit strategies.[42] The ECB started QE in 2015, with discussion centering around the mechanics of the policy, which is still in its infancy, rather than exit strategies.

Exit strategies have yet to be clearly pronounced upon and applied, and it is clear that the implications of the issues involved in their implementation and the expected outcome of returning to normalcy are still being theoretically debated. The purpose, in a nutshell, is to prevent the exit from QE reversing the positive macroeconomic impact achieved as a result of its implementation. The issues involved in exit strategies can be summarized as follows: the basis of the decision to exit, the announcement of the new strategy, the methods used to reverse QE, the speed of the implementation, and the possible reversal of the successful outcome of the entry.

The first issue relates to whether the policy has achieved its purpose or whether the outcome is conflicting with other goals. QE policies can be tied to certain rules related to the size of the recovery or to the impact of the policy on a conflicting goal. Some policy-makers may establish explicit policy rules advocating witnessing a full recovery or a return to the pre-crisis situation before QE is ceased, while others may tie it to the beginning of a reversal in the right direction before easing QE on the way to a full exit. On the other hand, central banks may adopt unconditional QE by not referring initially to any exit strategy or rules. This was the case in the US, when the asset purchase program did not have a state-contingent character. Bullard states that there is nothing optimal about simply announcing a figure for assets to be purchased rather than adjusting QE as macroeconomic information arrives.[43] He goes on to state that, in the same way the Taylor rule, among others, is used for conventional monetary policy reflected in interest rate cuts, QE should become state contingent if the Fed is adopting two policy instruments, with both adjusted in response to current information. Additionally, central banks with dual mandates may watch for signs of both high employment and price stability, whereas ones with a hierarchical mandate such as the achievement of price stability may cease QE if inflation starts to approach its target level. The BoE, which watches both full employment and price stability, has stated on several occasions in its Remits that it will continue the current highly expansionary policy until economic slowdown has been reduced as long as this does not constitute any risk to financial and price stability. Another case in point as regards a typical hierarchical mandate is the ECB, which has relied since the beginning of the crisis largely on interest rates cuts, setting one of them at negative levels in 2014 to stimulate economic activity before announcing the beginning of QE in January 2015, when the harmonized index of consumer prices (HICP) fell way below the announced level of price stability of less than 2 percent. The ECB also stated in reference to an exit strategy that asset-purchases programs will be carried out until the end of September 2016, when inflation rates will readjust to a level closer to 2 percent from below.

The second issue relates to the announcement of the new strategy. Some believe that the central bank ought to be methodical and transparent about its exit decisions. The literature shows that there could be a forward guidance and signaling channel in QE, implying that expectations about the stance of monetary policy may impact various outcomes. However, Wen, using a calibrated general equilibrium model framework, examines the response of the economy to both a fully anticipated exit and an unanticipated one.[44] The results show that it is optimal for the exit to be completely unanticipated by the public to preserve the maximum gains achieved in output and employment under QE; the conclusion reached is that it would be a mistake for the Fed to pre-announce the exit. This result appears to be in line with the belief that exiting a successful strategy may reverse the outcomes achieved from adopting it.

The third issue relates to the methods that can be used to implement the exit from QE. These methods take various forms, ranging from a gradual increase in key interest rates back to the levels prevailing before the crisis, to waiting for assets purchased to mature without being replaced in the portfolio of the central bank, to an outright reversal of QE through long-term asset sales or a reduction in the quantity of reserves via reserve repurchase agreements. Blinder summarizes and analyzes the Fed's early discussion about an exit strategy in the form of various speeches and testimonies by Chairman Bernanke in seven main points.[45] These points could serve as examples of exit strategies for central banks and are as follows: encouraging borrowers to reduce the use of extraordinary liquidity facilities; normalizing the terms of regular discount window loans; redeeming instruments as they mature or are repaid; raising the interest on reserves at the Fed; offering depository institutions term deposits that are not counted as reserves; reducing the quantity of reserves via repurchase agreements; and redeeming or selling securities in conventional open-market operations. The first three points are part of quantitative tightening, while the last two represent conventional monetary policy. The fourth and fifth points aim at draining further reserves from banks into the Fed.

The order of achieving this exit strategy is also crucial. The Fed stated on September 17, 2014 that in its normalization plan it will first raise its overnight interest rate target and then reduce its balance sheet to the order of pre-financial crisis levels. Williamson mentions that this order is puzzling, with no rationale provided for it by the FOMC; at the onset of crisis the Fed reduced the rate first and then conducted QE, making the reverse order a more natural policy in the event of exit, as it will now be trying to raise the rate with a large stock of reserves in the financial system.[46]

The speed of the implementation is a major issue addressed in the exit strategy debates. It is often mentioned that some central banks may wait for assets to mature before reducing their balance sheets and, given that long-term asset purchases were involved, it becomes clear that such plans for the exit strategy are gradual and deliberate. The rationale is that a speedy plan can pose many risks if conducted without a properly laid-out and effective framework. Thus, although the Fed announced the end of QE effective October 2014 it has yet to alter policy interest rates even slightly, accentuating the preparation of financial markets for the exit strategy. However, Wen, in a study mentioned earlier,[47] calls for a speedy implementation period, stating that if the exit is too gradual, long-run adverse effects of QE would arise, offsetting the gains from QE achieved in the earlier periods.

The last and most important issue is the possible reversal of the successful outcome of the entry after raising policy rates and reducing reserves back to their pre-crisis levels. Clearly, the causes that led to the adoption of QE were not the absence of it, meaning the levels of interest rates and reserves prevailing before the financial crisis in various economies (see Chapter 4 for the causes of the financial crisis). In the aftermath of the crisis, the whole international regulatory financial order has been modified in terms of governance, bank capital, and other financial sector practices, hopefully preventing the reoccurrence of the shocks that led to the crisis. QE served to reverse the negative macroeconomic impacts of the crisis and the exit strategy aims to normalize various economies after the unconventional policy of QE had achieved its purpose.

Concluding remarks and policy implications

The first decade of the twenty-first century ended with a wide-ranging financial crisis causing recessions in several major industrial countries. This global event necessitated the use of unconventional monetary policy arrangements redrawing the new central bank stabilization architecture. Though QE was used at the beginning of the decade to stimulate economic activity and prevent deflation in Japan, the coverage it received as a result of its use in the US, UK, and European Monetary Union made addressing the design and impacts of unconventional monetary policy the latest in monetary policy strategy and conduct, causing a myriad of literature to develop analyzing QE. The experiences of the countries adopting QE have been different, owing largely to their differing economic cycles and current economic conditions, the nature and levels of development of their financial markets, the availability, volume, and maturity of their financial instruments, and the mandates and goals of their central banks. Whereas the US announced the ending of QE effective October 2014, the ECB announced the beginning of QE in early 2015. The BoE re-emphasized time and again in its various monetary policy remits its continuing commitment to accommodative monetary policy through QE for the coming year of 2015–16.

The design of asset purchases also differed across countries. However, the objectives and aims were the same, stipulating an attempt to reduce long-term interest rates after reducing short-term ones to near zero and to affect credit conditions, other asset prices, financial markets, and expectations through forward guidance and signaling in order to activate the wide macroeconomy and prevent deflation. Using a transmission mechanism of a monetary policy framework, all channels provided mixed evidence according to econometric studies. However, there exists enough evidence, especially in counterfactual econometric research, of the improvements in the macroeconomy across countries to suggest that QE was to a degree effective. The gradual pre-announcements of strategies and tactics stating the volume and type of assets to be purchased, along with various maturities, could have also supported the effectiveness of the forward guidance channel of the transmission mechanism and for signaling. Policy-makers ought also to pay attention to the demand side of the money market in order to properly and effectively manage the rate of growth of the money supply in line with planned economic growth and inflation projected guidelines, given central bank mandates. Given zero bound interest rates, a decision by the public to hold more money, reducing velocity, may become detrimental to the growth in nominal GDP.

The debate over QE has also centered from the outset on various exit strategies and monetary policy normalization once the economy returns to pre-financial crisis levels. Five issues were highlighted in this chapter, encompassing the basis of the decision to exit, the announcement of the new strategy, the methods used to reverse QE, the speed of the implementation, and the possible reversal of the successful outcome of the entry when the exit is completed. As of February 2016, of the countries that adopted QE after the latest financial crisis only the US has started implementing the exit strategy. The Fed ceased its QE operations and developed an exit strategy starting with raising the federal funds rate, which began as of December 16, 2015. In its meeting on that day the FOMC judged that there had been considerable improvement in labor market conditions in 2015, and felt that it was reasonably confident that inflation would rise, over the medium term, to its 2 percent objective. Given the economic outlook, and recognizing the time it takes for policy actions to affect future economic outcomes, the FOMC decided to raise the target range for the federal funds rate from 0–0.25 percent to 0.25–0.5 percent. The stance of monetary policy remains accommodative after this increase, thereby supporting further improvement in labor market conditions and a return to 2 percent inflation. For all countries adopting QE, the basis of the decision to exit seems to be the improvement in the state of the macroeconomy, including careful attention to economic growth, unemployment, and price stability. We expect the other issues to be country specific, but also very similar in terms of the transparency of the announcements and the gradual implementation designed not to affect the outcome of the entry.

Notes

1 The figures reported are based on Fawley and Neely 2013. The study discusses the case of Japan and other countries extensively. Our study does not address the Japanese situation in detail and confines the analysis to the US and UK in this chapter and the experience of the ECB in the next one. However, some examples relating to Japan are mentioned when need arises.

2 Bullard 2010.

3 A very thorough analysis on which these figures are based is found in Sengupta and Tam Yu 2008. The authors detail the discussion of the LIBOR-OIS spread to highlight the severe credit crunch resulting from the financial crisis.
4 This information is based on Fuhrer 2015. The author mentions several sections of the Federal Reserve Act dealing with lending to depository institutions under Section 10(B), individuals, partnerships, and corporations under Section 13(3). The material also discusses the Federal open-market operations authorized in Section 14 of the Act.
5 These liquidity programs were compiled from various studies, namely Fuhrer 2015; Mishkin 2013; and Blinder 2010.
6 The information on QE in the US provided in this section was compiled from various sources, namely Bernoth et al 2015; Fuhrer 2015; Fawley and Neeley 2013; Blinder 2010; and Bullard 2010.
7 Information on the "Policy Normalization Principles and Plans" can be found on the Board of Governors of the Federal Reserve System web page at: www.federalreserve.gov/newsevents/press/monetary/20140917chtm
8 The information on QE in the UK provided in this section was compiled from various sources, namely the web page of the Bank of England at: www.bankofengland.co.uk; Bernoth et al 2015; Fawley and Neeley 2013; Bank of England 2012; and Joyce et al 2011a.
9 This information is based on the Remit of March 18, 2015 from the Bank of England web page at www.bankofengland.co.uk. The Remit was written by George Osborne, the Chancellor of the Exchequer.
10 This information is from the web page of the BOE on "Market Notice: Asset Purchase Facility: Gilt Purchases," August 6, 2015 at http://www.bankofengland.co.uk/markets/Documents/marketnotice150806.pdf
11 Mishkin 2010.
12 Bank of England 2013.
13 Shahin 2011.
14 Martin and Milas 2012.
15 Gagnon et al 2011.
16 Gagnon et al 2011.
17 Joyce et al 2011b.
18 Martin and Milas 2012.
19 Thornton 2014.
20 Bauer and Rudebusch 2011.
21 Butt et al 2014.
22 Neely 2015.
23 Glick and Leduc 2011.
24 Mishkin 2013.
25 Gagnon et al 2011.
26 Joyce et al 2011b.
27 The information on anecdotal evidence based on casual empiricism in the US provided in this section was compiled from various sources, namely Fuhrer 2015; Fawley and Neeley 2013; Blinder 2010; Bullard 2010; US Bureau of Labor Statistics and St. Louis Federal Reserve Bank.
28 The information on anecdotal evidence based on casual empiricism in the UK provided in this section was compiled from various sources, namely the web page of the Bank of England at: www.bankofengland.co.uk; Fawley and Neeley 2013; Bank of England 2012; Joyce et al 2011a; and data from the OECD at www.oecd.org
29 Joyce et al 2012.
30 Baumeister and Benati 2010.
31 Bridges and Ryland 2012.
32 Chen et al 2012.

33 Chung et al 2012.
34 Kapetanios et al 2012.
35 Chen et al 2012.
36 Martin and Milas 2012.
37 Anderson et al 2015.
38 Mishkin 2013.
39 Anderson et al 2015.
40 This information is summarized in Williamson 2015 from the "Policy Normalization Principles and Plans" found on the Board of Governors of the Federal Reserve System web at: www.federalreserve.gov/newsevents/press/monetary/20140917chtm
41 This information is summarized in Williamson 2015 from the "Policy Normalization Principles and Plans" found on the Board of Governors of the Federal Reserve System web at: www.federalreserve.gov/newsevents/press/monetary/20140917chtm
42 See, for example, the Remit of March 18, 2015 from the Bank of England web page at www.bankofengland.co.uk. The Remit was written by George Osborne, the Chancellor of the Exchequer.
43 Bullard 2010.
44 Wen 2014.
45 Blinder 2010.
46 Williamson 2015.
47 Wen 2014.

Bibliography

Anderson, R, Bordo, M and Duca, J 2015, "Money and velocity during financial crisis: from the Great Depression to the Great Recession," Working Paper 1503, Federal Reserve Bank of Dallas Research Department.

Bank of England 2012, "The distributional effects of asset purchases." Available from: www.bankofengland.co.uk

Bank of England 2013, "Monetary policy trade-offs and forward guidance." Available from: www.bankofengland.co.uk/publications/documents/inflationreport/2013/ir13augforwardguidance.pdf

Bank of England 2015, "Market notice: asset purchase facility: gilt purchases." Available from: http://www.bankofengland.co.uk/markets/Documents/marketnotice150806.pdf

Bauer, M and Rudebusch, G 2011, "The signaling channel for the federal reserve board purchases," Working Paper 211–21, Federal Reserve Bank of San Francisco.

Baumeister, C and Benati, L 2010, "Unconventional monetary policy and the Great Recession: estimating the impact of a compression in the yield spread at the zero lower bound," Working Paper 1258, European Central Bank.

Bernoth, K, Konig, P and Raab, C 2015, "Large-scale asset purchases by central banks II: empirical evidence," *DIW Roundup*, 61, pp. 1–8.

Blinder, A 2010, "Quantitative easing: entrance and exit strategies," *Federal Reserve Bank of St. Louis Review*, 92, 6, pp. 465–79.

Board of Governors of the Federal Reserve System 2014, "Policy normalization principles and plans," Monetary Policy Releases. Available from: www.federalreserve.gov/newsevents/press/monetary/20140917chtm

Bridges, J and Ryland, T 2012, "The impact of QE on the UK economy: some supportive monetarist arithmetic," WorkingPaper 442, Bank of England.

Bullard, J 2010, "Three lessons for monetary policy from the panic of 2008," *Federal Reserve Bank of St. Louis Review*, 92, 3, pp. 155–63.

Bureau of Labor Statistics, "Annual inflation rate in the United States (indicator)." Available from: http://www.bls.gov/data/

Butt, N, Churm, R, McMahon, M, Morotz, A and Schanz, J 2014, "QE and the bank lending channel in the United Kingdom," Working Paper 511, Bank of England.

Central Bank Rates, "Bank of England (BOE)." Available from: http://www.cbrates.com/

Chen, H, Curdia, V and Ferrero, A 2012, "The macroeconomic effects of large-scale asset purchase programs," *Economic Journal*, 122, 564, pp. F289–F315.

Chung, H, Laforte, JP, Reifschneider, D and Williams, J 2012, "Have we underestimated the likelihood and severity of zero lower bound events?" *Journal of Money, Credit and Banking*, 44 (supplement s1), pp. 47–82.

Fawley, B and Neely, C 2013, "Four stories of quantitative easing," *Federal Reserve Bank of St. Louis Review*, 95, 1, pp. 51–88.

Federal Reserve Bank of St. Louis, "Economic Data." Available from: http://research.stlouisfed.org/fred2

Federal Reserve, Board of Governors of the Federal Reserve System, "Data Chart, US Federal Funds Effective Rate." Available from: http://www.federalreserve.gov/releases/H15/data.htm

Fuhrer, J 2015, "Extraordinary FED policies during the financial crisis," in *Continuing Education Program Material on Monetary Policy*, American Economic Association.

Gagnon, J, Raskin, M, Remache, J and Sack, B 2011, "The financial market effects of the federal reserve's large scale asset purchases," *International Journal of Central Banking*, 7, 1, pp. 3–43.

Glick, R and Leduc, S 2011, "Central bank announcements of asset purchases and the impact on global financial and commodity markets," Working Paper 2011–30, Federal Reserve Bank of San Francisco.

International Monetary Fund, "IMF Data, US GDP Growth Rate." Available from: http://www.imf.org/en/data

Joyce, M, Tong, M and Woods, R 2011a, "The United Kingdom's quantitative easing policy: design, operation and impact," *Bank of England Quarterly Bulletin*, Quarter 3, pp. 200–12.

Joyce, M, Lasaosa, A, Stevens, I and Tong, M 2011b, "The financial market impact of quantitative easing in the United Kingdom," *International Journal of Central Banking*, 7, 3, pp. 113–61.

Joyce, M, Miles, D, Scott, A and Vayanos, D 2012, "Quantitative easing and unconventional monetary policy: an introduction," *TheEconomic Journal*, 122, pp. F271–F288.

Kapetanios, G, Mumtaz, H, Stevens, I and Theodoridis, K 2012, "Assessing the economy-wide effects of quantitative easing," *The Economic Journal*, 122, 564, pp. F316–F347.

Martin, C and Milas, C 2012, "Quantitative easing: a skeptical survey," *Oxford Review of Economic Policy*, 28, 4, pp. 750–64.

Mishkin, F 2013, *The Economics of Money, Banking and Financial Markets*, 10th edn, Pearson Publishers.

Neely, C 2015, "Unconventional monetary policy had large international effects," *Journal of Banking and Finance*, 52, pp. 101–11.

OECD 2016, "Broad money (M3) (indicator), GDP Growth Rate (indicator), Unemployment Rate (indicator), Inflation Rate (indicator)." Available from: https://data.oecd.org/

Osborne, G 2015, "Remit for the monetary policy committee," Bank of England. Available from: www.bankofengland.co.uk

Sengupta, R and Tam Yu, M 2008, "The LIBOR-OIS spread as a summary indicator," *Synopses*, 25, Federal Reserve Bank of St. Louis.

Shahin, W 2011, "Channels and environments of monetary policy and their implications for its conduct in GCC Countries," in eds D Cobham and G Dibeh, *Money in the Middle East and North Africa*, Routledge, pp. 172–96.

Thornton, D 2014, "QE: is there a portfolio balance effect?" *Federal Reserve Bank of St. Louis Review*, 96, 1, First Quarter, pp. 55–72.

Wen, Y 2014, "When and how to exit quantitative easing?" *Federal Reserve Bank of St. Louis Review*, 96, 3, pp. 243–65.

Williamson, S 2015, "Monetary policy normalization in the United States," *Federal Reserve Bank of St. Louis Review*, 97, 2, pp. 87–108.

8 Monetary policy in an era of monetary unions, and central banks' holdings of foreign reserves

Introduction

The twenty-first century witnessed the rise of the European Monetary Union (EMU) and European Central Bank (ECB), shaping the conduct of monetary policy for nineteen countries currently forming the euro area with a common euro currency. This monetary union was not coupled with a fiscal union, making the ECB operate in an environment in which it faces many fiscal authorities instead of one, which was the traditional form of monetary policy until the year 2000. This monetary union operates in a euro area that is sometimes divided into a two-tier system characterized by widely divergent unemployment and growth rates. Inflation rates are calculated based on a harmonized index of consumer prices (HICP) aiming at an average for the nineteen countries below but close to 2 percent to achieve the price stability objective as per the Maastricht Treaty. The differences in the macroeconomic indicators cause the common monetary arrangements to be loose for some countries and tight for others, making policy interest rates relatively too low for one group and too high for the other. Differences in economic fundamentals sometimes cause the euro to be overvalued for one group and undervalued for the other, impacting trade activities within the euro area and with the rest of the world. Additionally, the lack of a fiscal union or some type of disciplined fiscal integration has been perceived by many as leaving member countries with fiscal imbalances prone to inflows of shocks and crisis, causing declines in aggregate demand and contagious systemic dangers across the eurozone. These salient features require appropriate monetary policy arrangements, and these are different than the ones practiced by central banks facing one fiscal authority, given that the aim is to achieve the price stability objective and a macroeconomic environment characterized by high output and employment growth across various members. On another hand, the twenty-first century also witnessed a major financial crisis that has reshaped the international financial architecture. This crisis caused many central banks across the world to hold additional reserves for both precautionary reasons, reflected in responses to various market shocks and prevention of disorderly market conditions, and non-precautionary reasons, to protect fixed pegged exchange rate arrangements and provide international liquid assets. This reserve accumulation is believed to have a social cost when inappropriate amounts of reserves are accumulated. Thus, a literature is developing dealing with reserve adequacy or the determination of the optimal amount of reserves to be held by central banks.

This chapter thus aims at covering two main topics. First, it deals with monetary policy arrangements in monetary unions without fiscal unions by using the EMU as a case study. Then it examines the social cost of reserve accumulation using a set of countries from the Middle East and North Africa region (MENA). In doing so, it is organized as follows. The second section deals with monetary unions without fiscal unions, and the third section addresses the monetary policy conduct of the ECB from its inception until the decision to conduct policies of quantitative easing. This is followed by a section dealing with the assessment of central banks' reserve adequacy using a sample of MENA countries. The last section contains concluding remarks and policy implications.

Monetary unions without fiscal unions

To establish successful monetary unions strategies are commonly developed to support the arrangements through a coordination of monetary policies and the achievement of some common fiscal indicators by all member countries without necessarily considering a fiscal union or some type of disciplined fiscal integration. These strategies are built on meeting a set of convergence conditions or criteria outlined in the treaties in which the unions are established. These criteria are usually based on rules governing exchange rates, inflation rates, interest rates, budget deficits, and government debt. The purpose of setting up the convergence criteria in the EMU in the early 1990s, for example, was to achieve a high level of policy coordination on the road to realizing price stability and sound public finances across member states after establishing economic and institutional unity. This ensures that countries with high inflation and interest rates and/or ones with high budget deficits and public debt will not qualify to join a union requiring exchange rate coordination, low inflation levels, and sound public finances.[1] Using another example, the history of policy coordination among some Arab nations started as early as 1981, with the establishment of the Gulf Cooperation Council (GCC), composed of Bahrain, Kuwait, Oman, Qatar, Saudi Arabia, and the United Arab Emirates, and the creation of the GCC Free Trade Area. By the end of 2001 GCC countries decided to establish a common market and economic and monetary union by 2010. In fact, the common market was launched at the beginning of 2008, whereas plans for the monetary union are currently stalled, especially after the decision of Oman and the United Arab Emirates not to join. To achieve this union the GCC countries introduced mechanisms for international monetary coordination similar to the convergence criteria of the EMU. However, the convergence criteria that the GCC set up represent a slightly modified version of the ones used by the EMU.[2] One fact remains, though, which is that, in both of these cases, achieving some fiscal indicators was required but fiscal union was not attempted.

As far as the EMU is concerned, existing data show that many countries have recently missed the fiscal policy indicators reflected in debt to GDP ratio of 60 percent and deficit to GDP ratio of 3 percent. This applies not only to member countries that were perceived to have witnessed macroeconomic problems, such as Greece, Italy, Ireland, Portugal, and Spain (GIIPS), but also to some other members. In fact, public debt in the EMU as a share of GDP increased to an average of 95 percent in 2014, close to 30 percentage points above its average pre-crisis level.[3] Deviating from the debt to GDP criterion was one of the major factors contributing to the beginning of the crisis in Greece. Additionally, broadly speaking, there seems to have existed a two-tier system of countries in the eurozone based on economic indicators long before the financial crisis of 2008. On one hand stand the GIIPS countries, while the other tier consists Europe's northern members, Austria, Belgium, France, Germany, and the Netherlands. Given a single monetary policy, policy interest rates, according to some analysts, for the period 2001–6 were approximately 50 basis points too high for Germany but between 300 and 400 basis points too low for Ireland, Greece, and Spain.[4] The GIIPS countries witnessed an increase in unit labor costs of 32 percent for the period 1997–2007, compared with 12 percent in the northern member states. Additionally, the lack of fiscal integration coupled with undervalued borrowing costs in the GIIPS and high tax revenues from a boost in domestic demand caused an increase in government spending. To cite a few examples, between 1997 and 2007 per capita government spending rose by an average of 76 percent and the share of government spending in GDP by 3.5 percent in the GIIPS, whereas the same figures were 34 percent and no change in the northern countries.[5] With the advent of the global financial crisis, tax revenues declined drastically, exacerbating the crisis in the GIIPS and leading some analysts to call for fiscal integration to prevent future divergent expenditure paths among the eurozone members. At the same time, despite the fact of a single monetary policy and one exchange rate with a price stability objective, real sector variables reflected in output growth and unemployment have also significantly diverged among members. In 2014 unemployment rates were 5 percent in Germany and 5.6 percent in Austria, whereas they stood at 26.5 percent in Greece and 24.5 percent in Spain.[6] This implies that the crisis has affected different countries in the eurozone differently. Thus, many believe that the same currency has become overvalued for the countries with weaker performance, preventing them from increasing their exports to improve their economies, and undervalued for countries with the stronger performance, allowing them to increase their exports and growth rates further. To buttress the impact of the problems faced in the GIIPS on the other eurozone countries and prevent contagion, it could be argued that, in the spirit of cooperation, given the same monetary policy, countries with the stronger performance could inflate their economies slightly through increasing government expenditures to make their goods more expensive for exports, and import more from countries with the weaker performance. This would possibly require at least some fiscal policy cooperation, if not full integration. On the integration issue, two major questions arise in the wake of the latest financial crisis. The first question concerns whether fiscal policy coordination on the way to a full-fledged fiscal union could have averted the negative fiscal impacts of such crisis in some of the eurozone countries that had expanded their government expenditure out of the range of the northern members, while the second centers on whether a fiscal union could prevent adverse spillover effects to other member countries in the event of a crisis.

Studies on such issues have been conducted mainly by the International Monetary Fund (IMF) (International Monetary Fund 2013b), in which the mechanics of a fiscal union for the euro area have been developed. It is believed, using arguments supportive of more fiscal integration, that zone-wide insurance mechanisms are to be established, such as fiscal integration, to reduce the severity of a crisis. The integration can provide a pre-determined framework for fiscal discipline to contain shocks. This may prevent the undermining of the no-bailout clause in the Maastricht Treaty, given stronger enforcement powers by the center. The IMF analysis stipulates that the minimal elements for a fiscal union reducing the severity of a future crisis are as follows: building surplus buffers as one of the aims of national policies; developing temporary transfers or joint provisions of public goods and services organized by a central budget for the whole union to improve fiscal risk-sharing; creating backstops for the euro area banking sector to reduce the sovereign-banking mechanism in the financial system; and, finally, providing some form of common borrowing backed by common revenue to finance risk-sharing and provide a common safe asset, reducing the potential for asset reallocation among sovereigns (International Monetary Fund 2013b). In the absence of fiscal integration, governments do not pool sovereign risks, leading to the absence of risk-free assets except for the central bank's own liabilities. Thus, all other assets used in conducting open-market operations purchases carry credit risk.[7] These four components of fiscal integration are believed to reduce the frequency and severity of a crisis, making it less prone to systemic spillover effects. A partly centralized fiscal policy would reduce the risk of individual idiosyncratic national policies, increase the available countercyclical tools, and allow for better fiscal coordination, though at the expense of some national sovereignty over budget expenditure. Over sufficiently long periods all union members can benefit from transfers at some point in time, reducing the burden of risk-sharing mechanisms on countries with stronger traditions of fiscal discipline and prudence that usually experience better cyclical conditions. On the other hand, in the absence of fiscal unions or integration, monetary policy remains independent, with one central bank and many fiscal authorities and budgets. In such environments of monetary policy dominance or independence, the objective of monetary policy remains to ensure price stability rather than monetizing deficits and inflating away debts. The return on the balance sheet of the central bank through seigniorage operations is not used in support of the fiscal policies of various union members. The mechanics of how such a monetary policy for monetary unions without fiscal integration is implemented are addressed in the next section, using the EMU as a case study. On that topic, it is noteworthy that the ECB made a decision in 2015 to expand its asset purchase program to include the buying of public sector securities. This program is designed to preserve monetary dominance and independence while considering the fiscal set-up of the eurozone. In designing such a program without allowing the fiscal policy considerations of individual countries to affect the independence of the ECB, four crucial elements were introduced to stress the monetary policy dominance.[8] First, loss-sharing in the purchase of public sector securities is reserved for the purchases done by the ECB. Thus, the terminology used refers to "limited loss-sharing," as 80 percent of all purchases, on which no loss-sharing is available, are done by the national central banks. This is to preserve the necessary incentives for fiscal discipline among various central governments in the eurozone. Second, the purchases are allocated across eurozone countries based on the ECB's capital key limiting the degree of discretion towards individual governments, which preserves fiscal incentives for these authorities. Third, purchase limits on the issue and issuers of public sector securities have been introduced to ensure the prohibition of monetary financing. Finally, as a rule, the purchases include only sovereign securities that are assigned an external investment grade by credit assessment institutions to ensure that the ECB and the national central banks acquire more protection against governments with unsound fiscal policies.

Monetary policy of the European Central Bank: quantitative easing at last

Most central banks, such as the Federal Reserve System in the US and the Bank of England in the UK, adopt a dual mandate of high employment and low inflation. The ECB's monetary policy strategy, however, has been governed since 1999 as stipulated in the Maastricht Treaty by a hierarchical mandate aimed at achieving a price stability objective based on a quantitative definition of less than but close to a 2 percent inflation rate for the whole euro area harmonized index of consumer prices over the medium term. This strategy comprises a two-pillar approach used to analyze the risks to price stability. These pillars involve an economic analysis and a monetary analysis, providing a framework within which decisions are made concerning the appropriate level of short-term interest rates consistent with the policy goal.

In the economic analysis the emphasis is on evaluating and forecasting real activity, financial conditions, output growth, employment levels, various fiscal policies in the euro area, balance-of-payments developments, and external shocks. The monetary analysis relates to long-term links between money and prices through an evaluation of monetary and credit developments to assess their implications for future inflation and economic growth. This analysis uses a broad set of tools and instruments that are refined and expanded on a regular basis. The monetary analysis thus focuses on a longer-term horizon than its economic counterpart. The remaining parts of this section analyze the monetary policy of the ECB between the beginning of the crisis of 2008 and the present—the asset purchase program that started in 2015 and its expected transmission mechanisms, the performance of some macroeconomic indicators in the eurozone, and the possible exit strategy from quantitative easing (QE).

Early response to the financial crisis: standard and non-standard measures of the monetary policy of the ECB

The first major crisis faced by the ECB since its inception was the financial crisis of 2008. The eurozone witnessed major declines in growth rates, reaching negative levels of –4 percent from highs of 6 percent before the crisis and major increases in unemployment rates, reaching over 12 percent from lows of below 7.5 percent (see Figures 8.4–8.6). Inflation rates also started to fall drastically at the end of 2008, helping the ECB to cut interest rates to stimulate economic activity without endangering price stability.

The ECB responded to the financial crisis using both standard measures reflected in interest rate adjustments and non-standard measures in the form of credit support to the banking system. As Figures 8.1–8.3 show, interest rates banks receive on deposit facility at the ECB, rates charged through the main refinancing

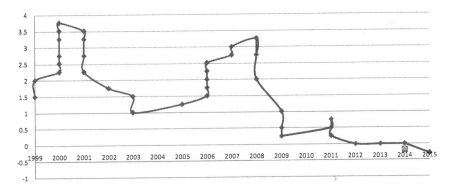

Figure 8.1 Interest rates on deposit facility.

Source: http://www.ecb.europa.eu/stats/monetary/rates/html/index.en.html

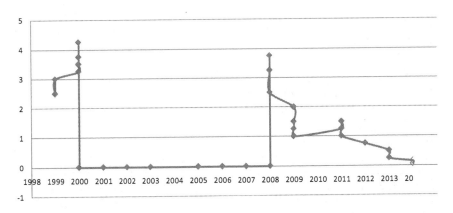

Figure 8.2 Interest rates on main refinancing operations.

Source: http://www.ecb.europa.eu/stats/monetary/rates/html/index.en.html

Figure 8.3 Interest rates on marginal lending facility.

Source: http://www.ecb.europa.eu/stats/monetary/rates/html/index.en.html

operations on funds regularly lent to banks, and rates paid on marginal lending facility for overnight lending to banks were reduced four times between October and December 2008, and another four times in 2009, reaching historically low levels. They were slightly increased twice at the beginning of 2011, as the euro area inflation rates crossed 2 percent, before being reduced continuously since then, twice in 2011, once in 2012, twice in 2013, twice in 2014, and once in 2015. Most importantly, after reducing the interest rate on deposit facility at the ECB to 0 percent in 2012, it was reduced to negative levels in 2014, reaching –0.3 percent in 2015 and early 2016. The rate on the main refinancing operations stands at 0.05 percent in 2016, while that on the marginal lending facility stands at 0.3 percent. To preserve the functioning of a money market in which banks lend to each other, the three interest rates cannot be the same or even very close to each other. Thus, when the rate on the main refinancing operations was reduced to 0.05 percent the rate on deposit facility had to be reduced to negative levels of –0.3 percent to preserve a spread of around 35 basis points and maintain a corridor necessary for functioning markets. The interest rate cuts represent standard measures designed to raise inflation rates back up to slightly less than 2 percent, ensuring price stability over the medium term, which is believed to be necessary for sustainable growth.

The non-standard measures comprised five consistent elements: unlimited liquidity provisions to banks at fixed interest rates against adequate collateral; increasing the maturity of the refinancing operations from three months to one year; the extension of assets accepted as collateral; the provision of liquidity in foreign currencies partly conducted through liquidity swaps with the US Federal Reserve System; and asset purchases in the covered bond market.[9] Thus, the expansion of the ECB's monetary base resulted mainly from the provision of loans against collateral. Providing loans to banks was necessary because some banks in some peripheral countries of the eurozone experienced an outflow of deposits towards other euro area countries, necessitating liquidity funding by the ECB to alleviate the difficulties.[10] This is different from the operations conducted by other central banks, such as those of the US and the UK discussed in the previous chapter, where the aim of the non-standard operations was mainly to reduce various asset yields. In fact, the ECB's actions started in October 2008, when it announced that it would provide all necessary loans to banks at fixed-rate tenders against an expanded list of eligible collateral. The ECB filled all main refinancing operations and long-term refinancing operations loan requests at the main refinancing rate, causing a major spike in lending following the availability of unlimited funds at this rate.[11] This rate was reduced between October 2008 and May 2009 from close to 4 percent to 1 percent (Figure 8.2). Additionally, the ECB introduced in May 2009 twelve-month long-term refinancing operations and the covered bond purchase program (CBPP), as commercial banks showed a preference for borrowing at longer maturities. Covered bonds provided security for their holders in case of default, which motivated their purchase, as the ECB committed to purchase €60 billion of these bonds for the first time in May 2009, in a program called CBPP1 (which ended in 2010, after all purchases were completed), to be followed by another €16.7 billion in November 2011 in a program called CBPP2 (which ended in 2012 after all purchases were completed). The assets bought under both covered bonds programs were held by the ECB until maturity.[12]

Quantitative easing: the asset-purchase program 2015–present

The ECB decided to embark on QE policies or asset purchase programs in January 2015. The decision to pursue this new policy was based on two main considerations: the weak recovery, which lowered inflation rates undesirably near zero or well below the 2 percent level; and the uncertain impact of the traditional expansionary monetary policy based largely on interest rates reduction. Given weak growth, high unemployment, and extremely low inflation approaching deflation, reducing interest rates further, given their current level approaching zero and negative, was shown not to be enough to steer inflation closer to 2 percent. With no room to cut interest rates any further, the asset purchase program was the only tool that might enable the ECB to achieve its objectives. Thus, the ECB reinforced the current monetary policy with more quantitative predictability. Additionally, one of the main aims of QE was to provide credit to the non-bank public by mitigating the adverse effects that malfunctioning money markets were having on bank liquidity and credit conditions.

All national central banks as well as the ECB participate in the asset purchases. The ECB coordinates the total amount to be purchased by various national central banks centrally. These amounts are allocated based on the institutional structure of the euro area, reflecting a common monetary policy, a single currency, a goal of price stability, and nineteen national fiscal and economic policies.

The asset-purchase programs were described by the ECB as non-standard measures amounting to €60 billion per month starting March 2015. These purchases were initially intended to be carried out until the end of September 2016, when it was expected that the inflation rates will readjust to a level closer to but still less than 2 percent. However, in its meeting of December 3, 2015, which was reconfirmed in the press conference of the President of the ECB Mario Draghi on January 17, 2016, the ECB decided to extend the asset-purchase program at least until March 2017. In the December meeting the Governing Council made five major decisions concerning traditional and non-traditional monetary policy.[13] First, the interest rate on the deposit facility was lowered by 10 basis points to –0.30 percent, while other interest rates were unchanged. Second, the asset purchase program was extended until the end of March 2017, or possibly further if need arises in line with the ECB's goal of price stability. Third, a decision was made to reinvest the principal payments on the securities purchased to achieve a favorable liquidity condition. Fourth, it was decided to include in the list of purchased assets by the national central banks euro-denominated marketable debt instruments issued by regional and local governments located in the euro area. Fifth, a decision was made to continue for as long as necessary, as fixed rate tender procedures, the main refinancing operations and three-month longer-term refinancing operations. Thus, it seems that the ECB is planning to remedy the impact of the financial crisis through policies of QE consisting of asset-purchase programs, with the list of assets being extended regularly to provide the necessary liquidity and diversified to include new assets. The expanded asset-purchase program that had started in March 2015 will include the third covered bond purchase program CBPP3 (after €60 billion in 2009 and €16.7 billion in 2011), the asset-backed securities purchase program, and the public sector purchase program. The securities covered by the public sector purchase program include: nominal and inflation-linked central government bonds and bonds issued by recognised agencies, international organisations, and multilateral development banks located in the euro area. The eurosystem intends to allocate 88 percent of the total purchases to government bonds and recognised agencies and 12 percent to securities issued by international organisations and multilateral development banks.[14]

The transmission mechanisms of monetary policy through which asset purchases aim to influence economic activity, according to the ECB, operate through three main channels.[15] The first is a credit channel which the ECB refers to as a direct pass-through channel, involving buying asset-backed securities and covered bonds, both linked to loans. The increased demand for these assets drives up their prices, encouraging banks to make more loans linked to them, generating more asset-backed securities and covered bonds and thus more loans. This is expected to provide more liquidity in the economy, bringing down the cost of borrowing. The second channel is a portfolio rebalancing one in which the sellers of instruments in the open market operations invest the funds in other assets, bringing up the overall asset prices and reducing various asset yields. Both channels serve to stimulate real sector activity in the economy and prevent deflation. The third channel is one that was shown to be significant in the US and the UK: signaling effects. The reassurance that QE policies will remain active at least until 2017 and will be reconsidered then for possible renewal will provide market participants with more certainty regarding the cost of capital and investment decisions.

The use of these channels of transmission mechanisms is being reinforced by some empirical studies showing that the monetary policy of the ECB has been effective in supporting and stimulating the eurozone economy since the beginning of the financial crisis. In fact, unconventional monetary policies seem to have had significant impacts on loans and interest rates and on boosting the real sector and inflation, albeit with a delay. Industrial production in some studies was shown to be 2 percent higher than it would have been and the unemployment rate 0.6 percent lower owing to the ECB's monetary policy.[16] The current macroeconomic performance in the eurozone is depicted in Figures 8.4–8.6. Eurozone growth rates fell to unprecedented negative levels with the advent of the financial crisis, reaching –0.4 percent in 2009. Since this period, this rate has recovered to positive levels, standing at around 3 percent in 2015. The unemployment rate also began to adjust downwards from a high of 12 percent in 2013 to 10.5 percent at the end of 2015. The inflation rate stands currently at slightly above zero levels, having reached negative ones in the first quarter of 2015. These conditions require further monetary policy accommodation to prevent the reoccurrence of deflation while reducing unemployment and increasing the rate of growth possibly to levels available before the crisis of around 6 percent. Figure 8.7 shows that the ratio of broad money measured by M3 to GDP has more or less stabilized over the last four years rather than decreasing if the GDP growth rate were higher than the growth rate of M3, due possibly to a positive growth rate in velocity. This stable figure could be attributed to the fact that money supply velocity also stabilized in the last three years (Figure 8.8). A stable velocity possibly resulting from a stable

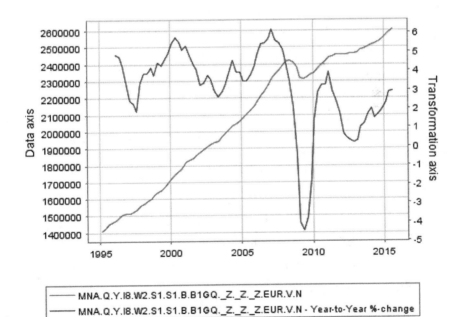

Figure 8.4 GDP growth rate.

Source: http://www.ecb.europa.eu/

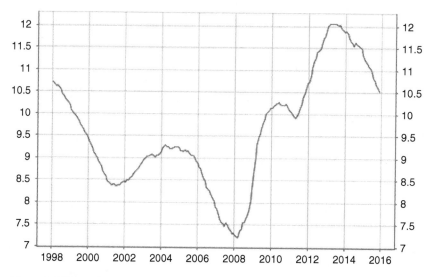

Figure 8.5 Unemployment rate: seasonally adjusted.

Source: http://www.ecb.europa.eu/

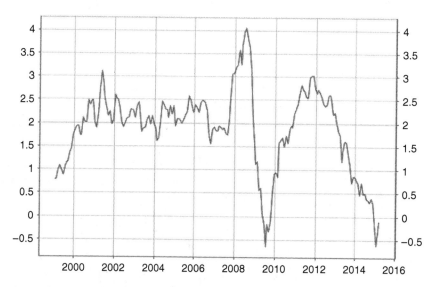

Figure 8.6 Inflation rate: overall inflation.

Source: http://www.ecb.europa.eu/

level of interest rates could perhaps be maintained, as interest rates cannot be decreased further, having reached close to zero or negative levels. Given a stable or even a constant velocity, there have been calls for major consecutive increases

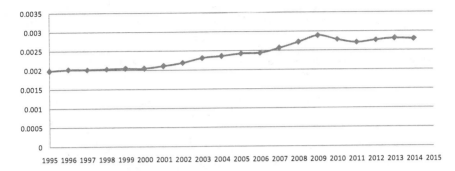

Figure 8.7 M3/GDP ratio.

Source: https://data.oecd.org/money/broad-money-m3.htm

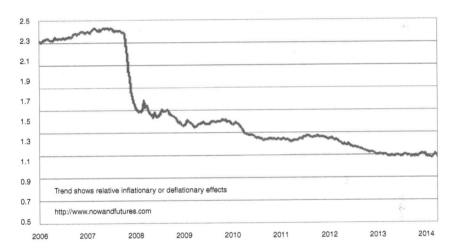

Figure 8.8 Velocity of M3.

in broad money to raise prices and output back up to desired levels. This necessitates extending the asset-purchase program through the injection of significant funds into the eurozone banking and financial systems for long enough periods of time to achieve the desired monetary policy outcomes. As the President of the ECB, Mario Draghi, stated: "The Governing Council will closely monitor the evolution in the outlook for price stability and, if warranted, is willing and able to act by using all the instruments available within its mandate in order to maintain an appropriate degree of monetary accommodation. In particular, the Governing Council recalls that the asset-purchase program provides sufficient flexibility in terms of adjusting its size, composition and duration."[17] Thus, it is too early to discuss various forms of exit strategy at this stage, as the asset-purchase program will be pursued at least until the end of March 2017, and certainly until the monetary authority sees an increase in the inflation rate back to levels below, though close to, 2 percent over the medium term.

An assessment of central banks' reserves adequacy: the case of MENA countries

The conduct of monetary policy in many countries is based on achieving the goal of exchange rate stability through some type of pegged exchange rate arrangement. Thus, the aim of monetary policy is to preserve the peg through regular interventions in foreign exchange markets to alleviate the pressure on domestic currency when necessary. This strategy necessitates the holdings of large amounts of foreign currency reserves in the portfolio of various central banks to support the conduct of monetary policy. These reserves are termed "non-precautionary reserves," as their purpose is to be actively and regularly adjusted to achieve currency stability. Holding non-precautionary reserves can also be intended to provide international liquid assets for intergenerational equity or be the result of large export earnings that rely on sterilized intervention to enhance external competitiveness.[18] Another major motive for reserves holdings is precautionary, in the sense that this type of reserves helps countries to respond to various economic shocks and prevent disorderly market conditions. Shortages of foreign currencies can cause market dysfunctions and limit the ability to alleviate a crisis in the external sector resulting from various shocks to the balance of payments current and capital accounts. Thus, the increase in foreign currency reserves held by central banks over the last decade has resumed for both precautionary and non-precautionary reasons in the wake of the global financial crisis. It is estimated that the reserves to GDP ratio for emerging countries is four times greater than its size in the 1990s. However, there is little consensus on what constitutes an adequate level of reserves for both precautionary and non-precautionary reasons. Therefore, while large amounts of reserves may serve to achieve currency stability, lower sovereign risk, and mitigation of the impacts of financial crises, the cost of holding these reserves could be high from several perspectives, especially if these reserves increase beyond adequate levels. This cost is measured as the difference between the rate at which a given country borrows to accumulate reserves and the risk-free rate at which reserves are invested either in central bank vaults or in risk-free assets. However, some believe that this spread is expected to decline as reserve accumulation increases, thus adding to the marginal benefit of holding reserves, which reduces reserves cost. This section discusses first the literature analyzing and assessing the adequate amounts of reserves held by various central banks. Then it applies the concepts in the literature to a group of Middle Eastern countries that mainly follow some type of pegged exchange rate arrangement, before drawing conclusions on the adequacy of their reserves held. Even though these reserves are necessary to achieve the objectives of monetary policy, their rising social cost ought also to be taken into consideration.

Literature review: central banks' holdings of foreign reserves

The literature on assessing reserve adequacy and the cost of reserves[19] addressed several issues, among which are four main ones: the adequate and optimal amount of reserves to be held for precautionary and non-precautionary reasons using various measures and criteria irrespective of the cost; the cost of holding reserves; the impact of reserve accumulation on this cost; and a reconsideration of the optimal amount of reserves to be held given the cost. Rodrik has estimated that, in the last decade, reserves holdings have climbed to almost 30 percent of developing countries' GDP and eight months' worth of imports.[20] Prior to financial globalization, central banks used to hold a quantity of reserves equivalent to three months' worth of imports, which is still the case in industrial countries. The main methodology used to measure optimal reserves is based on the Guidotti–Greenspan–IMF rule, which states that countries should hold liquid reserves equal to their foreign liabilities. According to Rodrik's calculations, most emerging market countries had insufficient reserves in 1990 and sufficient in 2004. Rodrik then estimates the measure necessary to compute the cost of holding reserves, which is equal to the spread between the private sector's cost of short-term borrowing abroad and the yield that the central bank earns on its liquid foreign assets. This spread is used as a percentage of GDP to compute the social cost and thus determine the optimal reserves holding, which is estimated as the holding that generates a cost of around 1 percent of GDP.

Levy has developed a mathematical model and empirically tested it to determine the cost of reserves.[21] This cost is estimated in his study as the sovereign spread over the risk-free return on reserves paid on the debt issued to purchase them, which ignores the benign effect of reserves on the spread. The empirical results show that these costs may have been overstated, as holding additional reserves has contributed to the decline of the spread by more than 50 percent, according to the calculations. The calculations also provide lower bounds to the benefits of reserves in terms of lower financing costs, as they do not include the savings to the private sector where borrowing costs are typically reduced given the decline in the cost of the sovereign. Thus, the paper underscores the fact that the cost of reserves to countries holding large reserve amounts may have been considerably overstated.

Jeanne presents a simple welfare-based model of the optimal level of reserves.[22] Based on the model, the author derives formulas for the optimal level of reserves and compares them with the Guidotti–Greenspan–IMF rule. The results suggest that the optimal level of reserves is subject to considerable uncertainty because it is subject to hard-to-measure variables. However, when the optimal level is approximated by plausible estimates from the model it is shown that the current build-up of reserves is not justified for precautionary reasons. This has some implications for reserve management in the sense that liquid foreign assets should be invested in market yielding assets, rather than the low yielding foreign assets in which central banks tend to invest.

The IMF, building on earlier publications,[23] believes that considering only one factor such as reserve adequacy without factoring in the cost of holding reserves biases the assessment of the holdings of reserves in one direction, meaning it is necessary to consider both the benefits and the costs of various types of reserve holding.[24] Additionally, reserve adequacy evaluations should be adjusted differently for different economies. The studies by the IMF therefore divide countries broadly into three categories: emerging markets in which reserves holdings are aimed at reducing the possibility of currency crisis; advanced economies in which reserve buffers are associated with a lower risk of banking crisis and market dysfunction; and low-income countries in which reserves smooth domestic absorption of current account shocks. Within each category, four metrics for reserve adequacy are used: reserve coverage of at least three months of imports; the Guidotti–Greenspan–IMF rule; the ratio of reserves to broad money; and a composite metric. This last metric comprises four components, including: export income to accommodate terms of trade shocks; broad money reflecting capital flight; short-term debt showing debt roll-over risks; and other liabilities for other portfolio outflows. Reserves in the range of 100–150 percent of the composite metric are considered broadly adequate for precautionary reasons. These metrics were then applied to the various groups of countries to determine reserve adequacy.

To summarize, the literature examining the cost and optimal amount of reserves suggests that the cost of reserves may be over-estimated and the amount of reserves held more than optimal. This is also apparent in some optimal reserve models recently developed to integrate both cost and benefit considerations. The policy implications of the analysis are many. Given that the countries under consideration hold adequate amount of reserves for the most part, the issue centers on whether this holding reduces the cost of reserves. If empirical investigation shows that this cost has been reduced, then the additional reserves held should not be perceived as having the social cost they are expected to have. A different management strategy for these excess reserves over the optimal level becomes warranted, in the sense of investing them in higher-yielding assets. On the other hand, if excess reserves are not shown to reduce the cost of reserves, then countries ought to weigh the benefits from holding these reserves purely as insurance in case of a financial crisis against the direct and social costs of holding these reserves. In this sense, reserves ought not to exceed the optimal level, as there are no tangible additional benefits from holding them in the sense of a reduction in the social and private costs of reserves.

Central banks holdings of foreign reserves in MENA countries

MENA countries have historically followed pegged exchange rate regimes either to single currencies or to composite indices or to baskets of currencies. Thus, their monetary policies have largely been based on preserving different exchange rate arrangements. This section first describes the current de facto and de jure exchange rate arrangements of various MENA countries, summarized in Table 8.1. Then it applies the various measures of reserve adequacy to a sample of these countries in line with the literature in order to arrive at some policy implications regarding the optimal amount of reserves held and the approximate cost of holding these reserves.

The de facto practice highlighted in Table 8.1 shows that, for the most part, MENA countries have historically adopted and continue to adopt some type of pegged exchange rate arrangements. Thus, their monetary policies are based on protecting the peg to achieve exchange rate stability.

Table 8.1 Exchange rate arrangements of MENA countries.

	Officially announced (de jure)	*Actual arrangement (de facto)*
GCC		
Bahrain	Limited flexibility vis-à-vis a single currency.	Classified under **Other Conventional Fixed Peg Arrangements** where the country pegs its currency at a fixed rate to a major currency or a basket of currencies and where the exchange rate fluctuates within a narrow margin of at most +/− 1 percent around a central rate. The peg is against a single currency
Kuwait	Pegged against a currency composite.	Classified under **Other Conventional Fixed Peg Arrangements**. The peg has been against a composite until 2001, but changed later to against a single currency
Oman	Pegged against a single currency.	Classified under **Other Conventional Fixed Peg Arrangements**. The peg is against a single currency
Qatar	Limited flexibility vis-à-vis a single currency.	Classified under **Other Conventional Fixed Peg Arrangements**. The peg is against a single currency
Saudi Arabia	Limited flexibility vis-à-vis a single currency.	Classified under **Other Conventional Fixed Peg Arrangements**. The peg is against a single currency
UAE	Limited flexibility vis-à-vis a single currency.	Classified under **Other Conventional Fixed Peg Arrangements**. The peg is against a single currency
North Africa		
Algeria	Managed floating	Starting 1994, classified under **Managed floating with no pre-announced path for exchange rate. From 1990 to 1993, conventional fixed peg against a composite**

(Continued)

Table 8.1 Exchange rate arrangements of MENA countries. (Continued)

	Officially announced (de jure)	Actual arrangement (de facto)
Egypt	Managed floating	Starting 2002 classified under **Managed floating with no pre-announced path for exchange rate. The same classification applies to 1999–2000. Classified under Pegged exchange rates within horizontal bands (1991–6, 2001)** where the value of the currency is maintained within margins of fluctuation around a formal or de facto fixed peg that are wider than +/– 1 percent around a central rate. Much earlier classified under **Other Conventional Fixed Peg Arrangements (1990, 1997, 1998)** with the peg being against a single currency
Libya	Domestic currency pegged to SDR	Starting 2001 classified under **Other Conventional Fixed Peg Arrangements** with the peg being against a composite. Earlier classified under **Pegged exchange rates within horizontal bands**
Morocco	Domestic currency pegged to a currency composite other than the SDR	Classified under **Other Conventional Fixed Peg Arrangements**. The peg is against a composite
Tunisia	Managed floating	Classified under **Managed floating with no pre-announced path for exchange rate (2000, 2001, 2005)**. Classified under **Crawling pegs (1990–99, 2002–4)** where the currency is adjusted periodically in small amounts at a fixed, pre-announced rate
Other MENA		
Yemen	Independently floating	Starting 1996, classified under **Independently floating. A conventional fixed peg arrangement against a single currency existed from 1990 to 1995**
Jordan	Currency pegged to a currency composite	Classified under **Other Conventional Fixed Peg Arrangements**. The peg is against a single currency starting 1995 and against a composite from 1990 to 1994
Lebanon	Independently floating	Starting 1998, classified under **Other Conventional Fixed Peg Arrangements**. The peg is against a single currency. A crawling peg regime existed 1993–7 following a managed floating regime with no predetermined path for the exchange rate from 1990 to 1992

(Continued)

Table 8.1 Exchange rate arrangements of MENA countries. (Continued)

	Officially announced (de jure)	Actual arrangement (de facto)
Syria	Domestic currency pegged to USD	Classified under **Other Conventional Fixed Peg Arrangements**. The peg is against a single currency
Turkey	Managed floating	Starting 2001, classified under **Independently floating**. Earlier classified **under Crawling pegs**
Iran	Managed floating	Starting 2002, classified under **Managed floating with no predetermined path for the exchange rate**. Earlier classified under **Other Conventional Fixed Peg Arrangements**. The peg is against a single currency from 1993 to 2001 compared to against a composite from 1990 to 1992

Source: computed by the authors from International Financial Statistics (www.imf.org)

Such policies require major foreign reserve accumulation to prevent real exchange rate appreciation or currency overvaluation. Thus, in addition to their holdings of precautionary reserves, these countries also have to accumulate non-precautionary reserves. Countries in the GCC have accumulated reserves as they peg to the US dollar, except for Kuwait, which pegs to a basket of currencies, but have also made minimum reserves holdings in excess of four months' worth of imports a criterion for joining the Gulf monetary union.

The foregoing analysis examines the holdings of reserves of several MENA countries, including the six GCC countries (Bahrain, Kuwait, Oman, Qatar, Saudi Arabia, and the United Arab Emirates), along with Lebanon, Jordan, Egypt, and Turkey. We first analyze the amount of reserves held by these countries against several measures, such as the Guidotti–Greenspan–IMF rule of reserves to foreign liabilities, reserves to import ratios, and reserves to GDP ratios, to estimate the optimal amount of reserves based on these rules.

The ratio of short-term external debt to reserves in the group of selected countries is shown in Figures 8.9–8.10. The Guidotti–Greenspan–IMF principle stipulates that this ratio ought to be in the region of 1, allowing a country to have the ability to cover all maturing debt in a given year with its foreign reserves. The figure has continuously been less than 1 for the group except in 2011 and 2012, when it was significantly equal to 1. This reflects the fact that countries were possibly holding more reserves than the rule stipulates. In fact, this figure has declined drastically more recently, in 2013 and 2014, largely owing to the unprecedented holdings of reserves by Saudi Arabia as it started computing the sovereign wealth fund in its reserves. On a country-by-country basis, all the figures stand below 1 except for Turkey's.

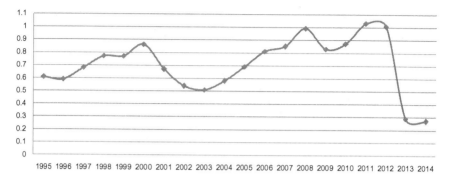

Figure 8.9 Short-term debt/reserves in selected Middle Eastern countries.

Source: Calculations from IFS

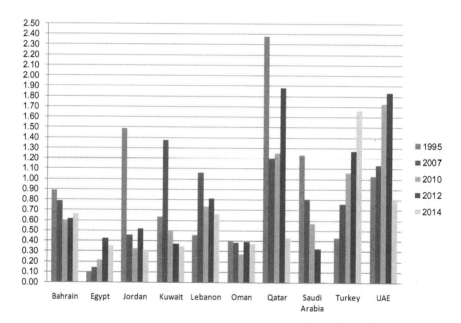

Figure 8.10 Short-term debt/reserves in selected Middle Eastern countries.

Source: Calculations from IFS

The reserves to GDP ratios highlighted in Figures 8.11–8.12 show an increase in the last two years due to those of Saudi Arabia approaching a one-to-one correspondence. For the other nine countries, these figures are 20 percent or less for six of the countries under consideration, except for Jordan, at 43 percent, the UAE, at 27 percent, and Lebanon, at 79 percent. Lebanon has, since 2009, accumulated large amounts of foreign reserves owing to the large capital inflows to the country's financial system translated into foreign reserves held at the central bank. The relative stability of the Lebanese banking sector in the wake of the financial

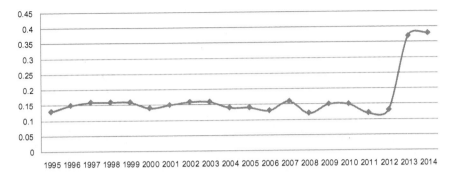

Figure 8.11 Reserves/GDP in selected Middle Eastern countries.

Source: Calculations from IFS

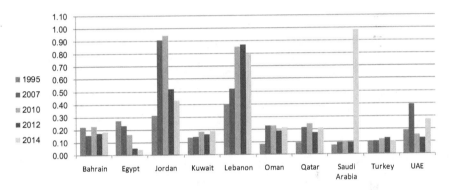

Figure 8.12 Reserves/GDP in selected Middle Eastern countries.

Source: Calculations from IFS

crisis contributed to this factor. The Lebanese central bank pays interest on these reserves and issues certificate of deposits to banks in foreign currency to sterilize capital inflows.

Figures 8.13–8.14 show the reserves to import ratios, which is recommended to be in the region of three to four months' worth of imports. The weighted average hovered between six to eight months for the period 1995–2012, falling slightly to over four months only in 2008 and 2011–12. This ratio increased to one year of imports as a result of the inclusion of Saudi Arabia's data. On a country-by-country basis (Figure 8.14) this ratio differs drastically, but it is greater than four months in all cases but Turkey and Egypt. A ratio greater than four months' worth of imports is necessary for the six GCC countries as a convergence criterion for entry to the Gulf monetary union.

The positive results reflecting the adequate holdings of foreign reserves for most of the countries considered usually come at a social cost. This cost, as stated above, results from the fact that countries attract reserves paying the

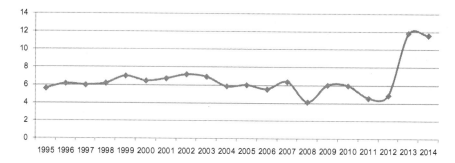

Figure 8.13 Reserves/imports in selected Middle Eastern countries.

Source: Calculations from IFS

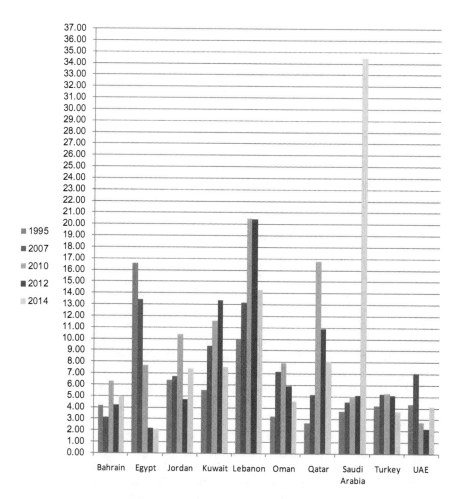

Figure 8.14 Reserves/imports in selected Middle Eastern countries.

Source: Calculations from IFS

market rate and hold them either in idle forms or invest them at a rate lower than the rate paid on reserves flowing in. In Lebanon, for example, the ratio of reserves to imports reached 20.38 months in 2012 and 14.27 in 2014, and the reserves to GDP ratio stood at 0.87 and 0.79 for the same two years respectively. This large accumulation of reserves took effect during and after the financial crisis as capital flew into the relatively stable financial system of Lebanon, especially its banks. Given that the banks could not reinvest the whole amounts in earning assets, the central bank of Lebanon issued its own certificate of deposits to banks to acquire the funds and was not able to invest them in interest-paying assets covering the interest cost of these reserves. Thus, the difference between the cost of reserves and the earnings on them amounts to the social cost of holding reserves expressed in terms of GDP. That is, the cost of reserves can be estimated as the difference between the rate at which the country borrows international reserves and the rate at which the central bank invests these liquid assets as a percentage of GDP. Figures 8.15–8.17 reflect the social cost for holding reserves for the selected group of countries. We first subtract four months' worth of imports from the reserves held to compute the precautionary reserves needed, irrespective of the cost, especially in developing and emerging economies. The remainder are assumed to be held for non-precautionary reasons. Following the literature reviewed earlier, this amount is multiplied by 3 and 5 percent respectively, reflecting the excess in the two interest costs over the interest revenue from investments. To compute the social cost, the computed figures are expressed as a percent of GDP for various countries. According to Figures 8.16–8.17, the social cost in 2014 was highest for Saudi Arabia, standing at 2.7 percent when the

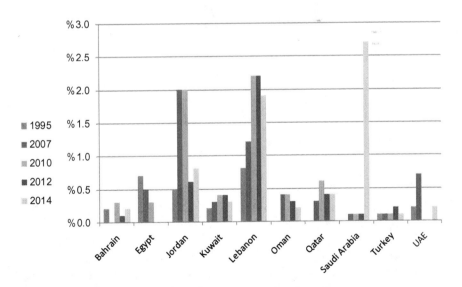

Figure 8.15 Social cost of excess reserves in selected Middle Eastern countries (spread=0.03).

Source: Calculations from IFS

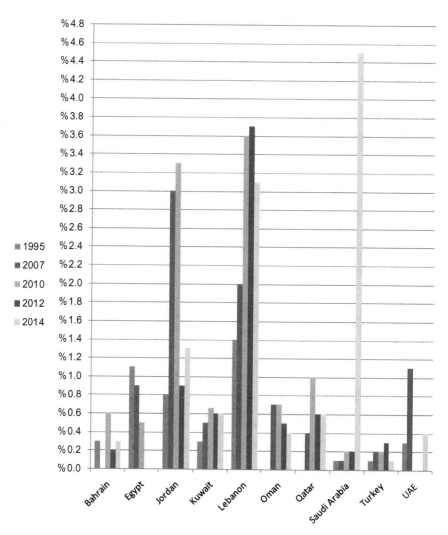

Figure 8.16 Social cost of excess reserves in selected Middle Eastern countries
    (spread=0.05).

Source: Calculations from IFS

excess cost over return is 3 percent and at 4.5 percent when it is 5 percent. This
is followed by Lebanon, at 1.9 percent and 3.1 percent respectively. For all other
countries except Jordan, for the case of 5 percent the social cost was significantly
below 1 percent in 2014.

To recommend a reserve management strategy for the future, given that the
results differ across countries, the model should be tested for the countries under
consideration to examine and investigate the impact of reserve accumulation on
the cost of reserves. If holding additional reserves causes a decline in the cost

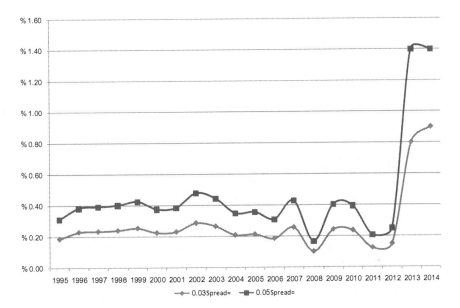

Figure 8.17 Social cost of excess reserves in selected Middle Eastern countries.

Source: Calculations from IFS

of reserves, this reduces the spread mentioned earlier and thus the social cost, implying that the marginal benefit of holding additional reserves outweighed part of this cost. This could be the subject of a future econometric analysis, which is, however, beyond the scope of this chapter.

Concluding remarks and policy implications

The conduct of monetary policy in monetary unions facing several fiscal budgets and arrangements becomes very challenging when the aim is to harmonize the inflation rate in member countries around a quantitative measure and to try to achieve some type of stable growth and employment in the region. This becomes of additional interest in a two-tier system of countries characterized by divergent macroeconomic indicators, monetary policy that is loose for some and tight for others, and possibly overvalued exchange rates for members experiencing fiscal imbalances and worsening economic fundamentals. The financial crisis of 2008 exposed various economies in the eurozone to negative growth and high unemployment rates coupled with very low inflation rates approaching deflation. This necessitated the adoption of a common monetary policy using standard and non-standard approaches to stabilize the economies and maintain the price stability objective quantified as an inflation rate close to but below 2 percent in the medium term, based on a harmonized index of consumer prices for the nineteen member countries. The standard measures aimed largely at cutting the policy interest rates, which have recently reached close to zero and negative levels. Unconventional measures first took the form of credit support to the banking system, with unlimited liquidity provisions in domestic and foreign currencies to banks against an extended list of adequate collateral, increasing the maturity of refinancing operations, and the introduction of several programs of asset purchases in the covered bonds markets. From 2015 the ECB embarked openly on policies of QE through the adoption of an asset-purchase program, including the buying of covered bonds, asset-backed securities, and public sector securities. This program is expected to be continued for a few more years, until the economies resume their path back to the inflation target with sustained economic growth and recovery. The financial crisis also led many central banks to hold additional amounts of reserves for both precautionary and non-precautionary reasons. The analysis in this chapter was applied to ten countries from the MENA region to determine adequate reserves held based on optimal economic indicators. The results reached show that these countries are, for the most part, holding more than adequate reserves, leaving room to estimate the social cost of holding these reserves. Additional policy implications may be investigated via the empirical testing of the model for various economies to further investigate the impact of reserve accumulation on the cost of reserves. There could be a marginal benefit to holding additional reserves reflected in the reduction of the sovereign interest rates, thus outweighing part of the cost; this could be the subject of a future econometric analysis.

Notes

1 The convergence criteria used by the European Monetary Union are five, outlined as follows: first, for at least two consecutive years, each country's exchange rates against currencies of countries that are members of the European monetary system's exchange rate mechanism must have remained within this mechanism's band without a devaluation of its central parity. Second, a country's inflation rate must not exceed by more than 1.5 percent the average of the three countries with the lowest inflation rates. Third, the long-term interest rate of any member state must not exceed by more than 2 percent the average of the three member countries with the best inflation performance. Fourth and fifth, member countries are to keep their budget deficit to GDP ratio at no more than 3 percent and their total public debt to GDP ratio at a maximum of 60 percent (Shahin 1997).
2 The conditions or convergence criteria that the GCC set up represent a slightly modified version of the one used by the European Monetary Union. There are five, outlined broadly as follows: first, a country's inflation rate must not exceed the average rate of the six countries by more than two percentage points. Second, the long-term interest rate of any member state must not exceed the average interest rates of the three member countries with the lowest rates by more than two percentage points. Third, foreign exchange reserves should be at least in excess of four months' imports. Fourth and fifth, member countries are to keep their budget deficit to GDP ratio at no more than 3 percent or 5 percent when oil prices are weak and their total public debt to GDP ratio at less than 60 percent (Shahin and El-Achkar 2013).
3 European Commission various years.
4 See Dadush et al 2010, where he reports these figures based on OECD estimates.
5 Dadush et al 2010.
6 EuroStat, various years.
7 Praet 2015.

8 In addition to the ECB website (www.ecb.europa.eu/mopo/implement/html/index.
en.html), these four points are also highly elaborated in Praet 2015.
9 This information is provided and discussed in the ECB *Monthly Bulletin*, July 2012.
10 Joyce et al 2012.
11 Fawley and Neeley 2013.
12 www.ecb.europa.eu/mopo/implement/html/index.en.html
13 Refer to the two press conferences in Draghi 2015; and Draghi 2016.
14 https://www.ecb.europa.eu/mopo/implement/html/index.en.html
15 www.ecb.europa.eu/mopo/implement/html/index.en.html
16 Joyce et al 2012.
17 Draghi 2015.
18 International Monetary Fund 2015.
19 International Monetary Fund 2015; International Monetary Fund 2013a; International
Monetary Fund 2011; Jeanne 2010; Levy 2008; Rodrik 2006.
20 Rodrik 2006.
21 Levy 2008.
22 Jeanne 2010.
23 International Monetary Fund 2013a; 2011.
24 International Monetary Fund 2015.

Bibliography

Dadush, U, et al 2010, "Paradigm Lost: The Euro in Crisis," Carnegie Endowment for International Peace, Washington, DC.
Draghi, M 2015, "Press Conference," Frankfurt am Main, 3 December.
Draghi, M 2016, "Press Conference," Frankfurt am Main, January 17.
ECB Monthly Bulletin 2012, "Monetary and Fiscal Policy Interaction in a Monetary Union," July. Available from: www.ecb.int
European Commission various years, *Annual Macroeconomic Data Base*, Economic and Financial Affairs.
EuroStat various years. Available from ec.europa.eu/eurostat
Fawley, B and Neely, C 2013, "Four stories of quantitative easing," *Federal Reserve Bank of St. Louis Review*, 95, 1, pp. 51–88.
International Monetary Fund, *Annual Reports*, various issues. Available from: www.imf.org
International Monetary Fund, *International Financial Statistics*, CD-ROM.
International Monetary Fund, *World Economic Outlook*, Database.
International Monetary Fund 2011, "Assessing Reserve Adequacy," prepared by Monetary and Capital Markets, Research and Strategy, Policy and Review Departments, International Monetary Fund.
International Monetary Fund 2013a, "Assessing Reserve Adequacy—Further Considerations," Policy Paper, International Monetary Fund.
International Monetary Fund 2013b, "Toward A Fiscal Union for the Euro Area," IMF Staff Discussion Note 13/09 September.
International Monetary Fund 2015, "Assessing Reserve Adequacy-Specific Proposals," Policy Paper, International Monetary Fund.
Jeanne, O 2010, "International reserves in emerging market countries: too much of a good thing?" in ed C Crow, S Johnson, JD Ostry and Z Jeromin, *Macrofinancial Linkages*, International Monetary Fund, pp. 473–521.

Joyce, M, Miles, D, Scott, A and Vayanos, D 2012, "Quantitative easing and unconventional monetary policy: an introduction," *TheEconomic Journal*, 122, pp. F271–F288.
Levy, YE 2008, "The cost of reserves," *Economics Letters*, 100, pp. 39–42.
Michael, J, Miles, D, Scott, A and Vayanos, D 2012, "Quantitative easing and unconventional monetary policy: an introduction," *The Economic Journal*, 122, pp. F271–F288.
Praet, P 2015, "Public sector security purchases and monetary dominance in a monetary union without a fiscal union," Speech at the conference "The ECB and its Watchers XVI," Frankfurt am Main, March 11.
Rodrik, D 2006, "The social cost of foreign exchange reserves," *International Economic Journal*, 20, 3, pp. 253–66.
Shahin, W 1997, "International monetary coordination between Lebanon and the EMU: the convergence criteria," in eds W Shahin and K Shehade, *Pathways to Integration: Lebanon and the Euro-Mediterranean Partnership*, The Konrad Adenauer Foundation.
Shahin, W and El Ashkar, E 2013, "Prospects for monetary coordination in the Mediterranean region: more or larger monetary unions?" in eds TM Peeters, N Sabri and W Shahin, *Financial Integration: A Focus on the Mediterranean*, Springer Publishers.

9 Concluding remarks and policy implications

This book was motivated by the changes and developments in the global financial environment witnessed in the twenty-first century. As the analysis has shown, the financial world experienced three major developments: changes in the financial environment governing financial and economic crimes, the global financial crisis, and changes in monetary policy conduct given the rise of monetary unions without fiscal unions, unconventional monetary policies such as quantitative easing, and central banks' holdings of foreign reserves. The book was thus divided into three parts covering these developments.

As far as the expansion in the size, type, and sophistication of economic and financial crimes is concerned, we concluded that there will always exist politically exposed persons aiming to build global retirement funds outside their jurisdictions and a corrupt component of the private sector seeking secret vehicles to launder its ill-gotten money. This demand-side for secrecy necessitates a supply-side for the secret market to develop, interact, and flourish. Financial secrecy is fascinating in terms of both its demand and its supply components for actors from all segments of life pursuing illicit gains. The variety of the financial and economic crimes addressed in this book, ranging across money laundering, terrorist financing, organized crime, bribery, corruption, fraud, cybercrime, financing proliferation, human trafficking, the smuggling of migrants, identity theft, tax evasion, whistle-blowing, stolen assets and politically exposed persons, represent major issues on both the demand and supply side of criminal activities, with the very few topics not addressed here falling largely into organized crime and corruption. However, the latest criminal activities may not necessarily represent "new wine in old bottles." The criminal vehicles—or bottles—are also changing, necessitating dynamic policy responses requiring permanent updating, enhancement, implementation, and coordination. Organized crime is not stagnant, but adapts as new crimes emerge and as relationships between criminal networks become both more flexible and more sophisticated, with ever-greater reach around the globe. This underscores the dynamics of the dialectic discussed in the Introduction, where regulators need innovation in the rules and marketplace to remain abreast of and capable of abating crime. On the performance front, the regulatory authorities have to a large extent succeeded in developing various conventions and rules to combat ill-gotten money, especially within countries. Chapter 2, on compliance, detailed these various measures. The regulatory model has attempted to combat the supply side of secrecy, as supply in this case motivates its own demand and curtailing it can reduce financial crime. Limiting the supply through various international and global coordinated measures is only the beginning, however, as additional challenges remain in enforcement and implementation. The evidence for the modest success of these measures is found in the figures on asset recovery, which show that only minimal amounts were recovered from public- and private-sector corruption. Fighting a dynamic and evolving enemy gives a new meaning to "more is less," where more standard and deliberate reactions by regulators are lagging behind the adventurous profit-motivated actions of the criminals and perpetrators. As Lewis Carroll stated in *Through the Looking-Glass*, "It takes all the running you can do to keep in the same place. If you want to get somewhere else, you must run at least twice as fast as that!" Thus, in order to strengthen the fight against criminal activities, the international bank regulatory and supervisory landscape has in the last two decades gone through a drastic but gradual change in response to political and regulatory concerns and pressures to fight tax evasion, money laundering, terrorism financing, and other types of financial crime, and to protect international economic and financial integrity and stability. The change has been more pronounced, however, in the years following the 2008 global financial crisis. In this environment, banks and financial institutions found themselves under the threat of a double-edged sword: on one edge, the prohibitive cost and damage of non-compliance with regulations; and on the other the soaring cost and repercussions of meeting compliance requirements, including the regulatory cost of constrained revenue avenues and profit opportunities. Thus, cost benefit analysis and other considerations drove some banks, at the level of bank executives or their subordinates, to take the risk and partially comply, while others were compelled to fully abide by a mass of often complex and frequently changing regulations involving ascending diverse challenges and direct and opportunity costs. Examples of compliance unit errors and the 'improper or unacceptable' conduct of a small number of employees or executives are many, and such errors and misconduct could be very harmful to the banking institution at both domestic and international levels. Thus, promoting a sincere compliance culture from top to bottom in the banking firm, demonstrating zero tolerance for misconduct, and investing in compliance programs, systems, and control measures are both necessary and beneficial to the reputation and growth of the financial services firm. Compliance, despite raising operational costs at banks, is therefore a better choice than non-compliance.

Yet the question is how to cope with burdening and excessive compliance and avoid or smoothen some of its undesirable implications, such as business discontinuity or exit pressure. The new regulatory environment increased demand for compliance officers and experts, and, given the limited supply at least in the short run, created a major difficulty for banks in general and small ones in particular not only in recruiting but also in retaining compliance staff. Small banks struggle more, too, in getting the right systems and infrastructure in place and thus their rising compliance regulatory burden threatened their competitive position, their continuity, and even their existence.

Many consider that most banks can and must survive the exorbitant compliance requirements and overcome the anxiety created and the impediments to their continuity and growth by adapting to and managing the imposed shift or evolution, as they have done before when faced with similar challenges and changing regulatory environments. A smooth transition to compliance and the outsourcing of some of the compliance tasks could play a role in this respect. In addition, banks are invited not only to effect the necessary adjustments in policies and procedures and integrate the compliance requirements in their business as a normal part of meeting regulatory demands but also to create value and business from the whole process. Successful adaptation to change, therefore, requires taking a fresh look at the issue and making use of the new technology infrastructure put in place to comply with new regulations; data gathering, management, and storage improvements; and upscaled internal organization in order to improve activity and performance and better serve their customers. That is, they should make use of upgraded KYC procedures and enhanced data collection to market and provide client-focused and tailored financial products and services; thereby, the bank would be meeting compliance needs and expanding its business simultaneously.

Yet, de-risking associated with stepping up compliance, enforcing stronger risk management practices; and maintaining strong AML/CFT standards at banks under heightened fear of imposed penalties can lead to unintended and undesirable consequences for some communities and countries. Banks and the financial sector cannot be the only ones responsible for addressing the possible negative impact that de-risking may have on, particularly, economically deprived societies and the possible distressing effects on financial inclusion. Financial services firms have the right to reduce the level of risk to which they are exposed and to decide whether it is more cost effective and less troublesome to stop doing business with certain customers and in some markets. However, we believe that they should be given the necessary incentives to consider the strategy of imposing stronger risk management and control on high-risk customers and markets, rather than pursuing a strategy of complete avoidance. Government officials, including regulatory and supervisory bodies, must also play a role in alleviating any adverse side-effects of newly imposed regulations and must assess carefully the negative impacts of standards' enforcement with a view to preventing unplanned outcomes. This would not mean that concerned authorities should lessen global standards, loosen laws, scale back regulations, or reduce the importance of enforcement. Forcefully compelling compliance with laws and regulations to prevent wrongdoing and protect financial markets and stakeholders should remain a main concern but not to the point of over-regulation and at the expense of consumer protection. It is a dilemma and there should be a trade-off somewhere. Research that sheds further light on this quandary could provide valuable input for decision- and policy-makers on the way to achieving a balance between excess regulatory requirements and protection of banks' clients.

As far as the second global development in the financial architecture—the global financial crisis—is concerned, this book generated major policy implications resulting from this crisis by examining the historical origins and causes of various worldwide crises, lending policies during the latest crisis of 2008, and the changes in the regulatory environment at the level of bank governance and capital adequacy. Starting with the origins of various crises, it was shown that the literature on the determinants of banking crises has identified a number of factors that eventually affect adversely the quality of assets at banks and therefore contribute to their weakness, generally by causing or inciting excessive risk taking by banks. Such factors include poorly designed safety nets and financial liberalization processes, poorly regulated and supervised banking sectors, and the adoption of certain exchange rate and inflation stabilization policies. These potential causes of banking crises require policy-makers to attempt to forge appropriate solutions based on policy recommendations tailored to the peculiarities and characteristics of each economy. Other determinants of banking crises have been found to impact directly the financial position of borrowers and eventually of banks. These could be cyclical economic downturns, high inflation and real interest rates, shifts in the terms of trade, real exchange rate appreciation, currency mismatches, currency crises, and collapses in asset prices. However, several positive lessons could be learned from facing and managing a crisis. The term "crisis" in the Chinese language is "Wei Ji," meaning risk (Wei) and opportunity (Ji). Each crisis, if analyzed and assessed properly, can bear the seeds needed to grow the reforms necessary to prevent its re-occurrence and to adjust policy to reverse its trajectory. Therefore, the challenge is to properly understand the impact of every crisis. With that aim, the book examined the impact of the financial crisis of 2008 on the credit availability in eight countries and established that there was a decline in credit after the crisis. The analysis continued by addressing, in line with the literature on credit crunch using disequilibrium analysis, the effects of the crisis on the demand and supply of credit. The correct identification of the cause of credit slowdown or retreat has important policy implications. If the credit decline is related to weak demand for bank loans, whether due to pessimistic economic perspectives, deteriorations in borrowers' balance sheets, excessive leverage, or other factors, then policies aiming at stimulating aggregate demand could be effective. If, on the other hand, the decline is due to banks' inability and reluctance to lend because of a decline in deposits, capital losses due to loan losses, or asset price collapses and increased riskiness then other sets of measures, including easy monetary policy, are needed to revive bank lending and foster investment. The results reached suggest that the recent credit slowdown for the eight countries was largely caused by credit supply factors. Banks seem largely to have been affected by liquidity shortage and heightened risk. The results also showed that credit demand declined as well for, reasons probably related to the global economic recession and regional slowdowns in economic activity. However, the demand impact was less significant. The results are in line with many studies in the literature, confirming that, in order to motivate lending, policy-makers must emphasize policies aimed at stimulating credit supply with an eye also on affecting loan demand.

The latest global financial crisis seems also to have shaped the architecture of bank corporate governance and bank capital adequacy. Corporate governance at banks could be regarded as one form of the financial safety net and an extension to the existing forms established by governments, particularly explicit deposit insurance schemes and the lender of last resort function, created initially with the intention of protecting bank depositors and other creditors, preventing bank failure, and safeguarding the banking system. This additional private sector element of the safety net, like the other elements, can be a mixed blessing, as an inappropriately designed or inadequate net can increase moral hazard incentives or incentives to take on greater risks, thus harming banks' performance and banking sector stability. Therefore, adequate corporate governance structures can reduce the risk of failure of banking institutions and thus the risks of government bail-outs, unnecessarily burdening taxpayers. Conversely, a poorly thought-out or an ineffective corporate governance framework can result in excess risk that could weaken public confidence and perhaps contribute to the failure of financial firms. This would mean that bank regulatory and supervisory authorities have a crucial role to play in ensuring that banks, which they regulate and supervise, have effective boards with strengthened practices, roles, and responsibilities, and strong senior management oversight. Strong, skilled, and independent supervisory authority is also a must for reinforcing adequate and strong internal governance. Supervisors have to ensure banks' compliance with corporate governance regulations, enforce corrective actions, and provide inputs into legislation and regulations. Boards and senior management, for their part, must also assume the responsibility of translating regulatory guidelines and bank management policies and rules into operational practices, show strong commitment, and reflect periodically on the effectiveness and relevance of the governance arrangement and practices in place, in line with the changes in the scale and scope of the business and the changing operating environment. The governance of banks, it appears, will always remain a dynamic and difficult issue, under constantly changing financial and operating conditions, in spite of the progress that has been made over the last two decades. In fact, many governance practices become less useful with the passage of time in a rapidly changing world, and it would seem that there is always a race between risk-taking and risk-prevention measures and therefore between stability and instability.

Nevertheless, the commitment to efficient corporate governance would always remain an important issue for banking system stability and by promoting sound governance practices countries also promote financial stability. Corporate or internal governance must ensure that the appropriate owners or managers are in place and that the quality of risk management and control systems is high. Sound banking requires that the role and responsibilities of directors and management be clearly defined and the competency of those people be verified. In this respect, regulatory authorities are often delegated the responsibility of approving shareholders and the appointment of directors and top management of a bank when licensing or whenever there is a change in ownership. The corporate governance of banks is also improved when regulation allows and encourages banks to establish appropriate internal risk-management and control systems to restrict or set appropriate levels of exposure to different types of risk. Letting banks set the appropriate level of credit, liquidity, exchange rate, and interest rate risk is a recent trend and contrasts with the traditional approach, in which regulators specify through prudential regulation the levels of exposure or set certain standards. Setting appropriate rules, procedures, and policies for controlling risk and minimizing the organizational hazards would make the bank's management more involved in risk management and control. Better internal governance is also achieved when banks are required to have clearly defined internal audit functions with externally audited annual accounts. This would help managers, directors, and owners detect failures or weaknesses and act accordingly. Sound internal governance also requires ensuring adequate incentives for directors and managers to operate the bank in a safe or sound manner and prevent any inclination on the part of owners–managers to hide problems.

The Basel III Accord on capital adequacy required by banks in light of the latest financial crisis seems to cause many challenges to banks, relating mainly to raising more capital, improving the quality of capital, and meeting the liquidity capital requirements on coverage ratio and liquidity requirement tools. At a time when many worldwide banks are still trying to meet the Basel II capital adequacy requirements, banks are asked to address the composition and quality of their capital as well as create buffer capital zones to address pro-cyclicality. Specifically, it is very challenging for banks that are not operating as public ones to raise the share of common stock in their Tier 1 capital and apply the stricter definition of this equity. It is also difficult to create a capital conservation buffer of common equity to withstand future periods of stress. Such requirements are believed to influence the way banks do business in most countries, especially if Basel III has possible effects on financial markets and monetary policy implementation. The literature on the impact of the new accord shows that, for the most part, raising more capital and holding more liquidity, as required by Basel III, seem to cause a rise in the cost of financial intermediation, a decline in the availability of credit, an increase in operating costs, and a reduction in profitability. However, the true impact cannot be predicted with certainty, as many countries have yet to attempt application and enforcement of the new capital standards.

The first decade of the twenty-first century also witnessed the rise of unconventional monetary policies to reverse the recessionary and deflationary impacts of the widespread financial crisis. These new policies of quantitative easing (QE) redrew the new central bank stabilization architecture. Although QE was used at the beginning of the decade to stimulate economic activity and prevent deflation in Japan, the coverage it received from its use in the US, the UK, and the countries of the EMU made addressing the design and impacts of unconventional monetary policy the latest in monetary policy strategy and conduct. The experiences of the countries adopting QE have been different owing largely to the differing economic cycles and conditions faced by those countries, the nature and levels of. development of their financial markets, the availability, volume, and maturity of their financial instruments, and the mandates and goals of their central banks. So, for example, while the US announced the ending of QE effective October 2014, the ECB announced the beginning of QE adoption in early 2015 and the BoE re-emphasized in its various monetary policy remits its commitment to QE for the coming year of 2015–16.

The design of asset purchases also differed across countries. However, the objectives and aims were the same, involving an attempt to reduce long-term interest rates after reducing short-term ones to near zero and to affect credit conditions, other asset prices, financial markets, and expectations through forward guidance and signaling in order to activate the wide macroeconomy and prevent deflation. Using a transmission mechanism of monetary policy framework, all channels, according to econometric studies, provided mixed evidence. However, there exists enough evidence, especially in the results of the counterfactual econometric research and given the improvements in the macroeconomy across countries, that QE was somewhat effective. The gradual pre-announcements of strategies and tactics stating the volume and type of assets to be purchased, along with various maturities, could have also supported the effectiveness of the forward guidance channel of the transmission mechanism and for signaling. Policy-makers ought also to pay attention to the demand side of the money market in order to properly and effectively manage the rate of growth of the money supply in line with planned economic growth and inflation projected guidelines, given central bank mandates. Given zero bound interest rates, a decision by the public to hold more money, reducing velocity, may become detrimental to the growth in nominal GDP.

The debate over QE has also centered from the outset on various exit strategies and monetary policy normalization once the economy returns to pre-financial crisis levels. Five issues were highlighted: the basis of the decision to exit, the announcement of the new strategy, the methods used to reverse QE, the speed of the implementation, and the possible reversal of the successful outcome of the entry when the exit is completed. As of February 2016, of the countries that adopted QE after the latest financial crisis only the US has started implementing the exit strategy. The FED ceased its QE operations and developed an exit strategy starting with raising the federal funds rate, which began as of December 16, 2015. In its meeting on that day the FOMC judged that there had been considerable improvement in labor market conditions in 2015, and felt that it was reasonably confident that inflation would rise, over the medium term, to its 2 percent objective. Given the economic outlook, and recognizing the time it takes for policy actions to affect future economic outcomes, the FOMC decided to raise the target range for the federal funds rate from 0–0.25 percent to 0.25–0.5 percent. The stance of monetary policy remains accommodative after this increase, thereby supporting further improvement in labor market conditions and a return to 2 percent inflation. For all countries adopting QE, the basis of the decision to exit seems to be the improvement in the state of the macroeconomy, including careful attention to economic growth, unemployment, and price stability. We expect the other issues to be country specific, but also very similar in terms of the transparency of the announcements and the gradual implementation designed not to affect the outcome of the entry.

The twenty-first century also witnessed the rise of a major monetary union without a fiscal union, namely the European Monetary Union, relying on the European Central Bank (ECB) to conduct monetary policy. The practice of this policy in monetary unions that are required to deal with several fiscal budgets and arrangements becomes very challenging when the aim is to harmonize the inflation rate in member countries around a quantitative measure and to try to achieve some type of stable growth and employment in the region. This becomes of additional interest where a two-tier system of countries exists, characterized by divergent macroeconomic indicators, monetary policy that is loose for some and tight for others, and possibly overvalued exchange rates for members experiencing fiscal imbalances and worsening economic fundamentals. The financial crisis of 2008 exposed various economies in the eurozone to negative growth and high unemployment rates coupled with very low inflation rates approaching deflation. This necessitated the adoption of a common monetary policy using standard and non-standard approaches to stabilize the economies and maintain the price stability objective, quantified as an inflation rate close to but below 2 percent for the medium term based on a harmonized index of consumer prices for the nineteen member countries. The standard measures aimed largely at cutting the policy interest rates had recently seen rates reach close to zero and negative levels. Unconventional measures took the form first of credit support to the banking system with unlimited liquidity provisions in domestic and foreign currencies to banks against an extended list of adequate collateral, increasing the maturity of refinancing operations, and the introduction of several programs of asset purchases in the covered bonds markets. Beginning in 2015, the ECB embarked openly on policies of QE through the adoption of an asset-purchase program, including the buying of covered bonds, asset-backed securities, and public sector securities. This program is expected to be continued for few more years, until the economies resume their path back to the inflation target with sustained economic growth and recovery.

The financial crisis also led many central banks to hold additional amounts of reserves for both precautionary and non-precautionary reasons. The analysis used in this book was applied to ten countries from the MENA region to determine the adequate amount of reserves held based on optimal economic indicators. The results show that these countries are, for the most part, holding more than adequate reserves, leaving room to estimate the social cost of holding these reserves. To determine additional policy implications the model should be empirically tested across various economies to further investigate the impact of reserve accumulation on the cost of reserves. There could be a marginal benefit of holding additional reserves reflected in the reduction of the sovereign interest rates and outweighing part of the cost; this could be the subject of a future econometric analysis.

Overall, the three main developments in the financial environment facing banks and central banks seem to have permanently shaped international regulatory strategies for combatting financial and economic crimes, the lending policies of many financial intermediaries, corporate governance structures, and the capital adequacy framework of various financial institutions. The practice and conduct of monetary policy has drastically changed in favor of unconventional approaches adopted by central banks to stabilize various macroeconomies in terms of high employment, output growth, and deflation prevention. The conduct of one monetary policy for a large monetary union facing several budget constraints instead of one fiscal authority is a new development. It remains to be seen whether coupling monetary unions with fiscal unions or major fiscal coordination or even integration becomes necessary for the prevention of contagion and systemic risk across the economies of union members. In the meantime, central banks seem to be holding high levels of foreign reserves, despite their social costs, for precautionary reasons aimed at protecting their economies from various future shocks and potential global crises.

Author index

Subject index